UN Law on International S

Peter Schlechtriem · Petra Butler

UN Law on International Sales

The UN Convention
on the International Sale of Goods

Peter Schlechtriem[†]
Universität Freiburg

Petra Butler
Victoria University
Law Faculty
Lambton Quay 15
Wellington/New Zealand
petra.butler@vuw.ac.nz

ISBN 978-3-540-25314-3   e-ISBN 978-3-540-49992-3
DOI 10.1007/978-3-540-49992-3

Library of Congress Control Number: 2008928511

Cover design: WMXDesign, Heidelberg, Germany

Printed on acid-free paper

9 8 7 6 5 4 3 2 1

springer.com

Foreword

This book is dedicated to Professor Schlechtriem and his tremendous life time work on the United Nations Convention on the International Sale of Goods (CISG) and all past, present, and future participants of the Willem C Vis Moot for whom hopefully the book will be of some use.

To have been asked to adopt Professor Peter Schlechtriem's German text book *Internationales UN-Kaufrecht* (4 ed, Mohr Siebeck, Tübingen, 2007) for the English speaking student, academic, and practitioner and to work with Professor Schlechtriem on this edition has been a great honour. Unfortunately this book has been longer in the making than originally planned and more unfortunately still was not finished in time for Professor Schlechtriem to see its publishing.

The aims of this book are more modest than other compendious treatments of the CISG. The main aim above all others has been to facilitate discussion on the use and application of the provisions of the CISG. As the CISG itself was the outcome of nearly a decade of debate between nations polarised in ideology, the importance of continuing discussion cannot be understated. This is especially true in regard to common law countries like Canada, Australia, and New Zealand which have all ratified the CISG many years ago but where its use and jurisprudence are rather underdeveloped. To show that common law jurisdictions should not fear the use of the CISG, references to further views (both for and against) are given along with the parallel provisions of the United Kingdom Sale of Goods Act 1979 (SOG), the US Uniform Commercial Code (UCC) and Canadian, Australian and New Zealand legislation and jurisprudence. This allows a reader used to the common law approach to sale of goods law to undertake a meaningful comparative analysis in the hope that domestic law within common law nations may be coloured by the principles of the CISG and hence achieve greater uniformity.

This book could have not been written without the help of several people whom it is my pleasure to acknowledge here. My personal assistant, Yana Khatchian, became an expert not only in reading my hand-writing but also in the editing and formatting of the text. She always provided cheerful encouragement and without her the book would not have been possible. A special thank you has to go to Nicholas Whittington and Cathy Nijman whose research assistance was invaluable and who spent long hours proof-reading the manuscript and to Arjun Harindranath. Arjun was especially involved in the last year of the project and not only provided invaluable research assistance and spent long hours proof-reading he also provided the calmness, patience, and the good sense of humour necessary to finish the book.

I also would like acknowledge the support and perseverance of Brigitte Reschke from Springer whose emails were always encouraging despite the fact that the book took me a little longer to print than I anticipated.

Last but not least, a special thank you has to go to my children Clara, Conor, and Cillian and my husband Andrew – their support was often the life-line needed for a substantial project.

Petra Butler
Wellington, April 2008

Contents

Abbreviations

ABGB	Allgemeines Bürgerliches Gesetzbuch (1 June 1811 (Austria)
AC-CISG	Advisory Council on the CISG
AcP	Archiv für die civilistische Praxis
AG	Aktiengesellschaft (share company); Amtsgericht (District Court)
AGB	Allgemeine Geschäftsbedingungen
AGBG	Gesetz zur Regelung des Rechts der Allgemeinen Geschäftsbedingungen (9 Dec 1976), BGBl. I, 3317 (Act to regulate Standard form contracts)
Am J Comp L	American Journal of Comparative Law (USA)
approx	approximately
Arab Law Quarterly	Arab L Q
Art	Article
Artt	Articles
ass plén	assemblée pléniere
BB	Der Betriebsberater
BBl.	Bundesblatt (Switzerland)
BG	Bundesgericht (Supreme Court of Switzerland)
BGB	Bürgerliches Gesetzbuch (German Civil Code)
BGBl	Bundesgesetzblatt
BGE	Entscheidungen des Schweizerischen Bundesgerichts (amtliche Sammlung) (Decision of the Swiss Supreme Court)
BGH	Bundesgerichtshof (decision of the German Supreme Court)
BGHZ	Entscheidungen des Bundesgerichtshofes in Zivilsachen (amtliche Sammlung)
BJM	Basler Juristische Mitteilungen (Switzerland)
BT-Drs	Bundestagsdrucksache
Brussels Convention	Brussels Convention on Jurisdiction and the Enforcement of Judgments in Civil and Commercial Matters 1968.
Brussels Regulation	Council Regulation (EC) No 44/2001 of 22 December 2000 on jurisdiction and the recognition and enforcement of judgments in civil and commercial matters

CA	Cour d'appel, Court of Appeal
Canadian Bar Rev	Canadian Bar Review
Cass.	Cour de cassation
Cc	Code civil (France)/Codice civile (Italy)
Cf	Refer to
cic	culpa in contrahendo
CIETAC	China International Economic and Trade Arbitration Commission
CIF (auch cif)	cost, insurance, freight (Incoterm)
Cir	US Circuit Court
CISG	United Nations Convention on Contracts for the International Sale of Good
CISG-online	Data-bank http://www.cisg-online.ch
Civ	Chambre civile (der Cour de cassation)
CLOUT	Case Law on UNCITRAL
CLR	Commonwealth Law Reports (Australia)
CMEA	Council of Mutual Economic Assistance
CMR	Convention relative au Contrat de transport international de marchandises par route
Corp	Corporation
CR	Computer und Recht
Ct App	Court of Appeal
D	Recueil Dalloz Sirey (Frankreich)
DC	District Court
Diss	Dissertation, PhD
DtZ	Deutsch-Deutsche Rechts-Zeitschrift
EAG	Einheitliches Gesetz über den Abschluß von internationalen Kaufverträgen über bewegliche Sachen
ECJ	European Court of Justice
EGBGB	Einführungsgesetz zum Bürgerlichen Gesetzbuch
EKG	Einheitliches Gesetz über den internationalen Kauf beweglicher Sachen (17 Jul 1973)
et seq	and following
etc	et cetera
EuGH	Gerichtshof der Europäischen Gemeinschaften
EuGVO	(auch EG-VO) Verordnung (EG) Nr. 44/2001 des Rates über die gerichtliche Zuständigkeit und die Anerkennung und Vollstreckung von Entscheidungen in Zivil- und Handelssachen v. 22. 12. 2000, ABl. EG 2001, Nr. L 12, S. 1.
EuGVÜ	Europäisches Übereinkommen über die gerichtliche Zuständigkeit und die Vollstreckung gerichtlicher Entscheidungen in Zivil- und

	Handelssachen vom 27. 9. 1968, BGBl. 1972 II, S. 774
European L Forum	European Law Forum
European L Rev	European Law Review
EwiR	Entscheidungen zum Wirtschaftsrecht
F Supp	Federal Supplement
F	Federal Reporter
FCA	Federal Court of Australia
Fn	Footnote
FOB (auch fob)	free on board (Frei an Bord) (Incoterm)
FS	Festschrift
G it	Giurisprudenza italiana
Ga J Int'l & Comp L	Georgia Journal of International and Comparative Law
GPR	Zeitschrift für Gemeinschaftsprivatrecht
HGB	Handelsgesetzbuch
Hoge Raad	Supreme Court of the Netherlands
ICC	International Chamber of Commerce
ie	id est = that means, that is
IHR	Zeitschrift für Internationales Handelsrecht
Incoterms	International Commercial Terms der IntHK von 1936, ergänzt und neu ausgelegt 1953, 1974, 1976, 1980 und 1990, IntHK-Publikation Nr. 460
InfoVO	Verordnung über Informationspflichten nach bürgerlichem Recht v. 2. Januar 2002, BGBl. I S. 342
Int'l & Comp LQ	The International and Comparative Law Quarterly (Großbritannien)
IPRax	Praxis des Internationalen Privat- und Verfahrensrechts
IR	Informations rapides (Rubrik in Recueil Dalloz Sirey)
J L & Com	The Journal of Law and Commerce (USA)
JCP	Juris-Classeur Périodique (Frankreich)
JDI	Journal du Droit International (Frankreich)
JBl	Juristische Blätter (Österreich)
JMBl NW	Justizmitteilungsblatt Nordrhein-Westfalen
JR	Juristische Rundschau
JuS	Juristische Schulung
JZ	Juristenzeitung
KG	Kammergericht (Court of Appeal Berlin)
L Rev	Law Review
LG	Landgericht (High Court)
LIBOR	London Interbank Offered Rate
LJ	Lord Justice

LMK	Kommentierte BGH-Rechtsprechung, Lindenmayer/Möhring
Ltd	Limited
MMR	MultiMedia und Recht
MünchKomm	Münchener Kommentar zum Bürgerlichen Gesetzbuch
NDNY	Northern District of New York
NY	New York/New York Reports
NIPR	Nederlands Internationaal Privaatrecht (Niederlande)
NJW – RR	Neue Juristische Wochenschrift – Rechtsprechungsreport Zivilrecht
NJW	Neue Juristische Wochenschrift
No	number
Nordic J Comm L	Nordic Journal of Commercial Law
NZ Jurist	New Zealand Jurist
NZBLQ	New Zealand Business Law Quarterly
NZLJ	New Zealand Law Journal
NZLR	New Zealand Law Review
NZSGA	New Zealand Sale of Goods Act
NZULR	New Zealand Universities Law Review
OR	Official Records (s. Literaturverzeichnis, Literatur zu CISG: United Nations Conference on Contracts for the International Sale of Goods)
OGH	Oberster Gerichtshof (Austria)
OLG	Oberlandesgericht (Austria/Germany)
Or App	Oregon Court of Appealsöst.österreichische (r/s)
P2d	Pacific Reporter, Second Series (USA)
PECL	Principles of European Contract Law.
PICC	UNIDROIT-Principles of International Commercial Contracts.
ProdHaftG(auch PHG)	Gesetz über die Haftung für fehlerhafte Produkte (Produkthaftungsgesetz) vom 15. 12. 1989, BGBl. I, S. 2198
RabelsZ	Rabels Zeitschrift für ausländisches und internationales Privatrecht
Rb	Rechtbank
Rev jurispr com	Revue de jurisprudence commerciale
RG	Reichsgericht
RGZ	Entscheidungen des Reichsgerichts in Zivilsachen
RIW	Recht der Internationalen Wirtschaft, Außenwirtschaftsdienst des Betriebsberaters
Rome Convention	Convention on the Law Applicable to Cotractual Obligations (19 June 1980) (80/934/EEC)

s	Sentence
SDNY	Southern Disctrict of New York
SchRModG	Gesetz zur Modernisierung des Schuldrechts v. 26.11.2001, BGBl. I, S. 3138
Sekretariatskommentar	Commentary on the Draft Convention on Contracts for the International Sale of Goods (s.a. Literaturverzeichnis, Literatur zu CISG: Commentary)
SGA	Sale of Goods Act
SJZ	Schweizerische Juristen-Zeitung
SSGA	Sale and Supply of Goods Act
Sup Ct	Supreme Court
Syracuse J. Int.'l	L.&Com. Syracuse Journal of International Law and Commerce (USA)
SZIER	Schweizerische Zeitschrift für Internationales und Europäisches Recht (Schweiz)
Tul J Int'l and Comp L	Tulane Journal of International and Comperative Law
Tul Civ LF	Tulane Civil Law Forum (USA)
US Ct App	United States Court of Appeals
UCC	Uniform Commerical Code
ULF	Uniform Law on the Formation of Contracts for International Sale of Goods
ULIS	Uniform Law on International Sale of Goods
UN	United Nations (Vereinte Nationen)
UNCITRAL YB	UNCITRAL Yearbook
UNCITRAL	United Nations Commission on International Trade Law
UNIDROIT	Institut International pour l'Unification du Droit Privé/International Institute for the Unification of Private Law
UNILEX	Database on the UN Convention on Contracts for the International Sale of Goods
USA	United States of America
Verjährungsübereinkommen 1974	Convention on the Limitation Period in the International Sale of Goods (Übereinkommen über die Verjährung beim internationalen Warenkauf) (A/CONF.63/15), YB V (1974), 210–215 = CISG-online, materials/text/other useful texts
VertragsG	Gesetz zu dem Übereinkommen der Vereinten Nationen vom 11. April 1980 über Verträge über den internationalen Warenkauf sowie zur Änderung des Gesetzes zu dem Übereinkommen vom 19. Mai 1956 über den Beförderungsvertrag im internationalen Straßengüterverkehr

	(CMR) vom 5. 7. 1989, BGBl. II, S. 586, i. d. F. des SchRModG v. 26. 11. 2001, BGBl. I, S. 3138.
VUWLR	Victoria University of Wellington Law Review
WLR	The Weekly Law Reports (Großbritannien)
WL	West Law
WM	Wertpapier-Mitteilungen
YbComArb	Yearbook Commercial Arbitration
Z Transp R	Zeitschrift für Transportrecht
Zahlungsverzugsrichtlinie	Richtlinie 2000/35/EG des Europäischen Parlaments und des Rates vom 29. Juni 2000 zur Bekämpfung von Zahlungsverzug im Geschäftsverkehr, ABl EG Nr. L 200 S. 35.
ZEuP	Zeitschrift für Europäisches Privatrecht
ZfRV	Zeitschrift für Rechtsvergleichung (Österreich)
ZPO	Zivilprozeßordnung

Table of Cases

Argentina

Parties, Date	Source	Para
Inta SA v MCS Officina Meccanica, SpA (1 Apr 1993)	CISG-online 543 = El Derecho (25 Apr 1994)	86
Juzgado Nacional de 1° Instancia en lo Comercial N°10, Buenos Aires (23 Oct 1991)	CISG-online 460	319
Juzgado Nacional de Primera Instancia en lo Comercial (20 May 1991)	CISG-online 461	61

Australia

Parties, Date	Source	Para
Angelopoulos v Sabatino	(1995) 65 SASR 1	70c
Downs Investments Pty Ltd v Perjawa Steel SDN BHD (17 Nov 2000) (SC, Queensland)	CISG-online 859	115, 273, 310
Akai Pty Ltd v People's Insurance Co Ltd	(1996) 188 CLR 418, 440	34
Empirnall Holdings Pty Ltd v Machon Paull Partners Pty Ltd	(1988) 14 NSWLR 523	83
Felthouse v Bindley	(1862) 11 CB(NS) 869; 142 ER 1037	83

Austria

Court, Date	Source	Para
OGH (22 Oct 2001)	CISG-online 614 = IHR 2002, 24	15, 54, 211
OGH (13 Sep 2001)	CISG-online 644 = IHR 2002, 74	54
OGH (5 Jul 2001)	CISG-online 652 = IHR 2002, 73	108
OGH (25 Jan 2001)	CISG-online 1223 = IHR 2006, 110	139
OGH (7 Sep 2000)	CISG-online 642	34
OGH (28 Apr 2000)	CISG-online 581 = IHR 2001, 206	243
OGH (13 Apr 2000)	CISG-online 576	139
OGH (21 Mar 2000)	CISG-online 641 = IHR 2001, 40	61
OGH (27 Aug 1999)	CISG-online 485 = IHR 2001, 81	154
OGH (29 Jun 1999)	CISG-online 483 = Transp R – IHR 1999, 481	331
OGH (14 Oct 1997)	öst JBl 1996, 577	32
OGH (24 Apr 1997)	CISG-online 291 = Forum International 1997, 93	41
OGH (6 Feb 1996)	CISG-online 224 = öst ZfRV 1996, 248	58, 108, 297
OGH (10 Nov 1994)	CISG-online 117 = JBl 1995, 253	75
OGH (27 Oct 1994)	CISG-online 133 = öst ZGRV 1995, 161	27a
OGH (28 Apr 1993)	öst JBl 1993, 782	62
OLG (8 Aug 2005)	CISG-online 1087	11

Belgium

Court, Date	Source	Para
Rechtbank van Koophandel (8 Dec 2004)	CISG-online 980 = IHR 2005, 114	58

France

Germany

Court, Date	Source	Para
LG Baden-Baden (14 Aug 1991)	CISG-online 24 = RIW 1992, 62	91
LG Dortmund 23 Sep 1981	RIW 1981, 854	84
AG Duisburg (13 Apr 2000)	IHR 2001, 114	41
AG Frankfurt (31 Jan 1991)	CISG-online 34 = IPRax 1991, 345	42e, 266
AG Oldenburg (24 Apr 1990)	CISG-online 20 = IPRax 1991, 313	130
RG	RGZ 78, 239	81
Hans OLG Hamburg (28 Feb 1997)	CISG-online 261	309
KG (24 Jan 1994)	CISG-online 130 = RIW 1994, 683	211
LG Neubrandenburg (3 Aug 2005)	CISG-online 1190	75

Hungary

Parties, Date	Source	Para
Hungarian Chamber of Commerce (5 Dec 1995)	NJW – RR 1996	27
Supreme Court of Hungary (25 Sep 1992)	CISG-online 63	76
Fövarosi Biróság (24 Mar 1992)	CISG-online 61, Vida, IPRax 1993, 263	65
Pratt & Wittney v Malev Hungarian Airlines, (Court of the Capital City Budapest) (10 Jan 1992)	CISG-online 43 = 1992 JL & Com 49-78	29

Italy

Court, Date	Source	Para
Al Palazzo Srl v Bernardaud di Limoges SA (Tribunale di Rimini) (26 Nov 2002)	CISG-online 737	154
Appelate Court Milan (11 Dec 1998)	CISG-online 430 = Riv. dir. int. priv. proc. 1999, 112	243
LG Padova (25 Feb 2004)	CISG-online 819 = IHR 2005, 31	20
Pretura di Parma-Fidenza (24 Nov 1989)	CISG-online 316	113
Tribunale Civile Monza (14 Jan 1993)	CISG-online 540 = G.it. 1994, I, 145 (comment by Bonell)	291
Rheinland Versicherungen v Atlarex (12 Jul 2000) (Tribunale di Vigevano District Court Vigevano)	http://cisgw3.law.pace.edu/cases/0 00712i3.html CLOUT case No 378 with editorial from Charles Sant 'Elia	8

Mexico

Court, Date	Source	Para
Comisíon para la Proteccíon del Comercio Exterior de Mexico (29 April 1996)	CISG-online 350 = (1998) 17 J Law & Comm 427	131

Netherlands

Court, Date	Source	Para
Hoge Raad (28 Jan 2005)	CISG-online 1002	58
Rechtbank Roermond (19 Dec 1991)	CISG-online 29 = 10 NIPR (1992) No 394	151

New Zealand

Russia

Court, Date	Source	Para
Tribunal of International Commercial Arbitration at the Russian Federation Chamber of Commerce and Industry (21 Dec 2004)	CISG-online 1187	11
Tribunal of International Commercial Arbitration at the Russian Federation Chamber of Commerce and Industry (17 Oct 1995)	CISG-online 207	289a
Tribunal of International Commercial Arbitration at the Russian Federation Chamber of Commerce and Industry (4 Apr 1998)	CISG-online 1334	115
Tribunal of International Commercial Arbitration at the Russian Federation Chamber of Commerce and Industry (17 Oct 1995)	CISG-online 207	289a

Spain

Court, Date	Source	Para
Audiencia Provincial Barcelona (7 Jun 1999)	CISG-online 499	14

Switzerland

Court, Date	Source	Para
Appellationshof des Kantons Bern (11 Feb 2004)	CISG-online 1191 = IHR 2006, 149	50, 145, 155
BG (11 Jul 2000)	CISG-online 627	11

Court, Date	Source	Para
BG (13 Nov 2003)	CISG-online 840 = IHR 2004, 215, with comment from Mohs	43, 155
BG (5 Apr 2005)	CISG-online 1012 = IHR 2005, 204	70a, 92
BG (7 Jul 2004)	CISG-online 848= IHR 2004, 252	145
Bonaldo v AF (29 Jun 1994) Kantonsgericht Valais	http://cisgw3.law.pace.edu/cases	120
Cour de Justice de Genève (9 Oct 1998)	CISG-online 424	31
Handelsgericht des Kantons Zürich (10 Feb 1999)	CISG-online 488	153, 177
Handelsgericht des Kantons Zürich (21 Sep 1998)	CISG-online 416	153
Kantonsgericht Appenzell Ausserrhoden (10 Mar 2003)	CISG-online 852	42d
Kantonsgericht Wallis	Zeitschrift für Walliser Rechtsprechung 1994, 125	11
Kantonsgericht Wallis (19 Sep 2005)	CISG-online 1137	11
Kantonsgericht Zug (11 Dec 2003)	CISG-online 958	41
Kantonsgericht Zug (2 Dec 2004)	CISG-online 1194 = IHR 2006, 158	91
Kreisgericht Bern-Laupen (29 Sep 1999)	CISG-online 701	27a
OG Luzern (8 Jan 1997)	CISG-online 228 = SZIER 1997, 132	154
Pretura di Locarno-Campagna (27 April 1992)	CISG-online 68 = SZER 1993, 665	203
Zivilgericht Basel	BJM 1993, 310	62

UK

Parties, Date	Source	Para
Falck v Williams	[1900] AC 176 (PC)	70a
Financings Ltd v Stimson	[1962] 3 All ER 386 (CA)	95a
Gough v Everard	(1863) 2 H & C 1	189
Grant v Australian Knitting Mills	[1936] AC 85	40
Hadley v Baxendale	(1854) 9 Ex. 341, 156 Eng Rep 145 (Chancery)	302, 305
Hain SS Co Ltd v Tate & Lyle Ltd	[1936] 2 All ER 597 (HL(E))	106
Harlington & Leinster Enterprises Ltd v Christopher Hull Fine Art Ltd	[1990] 1 All ER 737 (CA)	117
Haugland Tankers AS v RMK Marine	[2005] 1 All ER (Comm) 679	83
Hedley Byrne & Co Ltd v Heller and Partners Ltd	[1964] AC 465 (HL)	42
Henderson v Merrett Syndicates Ltd	[1995] 2 AC 145 (HL)	40
Henthorn v Fraser	[1892] 2 Ch 27	95
Hilton v Tucker	(1888) 39 Ch D 669	189
Howard v Pickford Tool Co Ltd	[1951] 1 KB 417 (CA)	108
Jackson v Rotax Motor and Cycle Co	[1910] 2 KB 937	277a
King v Reedman	(1883) 49 LT 473	219
Lloyds Bank Ltd v Swiss Bankverein, Union of London and Smith's Bank Ltd v Swiss Bankverein	(1913) 108 LT 143	189
Lord Kennedy v Panama, New Zealand and Australian Royal Mail Co (Ltd)	(1867) LR 2 QB 580 (QB)	117

European Court of Justice

Arbitral Awards

Award	Source	Para
Arbitral Award International Arbitral Tribunal of the Österreichschen Bundeskammer der gewerblichen Wirtschaft (15 June 1994)	CISG-online 120, 121 = RIW 1995, 590 http://cisgw3.law.pace.edu/cases	48, 52, 152, 157, 318
Arbitral Tribunal International Chamber of Commerce, Paris (23 Aug 1994) No 7660/JK	CISG-online 129	192
Arbitral Tribunal of the Hamburg Chamber of Commerce (21 Mar 1996)	CISG-online 187= NJW 1996, 3229	24a
Arbitral Tribunal of the Hungarian Chamber of Commerce, Award (20 Dec 1993)	reported by Vida in IPRax 1995, 52	192
CIETAC (10 May 2005)	CISG-online 1022	115
CIETAC (7 Apr 1997)	http://cisg3.law.pace.edu	133
Hungarian Chamber of Commerce (5 Dec 1995)	NJW – RR 1996	27
ICC Paris (1 Jan 1992)	CISG-online 36 = JDI 1993, 1028	50, 318
ICC Paris (1 Jan 1993)	CISG-online 71 = JDI 1993, 1040, 1048 (in regard to Art 84 CISG)	50, 318
ICC Paris (1 Jan 1994)	CISG-online 565	70b

Statutes and Conventions

Introduction

1 History and Aims

1. An essential feature of the law on contemporary trade and sale of goods is consensus among the parties. Although contract law governed interactions like the selling of goods among persons within states, consensus was not taken for granted in the case of transactions across borders. Yet although many states' domestic commerce and trade had depended on the efficacy of their agreements, there was no attempt to unify the law governing these agreements until the last half of the 20th Century.[1]

As with any nascent branch of law, the early periods are fraught with controversy. Therefore, the success and wide acceptance of the UN Convention on the International Sale of Goods (CISG) is in some sense surprising, given that earlier attempts at the unification of sales of goods law had received sparse recognition. Both Hague Conventions, the Uniform Law on the International Sale of Goods (ULIS) and the Uniform Law on the Formation of Contracts for the International Sale of Goods (ULF), were only accepted by 9 states and were missing key signatory powers (like France and the United States), whose influence would have been invaluable in the development of these provisions. Furthermore, the ULIS and the ULF failed to take into account perspectives from developing nations in two ways. First, they were not present at the earlier drafting process of the conventions and hence were unable to voice their concerns. Secondly, and as a result of the first point, the approach taken by those present lacked the objectivity with regards to general contract principles[2] as they served allegedly biased interests. The resulting dissent from the Conventions by developing states led to the eventual demise of the Hague Conventions.

In saying this, the lukewarm acceptance of the Hague Conventions by the international community did not leave the ground for international sales law entirely effete. Instead, both Conventions served as an unlikely muse for UNCITRAL,[3] a subsidiary body of the General Assembly of the UN, to begin work on a new codification of international sales law. Established in 1966, UNCITRAL sported the mandate to "further the progressive harmonization and unification of the law

---

[1] Ernst Rabel made the first significant advance to unify sales law when delivering a report on this topic to the International Institute for the Unification of Private Law in Rome in 1929. See Rabel, *Rapport sur ledroit comparé en metière de vente*, see also the original *Report A* of the Institute in RabelsZ 3 (1929) 402, 406.
[2] Maskow, *Convention on the International Sale of Goods*, 45.
[3] United Nations Commission on International Trade Law.

of international trade"; the term "progressive harmonization" here meaning the reshaping of domestic laws in the aim of ensuring certainty in commercial transactions, and "unification" as the aim of ensuring that States adopt these common legal standards.[4] In light of the Hague Conventions' failure, UNCITRAL took two important steps towards realising these aims. First, it chose to incorporate both procedural and substantive aspects of international sales law into one comprehensive document, leaving behind the bisected approach of ULF and ULIS. Secondly, on the strength of a Working Group boasting greater representation, UNCITRAL achieved a finer balance between developed and developing nations, thereby removing a crucial fetter that plagued the Hague Conventions. Furthermore, Article 99 of the final text (approved at the Vienna Conference 1980) ensured that the CISG would only come into force if 10 States were to either ratify or accede to it. Hence, the membership was guaranteed not to be any lower than that of the Hague Conventions. The CISG came into force on the 1st of January 1988 and, to date, 70 countries have ratified the convention.[5]

Although the dialogue preceding the inception of the CISG broadly canvassed many issues, opinions starkly divided over a number of provisions, the vote over the final text received unanimous assent.[6] And though there remained differences between developing and industrialised states, unlike the Hague Conventions, the impasse was not fatal. The unanimity in consensus might serve as cautious optimism that a uniform law governing contracts for the sale of goods is not only theoretically possible, but capable of practical realisation as well.

2   Structure of the CISG

2.   The layout of the CISG differs from, and is often viewed independently from the Hague Conventions. The latter instruments separated the rules governing formation and those governing the substantive aspects of the contract. On the other hand the CISG collates both formation and substantive rules under Parts II and III respectively. Furthermore, unlike the Hague Conventions, the CISG adopts a 'horizontal' structure whereby the seller's obligations are followed by the buyer's remedies in the event of a breach of an obligation. This is followed by the buyer's obligations and corresponding remedies for the seller. The layout of the CISG is divided into four parts, each of which will be introduced in turn:

PART I – Sphere of Application and General Provisions.
PART II – Formation of the Contract.

---

[4]   http://www.uncitral.org/uncitral/en/about/origin_faq.html.
[5]   http://www.uncitral.org/uncitral/en/uncitral_texts/sale_goods/1980CISG.html.
[6]   Honnold, *Uniform Law for International Sales*, § 10, pp. 10–12. This Commentary provides an invaluable source of the internal workings of the process as the author himself was party to the proceedings as the representative from the United States.

PART III – Substantive Rules for the Sale of Goods. This part also contains rules on the avoidance of contract, the passing of risk, interest, and exemptions to liability.

PART IV – Final Provisions. This section contains the final public international law provisions.

3 Part I – Sphere of Application and General Provisions

3.   Consider a sales contract between parties A and B, neither of whom resides in the same state. Does the CISG apply to their contract? This is the question that Chapter 1 of Part I CISG concerns itself with. Broadly speaking, there are three situations in which the CISG (either in its entirety or a portion of its provisions) would cease to apply.

The CISG affirms and preserves the absolute autonomy of the parties to determine the content of their contract. Hence, the first situation in which the scope of the CISG can be limited is where the parties A and B themselves, expressly or impliedly, choose to derogate from some or all of the provisions (Article 6 CISG).

Second, even if the parties chose the CISG as the appropriate law, the Convention itself may limit its applicability. For example, Article 2 CISG outlines certain types of sales contracts where the Convention would not apply (like sales contracts for ships, Article 2(e) CISG). Further to this, the CISG clarifies that its only concerns are the formation of the contract and the obligations of the parties. Any factors outside of these affecting the validity of the contract remain firmly outside the Convention's scope (Article 4(a) CISG). Finally, the liability of the seller for any death or personal injury caused by the goods will not be covered under the Convention (Article 5 CISG).[7] As a result of this exclusion, domestic consumer protection legislation is preserved under the CISG.[8]

The States to which A and B belong to may also play a part in limiting the scope of the Convention. The most obvious way in which to deny the CISG any effect is not to ratify or accede to it. However, the application of the CISG may also extend to parties that do not have their place of business in a Contracting State by virtue of Article 1(1)(b) CISG.[9] The Convention's reference here to the parties' place of business provided a simple and more effective test than the Hague Conventions, which also included inquiries as to where the offer and acceptance were established. Such further inquiries, however, convoluted what needed to be a concise and lucid test.[10] A state may also make various declarations limiting the scope of the CISG; though these are dealt with in Part IV.

---

[7] These instances of the CISG confining its own bounds are not exhaustive. For a more thorough treatment see paras 33 et seq.

[8] Art 2(a) CISG also results in the same preservation in that it excludes contracts of a personal nature from the sphere of application.

[9] See paras 14 et seq.

[10] See Honnold, *Uniform Law for International Sales*, § 40, p. 30.

The second chapter of Part I CISG specifically deals with issues of interpretation, trade usages and other general provisions regarding contractual form.

The general principles within the CISG regarding interpretation and trade usage may be enumerated as follows:

Interpretation of the CISG: regard must be given to the international character, the need to promote uniformity in application of the Convention and the observance to good faith (Article 7(1) CISG).[11]

Interpretation of the parties' conduct: Statements or conduct are to be interpreted according to the intention the other party gleaned (or ought to have gleaned) or, failing this, interpreted in relation to the reasonable person standard. In either case, no fetter is placed on the source of the statements or conduct and the intention can stem from negotiations and subsequent conduct (Article 8, CISG).[12]

Parties may bind themselves by any practices they have either established between themselves (Article 9(1) CISG) or are widely known in the type of contract they have entered (Article 9(2) CISG).[13]

In the absence of any principle within the CISG to aid interpretation, courts are allowed to construct a principle by way of analogy with one of the other provisions in the Convention or private international law (Article 7(2) CISG). However, how such "gap-filling" provisions like Article 7(2) CISG are to establish principles not explicitly within the CISG, remains an open and important question in the literature.[14] In fact the preservation of uniformity may hinge on an adequate solution to this question. For example, if courts reverted to domestic law wherever general principles were unavailable (and a cursory attempt to find an analogy provides little help) then the aim of uniformity may erode.

Most importantly, there are no strict requirements as to contractual form and the contract can be evidenced by any means whatsoever (Article 11).[15] Many commentators also recommend the term 'writing' to be interpreted so as to include e-mail correspondence.[16]

4   Part II – Formation of the Contract

4.   Whether there is a contract or not is the main inquiry within Part II. These provisions relate to the offer (Articles 14-17 CISG), the acceptance (Articles 18-22 CISG) and the timing of the conclusion of the contract. The rules on offer and acceptance are orthodox in their treatment and the revocability of an offer (so

---

[11] See paras 43 et seq.

[12] See paras 54 et seq.

[13] See paras 56, 59 et seq.

[14] See Honnold, *Uniform Law for International Sales*, § 21 and § 94.

[15] See paras 64 et seq.

[16] Currently the term writing only extends to telegram and telex (Art 13 CISG), a reflection of the technology present during the course of the drafting of the Convention.

long is it is before the other party has accepted) was a compromise to facilitate the common law view on revocation.[17]

Furthermore, these provisions make no reference to the incorporation of standard business terms which are of major practical importance. For example, the celerity with which many companies can make acceptances (via acknowledgement and order forms) often becomes a routine that amounts to a usage. In cases like this, problems emerge where defects arise or are found after the speedy transaction as to what the terms of the contract were.[18] Hence, the efficiency of business transactions (or the 'reality' of it as it is so often called) should be an important factor in interpreting these provisions.

5   Part III – Substantive Rules for the Sale of Goods

5.   Once a contract has been established, Part III (Chapters II and III) establishes the scope and extent of the rights and obligations of the buyer and seller.

Further to this, one can avoid a contract only in the event of a fundamental breach (Article 49(1)(a) CISG). Fundamental breach is defined in Article 25 CISG as a substantial deprivation of what one party has expected from the contract. Usually this will only be satisfied where there is a non-delivery, non-payment or a failure to take delivery. As with the ULIS, *peius* (non-conforming goods) and *aliud* (totally different goods) are treated the same way: as goods whose quality is not in accordance with the contract.

The CISG is extensive with respect to remedies in that it offers both performance and damages to the aggrieved party. Article 46(1) CISG gives the buyer the right to specific performance; a right often seen as the 'backbone' of obligation in civil law countries. But the granting of specific performance is subject to whether the seller has done something inconsistent with the right to specific performance (Article 46(1) CISG) and whether domestic courts would allow it (Article 28 CISG). Curiously, performance can still be granted where there is an impediment preventing a party from performing (Article 79(5) CISG).

6   Part IV – Final Provisions

6.   The final provisions relate to certain matters relating to public international law and some will rarely be of interest to either party to the transaction.[19] However, two provisions are worth noting here as they shed light on the CISG itself. First, Article 92 CISG allows any Contracting State to make a declaration that neither Part II nor Part III is to apply. Were a state to make such a reservation then they are not considered Contracting States in respect of matters to which the

---

[17] See in regard to the common law position *Adams v Lindsell* (1818) 1 B & Ald 681, 106 ER 250.
[18] See Honnold, *Uniform Law for International Sale,* § 165.
[19] Honnold, *Uniform Law for International Sales,* § 458, p. 529.

reservation applies (Article 92(2) CISG). In particular, States may make reservations with respect to formal requirements required of their domestic laws (Article
96 CISG). For example, the domestic law may require all contracts to be in writing and a State that has made a reservation under Article 96 CISG denies the
application of Article 29(1) CISG. At present these declarations serve as a hin-
drance to uniform application of the CISG and it is hoped that such reservations
are revoked within time.

Secondly, the fact that the CISG only took effect twelve months after the 10th
state had incorporated it (Article 99(1) CISG) shows that 'self-execution' is an
inherent aspect of the Convention. In contrast, the preceding Hague Conventions
had to be brought into force by way of annexing a treaty.

7   Achieving the Ideal – New Directions for the CISG

7.   In light of the provisions of the CISG, it is important to keep in mind the
ideals that the CISG accumulates for future application. The ideals to be achieved
can be broadly categorised as that of uniformity, flexibility, filtration and practicability.

Uniformity: In relation to the gap-filling provisions, it is important that principles are created in line with international literature and practice. In this way, states
must do more than just ratify the CISG but must incorporate its principles effectively (evading inconsistency) into its domestic law. Particular regard must be
given to uniform establishment of specific examples for indefinite legal concepts,
like that of "reasonable time" explained above. Further legal concepts like "foreseeable damage" also need to be petrified by way of concrete examples.

Two dangers to unification are, first, when courts revert to domestic law without adequately ascertaining whether it is possible to glean principle from the CISG
or private international law. Second, the rules may be threatened by the *lex fori*
which classifies certain sale of goods law under rules of validity. For example, in
one US case the Courts included the requirement of consideration into a contract
where the CISG applied as the Courts considered it a matter of validity, and hence,
outside the scope of the Convention (Article 4(1) CISG).[20] Furthermore, the
application could be disrupted by tort claims or *culpa in contrahendo*,[21] public law
or laws governing mistake.

The view that uniformity in international sale of goods law is a chimerical and
utopian ideal, incapable of realisation in practice, may find favour among those
who find any Convention that runs through this process of debate between nations

---

[20] *Shuttle Packaging Systems v Tsonakis INA SA et al.*, US DC Michigan (17 Dec 2001) CISG-
online 773.

[21] *Culpa in contrahendo* ("cic") is a judicially crafted doctrine of the German law of obligations.
Literally translated from the Latin, it means "culpable conduct during contract negotiations." The
doctrine was developed by the courts to impose a mutual duty of care upon persons who were not
yet in privity of contract. The doctrine is now codified in § 311(a) BGB. See in regard to case law,
for example, BGH (26 Oct 1961) NJW 1962, 31 et seq.

where there is a lack of representation by certain nations, hence resulting in either a concession to more dominant interests or an agreement to disagree. For example, such a view can be said of the Human Rights Conventions enacted following the Second World War II where many dominant interests were pursued at the expense of other nation's values.

First, it is important to notice that the ideal is not a contemporary one but one that underpins the doctrine of *lex mercatoria* which extends back to the 16th and 17th centuries. Secondly, by definition an agreement between two parties is very much about finding common ground. If it is accepted that international trade could not exist without effective solutions in the event of disputes then the above argument above cannot be sustained. Unlike the CISG, Human Rights Conventions impinge on the way of life of people within their own nations. However, the CISG governs relations between people from different states and hence should be the very subject of uniformity.

The ideal of uniformity can be achieved by employing a consistent approach to existing provisions of the CISG and filling gaps by way of article 7(2) CISG. With respect to existing provisions, common law states may be unwilling to forego domestic law in favour of the CISG. Two examples are that of the non-requirement of consideration and the favouring of specific performance over damages as a remedy. Both of these requirements can be seen as an inherent bias towards civil law. However, the more appropriate view may be that the shift is from looking at an agreement as a *contract* to viewing it as a *promise*.[22]

Flexibility: Is the CISG flexible? Professor Honnold maintains that the CISG must in general be willing to purge itself of 'old relics'.[23] For example, Article 13 CISG includes the outdated telegram as 'writing' but is silent as to electronic correspondence which furnishes modern economic reality. Other key definitions like 'goods' may also need extension so as to include intangibles like software programs and hence maintain in step with technological advances.

Another cause for concern revolves around the inadequate rules in Art 19 CISG. These rules are commonly termed under the category of 'battle of the forms' as the problem relates to when an acceptance is made in the middle of a myriad of complex transactions.[24] Issues surrounding contractual variations in the event of changed circumstances will also need further clarification.[25]

Filtration: Professor Schlechtriem argues that principles in the CISG must seep into domestic law, especially where the law falls silent on a point of contention.[26] Such integration has already been highly successful in Germany following the revision of the German Civil Code and the Baltic States. In doing so Professor Schlechtriem concludes that these states have enriched their domestic sales law

---

[22] The importance of viewing agreements in light of this distinction can be found in Shiffrin, (2007) 120 Harv L Rev, 3.

[23] Honnold, *Uniform Law for International Sales*, § 18.

[24] Lavers, (1993) Int'l Bus Law, 11, 12.

[25] Schlechtriem in Schlechtriem/Schwenzer, *Commentary*, Introduction, para 9. The common law position on this point can be found in *Williams v Roffey Bros & Nicholls (Contractors) Ltd* [1991] 1 QB 1.

[26] Schlechtriem in Schlechtriem/Schwenzer, *Commentary*, Introduction, para 9.

with CISG jurisprudence. Given that the rules are intended for universal application, there may be room for optimism that the CISG is capable of application to domestic disputes as well.[27]

Yet this view is in direct opposition with the doctrine of precedent whereby the common law courts look to previous decisions for filling gaps in favour international instruments like the CISG. However, the importance of interpreting domestic legislation consistent with international instruments is gaining favour in even the highest courts in common law jurisdictions. Furthermore, interpretations consistent with the CISG would also serve as a catalyst in producing more CISG-related precedent; the dearth of which has caused concern to the common law.[28]

Practicability: The CISG's attempts to unify sales law stands or falls on its successful implementation by both scholars and practitioners. Although there are examples of states that have embedded the CISG into their jurisprudence (like Germany, Scandinavia, and the Netherlands), further progress is needed. Some states, for example, still require their legislatures to embrace the Convention. One notable example is the failure of the United Kingdom to ratify the CISG. As UK jurisprudence is highly persuasive authority to other Commonwealth nations, failing to take the CISG into account serves as a fetter on the development of a uniform body of law in these nations as well.[29]

Furthermore, even in the event that a state has ratified the CISG, some commentators argue that the courts must forego any reluctance they may have in applying the CISG in favour of domestic law.[30] Such reluctance can, for example, be found in recent Canadian decisions.[31]

8   Structure and Aims of this Book

7a.   This book follows the same structure as the CISG for ease of use. However, where necessary, relationships between provisions or commentary of groups of provisions will also be dealt with rather than an isolated analysis of each article.[32] As the literature on the CISG grows the importance of separating the law and the authors' opinions of what the law ought to be accrues greater significance, especially to the student traversing this terrain for the first time. As this text is often the first port of call for many students, this ideal becomes all the more important. This book attempts to maintain this divide, clearly signposting which statements are established fact and which opinion.

---

[27]   Honnold, *Uniform Law for International Sales*, § 14.

[28]   Lavers, above fn 18, at 10–11.

[29]   Similar considerations may be said to hold of Brazil with respect to South America; see Grebler, 25 J L & Com, 467.

[30]   Sharma, (2005) 36 VUWLR, 847.

[31]   *Nova Tool and Mould Inc v London Industries Inc* [1998] CarswellOnt 4950 (Ontario Court of Justice), *La San Giuseppe v Forti Moulding Ltd* [1999] CarswellOnt 2837 (Ontario Superior Court of Justice).

[32]   The autonomous and isolated treatment of each article can be found in Schlechtriem/Schwenzer, above fn 25.

The aims of this book are more modest than other compendious treatments of the CISG.[33] The main aim above all is to facilitate discussion on the use and application of the provisions of the CISG. As the CISG itself was the corollary of nearly a decade of debate between nations polarised in ideology, the importance of continuing discussion cannot be understated. In its aid, references to further views (both for and against) are given along with the parallel provisions of the United Kingdom Sale of Goods Act 1979 (SOG), the US Uniform Commercial Code (UCC) and Canadian, Australian and New Zealand legislation and jurisprudence. This allows for a comparative analysis for a reader used to the common law approach to sale of goods law in the hope that domestic law within common law nations may be coloured by the principles of the CISG and hence achieve greater uniformity.

---

[33]   See for example, Schlechtriem/Schwenzer, *Commentary*.

Part I of the CISG – Sphere of Application and General Provisions

1 Application and Ambit of the CISG Articles 1-6

1.1 Introduction

8. The sphere of application of the CISG, that means its applicability to certain contracts, falls to be determined according to its own rules of application set out in Articles 1 to 6 CISG. To determine its applicability, the CISG relies on elements related to (a) the parties (and their connection to a Contracting State to the CISG) and (b) to the transaction itself. Only where Articles 1 to 6 CISG leave a gap, or specifically allow, are choice of law rules to be used to determine the application of the CISG to the contract in question.[1]

In addition to providing rules relating to the application of the CISG, Articles 1 to 6 CISG provide rules which limit its scope. These rules are of great importance because the unification of sales law of different legal jurisdictions' traditions through the CISG is only a partial one: the CISG only purports to regulate a section of the law, namely that concerning a sales contract and its performance. Therefore, in practice domestic law (which is determined by private international law rules) will be applicable together with the CISG. Accordingly, it is advisable to stipulate in a contract not only the applicability of the CISG but also the domestic law governing the contract.

1.2 Application Requirements

9. The first requirement for the application of the CISG is that the parties have their respective places of business in different states (Article 1(1) CISG). Article 10 CISG provides specific rules for situations where one or both parties have several or no places of business. In the case of several places of business the branch which has the closest connection to the contract and its performance is determinative (Article 10(a) CISG).[2]

---

[1] See *Rheinland Versicherungen v Atlarex* (12 Jul 2000) District Court Vigevano with editorial from Charles Sant 'Elia (http://cisgw3.law.pace.edu/cases/000712i3.html) Tribunale di Vigevano (12 Jul 2000) CLOUT case No 378.

[2] See for a more in depth discussion of Art 10 CISG Schlechtriem in Schlechtriem/Schwenzer, *Commentary*, Art 10.

Example: The buyer, Asante Technologies Inc, which has its principal place of business in California, bought from PMC-Sierra Inc, which was represented by a dealer whose place of business was also in California, ASICs (Application-Specific Integrated Circuits). The seller had been incorporated in Delaware and had a branch in California. However, the administration and its design and engineering functions were situated for the most part in Burnaby, British Columbia (Canada). The buyer had ordered directly from the seller's branch in Burnaby and delivery of the goods had been made from there. The buyer had been invoiced by the seller's Californian dealer.

The District Court decided that the CISG was applicable to the contract because the parties had their places of business in different countries, the USA and Canada. The main contacts with regard to the sale contracts in question existed with the seller's branch in Canada, the contacts to the dealer in California on the other hand were of lesser importance, so that according to Article 10 CISG the *closest relationship* was with the Canadian branch.[3]

The use of electronic communication means to the degree, as used today, had not been anticipated by the drafters of the CISG. How their use reflects the application of the CISG is partly answered by the UNCITRAL Model Law on Electronic Commerce. It referred to the issue at hand it should be noted that, in cases where the parties use electronic means for their communication, the place of the server is not determinative of where the closest connection of a contract with a branch lies.[4]

If a party does not have a place of business at all, its place of residence is decisive (Article 10(b) CISG).

10.   That the parties have their respective places of business in different states is the determinative "across borders" requirement for the application of the CISG. The "foreign connection", however, must also be apparent either from the contract, or from the dealings between, or information disclosed by, the parties during the negotiations (Article 1(2) CISG).

Example: If a German company with its branch in Germany buys something from the German agent of a Swiss company (which does not have a branch in Germany) then the German company must have been aware that the agent acted for the Swiss company and/or that the Swiss company has the closest connection to the contract and its performance, for the CISG to apply pursuant to Article 10(a) CISG. If the agent did not reveal that he/she contracted on behalf of the Swiss company and if it is not evident that the contract has a close connection with the Swiss company

---

[3]   *Asante Technologies Inc v PMC-Sierra Inc* US District Court (Northern District Court of California) (27 Jul 2001) CISG-online 616 = 164 F Supp 2d, 1142.

[4]   UNCITRAL Model Law on Electronic Commerce, 1996 (http://www.uncitral.org) (last accessed 1 Feb 2007), in regard to declarations by electronic means see below para 70b.

(either through previous dealings between the parties, the negotiations, or from the contract or its performance), the CISG will not be applicable. Instead, German law would apply.[5]

1.3   Application of the CISG in Accordance with Autonomous Requirements

11.   Even if the branches of the parties are in different states, the CISG only applies if these states are member states of the CISG and at the time of the conclusion of the contract the states had incorporated the CISG into their national law.[6] With the rising number of member states, the application of the CISG via Article 1(1)(a), namely that the CISG automatically applies to contracts of sale of goods between parties whose place of business are in different CISG member states has become more and more the norm.[7] In summary, if the requirements of "places of business of the parties in different member states" are met, then the CISG is generally applicable to the contract between the parties.[8]

12.   The nationalities of the parties or whether the parties are merchants is of no consequence in determining the application of the CISG (Article 4 CISG). First, there is no call for an inquiry into whether a party meets the legal requirements of

---

[5]   *Sarl Pelliculest et al., v GmbH Morton International et al.*, Cour d'appel de Colmar: CISG-online 578. Compare also Schlechtriem in Schlechtriem/Schwenzer, *Commentary*, Art 10 para 5 et seq.

[6]   See Art 100 CISG. As of 1 Feb 2007, 70 states have adopted the CISG. Pursuant to Art 99(1) CISG, "This Convention enters into force, ... on the first day of the month following the expiration of twelve months after the date of deposit of the tenth instrument of ratification, acceptance, approval or accession." In December 1987, the People's Republic of China deposited the tenth ratification. The CISG entered into force, therefore, on 1 January 1988. See also *Ajax Tool Works Inc v Can-Eng Manufacturing Ltd* 2003 US District Court (NDI 11) (29 Jan 2003), Lexis 1306.

[7]   See, for example, *BP International, Ltd and BP Exploration & Oil, Inc v Empresa Estatal Petroleos de Ecuador, et al.*, US Ct Appeal (5th Cir) (11 Jun 2003) CISG-online 730 (parties in Pennsylvania, USA, and Ecuador). However, it should also be noted that the fact that the CISG "automatically" applies does not mean that parties and/or Courts are more aware of it. Anecdotal evidence from Australia and New Zealand suggests that often neither lawyer, judges nor businesses are aware of the CISG and, therefore, do not argue it but decide according to domestic law: see Lutz, 35 (2004) VUWLR, 711.

[8]   See the very precise remark in regard to the application requirements of the Swiss Kantonsgericht Wallis, Zeitschrift für Walliser Rechtsprechung 1994, 125, Kantonsgericht Wallis (19 Sep 2005) CISG-online 1137 (C10433), BG (11 Jul 2000) CISG-online 627, and OLG Linz (8 Aug 2005) CISG-online 1087 (3 R 57/05f).
Oberste Gerichtshof (24 May 2005) CISG-online 1046.
Vision Systems Inc et al., Vision Fire & Security Pty Ltd v EMC Superior Court of Massachusetts (28 Feb 2005) CISG-online 1005.
Tribunal of International Commercial Arbitration at the Russian Federation Chamber of Commerce and Industry (21 Dec 2004) CISG-online 1187.
Valero Marketing & Supply Company v Greeni Oy & Greeni Trading Oy US DC, NJ (15 Jun 2005) CISG-online 1028: The requirements of Art 1(1)(a) are fulfilled since on the one hand, the parties have their branches in different member states and on the other hand, the Convention came into force for Italy on 1 January 1988 and for Switzerland and 3 Mar 1991 so that in the area of international sale of goods a unifying law applies. See also *Chateau Des Charmes Wines Ltd v Sabate, USA Inc* http://www.yorku.ca/osgoode/cisg/ChateauDesCharmesWinesv.Sabate.htm.

a particular state in respect of the states of being a merchant.[9] Second, the fact that nationality does not play a role in determining the applicability of the CISG is an advantage with regard to the use of the CISG since it releases parties from an inquiry into the nationality of the other contracting party or parties, and in particular from the sometimes difficult question of the nationality of a legal person.[10]

The following discussion on the UCC rules in regard to "who is a merchant" illustrates the sometimes rather difficult inquiry into this issue: under the UCC merchants are professionals in business. The professional status may be based upon specialised knowledge of the goods, specialised knowledge of business practices, or both.

The UCC distinguishes between two types of merchants. First, under § 2-314 UCC a merchant is considered to be someone selling a specific good and having special knowledge about it. Secondly, a more relaxed type of merchant is envisaged by § 2-201(2), § 2-207, § 2-209 UCC which covers nearly everyone in business. Therefore, practically most sales of goods will be conducted by a merchant under the UCC.[11]

13. The above mentioned requirements will mean that for the most part, tribunals which have to decide upon its application to a particular matter will be in one of the member states to the CISG and the CISG, in turn, will be one of the laws which belongs to the natural realm of the tribunal.

However, the CISG can also be applied by a court of a non-member state. Take for example, a scenario where the parties' places of business are in different member states but the dispute comes before a tribunal in a non-member state[12] and the private international law of the tribunal in the non-member state leads to the application of the law of a member state to the CISG. In such a case, the tribunal or court will have to apply the CISG as the tribunal or court of the member-state would do.

1.4   Applicability Because of Private International Law Rules

14. The CISG can be applicable even if neither party has its seat in a member state. According to Article 1(1)(b) CISG, the CISG is applicable if the private international law rules of the forum state lead to the application of the law of a CISG member state. For example, the forum state could be a member state whose private international law rules determine that its own law, and therefore the CISG,

---

[9] Practically, the parties to contracts which fall under the CISG (because of Art 2(a) CISG) will nearly always contract within the bounds of commercial activity and, therefore, will satisfy the formal requirements of the merchant, for example, under German and French law.

[10] See discussion in UNCITRAL YB VIII (1997) 26.

[11] UCC §§ 2-104 (see also §§ 2-201(2), 2-207, 2-209 UCC), see also Willier/Hart, *Uniform Commercial Code*, §§ 2-104 para 2.

[12] In the course of the book "X" and "Y" will be used to signify non-member states instead of using existing states as examples since the ongoing ratifications of the CISG by states could otherwise render information on the status of states as non-member states obsolete.

is applicable.[13] The forum state could also be a non-member-state whose private international law rules refer to the law of a member state (for example, because one of the parties has its relevant place of business in a member state).[14]

15.   The reason for referring to the law of a CISG member state through the application of the forum state's private international law rules is irrelevant: whether the law of a member state is applicable because the contract has its most significant relationship[15] in that state or because of the parties' express or implied choice is not important. However, if the parties choose the law of a CISG member state, an issue sometimes arises as to whether the parties chose the law of that state *in toto*, or only the domestic sale of goods law and thereby intended to exclude the application of the CISG as permitted by Article 6 CISG. The question of whether a general reference to national law includes a reference to the CISG is disputed in the case law and academic writing.[16] In the authors' view, unless the parties have expressly referred to the domestic sales law of a state the reference to the national law of a member state either through private international law or by the choice of the parties includes the CISG.[17] In each individual circumstance, the intention of the parties should be considered by applying Article 8 CISG.[18]

Some authors are of the opinion that the reference to the national law of a member state must be read as excluding a reference to the CISG if Article 1(1)(a) is applicable (if, say, both parties have their seats in member states) because otherwise the parties' express choice of law could be rendered meaningless.[19]

---

[13] See for the application of its own substantive law by a forum state: BGH (26 Mar 1992) CISG-online 67 = WM 1992, 1715: seller has business in Germany (member state), buyer in Great Britain (non-member state); similar Audiencia Provincial Barcelona (7 Jun 1999) CISG-online 499: Spanish-English sales contract; the Court when determining its jurisdiction relied on the CISG as Spanish law in regard to the question of the place of performance which was determinative to decide jurisdiction.

[14] Even before the CISG was in force in Germany the courts were not shy to apply the CISG especially in regard to sale of goods contracts with Italy and France (where the CISG was in force before Germany), because Germany's private international rules lead to the application of the law of the seller.

[15] See Art 4(1) of the Rome Convention which uses the term "closest connection"; in English private international law the "closest and most real connection test" is used to determine the applicable law if the express or implied choice of the parties cannot be established (see *Amin Rasheed Corp v Kuwait Insurance* [1984] 1 AC 50 (HL); Dicey, *The Conflict of Laws*, para 32–006).

[16] Schlechtriem in Schlechtriem/Schwenzer, *Commentary* (with further overview of the dispute), Art 6 para 14.

[17] Compare *Ajax Tool Works Inc v Can-Eng Manufacturing Ltd* 2003 US District Court (NDI 11) (29 Jan 2003), Lexis 1306; *Asante Technologies Inc v PMC-Sierra Inc* US District Court (Northern District Court of California) (27 Jul 2001) CISG-online 616 = 164 F Supp 2d, 1142; OGH (22 Oct 2001) CISG-online 614 = IHR 2002, 24, 25. *American Mint LLC, Goede Beteiligungsgesellschaft, and Michael Goede v GO Software Inc* (6 Jan 2006) US DC MD (Pennsylvania) CISG-online 1175 (CivA 1:05-CV-650) "parties must affirmatively opt out"; further references Ferrari in Schlechtriem/Schwenzer, Art 6 paras 22 et seq; Magnus in *Staudinger*, Art 6 para 28; Winship, *Scope*, 1–35, 36; see for contrary opinion which holds that the CISG is not intended in a reference to the national law of a member state: Honnold, *Uniform Law for International Sales*, § 77.1 at the end.

[18] See para 54.

[19] Compare Neumayer/Ming, Art 6 No 6, p. 89 et seq. See also the contrary decision by the US courts: "agreement to include domestic law fails to specifically exclude application of the CISG"

However, in the authors' opinion this view is erroneous. There are often reasons why the parties might express a choice of law in their contract. For example, the CISG only provides for particular matters arising out of a sale of goods contract but it does not deal with others, such as set-off, assignment, and validity of the contract.[20] Therefore, a choice of law clause is always advisable in a sale of goods contract, even if the CISG is already applicable pursuant to Article 1(1)(a) CISG. The law concerning the areas not covered by the CISG has to be determined by private international law rules. In this respect the parties' choice of law is the most important.

16. The reference to the law of a member state can result in the application of the CISG even if the parties are from different states but neither of the parties has its seat in a member state. This scenario, anticipated in Article 1(1)(b) CISG, has been a concern since the parties are subjected to a sale of goods law, namely the CISG, which is not applicable to either of the parties as part of its national law. Article 1(1)(b) CISG was, therefore, very controversial during its drafting in Vienna.[21] However, Article 1(1)(b) CISG is justifiable in that it is easier for a judge to apply the CISG, which is easily accessible, is printed in many languages (six official languages and 13 unofficial languages), and has been subjected to jurisprudential and academic analysis on the world stage. The alternative is for a judge to have to apply a national law which might be inaccessible for him or her and in his or her view very obscure. This is also true for the parties. Even if the applicability of the CISG comes as a surprise to the parties, the CISG devises a legal paradigm for specific problems arising out of cross-border sales of goods contracts often more modern than a domestic sale of goods law. But importantly, the advantage of the domestic sale of goods law can only ever be afforded to one party whereas the CISG is more advantageous because it is "neutral" as between the parties.

17. Article 1(1)(b) CISG is sometimes wrongly interpreted: it is not itself a provision of private international law, but its application requires the use of the private international law rules of the forum state and the reference to the law of a

---

American Mint LLC, Goede Beteiligungsgesellschaft, and Michael Goede v GO Software Inc US DC MD (Pennsylvania) (6 Jan 2006) CISG-online 1175 (CivA 1:05-CV-650); *BP International, Ltd and BP Exploration & Oil, Inc v Empresa Estatal Petroleos de Ecuador, et al.,* US Ct Appeal (5th Cir) (11 Jun 2003) CISG-online 730;
Asante Technologies Inc v PMC-Sierra Inc US District Court (Northern District Court of California) (27 Jul 2001) CISG-online 616 = 164 F Supp 2d, 1142 (ND Cal 2001);
Ajax Tool Works Inc v Can-Eng Manufacturing Ltd 2003 US District Court (NDI 11) (29 Jan 2003), Lexis 1306;
Valero Marketing & Supply Company v Greeni Oy & Greeni Trading Oy US DC, NJ (15 Jun 2005) CISG-online 1028; and for arguments that "choice of national law excludes CISG" see: *Delchi Carrier SpA v Rotorex Corp* (6 Dec 1995) US Court of Appeals (2nd Circ) CISG-online 140 = 10 F 3rd 1024; *Viva Vino Import Corporation v Farnese Vini Srl* (29 Aug 2000) IHR 2002, 28 (US ED Pennsylvania) (Italian-US parties to a contract) or CISG-online 675;
Claudia v Oliveri Footwear Ltd, 1998 WL 164824 (SDNY) (7 Apr 1998);
American Biophysics v Dubois Marine Specialties a/k/a Dubois Motor Sports US DC Rhode Island, (30 Jan 2006) CISG-online 1176.

[20] See paras 34 et seq, 41 respectively.
[21] Schlechtriem in Schlechtriem/Schwenzer, *Commentary,* Art 1 para 36.

member state. As part of the national law of the referred to member state, Article 1(1)(b) CISG is a "distribution" provision which divides the law of the member state in the area of sale of goods into different strands: first, sale of goods law relating to domestic sale of goods contracts including special consumer protection laws; and second, sale of goods law relating to international sale of goods contracts.[22] Article 1(1)(b) CISG is, therefore, similar to § 2-102 UCC in its function.[23]

1.5   Reservation Against the Application Because of Private International Law Rules

18.   The reservations against and disagreements with regard to Article 1(1)(b) CISG resulted in the adoption of Article 95 CISG which allows member states to implement the CISG without being bound by Article 1(1)(b) CISG ("will not be bound by").[24] Therefore, when considering the application of the CISG, one has to keep in mind that member states, member states with an Article 95 CISG reservation, and non-member states exist side-by-side. If the CISG is only applicable because of private international law rules, confusing situations can occur.[25] However, as discussed above,[26] the function of Article 1(1)(b) CISG should be understood as being one of distributing the contract law of the member states: where a member state, because of an Article 95 CISG reservation, has made Article 1(1)(b) CISG inapplicable, then the member state signals that it wants, when private international law rules refer to its law, not that the CISG applies, but rather its domestic sale of contract law applies. In such a case, the CISG can only be applied if the requirements for the application of Article 1(1)(a) CISG are met (that is, both parties have their places of business in a member state). The decision of a national legislature in a "reservation member state" has to be respected even if it is a foreign court [27] whose private international law rules lead to the law of a reservation member state.

---

[22] Convincing also in regard to this question Teklote, *Einheitlichen Kaufgesetze*, 50: internal norm of the applicable domestic law; see also: Willier/Hart, *Uniform Commercial Code*, paras 21–02.

[23] §§ 2-102 UCC states: "Unless the context otherwise requires, this Article applies to transactions in goods; it does not apply to any transaction which although in the form of an unconditional contract to sell or present sale is intended to operate only as a security transaction nor does this Article impair or repeal any statute regulating sales to consumers, farmers or other specified classes of buyers."

[24] For example important member states such as the US, Singapore and China have made the Art 95 CISG reservation. (See Appendix 2 – reservation States are marked *).

[25] Peter Winship constructed 54 different case scenarios, which demonstrate the unwieldy situations which may occur because of the Art 95 CISG reservation (the application of the CISG because of private international law rules). Winship, *Scope*, 1–26. Gabriel, *Contracts for the Sale of Goods*, 23 (with fn 94), 25. A comprehensive overview in regard to the different scenarios can be found in Pünder, RIW 1990, 869–873, Kren-Kostkiewicz/Schwander, *FS Neumayer*, 33 et seq, 42 et seq.

[26] See para 17.

[27] The question is controversial because the wording of Art 95 CISG could be interpreted to mean that Art 1(1)(b) CISG only binds the "reservation member state" but not other (non-reservation) member states. However, the principle stipulated in Art 7 CISG "to interpret the CISG in such a way as to promote its uniform application" means that Art 95 has to be interpreted so that decisions with the decisions harmonious of the "reservation member state" will be achieved. The German CISG ratification in 1989 ("Gesetz zu dem Übereinkommen der Vereinten Nationen vom 11. April 1980 über Verträge über den internationalen Warenkauf sowie zur Änderung des Gesetzes

Example: The buyer's place of business is in non-Member State X; the seller's in the "reservation Member State" USA. The private international law rules in X lead to US law. In these circumstances, the CISG is not applicable because the USA has made an Article 95 reservation in respect of Article 1(1)(b) CISG.

The German parliament has expressly provided for this exact solution, as set out above, in Article 2 of the "Gesetz zu dem Übereinkommen der Vereinten Nationen vom 11. April 1980 über Verträge über den internationalen Warenkauf sowie zur Änderung des Gesetzes zu dem Übereinkommen vom 19. Mai 1956 über den Beförderungsvertrag im internationalen Straßengüterverkehr (CMR)" of 5 July 1989 (BGB1 II 586).[28] Of course the CISG would not be applicable if the private international law rules of the forum state[29] lead to the law of state X where state X is not a member state and, therefore, the CISG is not part of its law.

However, if the parties have their places of business in a "reservation member state" and a member state respectively, then this issue with Article 1(1)(b) CISG does not arise. Instead the CISG will apply by virtue of Article 1(1)(a).

Example: A contract for sale is concluded between an US buyer and an Italian seller. The CISG is applicable because both parties have their place of business in member states. Italy and the USA are both member states,[30] although the USA has made a reservation in accordance with Article 95 CISG. Private international law rules do not have to be taken into account if courts in either the USA or Italy are seized of a case.[31]

1.6   Party Autonomy

19.   Article 6 CISG provides for the principle of party autonomy in relation to the choice of law and the choice of substantive law and corresponds in that regard with that of most countries in that contractual freedom is also the CISG rule.[32]

---

zu dem Übereinkommen vom 19. Mai 1956 über den Beförderungsvertrag im internationalen Stra-ßengüterverkehr (CMR)" of 5 Jul 1989 (BGB1 II 586), Art 2 states "if the private international law rules lead to the application of the law of a state, which made a reservation according to Art 95 of the Convention of 1980, Art 1(1)(b) of the Convention will be disregarded". See in regard to the controversy Schlechtriem in Schlechtriem/Schwenzer, Art 1 para 42, Art 95 para 4.

[28] This is the Act ratifying the CISG and making it German law. See for further discussion Schlechtriem in Schlechtriem/Schwenzer, *Commentary*, Art 1 paras 42–44.

[29] This is the state where the dispute is heard.

[30] See Appendix 2.

[31] See as well *Viva Vino Import Corporation v Farnese Vini Srl* (29 Aug 2000) IHR 2002, 28 (US ED Pennsylvania) (Italian-US parties to a contract) or CISG-online 675. *Filanto SpA v Chilewich International Corp* DC (SDNY) (14 Apr 1992) CISG-online 45 = 789 F Supp 1229 (contract between an Italian seller and US buyer).

[32] See, for example, Lookofsky, *Understanding the CISG*, § 2-7; see more general to the concept of party autonomy in contract law Cherednychenko, 8.1 (March 2004) EJCL http://www.ejcl.org/81/art81-3.html and general Lohmann, *Parteiautonomie*.

It is this Article which permits parties to opt out of the CISG in whole or in part.[33] This may be affected by the choice of a different law, or by the express rejection of the CISG without other choice of law. Unlike Article 3(2nd s) EKG[34] Article 6 CISG does not expressly deal with the possibility of an implied exclusion. The deletion of the word "implied" from an early draft convention should prevent courts from too easily implying an exclusion of the CISG.[35] The agreement to submit a dispute to an arbitral tribunal in a different country or the use of standard term contracts (which had been drafted before the coming into force of the CISG according to a particular domestic law) are by themselves not enough evidence to conclude that the parties impliedly excluded the CISG.

20   As discussed in para 15, in the authors' view, the choice of another legal system does not entail, the choice of a domestic substantive law, but includes the CISG if its requirements for its application are met. At the Vienna Conference, this was clarified and the suggestion that the choice of a domestic law should automatically be seen as the implied exclusion of the CISG was rejected.[36] For the choice of a domestic law to be regarded as excluding the CISG, and for only the domestic sale of goods law to be applicable, there must be clear indications that that was the parties' intention. For example, there must be a stipulation that the particular domestic law concerning liability for material defects should apply to the contract. Evidence of the negotiations, as stipulated by the domestic law, can be called before a court when interpreting a choice of law clause according to Article 8(3) CISG.[37]

The burden of proof for such an interpretation in the particular circumstances lies with the party who claims the exclusion of the CISG.[38]

---

[33] During the CISG consultations it was hotly debated (as it had been in regard to the Hague Uniform Sales laws ULIS and ULFIS) whether the CISG should only be applicable if the parties opted in. In the end, the autonomous applicability of the CISG was favoured with the possibility to opt out, see: Schlechtriem, *Einheitliches UN-Kaufrecht*, with materials (Mohr Siebeck, Tübingen, 1981) 21. Schlechtriem in Schlechtriem/ Schwenzer, *Commentary*, Introduction I, pp. 1–3; see general overview over Uniform Law on International Sale of Goods (ULIS) and Uniform Law on the Formation of Contracts for the International Sale of Goods (ULFIS) Schlechtriem, 18 Israel L Rev (1983), 309.

[34] Einheitliches Gesetz über den internationalen Kauf beweglicher Sachen vom 17 Jul 1973 (BGBl I, S 856). See discussion of the EKG in Lohmann, *Parteiautonomie*, 128.

[35] See Secretariat's Commentary OR 5 Art 6, Schlechtriem, *Einheitliches UN-Kaufrecht*, 22 fn 98. Also Schlechtriem in Schlechtriem/Schwenzer, *Commentary*, Art 6 para 8.

[36] Secretariat's Commentary OR p. 250.

[37] See in regard to Art 8(3) CISG para 56.

[38] Cour d'appel de Paris (6 Nov 2001) CISG-online 677, 2002, 2795 with comment by C Witz; see as well LG Padova (25 Feb 2004) CISG-online 819 = IHR 2005, 31 the CISG was not excluded because in the appeal statements the parties used domestic sale of goods law unless the parties knew that the CISG would apply.

1.6.1 Exclusion Through Private International Law

21. Whether the parties can exclude the CISG by agreeing on the private international law of a non-member state depends on whether this is permissible according to the private international law of the forum state and/or whether this conforms to the requirements of choice of law by the parties. According to English private international law rules the parties can choose the applicable law.[39] Article 3(1) of the Convention on the Law Applicable to Contractual Obligations ("Rome Convention") stipulates that "the choice must be expressed or demonstrated with reasonable certainty by the terms of the contract or the circumstances of the case." The German courts have even inferred a choice of law during trial if the parties base their legal arguments on a particular jurisdiction.[40] This practice, however, is questionable, especially where the parties did not intentionally choose to argue under the particular jurisdiction or did not appreciate the private international law dimension of the case.[41] However, in our view, under no circumstances can the fact that the parties have based their arguments on a domestic sale of goods law be regarded in itself as an exclusion of the CISG where its application requirements are otherwise met. The judge is not bound by the parties' wrong interpretation of the law – iuria novit curia – and has to decide according to the CISG. Of course, a prudent judge will inquire why the parties have based their arguments on that particular law as opposed to the CISG. If the parties have had the intention to apply that particular law instead of the CISG, then it is not a choice of law in accordance with private international law rules but a substantive agreement that the contract between the parties is to be governed by the particular law.[42] The choice of substantive law is of course as much within the parties' power as to choose any particular provisions of a domestic law. However, such an agreement on substantive rules governing the contract can only be inferred from the arguments presented by the parties in court (and it has to be noted that the agreement on a particular domestic law during trial after the conclusion of the contract constitutes an alteration of the contract) where the parties were aware of the applicability of the CISG to their contract and they intentionally did not want to apply the CISG to their contract or parts of their contract.

The exclusion or part exclusion of the CISG can clearly be stipulated in standard terms as far as they have been made part of the contract. However, a general

---

[39] Dicey, *The Conflict of Laws*, paras 32–004; the choice is limited if the choice would circumvent same mandatory rules. See s 187 of Restatement Second of Conflict of Laws, compare § 1-301 UCC, and comment by Willier/Hart, *Uniform Commercial Code*, para 1–301.

[40] Compare OLG Koblenz, IPRax 1989, 175; OLG Frankfurt (10 Sep 1991) RIW 1991, 865; OLG Koblenz (3 May 1991) RIW 1992, 59; BGH (21 Feb 1992) NJW 1993, 385, 386; see as well Piltz, IPRax 1994, 191–193. It needs to be noted that in all jurisdictions referred to parties are not allowed to escape mandatory or public policy provisions through their choice of law.

[41] Compare also the decision of the Cour de Cassation (26 Jun 2001) CISG-online 598 and 600 = Recueil Dalloz Dec 2001, No 44, 3607–3614 with critical comment by Claude Witz; Reifner, IHR 2002, 57 et seq; but see also para 20 in regard to negotiation according to national law as interpretation aid.

[42] See para 22.

reference in the standard terms to the party's national law is not sufficient to exclude the CISG.[43] Furthermore, the standard terms have to be validly agreed, that means account must be taken of the invalidity of a contract under domestic law.[44] In particular, given the widespread applicability of the CISG as a consequence of the large number of member states, a clause excluding the CISG in its entirety may be void or voidable because it would result in surprise or hardship if incorporated without express awareness by the other party.[45]

1.6.2 Exclusion Through Choice of Substantive Law

22.   A distinction needs to be drawn between the exclusion of the CISG by the choice of the jurisdiction of a non-member state and the parties' express agreement to exclude the CISG (or particular provisions of it) as part of the chosen substantive law. The latter is possible according to Article 6 CISG and is consistent with the principle of party autonomy which allows the parties to deviate from dispositive law. Modifications and amendments to CISG provisions are often agreed upon by the parties, just as they would agree upon commercial terms or Incoterms.[46] Limits to party autonomy are set by the law which governs standard terms or abusive clauses. Each individual modification or exclusion of a CISG provision by standard terms has to be in compliance with the domestic law governing standard form contracts.[47]

1.6.3 Substantive Agreement in Relation to Applicability

23.   In addition to expressly opting out of the CISG, parties can also opt in. In other words, even where the contract does not come within the CISG's application requirements, the parties may expressly agree to be governed by the CISG. Whether their choice of the CISG is valid cannot be ascertained from the CISG itself but must be ascertained from a consideration of the particular domestic law, especially its private international law rules and the principle of party autonomy (and its limits). The question arises whether the parties contracting domestically can agree to the application of the CISG as domestic law even if the requirements of its application are not (completely) fulfilled.[48] Of practical relevance for the choice of the CISG as the applicable law for the contract are mandatory norms of the domestic

---

[43]   OGH (14 Jan 2002) CISG-online 643 = IHR 2002. LG Düsseldorf (11 Oct 1995) CISG-online 180.

[44]   See Schlechtriem in Schlechtriem/Schwenzer, *Commentary*, Art 4 para 12 – Art 6 para 6.

[45]   See (§ 2-207(2)(b) UCC) Willier/Hart, *Uniform Commercial Code*, § 2-4, see also §§ 305c(1), 307(1) BGB and OLG Düsseldorf NJW – RR 1994, 506 holding a clause excluding the CISG in favour of English law as surprising and unfairly disadvantageous to the German party.

[46]   See New Zealand Law Commission, *United Nations Convention on Contracts*, paras 120 et seq. Compare Piltz, RIW 2000, 485, 487, 489.

[47]   See para 58.

[48]   Compare in regard to the Rules of the International Chambers of Commerce Paris: Chiomenti, (2005) European Legal Forum I, 141 et seq. The author correctly points out that in essence the question is which mandatory norms will be applicable. The author favours the choice of international rules only for arbitral tribunals (p. 147) and does not find that a choice of international rules meant an exclusion of the CISG.

law. Mandatory norms stay in force if the parties choose an applicable law; in case the applicable law is determined according to private international law rules mandatory rules only stay in force if they are acknowledged international mandatory rules.[49]

> Example: The proposed European Union Regulation implementing the Rome I Convention (KOM (2005) 650 (15 December 2005) would allow according to its Article 3(2) the choice of international rules like the Principles of European Contract Law (PECL) or the Unidroit Principles of International Commercial Contracts (PICC) but also the CISG.[50] That means that European electricity suppliers could agree for the CISG to be applicable for their contracts (despite Article 2(f) CISG).[51]

1.6.4 Ambit of CISG

Sale of goods contracts

24.   The CISG only applies to sale of goods contracts, that is, contracts where goods are exchanged for money. Contracts which exchange goods and back-to-back-sales do not fall under the ambit of the CISG.[52] If, however, a back-to-back-sale consists of two linked but legally severable contracts for the sale of goods then the CISG may apply to each of the contracts.[53]

24a. A special issue, for example, are distribution agreements: a distinction needs to be drawn between the framework contract and each of the contracts between the distributor and the supplier or manufacturer. The former generally does not fall under the CISG unless the parties have specifically chosen for the CISG to apply. However, the framework contract already obliges the dealer to purchase the goods but leaves everything else open, for example, the quantity or the delivery date, the framework contract itself can be a contract for the sale of goods.[54]

24b. Further, in the authors' view, CISG should be applicable to preliminary contracts and other framework contracts which bind the contracting parties to agree to a sale of goods contract if they contain the main rights and obligations of the parties in a way that the parties could sue out of those contracts without agreeing on the (main) sale of goods contract. A breach of the preliminary contract or the

---

[49]   See Rome Convention (19 Jun 1980), Art 7.
[50]   Compare Schäfer, GPR 2006, 54 et seq.
[51]   CISG, Art 2(f) states that the CISG does not apply to sales of electricity.
[52]   Compare in contrast to the general opinion Schlechtriem in Schlechtriem/Schwenzer, *Commentary*, Art 1 paras 14–19 with a comprehensive discussion on the issue.
[53]   Schlechtriem in Schlechtriem/Schwenzer, Art 1 para 18.
[54]   Compare in regard to distribution agreements BGH (23 Jul 1997) CISG-online 285, 276 = NJW 1997, 3304 and 3309 (Benetton I and II); OLG München (22 Sep 1996) CISG-online 208 = RIW 1996, 1035 with comment by Klima; Arbitral Tribunal of the Hamburg Chamber of Commerce (21 Mar 1996) CISG-online 187 = NJW 1996, 3229 see as well as the US division of the Federal District Court (Pennsylvania) in *Viva Vino Import Corporation v Farnese Vini Srl* (29 Aug 2000) IHR 2002, 28 (US ED Pennsylvania).

framework contract should then require the remedies of the CISG.[55] Similarly, the CISG might be applicable in regard to contracts stipulating a sales option.[56]

25. The legal nature of the sale of goods contract will not be changed because the parties stipulate their duties differently as set out in the CISG, for example, by agreeing on payment by instalments or delivery by instalments.[57] The applicability of the CISG will be in doubt, however, if instead of a contract where the ownership of the goods does not pass to the buyer until the final instalment is paid, the parties agree on a hire-purchase agreement (under which the buyer rents the good, the rental price equals an instalment payment and at the end of the rental time the buyer pays a final sum to purchase the good), or a leasing contract with an option to purchase. The key factor in considering whether a contract falls within the ambit of the CISG is whether, in an economic sense, the good is to be purchased, especially whether the instalments paid by the purchaser (including the down payment and the end payment) cover the intrinsic value of the goods and the financial cost. Therefore, either the contract must be directed towards the purchase of the good, or the use of the good during the agreed time must be such that the utility value of the good is exhausted.[58]

Delivery purchase, manufacture and delivery contracts, mixed contracts

26. Article 3 CISG deals with the question of whether a contract is a sale of goods where performance by the seller requires more than delivery of, and transferring property in, the goods.[59] For example, if the contract involves the provision of some kind of service in the wider sense, then the applicability of the CISG can be difficult.[60] Under Article 3(1) CISG, where the seller has to manufacture or produce the goods out of his or her own materials the CISG is applicable. In contrast, if the buyer supplies a substantial part of the materials necessary to manufacture or produce the goods the CISG is not supposed to be applicable because the seller in these circumstances is a provider of services rather than a

---

[55] Bridge, *International Sale of Goods Law*, para 2.18: "It seems pedantic to distinguish between contracts **of** sale and contracts **for** sale". They were good reasons "to avoid a clash between the CISG and any law applicable to such framework contracts".

[56] Schumacher, IHR 2005, 147, 149; see as well Cour de Cassation (30 Jun 2004) CISG-online 870: CISG applicable to a contract where the sales quota was determined by buyer. The decision is discussed by Schumacher.

[57] Schlechtriem in Schlechtriem/Schwenzer, *Commentary*, Art 1 para 15, see, for example BGH (28 Mar 1979) BGHZ 74, 193.

[58] In regard to the controversy concerning financial-leasing contracts, see Schlechtriem in Schlechtriem/Schwenzer, *Commentary*, Art 1 para 16; Magnus in *Staudinger*, Art 1 paras 34 et seq; with reference to UNIDROIT Convention on International Financial Leasing. In regard to software contracts for use without the additional purchase of the intellectual property see below para 32.

[59] CISG, Art 3: "(1) Contracts for the supply of goods to be manufactured or produced are to be considered sales unless the party who orders the goods undertakes to suuply a substantial part of the materials necessary for such manufacture or production. (2) This Convention does not apply to contracts in which the preponderant part of the obligations of the party who furnishes the goods consists in the supply of labour or other services."

[60] That means, including manufacturing.

seller of goods. However, the seller is not seen as a service provider where the buyer provides plans or know-how, even if they are very valuable. The rule only relates to material necessary to manufacture or produce the good.

Example: A firm with its place of business in France sold electronic parts to an Italian buyer. The electronic parts are supposed to be manufactured according to plans of the buyer. The *Cour d'appel Chambery* erroneously held that the buyer had contributed substantially to the manufacturing of the electronic parts and therefore did not apply Article 3 CISG.[61]

It is unclear how to determine when the buyer has fulfilled a substantial part of the contract and, therefore, the seller was a manufacturer rather than a seller f goods. Most scholars and courts have considered this question from a purely economic perspective, that is by comparing the economic value of the respective materials.[62] Some authors suggest that at least as a secondary criterion an "essential part" test should be used to determine whether the contract is a sale of goods contract in accordance with Article 3(1) CISG.[63] That the parties are nevertheless able to agree on the applicability of the CISG to a contract where the substantial part of the material has to be supplied by the buyer necessarily follows from the principle of party autonomy on which the CISG is based.[64] It is not relevant to the applicability of the CISG whether the good which has to be manufactured is one which is unique and cannot be exchanged for another or whether the good has no unique characteristics and can be substituted.[65] However, the similarity between sale of goods contracts and manufacturing contracts and the generous application of the CISG to contracts which have at least a manufacturing component means that the CISG of necessity will have some gaps in regard to questions arising from the manufacturing element peripheral to some sale of goods contracts.

Example: The Buyer X has ordered the manufacturing of a special machine which only needs to be delivered in year Z. A couple of months after the order, the buyer decides it does not need the machine anymore. It would be economically inefficient if, in these circumstances, the buyer could not

---

[61] Rev. jurispr. com 1995, 242.

[62] CISG-AC Opinion No 4, Contracts for the Sale of Goods to be Manufactured or Produced and Mixed Contracts (Art 3 CISG), 24 Oct 2004, Rapporteur: Prof Pilar Perales Viscasillas. Honnold, *Uniform Law for International Sale*, § 106; Schlechtriem in Schlechtriem/Schwenzer, *Commentary*, Art 3 para 3a with an overview of the different opinions; but see against this assessment Magnus in *Staudinger*, Art 3 paras 14; OLG München (3 Dec 1999) CISG-online 585/634 = RIW 2000, 712 where not only the economic value but also the function of the material played a role in the evaluation.

[63] Enderlein/Maskow, *International Sales Law*, 36, 37; Cour d'appel de Grenoble (21 Oct 1999) CISG-online 574.

[64] See above para 23.

[65] The distinction whether the good is unique or not plays a major role under German law to determine whether German sale of goods law or law in regard to a contract for manufacturing goods is applicable. If the contract for the manufacturing of a unique goods sale of goods law is applicable – compare §§ 433, 651 BGB.

terminate the contract, and instead the seller could wait until year Z to make the good and demand the purchase price as damages for non-acceptance.[66] By comparison § 651 of the German BGB, in conjunction with § 649 BGB, allows the buyer of a specific good to terminate the contract at any time. The seller has the right to receive the purchase price, but the seller must subtract from that price all expenses he or she has saved by not completing the manufacturing of the good. The lack of regulation of the seller's special duty to co-operate or express provision for the reasonable acceptance of a manufactured good – as opposed to simply getting possession of the good – has to be filled by interpretation of the CISG and its provisions in accordance with Article 7(1) CISG[67] or by gap-filling in accordance with Article 7(2) CISG.[68]

If, as part of a contract the buyer is required to put at the seller's disposal a property, on which the seller is to build, for example, a factory, the question whether this will constitute a substantial part of the contract for the purposes of Article 3(1) CISG will depend on the relevant property values at the time of contract formation, not the time of completion of the performance.

27. Article 3(2) CISG stipulates, comparable with Article 3(1) CISG, that where the contract is not only for the sale of goods, but also the provision of services, the application of the CISG will hinge on whether the substantial part of the contract is for services or for the goods.

Example: A buyer with its place of business in Passau (Germany) manufactured windows. It purchased from the seller, with its place of business in Rimini (Italy) a window-making machine which was supposed to be assembled on the buyer's premises. Since the service of assembling the machine was not a substantial part of the contract the CISG was applicable to the contract.[69]

Similarly to the test employed in Article 3(1) CISG,[70] the comparative values between the services and the goods will be determinative in deciding whether the contract is substantially for the sale of goods or for services. Take for example the repair of a machine, or a vehicle, by using spare parts where the labour needed

---

[66] The American Delegation had argued for a provision – similar to Art 77 CISG which obliged the parties to mitigate their losses but unfortunately it did not succeed, see Schlechtriem, *Einheitliches UN-Kaufrecht*, 92, see as well para 236. Cf the English case of *White and Carter (councils) Ltd v MacGregor* [1962] AC 413 (HL).

[67] See paras 43 et seq.

[68] See paras 43 et seq.

[69] Compare OLG München (3 Dec 1999) CISG-online 585/634 = RIW 2000, 712 with comment by Schroeter, (2001) 5 VJ, 130 and also in general: Schlechtriem in Schlechtriem/ Schwenzer, *Commentary*, Art 3 paras 4, 7a.

[70] See above para 21.

for the repair is minimal.[71] If the substantial part is for services the CISG will not be applicable.[72] However, there might be exceptions where the buyer has an over-whelming interest in a particular part of the performance without that part being the more valuable one.[73] The time of the formation of the contract is decisive. This is particularly so for contracts where the good has to be assembled on-site and/or where the good also has to be made operational and the seller for a limited time operates the good.

> Example: A company with its place of business in Italy sold a production line to a company in the Czech Republic. The entire production line consisted of three different parts. The parts were to be delivered directly to the buyer's client and assembled there by the seller ready for use. The Arbitral Tribunal of the International Chamber of Commerce in Paris held that the CISG was applicable to the contract.[74]

27a. The difference between Articles 3(1) and 3(2) CISG is that Article 3(2) CISG deals with mixed contracts, in which the obligation to deliver a good or goods is combined with the obligation to provide services. Article 3(2) CISG is not applicable if the manufacturing of the good entails certain services necessary for manufacture, such as, for example, the planning and design of the good. Such a situation falls under Article 3(1) CISG.[75] Where the buyer purchases solely the good, a comparison between the relative values of the design, the planning and the production, with the value of the end product is not necessary.[76]

In accordance with Articles 3(1) and 3(2) CISG where goods merely for pro-cessing purposes (for example, refinement) are handed over to another party and after processing handed back (the property in the goods staying with the original owner) the CISG does not apply.

---

[71] Compare in regard to repairs as a service: Hof van Beroep, Antwerpen (3 Jan 2005) CISG-online 1001.

[72] See Arbitral Awards of the Hungarian Chamber of Commerce (5 Dec 1995) NJW – RR 1996, 1145, 1146; LG Mainz (26 Nov 1998) CISG-online 563 = IHR 2001, 203 sub A.1 well reasoned.

[73] Magnus in *Staudinger*, Art 3 para 25; see for comprehensive discussion Pilar Perales, AC-CISG Opinion No 4 paras 3 et seq.

[74] ICC Paris (23 Aug 1994) CISG-online 129; OLG München (3 Dec 1999) CISG-online 585/634 = RIW 2000, 712; compare also the German Supreme Court (BGH) which held that in regard to delivery and assembly a solar energy system (in regard to the question whether sale of goods or provisions in regard to contracts for manufacturing were applicable) the value of delivery and as-sembly as were as special circumstances of the contractual agreed result (note the decision did not concern the CISG but German Civil law, however, the same reasoning applies).

[75] See CISG-AC Opinion No 4 Contracts for the Sale of Goods to be Manufactured or Produced and Mixed Contracts (Art 3 CISG), 24 Oct 2004, Rapporteur: Prof Pilar Perales Viscasillas.

[76] Persuasive (for industrial software which had to be produced) Marly, *Softwareüberlas-sungsverträge*, para 404; see as well Schäfer, IHR 2003, 118–121. See for a different view: Kreisgericht Bern-Laupen (29 Sep 1999) CISG-online 701; Heuzé, *Traité des Contracts*, 79, 80. The misunderstand-ing is aggravated by the difference of the French and English versions of the CISG: the French text of Art 3(2) CISG uses the word "obligation" in the singular whereas the English version uses the word "obligations" which in the authors' view reflects the intention of the drafters. See also CISG-AC Opinion No 4, Contracts for the Sale of Goods to be Manufactured or Produced and Mixed Contracts (Art 3 CISG), 24 Oct 2004, Rapporteur: Prof Pilar Perales Viscasillas, para 2.3.

Examples: An Austrian company contracted with a foreign trade organisation of
the former Yugoslavia whereby a Yugoslavian company was to manufacture brushes and brooms from material delivered by the Austrian
company. The value of the manufacturing of the brushes and brooms
was less than that of the material. Therefore, the CISG was, according
to Article 3(1) and 3(2), not applicable.[77]

A German company contracted a Swiss research institute to conduct
a study. Although the study was documented in writing and the written
document handed over to the German company, the core obligation was
one of service not of sale of goods.[78]

28.   The principle embedded in Article 3 CISG must also be applicable if the
seller has to deliver goods which fall under the CISG, and, in addition, other assets
(for example, know-how, securities, or shares of a business) that do not fall under
the CISG. The same is true for ancillary duties negotiated with the contract. If the
parties' intention is that the sale of different goods should be regarded as one sale,
then the CISG is to govern the sale of the different goods.[79] If the will of the parties cannot be ascertained, private international law rules will determine the law
applicable to the contracts for the sale of the goods which do not fall under the
CISG. The CISG and its remedies are also available if competition prohibitions
and re-import prohibitions in sale of goods contracts are breached.[80]

1.7   Goods

29.   The object of the sales contract must be goods. Examples from case law
include machines (for example a key-cutting machine[81]), food (for example,
mussels),[82] shoes,[83] clothes,[84] cars,[85] jet engines,[86] and even circus elephants.[87]

---

[77]   OGH (27 Oct 1994) CISG-online 133 = öst ZGRV 1995, 161 parallel to the contract of processing
the material delivered by the Austrian company a "real" contract for the sale of goods for which the
CISG was applicable.

[78]   Compare OLG Köln (26 Aug 1994) CISG-online 132 = RIW 1994, 970.

[79]   See Schlechtriem in Schlechtriem/Schwenzer, *Commentary*, Art 3 para 9.

[80]   See Ferrari in Schlechtriem/Schwenzer, Art 3 para 19. See as well jurisprudence: *Shuttle Packaging
Systems v Tsonakis INA SA et al.*, US DC Michigan (17 Dec 2001) CISG-online 773 (non-competition
clause valid even without consideration); OLG Frankfurt (17 Sep 1991) CISG-online 28 "exclusive
trademark protection"; Cour d'appel de Grenoble (22 Feb 1995) CISG-online 151 (re-import prohibition – breach equates to a fundamental breach); see also below para 114.

[81]   BGH (15 Feb 1995) CISG-online 149 = NJW 1995, 2101.

[82]   BGH (8 Mar 1995) CISG-online 144 = NJW 1995, 2099.

[83]   OLG Frankfurt (17 Sep 1991) CISG-online 28 = NJW 1992, 633; *Fercus Srl v Mario Palazzo
et al.*, US DC SDNY (8 Aug 2000) CISG-online 588.

[84]   Cour d'appel de Paris (18 Mar 1998) CISG-online 533; also OLG Köln (14 Oct 2002) CISG-online
709 = IHR 2003, 15–17.

[85]   OLG München (28 Jan 1998) CISG-online 339 = RIW 1998, 559, 560.

[86]   *Pratt & Wittney v Malev Hungarian Airlines*, Court of the Capital City Budapest (10 Jan 1992)
CISG-online 43 = 1992 JL & Com 49–78.

[87]   Cour d'appel de Paris (14 Jan 1998) CISG-online 347 = IHR 2001, 128.

29a. The sale of documents, such as storage certificates or bills of lading, which "represent" the good (in the sense of documenting the buyer's right to delivery of the goods) is a sale of goods and falls under the ambit of the CISG.[88] Since the legal differentiation between the sale of goods performed by the delivery of documents as a substitute for the goods on one hand, and the sale of documents themselves on the other hand is not always easy for business people to establish, the CISG should be applicable for both variations.

29b. Article 2 CISG, however, contains exceptions to the applicability of the CISG. The most important exception is Article 2(a) CISG, which generally excludes the sale of consumer goods. This exclusion avoids conflict with national consumer protection laws. A consumer good is one which is for personal, family or household use. Therefore, the term is defined by the intended private use of the goods.[89] However, it is a requirement that the seller knew or ought to have known that the good was for one of these uses at the time of contract formation. Accordingly, in exceptional circumstances the CISG can be applicable in cases of a sale of a consumer good.

Example: A German lawyer orders a desk chair on his/her law firm's letter-head from a furniture store in Strasbourg, France. The lawyer wants to use the desk chair at home which the furniture seller cannot know and should not reasonably be expected to know. The CISG will apply unless the fact of intended home use was specifically mentioned during contract negotiations.

EU directives concerning consumer protection[90] use an objective consumer definition (similar to the CISG, such as "for purposes which are outside his trade, business or profession"), making the knowledge of the seller of no legal consequence, and can conflict with the application of the CISG.[91]

Example: As with the previous example where the French furniture seller did not know and could not have known that the German lawyer did not want to buy the desk chair for the office. If the chair delivered does not conform to the contract, the CISG provisions (since the CISG is applicable unless specifically excluded) could conflict with the EU *Directive On Certain Aspects of the Sale of Consumer Goods and Associated Guarantees* as implemented by the national laws of the member states.[92]

---

[88] Compare Commentary of the UN-Secretariat to the UNCITRAL-draft 1978 (Report) p 40 para 8: the sale of such sale documents does not fall under the exclusion rule of Art 2(d); see further for a discussion on that part Schlechtriem *in Symposium Frank Vischer*, CISG-online: publications.

[89] Meyer in Hay (ed) 297–322, 305.

[90] For example: EU Directive 1999/44/EC (25 May 1999) On Certain Aspects of the Sale of Consumer Goods and Associated Guarantees; EU Directive 931, 131 EEC (5 Apr 1993) Unfair Terms in Consumer Contracts.

[91] See para 42c, see also comprehensively Meyer in Hay (ed) 304 et seq.

[92] However, in regard to the EU-Directive *On Certain Aspects of the Sale of Consumer Goods* this is very unlikely since the remedy regime devised by the directive for delivery of non-conforming goods is nearly identical to that of the CISG.

The use of the word "unless" in Article 2(a) CISG makes it clear that the burden of proof for demonstrating the lack of knowledge and its reasonableness lies with the seller.[93]

30. The other exceptions to the applicability of the CISG, Articles 2(b) to 2(g), CISG have political and historical bases. The exclusion of ships and aircrafts from the CISG (Article 2(e) CISG) can only be explained historically and poses some problems in regard to defining the exception clearly. Some authors exclude the purchase of the smallest boat from the ambit of the CISG[94] whereas other authors only exclude the application of the CISG in respect of sales of large ships.[95] Nonetheless, on the other hand, in the authors' view that the ship must be a means of locomotion before it will be excluded. Restaurant ships, oil rigs and porter bridges will come within the ambit of the CISG.[96] The exceptions in Articles 2(b) and 2(c) CISG acknowledge the existence of specific national rules for auctions and bankruptcy proceedings.[97] Particular mandatory rules also often exist for the trade of stocks and foreign currencies. However, insofar as such contracts concern documents which represent the good to be bought and sold, the CISG is applicable.[98]

31. There is no doubt that rights, such as intellectual property rights, (contractual) claims, or those of a shareholder in a company, do not come within the meaning of "goods" in the CISG.

Example: The CISG does not apply to an agreement between a Hungarian and a German party for the sale of shares in a company even if Hungarian company law talks about ownership in regard to the share of a member in a company.[99] An asset purchase on the other hand can fall within the ambit of the CISG if most of the assets of a company consist of movables.

A claim for delivery which is in writing, however, can be a good.[100] Historically, in the context of the unification of sale of goods law, goods have been understood

---

[93] For a more detailed discussion on the burden of proof see Magnus in *Staudinger*, Art 2 para 28. In the main commentary Peter Schlechtriem has another opinion about this issue, see Schlechtriem in Schlechtriem/Schwenzer, *Commentary* Art 2 para 15 fn 26.

[94] Audit, Vente internationale, 30; Honnold, *Uniform Law for International Sales*, § 54; Rézei, Rules of the Convention, 71.

[95] Schlechtriem, *Einheitliches UN-Kaufrecht*, 16; Strohbach in Enderlein/Maskow/Strohbach, *Internationales Kaufrecht*, Art 2 para 7.2.

[96] See for an overview of the different opinions: Schlechtriem in Schlechtriem/Schwenzer, *Commentary*, Art 2 para 33.

[97] Schroeter, ZEuP 2004, 25 et seq, in the authors' view correctly questions whether the exclusion of auctions, seen at the time of drafting as domestic matter, is still a valid view in light of the proliferation of internet auctions and the generally more international character of auctions; see also Schlechtriem in Schlechtriem/Schwenzer, *Commentary*, Art 2 paras 19, 20.

[98] Compare Magnus in *Staudinger*, Art 1 para 47; Bydlinski, AcP 198 (1998) 288, 308, 309.

[99] See Arbitral Tribunal of the Hungarian Chamber of Commerce, Award (20 Dec 1993) reported by Vida, IPRax 1995, 52, (not in English). Cour de Justice de Genève (9 Oct 1998) CISG-online 424, (English text on Pace website).

[100] See above para 29a.

to be movables.[101] The decisive factor is the fact that the good is movable at the time of delivery. The sale of a crop before it is harvested can fall under the CISG, as well as main parts of a building. In the latter the seller is also obliged to perform his/her contractual duties to ensure the property transfer of the building. Building materials which on delivery may become a fixture of the property regarded as movable for the purpose of the CISG.[102] However, authors and courts seem also to agree that material goods fall under the ambit of the CISG.[103]

32.   Software is generally regarded as a "good", if the software is saved on a data carrier such as a hard drive, disc or chip.[104] However, the distinction drawn between standard software and individualised software which is advocated particularly by German academics is in the authors' view not compatible with the CISG. Such a differentiation in the case of software would not marry with the principle found in Article 3(1) CISG that the CISG does not differentiate between standardised and individualised (especially manufactured for the buyer) goods.[105] Many authors and some courts have supported the application of the CISG to software.[106] This will result in a common legal framework applying to the cross-border purchase of computer software, removing the uncertainty for the parties and courts or tribunals to have to apply a (probably for them) foreign law which may not be particularly accessible. In the authors' view there are only two limits to the application of the CISG to software which will be discussed in the following paragraphs.

32a.   First, although the definition of "goods" in the CISG does not require the goods to be corporeal "movables" – and of the listed exceptions only electricity is not a "corporeal object"[107] – many of the provisions clearly envisage movable and

---

[101] Compare, for example, Artt 1(1) and 6 of the German Unifying Act in regard to the sale of movable goods (17 Jul 1993).

[102] Schlechtriem in Schlechtriem/Schwenzer, *Commentary*, Art 1 para 23.

[103] See next para.

[104] OGH (21 Jun 2005) CISG-online 1047. Compare Magnus in *Staudinger*, Art 1 para 44 with a comprehensive overview of the literature. See Cox, CISG-online and in (2000) 4 VJ, 3; See also generally Lookofsky, (2003) 13 Duke J of Comp & Int'l L, 263, 274–280; Mowbray, (2003) VJ, 121-150 (analysing the difficulties in applying the convention to e-commerce transactions and concluding that the Convention is not well-suited to electronic sales contracts); Vilus, (2003) 8 Unif L Rev, 163–1/2 97 (discussing the need for the development of uniform rules appropriate for electronic commerce in light of the rapid increase of the use of technology to engage in transactions and execute contracts).

[105] See para 26.

[106] Brandi-Dohrn, *Gewährleistung*, 4 et seq; Endler/Daub, CR 1993, 601, 606 (summary); Herber, Z TranspR 1999, 1, 5; Honnold, *Uniform Law for International Sales*, § 4 (Honnold takes into account the saving process on chips, hard drive, and disc – compare with books and CDs, where the purchase relates to contained information, but it still considered a "good" in accordance with the CISG); Lookofsky in Herborts/Blanpain (eds) *International Encyclopaedia*, 37; Neumayer/ Ming, Art 1 No 3, p 40; Piltz, *UN-Kaufrecht*, No 71; Schmitt, CR 2001, 145, 147, 148; Schmitz, MMR 2000, 256, 258; OLG Koblenz (17 Sep 1993) CISG-online 91 = RIW 1993, 934; *American Mint LLC, Goede Beteiligungsgesellschaft, and Michael Goede v GO Software, Inc* US District Court (16 Aug 2005) CISG-online 1104; *Evolution Online Systems, Inc v Koninklijke Ptt Nederland N.V et al.,* USCA (9th Cir) (27 May 1998) CISG-online 768.

[107] CISG, Art 2(g).

corporeal goods, such as the references to handing over,[108] or "passing of risk".[109] The application of the CISG to "non-corporeal", online-delivered computer software which might have been accepted by downloading would probably require a generous interpretation of the CISG or perhaps in some case even adaptation,[110] if possible.[111]

32b. Second, more problematic is the fact that software is generally only licensed for use and that the property-right in the software itself (i.e. a copyright) is not transferred.[112] However, in the authors' view two types of software purchases have to be distinguished. In the first category are software contracts where the software is licensed for a limited time. Once the agreed licence period ends, the contract can be renewed or terminated. The licensor might be obliged during the licence period to upgrade and service the software. At the end of the licence period the licence is terminated and the licensee must give back what is capable of being given back (such as manuals or discs). The CISG does not apply to such a contract. The second category concerns contracts where the buyer purchases the software licence indefinitely, that is, for an unlimited time period. In such cases the buyer, after paying the purchase price, can use the software as if it was his or her property. The licensor cannot interfere anymore. The buyer can delete, alter or gift the software. The buyer is only prohibited from selling the software. Having said that, limitations on resale can also result from rules prohibiting goods from being re-imported into the EU, or if certain goods cannot be sold to certain third parties (for example, nations subject to trade sanctions). Complete, indefeasible property in the good is not a requirement for a sale of goods contract to come under the CISG. Accordingly, the CISG will apply to software contracts coming within the second category.[113]

1.8   Substantive Ambit

33. Article 4 CISG limits the ambit of the CISG to the formation of the contract and the rights and obligations of the buyer and seller arising from the contract. Only in regard to these areas can "questions concerning matters governed by this Convention" arise within the meaning of Article 7(2) CISG. Contractual questions arising outside the substantive ambit of the CISG have to be dealt with according to domestic law which is determined by the private international law of the forum. These "external gaps"[114] contrast with "internal gaps" which are gaps within the substantive law regulated by the CISG. In regard to some areas the application

---

[108] CISG, Art 31(a).

[109] CISG, Art 36.

[110] See Cox, CISG-online and (2000) 4 VJ 3 – goes through domestic laws of EU/US and gives options for an international uniformity approach.

[111] Compare Schmitt, CR 2001, 145, 148. See Diedrich, cisgw3.law.pace.edu and in (2002) 6 VJ, 55.

[112] Compare Lorenz in Witz/Salger/Lorenz, Art 1 No 6; generally Marly, *Softwareüberlassungsverträge*, 20 et seq in regard especially to the CISG 177 et seq.

[113] Compare with comprehensive analysis OGH (14 Oct 1997) öst JBl 1996, 577, 580.

[114] Compare to "external gaps" para 41.

of the CISG is explicitly excluded.[115] In regard to other areas the CISG has "intentional" gaps because states could not agree on how to regulate a particular matter, for example, the amount of interest[116] or the problem of the battle of the forms.[117] Further gaps result unintentionally from both the working group and Conference missing the need to regulate a particular matter, such as the possibility of retracting declarations made pursuant to Articles 26 and 27 CISG,[118] or because some developments were not foreseeable at the time of drafting, in particular, the use of email, internet, and fax. The latter are considered "internal gaps".

1.8.1 Validity Requirements

34.   Article 4 (2nd s(a)) CISG specifically excludes questions of contract validity from the scope of the CISG unless they arise in conjunction with the questions of offer and acceptance which is regulated in Part II CISG.[119] Domestic law applies to the contract (through the private international law rules chosen) with respect to matters such as capacity to contract, consensus ad idem or mistake and their consequences. Generally, in common law countries the parties' expressed choice of law or, in the case of the failure to express a choice of law, their implied choice of law, will govern the contract. If the courts are unable to determine the choice of the parties they use the "closest and most real connection" test to determine the applicable law.[120] Similarly, in Europe, the Rome Convention on the Law applicable to Contractual Obligations of 1980 is based on the freedom to choose the applicable law (Article 3) and, in the absence of an expressed or implied choice of law by the parties, determines the applicable law to be that of the country most closely connected to the contract (Article 4).[121]

The invalidity of contracts as contrary to public policy or as violating mandatory national law will also depend primarily on the domestic law (once again determined by the private international law of the forum). In principle, regulatory laws, embargo laws (if an infringement carries invalidity of the contract with it) and consumer protection laws, which invalidate certain types of contracts, might apply to the contract in question depending on the applicable domestic law determined by the conflict of law rules of the forum. Nevertheless, before applying domestic mandatory law it needs to be ascertained whether the particular domestic law is capable of applying to cross-border sales of goods, that is, being mandatory for international sales. For example, safety laws (applicable by the private international

---

[115] For example see Art 4(a), 4(b) the validity of the contract and the transfer of property respectively.

[116] See CISG, Art 78.

[117] See in regard to amount of interest para 318 and the battle of the forms paras 51, 93.

[118] See Schlechtriem, *Bindung an Erklärungen*, 259, 265 et seq. See Schlechtriem in Schlechtriem/ Schwenzer, *Commentary*, Art 27 para 14.

[119] Compare CISG, Artt 14-24 and paras 73 to 95 et seq.

[120] See in regard to the private international law rule governing contract: *Amin Rasheed Shipping Corp v Kuwait Insurance Co* [1984] AC 50, 61 (per Lord Diplock); *Akai Pty Ltd v People's Insurance Co Ltd* (1996) 188 CLR 418, 440-442; Dicey, *The Conflict of Laws*, Vol 2, 1537 et seq; O'Brien, *Smith's Conflict of Laws*, 307 et seq.

[121] EC Convention on the Law Applicable to Contractual Obligations (Rome 1980) OJ C 27 of 26/01/1998.

law rules of the forum) of a country might prohibit the sale of a certain good to protect its consumers. That, however, does not mean that the importation of that good for on-sale to a third country is forbidden. German law, for example, prohibits the contractual exclusion of liability if the seller has given a guarantee.[122] In the authors' view this provision should not be extended to international sale of goods contracts under the CISG.[123] On the other hand, in EU member states Article 34 of the Rome Convention and its domestic counterparts may require application of internationally mandatory regulations not only of the forum state, but also of other states with a close connection to the contract. In general, however, the Rome Convention (and the domestic laws implementing the Convention), as mentioned above, give preeminence to the parties' choice and in the absence of choice, prefers the domestic law with the closest connection to the contract.[124]

The question of capacity, however, might be determined by special private international law rules, such as, for example the law of the domicile of the parties.[125] Another example where specialist private international law rules might apply is in regard to a contract being void or illegal which, according to German law, is governed by Articles 27 et seq EGBG which incorporate Article 4 of the Rome Convention into German law.

At common law the position is substantially the same as under the Rome Convention. Material validity is governed by the law which would govern if the contract was a valid contract.[126] In general, provisions which regulate the economy, such as some EU regulations based on the EU treaties or embargo regulations (if they result in invalidity), or consumer laws which stipulate invalidity for certain contracts, are applicable and supersede the general contract law rules if they are mandatory rules. However, in such cases the question whether such national laws are applicable must be examined. In addition, it has to be examined whether such national laws are applicable in regard to international, cross-border sales of goods, including whether such laws are mandatory in the international arena. For example, if the food safety rules of the country whose laws are applicable prohibit the sale of particular foods to protect its domestic consumers, it does not necessarily follow that the contracts of an importer who wants to on-sell the food to a third country are affected. In particular, domestic provisions invalidating unfair contract terms or terms with a certain effect, such as in standard form contracts, have to be applied to CISG contracts under Article 4 (2nd s(a)).[127] However, if the measure for the invalidity of

---

[122] BGB, § 444.

[123] See also Piltz, IHR 2002, 2, 5.

[124] See Rome Convention, Artt 3, 4(1) and O'Brien, *Smith's Conflict of Laws*, 328–347.

[125] See EGBGB, Artt 7, 12. However, it has to be noted that according to English law and the law in the United States the question of capacity is predominantly decided according to the law of the country with which the contract is most closely connected [Restatement, s 198; Dicey, *The Conflict of Laws*, Vol 2 paras 32–223]. See also *McFeetridge Stewarts* [1913] SC 773; *Kent v Salmon* [1910] TPD 637; *Bondholders Securities Corporation v Manville* [1933] 4 DLR 699 (Sask CA) which held that the place of contracting was decisive in regard to the question of capacity.

[126] Royal Exchange *Assurance Corp v Vega* [1902] 2 KB 384 (CA); Dicey, *The Conflict of Laws*, paras 32–169.

[127] See OGH (7 Sep 2000) CISG-online 642; Schlechtriem in Schlechtriem/Schwenzer, *Commentary*, Art 4 para 12; see in regard to German law §§ 307–309 BGB; New Zealand, Canada, Australia, the

a contractual term is a divergence from statute or case law then the CISG provides the measure (as far as it is applicable). In regard to contracts which are closely lin-ked to an EU member-state it has to be noted that contract provisions can be "safe" if they guarantee the minimum consumer protection of that member-state.[128]

35.   It does not matter for the application of domestic law in the area excluded by Article 4 (2nd s(a)) CISG whether the invalidity occurs ipso jure or because of a "legal act of the parties" (for example, through avoidance by mistake or revocation of consent under special consumer protection laws), because of a judicial decision, or because of a legal act of a state. It is also possible that the content of the contract could be changed by a court declaring part of the contract void.

36.   The reservation in favour of the national domestic provisions in regard to contract validity is only applicable as long as the CISG itself does not clearly govern the situation. "Clearly" does not mean that every CISG provision which differs from a domestic provision of contract validity must clearly indicate its every departure from the domestic provision or lead to the invalidity of the contract according to domestic law. The crucial question is whether a specific issue has been dealt with undoubtedly by the CISG. Gap filling additions to the CISG which have been developed through Article 7(2) CISG with the help of the core principles of the CISG are clearly dealt with by the CISG, at least if there is a large degree of consensus.

The specifics when an issue of validity is clearly governed by the CISG and, therefore, does not fall under Article 4 (2nd s(a)) CISG are, however, complicated and uncertain. Agreement exists probably in regard to the question of the validity of a contract because of the impossibility of regularising such a variety of circumstances in one document. The CISG prevails over national rules concerning the question whether a contract is invalid because the performance has been rendered impossible.

Example: The responsible Government department sells the cargo of a sunken ship (which does not exist) located outside its territorial waters to a salvage company. The domestic provisions which provide for invalidity if performance of a contract is impossible do not apply. Instead, the rights of the buyer are as stated in Articles 45 et seq CISG. The impossibility of the performance is only relevant in regard to Article 79 CISG.[129]

UK and the US have legislation which contains prohibitions that intervene in the market of the pre-market (like the Australia's Trade Practices Act 1974, New Zealand Fair Trading Act 1986), market, and after market stages (like the New Zealand Consumer Guarantees Act 1993). Misleading and deceptive conduct and pyramid schemes are prohibited and all the legislation contains product safety provisions.

[128] See in regard to the specific limitations of the choice of law in regard to consumer contracts and the more loosened rules Schlechtriem in *FS Lorenz*, 565, 566 et seq.

[129] The example is based on *McRae v The Commonwealth Disposals Commission* (1951) 84 CLR 377 which was a case where the CISG would not have been applicable because both parties were Australian. However, the applicability of the CISG would be doubtful anyway because of Art 2(c)

36a. Mistakes in regard to the characteristics of the goods or the future ability of the other party to perform are also issues provided for in the CISG: the question of responsibility for the characteristic performance of the contract is provided for in Articles 35 et seq and Article 45 CISG. A mistake concerning the ability of the other party to perform the contract in the future entitles the mistaken party, according to Article 71 CISG (only), to suspend its own performance. In certain circumstances the right to suspend the contract can develop into a right to avoid the contract in accordance with Article 72 CISG. However, there is no room to avoid the contract because of a mistake based on the ground that the goods do not possess the agreed characteristics.[130] Mistakes in regard to the transmission of a notice, request or a communication is regulated by Article 27 CISG as being at the risk of addressee.

36b. Especially problematic is the categorisation of national rights to revocation and rights to return. Some national revocation and return rights may protect the consumer in particular, and, therefore, do not fall within the ambit of the CISG (Article 2(a) CISG). However, some overlap between consumer oriented contracts and the CISG is possible. Three questions should be distinguished:

(1)   As far as national provisions which relate to the validity of the contract derive from, for example, European Union directives or regulations, the question arises whether European Union legal measures prevail, like international agreements according to Article 90 CISG, over the CISG. Directives are not international agreements and their basis in the European Union treaties is not enough to afford directives the same status as international agreements. Directives are also not applicable directly between private parties but need to be transposed into domestic laws.[131] However, in the authors' view a distinction has to be drawn in regard to regulations. Regulations are directly applicable in the European Union member states. Therefore, provisions which are derived from regulations prevail over the CISG according to Article 90 CISG.[132]

(2)   It is also unclear whether revocation and return rights can be at all qualified as validity norms since they do not destroy a contract but generally convert the

---

CISG. In regard to Art 79 CISG, which governs the scenarios when a party is exempt from performance see paras 288 et seq.

[130] However, this view is controversial; some commentators hold the view that rescission for mistake on the ground that the goods do not possess a particular characteristic, or that the other party will not have the ability to perform in the future is available concurrently with sales law remedies under the CISG. See Hartnell, (1996) 18 Yale J Int'l L, 77, who wishes to apply domestic law while taking international connections into account; Neumayer, RIW 1994, 99, 102 for German law; Magnus in *Staudinger*, Art 4 paras 48, 49.

[131] This is controversial: some commentators opine that regulations and directives have priority over the CISG as "international agreements" or "based on international agreements" under Art 90. See Herber, IHR 2001, 187 et seq; see also Magnus in *Staudinger*, Art 90 para 4 in regard to the argument that harmonisation of private law in Europe is a matter regulated by Art 94 CISG, thus requiring a declaration in order not to be bound by the CISG in the areas harmonised by the European legal measures.

[132] Ferrari in Schlechtriem/Schwenzer, Art 90 para 3; Fenge in Soergel Art 2 para 5 and Art 90 para 5. See especially the Directive on Late Payments (Directive 2000/35/EC) and the E-commerce Directive (Directive 2000/31/EC).

contract into an avoidance relationship. The decision in regard to the substantive question should not depend on the technical form of the instruments which are used to control contracts and their continuation. A revocation of a contract which lets lapse contractual duties which have not been fulfilled should, therefore, be treated as a measure which rescinds the validity of the contract.[133]

(3)   According to Article 4 (2nd s(a)) CISG revocation and return rights can only play a role in respect of the domestic validity provision if the legal arrangements are concerned with a subject-matter not covered by the CISG. A domestic provision which allowed for the revocation of a contract to provide the buyer (in the case of faulty goods) an easier way to rescind the contract would be in direct conflict with Articles 35 and 45 CISG and would need to be disregarded in an international sales contract. Revocation and return rights where the function is consumer protection generally only want to allow consumers additional time to think about exercising their rights and are in regard to their function rather comparable with discerning requirements. Therefore, they are comparable as well with Article 14 CISG and applicable if the sale falls within the ambit of the CISG.

1.8.2 Transfer of Property

37.   The CISG contains no provisions dealing with the transfer of the property of the sold goods and the necessary requirements of such transfer. As with the requirements in respect of a valid payment, the domestic law applicable governs the transfer of property (Article 4 (2nd s(b)) CISG). The law applicable to a transfer of property is generally the lex rei sitae.[134] The applicable property law determines whether the property in the goods has already transferred to the buyer with the conclusion of the contract, or whether, such as under German law, a special "transfer contract" is necessary to make the buyer the new owner and, if so, whether the special transfer contract is separate from the underlying sales contract so that even if one is invalid the other might not be.[135] In regard to retention of title clauses two issues have to be distinguished. First, retention of title clauses modify the seller's duties as such that the seller has no duty immediately to transfer the property but can wait until full payment has been made or other claims of the seller against the buyer satisfied. Modification of the seller's Article 30 duty catalogue, ie delivering the goods, handing over any documents relating to them, and transfer the property in the goods as required by the contract, is generally possible under Article 6 CISG. However, the modifications might be subject to control devices under domestic law, for example, public policy, unfair standard terms, or whether the deviation from the seller's duty under the CISG is unreasonable. The second issue is one of property law, namely whether the buyer in getting possession of the good acquires an interest in the property, whether with the payment of the sales price

---

[133] See above para 35.

[134] In regard to movables the lex rei sitae at the time of transfer, see Dicey, *The Conflict of Laws,* 1158 et seq, 1164 et seq.

[135] See Secretariat's Commentary OR p. 17, Art 4 No 4 in regard to the fact that the difference between French and English law in comparison to German law could not be bridged in the preparatory work by UNCITRAL.

the buyer automatically acquires the full ownership of the goods, or whether other requirements must be met before ownership vests in the buyer. The issues need to be determined according to the domestic law which is applicable according to private international law rules.

Example: The German seller sold the Swiss buyer a key embossing machine under a contract with a retention of title clause. On contract formation the buyer paid a deposit. The rest of the purchase price was to be paid in instalments. Between the seller and the seller's supplier, the manufacturer of the key embossing machine, a dispute arose and the supplier informed the Swiss buyer that the supplier was now its contractual partner in regard to the key embossing machine. The buyer paid the rest of the purchase price to the supplier. In such a situation, does the buyer become the owner of the key embossing machine?[136]

38.   Domestic law is only applicable in regard to the property aspects of a retention of title clause agreement. So far as the retention of title agreement results in a modification of the contractual relationship between buyer and seller[137] the CISG is applicable instead of the applicable domestic law.

In English law there is no objection to clauses under which the seller retains the title to the goods until, for example, the price is paid by the buyer (though in principle the seller could impose any terms it sees fit).[138] Nonetheless, if goods are subject to a retention of title clause are used in the manufacturing process to make other goods, or incorporated into other goods, the seller may lose the title to the buyer.[139] In New Zealand an agreement to sell subject to a retention of title clause creates a security interest under the Personal Property Securities Act 1999.[140] Several of the Canadian provinces have enacted similar Personal Property Securities legislation.[141]

On the other hand, if German law would be the underlying domestic law the retention of title clause does not mean that the seller has to rescind the contract[142] to let the buyer's right to possession of the good lapse, but that the seller has to avoid the contract according to Article 64 CISG.

Example: The Roder Zelt-Und Hallen Konstruktionen GmbH which had its seat of business in Germany sold tents to the Australian Rosedown Park Pty Ltd under a contract with a retention of title clause. The buyer became bankrupt, and the seller rescinded the contract, claiming damages and the

---

[136] Compare BGH (15 Feb 1995) CISG-online 149 = NJW 1995, 2101. The German Supreme Court did not discuss, however, how a transfer of property to the buyer if the payment was made to a third party would be affected, see in that regard Schmidt-Kessel, RIW 1996, 60–65.

[137] See above para 37.

[138] See *Aluminium Industrie Vaassen BV v Romalpa Aluminium Ltd* [1976] 1 WLR 676.

[139] See *Borden (UK) Ltd v Scottish Timber Products Ltd* [1981] 1 Ch 25 (CA).

[140] PPSA 1999, s 17(3).

[141] See Personal Property Security Act 1990 (Ontario), Personal Property Security Act 1993 (Manitoba), Personal Property Security Act 1996 (British Columbia) and Personal Property Security Act 2000 (Alberta).

[142] See BGB, § 323.

return of the already delivered tents. The Australian Federal Court (South Australia District, Adelaide) granted the claim. The avoidance of the contract was permissible according to Article 64(1) in conjunction with Article 25 CISG, because starting the bankruptcy proceedings indicated that the payment of the purchase price could not be expected. The non-payment of the purchase price was a fundamental breach (the buyer does not need to be given an opportunity to remedy the breach). The retention of title to the tents needed to be examined initially in accordance with German law, but after the arrival of the tents in Australia the relevant law was Australian property law and, according to that law, the retention of title clause was valid. Therefore, the claim to return the tents was allowed.[143]

Under Article 6 CISG, however, the parties can agree on a different regime in regard to avoidance of the contract in case of breach, to take account of the retention of title agreement including for example, less stringent requirements such as simply missing an instalment or the application of Article 64 CISG without extra agreement. If the buyer refuses to pay before the goods are due, Article 72(1) CISG is applicable (avoidance of contract). Articles 64 and 72 CISG also produce the avoidance rules for standard form contracts which often have a retention of title clause.[144]

1.8.3 Compensation for Personal Injury and Death

39.   Article 5 CISG excludes death and personal injury from the scope of the Convention. The reason is simple: the CISG has not incorporated product liability. In turn, domestic product liability law should not be disturbed and any conflict between the CISG and the domestic law should be avoided. Insofar as a domestic legal system sees product liability conceptually as a non-contractual duty (as in Germany),[145] Article 5 CISG declares that the domestic law supersedes the CISG – in this respect Article 5 CISG can be regarded as devising a conflict rule. Since, however, in some jurisdictions product liability is part of contract law the CISG needed to ensure that after its coming into force domestic contract law provisions superseded.

Whether a buyer, who has to compensate his or her purchasers for personal injury or death arising out of faulty goods supplied by a seller under a CISG contract can claim, under the CISG, against his or her seller is controversial.

Example: The German seller sold to the American buyer wood manufacturing machines, which the seller delivered directly to the American buyer's purchaser, a Russian company. Because of a defective machine an accident happened in which workers of the Russian company were

---

[143] *Roder Zelt-und Hallen Konstruktionen GmbH v Rosedown Park Pty Ltd* and Reginald Eustace van Doussa J 57, FCA (Sth Australia) (28 Apr 1995) 216 et seq, CISG-online 218.

[144] See in regard to avoidance paras 106 et seq.

[145] Produkthaftungsgesetz, BGB §§ 823 et seq.

injured. The American buyer claimed (inter alia) compensation for personal injury incurred because of liability to the Russian purchaser. These compensation claims against the German seller do not fall in the scope of the CISG because of Article 5 CISG.[146]

The English wording of Article 5 CISG "death or personal injury caused by the good **to any person**" seems to exclude the CISG in regard to claims by the buyer for redress[147] resulting from claims against the buyer for personal injury or death in regard to third persons.[148] Domestic legal systems generally offer not only contractual remedies (which potentially could fall under the CISG) for redress claims between liable persons who have caused a personal injury or death through a faulty product, but some, particularly common law jurisdictions, offer remedies in tort as well.[149] The buyer's liability, exclusively regulated through the CISG, would be vulnerable because of CISG rules, like Articles 38, 39 CISG, which are designed to facilitate a relatively swift avoidance of the contract. However, majority opinion states that the loss to the buyer in contrast to the injured third party is only pecuniary loss and therefore not excluded from the ambit of the CISG according to Article 5 CISG.

In the authors' view the problem turns on the question of whether the CISG, when applicable, is always lex specialis and, therefore, excludes other claims.[150] If the minority's view is taken, a buyer can only pursue a claim for redress pursuant to the CISG. The consequence would be that a lack of notice provided for in Article 39 CISG, or after the period of two years according to Article 39(2) CISG has elapsed, the buyer would have forgone his or her right to claim the loss, although personal injury or death, especially due to a faulty product, often only occurs at a later stage. If one, on the other hand, allows the buyer's claims according to the CISG but also concurrent claims according to the applicable domestic liability law determined in accordance with the private international law of the forum[151] then the question whether Article 5 CISG excludes claims for redress according to the CISG, loses its practical effect.

Concurrent claims are also necessary in regard to property damage which is the result of faulty goods.[152] The availability of the buyer's claim for redress for pecuniary loss under the CISG has the advantage of differentiating the buyer's

---

[146] Compare, however, the case OLG Düsseldorf (2 Jul 1993) CISG-online 74 = RIW 1993, 845 where the Court without any discussion applied the CISG.

[147] By "redress" the authors mean claims for recovery of all losses, both direct and consequential, arising from the on-sale of a faulty good that causes loss to third parties.

[148] See also the 3rd German edition of this textbook para 39; different OLG Düsseldorf (2 Jul 1993) CISG-online 74 = RIW 1993, 845 where the Court without any discussion applied the CISG.

[149] The injured person will be able to sue the seller in tort for negligence, though in New Zealand such a claim will be precluded by s 317 of the Injury Prevention, Rehabilitation, and Compensation Act 2001.

[150] See for this view: Piltz, NJW 2005, 2127 and 3128 with note on Rechtbank van Koophandel hasselt (6 Jan 2004) CISG-online 829, where tort claims (according to Belgian law) were not acknowledged and cumulative claims were held possible.

[151] Koller in Bucher et al., (eds) *Norm und Wirkung*, 422–447, 445–447.

[152] See para 40.

general liability (such as, for example, lawyers' fees, trial costs, and the damage caused directly by the goods to end-buyers) with the buyer's liability for personal injury and death or property damage resulting from the faulty product to end-buyers.[153]

1.8.4 Compensation for Damage to Property

40. Liability for personal injury and death is only one aspect, albeit the most important, of product liability. Damage to property is not excluded from the scope of the CISG by Article 5 CISG. At the Conference in Vienna delegates had thought to broaden the exception for product liability by choosing a different criterion, such as "claims from product liability". However, the delegates could not agree upon whether, and how far, in a case of property damage which resulted from the use of faulty goods, the CISG should be applicable. The ruin of half-manufactured goods by a faulty machine or the loss of materials which were manufactured together with faulty or unsuitable material is typical cases of the unfulfilled contractual expectations of a buyer. They belong to the core of what a sales law should regulate. In the authors' view, therefore, such damage should fall within the scope of the CISG and should be compensated in accordance with Article 74 CISG. Fire originating from a faulty machine which destroys the buyer's manufacturing premises was regulated, at the Vienna conference, as another example in which the seller would be liable for damages.[154]

For example, § 280 BGB which sets out the duty to pay damages for the breach of a duty[155] would not be necessarily applicable if German law is applicable as the proper law of the contract concurrently with the CISG. The private international law rules of the lex fori will determine the applicable domestic tort law. This is of practical relevance because how the domestic tort law interacts with contractual liability in product liability cases will differ between jurisdictions.[156] The claimant

---

[153] The authors note that the view expressed differs from the view expressed by Peter Schlechtriem as stated in the previous German editions of this textbook, see Schlechtriem, *Internationales UN-Kaufrecht*, para 39.

[154] See speech of the English delegate Feltham O R 346.

[155] BGB, § 280: (1) If the obligor breaches a duty arising from the obligation, the obligee may demand damages for the damage caused thereby. This does not apply if the obligor is not responsible for the breach of duty.
(2) Damages for delay in performace may be demanded by the obligee only subject to the additional requirement of s 286.
(3) Damages in lieu of performance may be demanded by the obligee only subject to the additioanal requirements of ss 281, 282, or 283.

[156] The French doctrine of *non cumul* excludes liability in tort as between contracting parties. See Durry, *La Distinction De La Responsabilité Contractuelle*. In New Zealand the Courts have followed English authority in holding that there is no reason why, in principle, concurrent liability in contract and in tort cannot exist. There will be no concurrent liability, however, where the contractual matrix can be said to exclude tortious liability. See generally *R M Turton & Co Ltd (In Liquidation) v Kerslake and Partners* [2000] 3 NZLR 406 (CA), *Rolls-Royce New Zealand Ltd v Carter Holt Harvey Ltd* [2005] 1 NZLR 324 (CA) and *Henderson v Merrett Syndicates Ltd* [1995] 2 AC 145 (HL).

can involve concurrently tort and the CISG.[157] According to German law, tort liability is only available if the non-conformity of the goods is at the same time a "defect" in regard to product liability, that means that the goods do not meet the safety standards expected[158] so that the putting into circulation of the goods amounts to a breach of a duty of care.[159] In New Zealand there is no special duty of care in respect of product liability; liability is determined under the ordinary principles of the tort of negligence. Liability for death or personal injury is dealt with under the Accident Compensation scheme, currently embodied in the Injury Prevention, Rehabilitation, and Compensation Act 2001. In England and Wales, the Consumer Protection Act 1987 imposes a regime of strict liability for damage caused by defective products (though the existing common law was preserved). In the United States strict liability in tort appears to have been accepted though the Uniform Commercial Code also imposes strict liability for breach of warranty.[160] In Australia, the Trade Practices Act 1974 (Cth) imposes a form of strict liability for defective products but, as in England and Wales, the common law is not disturbed.

Whether a "defect" is to be dealt with under contract or tort law is also in German law, for example, very controversial.[161] However, the question can be solved easily if one is able to differentiate correctly between two situations. First, contract law rules apply where there has been a failure of the delivered goods to conform to the contract. That requires the buyer to notify the seller of the non-conformity of the goods or the buyer risks the claim falling of a statute of limitations. Second, damage which is consequent on the buyer putting a defective good into circulation is a matter of tort law. The consequential damage has to be subtracted from the entire damage. Where, however, the buyer's performance interest can be claimed through tort law because of the goods' non-conformity with the contract the CISG should be applied ahead of tort law.

Example: A manufacturer sells woollen underwear to stores which contain an excessive amount of sulphites such that consumers will contract dermatitis if they wear them. In such a case the stores' remedy for any lost expectation interest should be recovered under the applicable contract law notwithstanding that a claim in tort would exist.[162]

---

[157] See an extensive coverage of the problem in: Köhler, *Haftung nach UN-Kaufrecht*, 71, 133. The claimant can involve concurrently with the CISG.

[158] Compare ProdHaftG, para 3.

[159] Prevailing view but very controversial; see in regard to contrary view Huber in Schlechtriem, *Kommentar zum Einheitlichen UN-Kaufrecht*, Art 45 para 61; in regard to the exclusion of domestic tort law see Schneider, *UN-Kaufrecht*; Herber, IHR 2001, 187 ff; as well as Schmid, RIW 1996, 904 et seq.

[160] See Prosser/Keeton, *On the Law of Torts*, at 690 et seq.

[161] In New Zealand the Courts have followed English authority in holding that there is no reason why, in principle, concurrent liability in contract and in tort cannot exist. There will be no concurrent liability, however, where the contractual matrix can be said to exclude tortious liability. See generally *R M Turton & Co Ltd (In Liquidation) v Kerslake and Partners* [2000] 3 NZLR 406 (CA), *Rolls-Royce New Zealand Ltd v Carter Holt Harvey Ltd* [2005] 1 NZLR 324 (CA) and *Henderson v Merrett Syndicates Ltd* [1995] 2 AC 145 (HL).

[162] *Based on Grant v Australian Knitting Mills* [1936] AC 85.

Another example based on a German Supreme Court decision is:[163] The proprietor of a fish farm has bought fish feed which contained illegal traces of an antibiotic. The sale as well as the use of the fish feed are contrary to the applicable Animal Food Act. In the authors' view, as far as the performance interest is at stake, the CISG should be applied before any claim in tort.

1.9 Limits of the Application: Additions and Filling the Gaps

1.9.1 Limits of the CISG ("External gap")

41. The ambit of the CISG is limited, as stated in Articles 4(a) and 4(b) CISG, to the formation of the contract and the rights and obligations of the seller and the buyer arsing from the contract. It excludes some substantive issues which can arise during a sale of goods, issues which also occur in regard to contracts other than sale of goods contracts, such as legal capacity and legal competence of the parties, legality of powers of attorney, set-off,[164] assignments of claims and receivables and the question whether a claim can be assigned,[165] the transfer of debts,[166] and the legal situation of joint debtors and their relations.[167] All of these issues have to be addressed by reference to the domestic law which is applicable according to the private international law of the forum. Whether or not the transfer of a whole contract is covered by the CISG is controversial.[168]

In the authors' view, jurisdiction and arbitration clauses do not fall within the ambit of the CISG as they are better seen as procedural law (despite being mentioned in Articles 19(3) and 81(1)(2) CISG). This position is supported by the Article 90 CISG which provides that the CISG does not prevail over matters governed by the CISG which are regulated by international conventions preceding the CISG.[169] Therefore, the Brussels Regulation has, for example, priority in Europe.

---

[163] BGH (25 Oct 1988) NJW 1989, 707, 709.

[164] See below para 42 and OLG Hamm (8 Feb 1995) CISG-online 141 with commentary from Schlechtriem, IPRax 1996, 197.

[165] See OLG Hamm (8 Feb 1995) CISG-online 141 with commentary from Schlechtriem, IPRax 1996, 197; see in regard to claims of the end purchaser against the manufacturer because of assigned claims (action directe) Krebs, (2001) 1 European L Forum, 16; see also if the assignment took place in the context of an international factoring contract governed by the (Ottawa) Convention on International Factoring of 28 May 1998; see also UN Convention on the Assignment of Receivables in International Trade (2002) 67 Unif L Rev 7:49 et seq.

[166] Compare AG Duisburg (13 Apr 2000) IHR 2001, 114 et seq; OGH (24 Apr 1997) CISG-online 291 Forum International 1997, 93 with a note by Ferrari, Magnus in *Staudinger*, Art 4 para 57 with more sources.

[167] LG München (25 Jan 1996) CISG-online 278.

[168] Compare BGH (15 Feb 1995) CISG-online 149 = NJW 1995, 2101. The replacement of a contractual party by assignment of the contract to a third person can be seen, according to Art 29 CISG, as a modification of the contract (see below para), see Schmidt-Kessel, RIW 1996, 60 et seq.

[169] Compare Kantonsgericht Zug (11 Dec 2003) CISG-online 958 sub 2.1.1.1; the lex fori was the Convention of *27 September 1968* on Jurisdiction and the Enforcement of Judgments in Civil and Commercial Matters (Brussels Convention) compare also the Convention of *16 September 1988* on

Formal requirements especially have to conform to the procedural law of the lex fori. Article 11 CISG is not applicable. However, insofar as domestic or international jurisdictions or arbitration provisions do not govern the formation of the jurisdiction or arbitration clause, Articles 14, 24 and 29 CISG are applicable, provided that the clause is or will be part of a sale of goods contract which falls within the ambit of the CISG.[170] Therefore, the question whether a jurisdiction or arbitration clause is valid can be a mixture between the procedural rules of the lex fori (for example Article 23 Brussels Convention) and the CISG (for example Articles 8, 19, 29 CISG).[171]

It might be already apparent from the forgoing discussion but Article 4 CISG, is too narrowly formulated: For example, CISG not only governs the formation of a contract but also its possible modification.[172] Further, questions of dispute settlement arising out of a sale of goods contract which is governed by the CISG, unilateral releases, or the prolonging of payment dates are covered by the CISG.[173]

42. A number of controversial issues remain. Already mentioned is that rescission for mistake must be treated as a question of validity and is, therefore, not governed by the CISG according to Article 4 (2nd s(a)), but instead is governed according to the applicable domestic law. However, the CISG does govern mistakes which are specifically regulated by the CISG, such as mistakes in respect of the other party's capacity to perform which become apparent after the conclusion of the contract, or mistakes regarding the conformity of the goods with the contract. Similarly, in regard to the liability of the parties for pre-contractual behaviour/dealings, the CISG is applicable (instead of the domestic tort law or culpa in contrahendo liability).[174] As far as pre-contractual information duties concern the

---

Jurisdiction and the Enforcement of Judgments in Civil and Commercial Matters (Lugano Convention).

[170] Compare in regard to the consensus about an arbitration clause *Filanto SpA v Chilewich International Corp* District Court (SD NY) (14 Apr 1992) CISG-online 45 = 789 F Supp 1229; in regard to a jurisdiction clause see *Chateau des Charmes Wines Ltd v Sabate, USA Inc* US Ct of Appeals (9th Cir) (5 May 2003) CISG-online 767.

[171] Compare OLG Köln (24 May 2006) CISG- online 1232 = IHR 2006 in regard to the inclusion of a jurisdiction clause in a standard form contract according to 23 Brussels Convention, in regard to conflicting standard form contracts Art 19 CISG was held applicable.

[172] CISG, Art 29, see paras 96 et seq.

[173] Compare Magnus in *Staudinger*, Art 4 para 62 (settlement), para 55 (unilateral release), and para 56 (prolongation of payment dates); see also Schlechtriem in Schlechtriem/Schwenzer, *Commentary*, Art 4 para 25.

[174] Liability for damages occurring during pre-contractual negotiations are either quasitortor in some instances even seen as restitutionary whereas in the Germanic legal tradition they are seen as quasi-contractual and fall under the concept of culpa in contrahendo. At common law, as there is no general duty of good faith in contractual negotiations, liability arising out of pre-contractual negotiations is unlikely unless a party can show a misrepresentation on the part of the other party. In New Zealand this area is complicated by the Contractual Remedies Act 1979 (NZ). A misrepresentation in the course of negotiations which induces entry into a contract is actionable as if it were a term of the contract: see s 6. However, if no contract results from the negotiations, a claim under the Contractual Remedies Act is not available because there is no contractual relationship to which a claim can be attached. In such cases, there may be a claim under the *Hedley Byrne* principle (see *Hedley Byrne & Co Ltd v Heller and Partners Ltd* [1964] AC 465), under the tort of deceit, or

conformity of the goods (factual and legal) or documents, the CISG applies before the domestic law. Also, as regards liability for damage caused by the breaking off of negotiations, the CISG provisions concerning irrevocability of an offer and the timing of the formation of a contract constitutes a legal framework which should not be undermined by domestic damages law which binds the parties earlier. In regard to other scenarios, for example, pre-contractual duties in regard to the protection of property of the parties to the contract, or the liability of an intermediary, the domestic law applies.[175]

42a. The impact of domestic pre-contractual informational duties on contracts under the CISG is uncertain. In Europe, such duties are often based on EU regulations and contain an array of duties relating to information between the parties and in connection with the formation of a contract. Examples are § 312c[176] and § 312e BGB which and the Information Regulation[177] which on which § 312c and § 312e BGB are based. Since § 312e BGB applies not only to consumer contracts but also to any contract with a "client" of a company, § 312e BGB's relationship with the CISG has to be considered. In the authors' view it is not decisive whether and how far the information duties are based on EU regulations since those do not take precedence over the CISG.[178] Article 4 (2nd s(a)) CISG cannot be a "gateway" for domestic law since a breach of informational duties generally does not render the contract void. In regard to the BGB and the Information Regulation it has to be noted that the legal consequences of a breach of the duties to inform has not been regulated extensively.[179] Only insofar as a mistake of a party caused by a breach of an informational duty during contract formation permits that party to avoid the contract can the duties to inform be taken indirectly into account in accordance with Article 4 (2nd s(a)) CISG.

42b. In the authors' view a distinction must be drawn between informational duties in regard to contracts formed by electronic means and informational duties in respect of international sales contracts. Electronic commerce is not regulated by

---

under the Fair Trading Act 1986 (NZ). Some particular circumstances may disclose a fiduciary relationship or duty of confidence between the parties, such as in *LAC Minerals Ltd v International Corona Resources Ltd* [1989] 2 SCR 574, but this is unlikely in an arms length business transaction. In such a case restitutionary or equitable remedies may be available.

[175] Extensively Köhler, *Haftung nach UN-Kaufrecht*, 212 et seq; in parts different Bonell, RIW 1990, 693, 701; following Bonell: Magnus in *Staudinger*, Art 4 para 43: if a party creates the good faith expectation that a contract will be formed the party will be liable for the damage incurred by the party relying on the contract formation.

[176] § 312c BGB stipulates inter alia, the duties of the businesses in regard to the information it has to communicate to the consumer when using modern mean of communication. Furthermore, it stipulates which contractual terms and standard form provisions the supplier has to make available to the consumer.

[177] Directive 97/7/1 EC of the European Parliament and of the Council (20 May 1997), on the Protection of Consumer in respect of Distance Contracts; § 312e BGB states the duties of the supplier in regard to e-commerce, for example, technical assistance, duties in regard to availability of contractual terms and standard form contracts.

[178] See para 345a.

[179] See Janal, *Sanktionen und Rechtsbehelfe*, 144 et seq.

the CISG. Issues arising from the use of electronic communication during contract formation, such as questions of form,[180] or the point at which electronic communications reach the addressee,[181] can be solved either by an ambulatory interpretation of Articles 14 et seq CISG or by filling the gap pursuant to Article 7(2) CISG. Insofar as the purpose of the information duties is to safeguard the transparency of electronic contract formation[182] the CISG does not deal with the issue and, therefore, cannot be interpreted accordingly. Therefore, the domestic law applicable to the contract will need to be applied in order to determine the legal consequences of a breach of such informational duties.[183] If, for example, German law is the proper law of the contract, the company has to provide the means of correcting data entry mistakes[184] or has to inform about the technical steps which lead to the contract formation.[185]

According to § 312e (1) No 3 BGB electronic acknowledgement of receipt has to be provided to the other party, but this does not have any effect on contract formation.[186]

42c. Provisions such as § 312c (1)(1st s) No 1 BGB in conjunction with § 1 (1) Nos 1-10 Information Regulation[187] are designed to protect the consumer and should, therefore, notwithstanding Article 2(a) CISG, fall outside the ambit of the CISG since mistakes of the parties concerning their intentions in respect of contract formation and their consequences fall under the applicable domestic contract law, which is determined by the private international law rules of the forum.[188] Nevertheless, a certain intertwining with the CISG can occur, for example, if the seller according to § 312c (1)(1st s) No 1 BGB in conjunction with § 1 (1) No 3 Information Regulation has to inform the buyer about essential characteristics of the goods and, therefore, expresses the basic requirements for an agreement of "quality" in Article 35(1) CISG (should the CISG be applicable). In the authors' view, if a consumer contract falls under the CISG in exceptional circumstances and German law is the proper law of the contract, such an intertwining would be

---

[180] See paras 64 et seq.

[181] See para 95.

[182] See, for example, § 312e (1) (1st s) Nos 1 & 2 in conjunction with § 3 Nos 1, 3, 4 Information Regulation: the first refers to technical assistance, the second to the clarity of the information in regard to the contact. The Information Regulation states what information in case of distance contracts has to be made available, by the supplier, for example: identity of the contracting party, address, main characteristic of the goods; minimum duration of the contract if the contract is for a permanent or renewable goods; additional costs; the arrangements for payment, delivery or performance; the period for which the offer or the price remain valid.

[183] See in regard to German law with an overview over the available remedies: Janal, *Sanktionen und Rechtsbehelfe*, 145 et seq; see also Hoeren, WM 2004, 2461–2470.

[184] See § 321e (1) No 1 BGB.

[185] See § 3 No 1 Information Regulation.

[186] See to the possible interpretation of the acknowledgement as acceptance: Leible/Sosnitza, BB 2005, 725, 726.

[187] § 312c BGB in conjunction with § 1 Information Regulation stipulates the information the supplier has to provide to the consumer, for example, the identity of the supplier, arrangements for payment, additional costs.

[188] See further Janal, *Sanktionen und Rechtsbehelfe*, 192 et seq.

compatible with the CISG. On the other hand, the duties provided in § 312c (2) BGB in conjunction with §§ 1(2), (3) Nos 1, 3, 4 Information Regulation or § 312e (1) No 4 BGB which protect the legal position of the consumer or client[189] and which compel the seller to give the buyer certain information in writing are additional duties for the seller and not compatible with the CISG (despite the fact that those provisions do not devise a mandatory formal requirement which would be contrary to Article 11 CISG). Information in writing which diverts from the content of a contract does not generally alter a contract's content, but if the purpose of the additional information is intended to achieve a modification of the contract, Article 29 CISG would have to be satisfied.[190] Only insofar as such duties (again) protect the forming of the buyer's intention in regard to contract formation and the breach of those duties results (or can result) in mistakes or in prolonged revocation periods, do those duties as stipulated by, for example, the Information Regulation lie outside the ambit of the CISG. Where this is the case, the provisions of the applicable domestic law or, for example, regulations like the Information Regulation, are applicable even though the contract would otherwise fall under the ambit of the CISG. On the whole it is regrettable that the drafter of the Information Regulation and the German legislature has ignored the potential conflict which arises out of the numerous differing duties for the parties of a contract whose legal relations fall under the ambit of the CISG.

42d. Domestic law applies to the buyer's and seller's rights to withhold performance except where the CISG provides for a particular right to withhold performance, as with, for example, the concurrent payment and handing over of the goods under Article 58(1) CISG; the rights and obligations of the parties consequent upon the avoidance of the contract under Article 81(1)(2nd s) CISG; or the right to suspend performance of obligations if it becomes apparent that the other party will not perform a substantial part of its obligations under Article 71(1) CISG. These provisions indicate that the CISG recognises the principle that the parties have the right to withhold performance in addition to their other legal rights in accordance with Article 7(2) CISG, in certain circumstances and in regard to duties and obligations stipulated by the CISG.[191] The property dimension of rights to withhold, disposal rights which impact on the rights of third parties and priority rights in insolvency proceedings fall under the ambit of the domestic law which is applicable according to the private international law rules of the forum.

Example: The seller does not let the buyer know the date for the pick up of the machine sold which he/she was required by the contract to do 14 days

---

[189] See Janal, *Sanktionen und Rechtsbehelfe*, 138, 139, 234 et seq.

[190] In regard to consumer contracts see Janal, *Sanktionen und Rechtsbehelfe*, 264, 265.

[191] See also para 205 in regard to the buyer's right to withhold his/her performance and paras 250, 251 in regard to the seller's right to withhold' see also in the affirmative: OGH (8 Nov 2005) CISG-online 1156 (gap-filling in accordance with Art 71(1) CISG); from the literature: Kern in Will (ed) *Rudolf Meyer*, 73 et seq; Kern, ZEuP 2000, 837 et seq; Schlechtriem in *Symposium Frank Vischer* (11 Mar 2004) CISG-online (publications); Witz in *FS Schlechtriem* 293 et seq.

before the date of performance. When the seller makes demand for the sale price, the buyer can withhold payment.[192]

42e. It is doubtful that parties have the possibility of set-off claims the have against each other and how such a set-off would be effected, for example whether the parties would have to declare the set-off or whether the principle of ipso iure compensatur would apply, or whether as under Article 1290 of the French Code Civil claims will be set-off against each other automatically if they fulfil the requirements of set-off. As far as claims derive from contracts to which the CISG does not apply are concerned, the domestic law applicable to the contract according to the private international law of the forum will determine whether and what the requirements of a set-off are. In the authors' view, however, even claims arising out of "CISG contracts" have to meet the requirements for set-off of the applicable domestic law[193] since the CISG is silent as to whether a set-off can be done ipso iure or by party declaration and from which point in time the claims are extinct. The answers or principles cannot be drawn together by way of gap-filling under Article 7(2) CISG, since no clear principles as to set-off can be extracted from the CISG.[194] The prohibition of set-off in certain circumstances in domestic laws can neither be ignored nor substituted. However, a rejection of set-off agreed to by the parties must be evaluated according to Article 6 CISG, for example, whether Articles 11, 14 et seq CISG are met. National rejections of set-off, however, can come into play through Article 4 (2nd s(a)) CISG.[195]

Example: An Italian shoe manufacturer sold shoes in January to a German buyer for the summer season. The seller, however, only delivered the shoes at the end of June, after the buyer had paid part of the purchase price. The Italian seller asserted its right to withhold delivery according to Article 71(2) CISG. The Court saw in the invocation of Article 71(2) CISG a breach of contract by the Italian seller and allowed a set-off of the remaining purchase price with the damages claim of the buyer according to Article 45(1) (b) CISG (the shoes could only be sold at a lower price because of the late delivery in the summer sales). The set-off was based on § 387 et seq BGB although according to the German private international law rules (Article 32 No 2 EGBGB) the domestic law of the main claim determines the applicable law of the set-off: in this case

---

[192] Example according to Kantonsgericht Appenzell Ausserrhoden (10 Mar 2003) CISG-online 852.

[193] Saenger/Sauthoff, IHR 2005, 189-195, 190 et seq with further references; see also Schlechtriem in Schlechtriem/Schwenzer, *Commentary*, Art 4 para 22a with a comprehensive overview of the issue.

[194] Different view: Hornung in Schlechtriem/Schwenzer, Art 81 para 16 ("trying to achieve"); Magnus in *Staudinger*, Art 4 para 46 with further references; OLG München (9 Jul 1997) CISG-online 282; in agreement: Tallon in Bianca/Bonell, Art 81 para 2.6; Kindler, IPRax 1996, 16, 19 comment on LG München (20 Mar 1995) CISG-online 164; Saenger/Sauthoff, IHR 2005, 189, 190 et seq; OLG Hamm (9 Jun 1995) CISG-online 146; OLG Stuttgart (21 Aug 1995) CISG-online 150.

[195] Compare, for example, § 309 No 3 BGB which prohibits a prohibition of set-off in standard form contracts.

the main claim was the claim for the purchase price and, therefore, the Court should have determined the set-off according to Italian law.[196]

42f. The question where secondary duties (for example, the continuing rights and obligations after the avoidance of a contract) have to be performed, falls without doubt within the ambit of the CISG even though the CISG does not provide for secondary duties expressly. In the authors' view domestic law is not applicable in these cases. The gap has to be filled in accordance with Article 7(2) CISG, that means, by rules which have to be determined in accordance with the principles stipulated in the CISG.

1.9.2 Interpretation of the Convention

43. Article 7(1) CISG provides general principles for the interpretation, use and filling of gaps within the CISG.[197] In particular, regard is to be had to its international character, to the need to promote uniformity in its application and the observance of good faith in international trade. Similar provisions can be found in other international agreements.[198] The requirement to take into account the international character of the CISG seeks to secure the principle of autonomous interpretation of the principles of the CISG and prohibits the use of technical terms and principles of domestic laws, especially the domestic law of the user.[199] This means the analysis of the function of specific terms within the CISG has to be autonomous and does not reflect the subjective understanding which the user (for example) the court, has based on its domestic law and experience.[200] Only insofar as certain solutions and terms in the CISG are clearly influenced by a particular legal system is it permissible to look to this legal system for interpretation and understanding. For example, Article 74(2nd s) CISG states that "damages may not exceed the loss which the party in breach foresaw or ought to have foreseen at the time of the conclusion of the contract ...". The limitation of compensation to foreseeable losses, is the corollary to the parties' strict liability.[201] The model of strict liability provided for in Article 74(1st s) CISG follows the Anglo-American model where the promisor is in principle liable for all losses arising

---

[196] Compare AG Frankfurt (31 Jan 1991) CISG-online 34 = IPRax 1991, 345 with comment from Jayme.

[197] See in regard to the methods of interpretation: Schlechtriem in Schlechtriem/Schwenzer, *Commentary*, Art 7 paras 19–26, in regard to the importance of the English and French language BG (13 Nov 2003) CISG-online 840 = IHR 2004, 215, 217 (para 4.3) with comment from Mohs; see also Huber/Mullis, *The CISG*, 7 et seq.

[198] UNIDROIT "Principles of International Commercial Contracts" (2004) Art 1.6. Commission on European Contract Law "Principles of European Contract Law" (1998) Art 5:102(g).

[199] Schlechtriem in Schlechtriem/Schwenzer, *Commentary*, Art 7 paras 6, 7, 11; Ferrari, (1994) 24 GA J Int'l & Comp L, 183, 200: "the Convention opted, in other words, for an 'autonomous interpretation'"; see also Kramer, öst JBl 1996, 137 et seq especially 140 et seq.

[200] Compare Ferrari, (1994) 24 GA J Int'l & Comp L, 183, 209 who, however, argues against the qualification through a comparative analysis, since a comparative analysis could result in a qualification which could be against the spirit of the CISG.

[201] Witz in Witz/Salger/Lorenz, Art 74 para 2; Huber, *Leistungsstörungen*, 72 ("theoretically and practically inseparable"); Vékás, (2002) 43 Acta Juridica Hungarica 159.

from non-performance, irrespective of fault, unless exempted in accordance with Articles 79 and 80 CISG.[202] Therefore, Anglo-American jurisprudence can be considered when interpreting "foreseeable losses" in Article 74(2nd s) CISG.

It goes without saying that courts and tribunals interpreting the CISG should take into account foreign judgments and literature which are accessible through commentaries and databases[203] to aid and to inform the uniform interpretation of the CISG. Although no precedent system comparable to common law is mandatory under the CISG, the term "to promote uniformity in its application" in Article 7(1) CISG obliges the taking into account of foreign literature and especially jurisprudence.[204] If a question of substance in regard to the CISG has been considered by the highest court of a member state then the decision should be regarded as "persuasive authority" by other courts and arbitral tribunals, even though they might otherwise tend to another interpretation. If a generally uniform opinion in regard to a question has been formed in the literature and jurisprudence then this should be treated like "precedent" and followed in the interest of uniform application of the CISG. An example is the view described above at para 15 that the choice of a domestic law, if in doubt, includes the choice of the CISG. This approach allows for the development of the CISG even though its basic structure was developed in the 1930s and technical developments like, for example, electronic communication and modern legal solutions have threatened to outdate it. In this way, the development of the CISG can occur without having to call a conference of all member states to amend the CISG and to wait for the amendments' ratification, neither of which is likely to come to fruition. Therefore, if, for example, a general or dominant opinion should develop in relation to the issue of the application of the CISG to a software contract, then this opinion should be followed having regard to the "uniform application" advocated in Article 7(1) CISG.[205]

44. Article 7(1) CISG only stipulates the interpretation of the CISG and is not stipulating a general principle in regard to the conduct of the parties during contract formation and the performance of the contract or in regard to the interpretation of the parties' statements. The principle of good faith in regard to the interpretation of the CISG can be found in a couple of CISG provisions.[206] The drafters of the CISG debated for a long time whether the obligation to act in good faith should also apply to the parties. However, they rejected the advancement of good faith on party conduct in the end. It was feared that the potential to apply such a

---

[202] Still/Gruber in Schlechtriem/Schwenzer, *Commentary*, Art 74 para 2.

[203] See for example, case law on UNICTRAL texts (CLOUT) www.uncitral.org/uncitral/en/case_law.html; Baasch Andersen, (2005) 24 J L & Comm, 159 (available at www.cisg.law.pace.edu); the UNCITRAL Digest of Case Law on the United Nations Convention on the International Sale of Goods A/CN.9/SER.C/DIGEST/CISG/7 (8 Jun 2004) www.cisg. law.Pace.edu/cisg/text.

[204] Recent studies have shown that despite certain differences in terminilogy many legal systems use similar standards or tools when interpreting statuory texts. Huber/Mullis, *The CISG*, 9 with fn 17.

[205] van Alstine, (1998) 146 U Pa L Rev, 687, 726 et seq.

[206] Compare the catalogue in UNCITRAL Secretariat "Commentary on the Draft Convention on Contracts for the International Sale of Goods Prepared by the Secretariat" (14 Mar 1979) A/Conp/97/5, Art 6, 3; see also Ferrari, (1994) 24 GA J Int'l & Comp L, 183, 210 et seq.

principle differently would be great; that domestic jurisprudence on good faith would heavily influence its interpretation; and that sanctions were missing. However, during the drafting sessions it was continuously emphasised that it would be desirable to take account of the principle of good faith in regard to the conduct of the parties.[207] In the international literature views are divided over whether Article 7(1) CISG can be used as a basis for the application of good faith to particular contracts and their interpretation or whether in regard to gap-filling other suitable principles from other CISG provisions have to be used. The difference in opinion in regard to Article 7(1) CISG is only of minor importance, because general principle can and has to be developed in accordance with Article 7(2) CISG.[208] It is important to note that domestic jurisprudence and principles concerning the principle of good faith should not be incorporated unreflected into the CISG since they are often developed because of deficiencies in the domestic legal system. An example is the German ancillary duties to a contract (which in common law are often tortious and not contractual duties) such as a duty to inform about a product, to create a safe environment for the party which concluding the contract.[209] The obligation in Article 7(1) CISG to observe "good faith in international trade" takes account of rules and trade practice in international trade and/or a particular trade, in usages not (yet) meeting the requirements of Article 9(2) CISG, and in widely used standard forms and trade terms, which can be found (but not exclusively), for example, in the UNIDROIT – principles, Incoterms, certain generally accepted contract forms (for example, like the GAFTA contract example/form No 100 for the delivery of forage cereal,[210] or the *Uniform Customs and Practice for Documentary Credits (UCP 500)* issued by the International Chamber of Commerce).

1.9.3 Gap-filling

45.   As discussed in para 33, since no legislator is blessed with perfect foresight and the CISG is sometimes the product of compromise between the different positions of different legal cultures, the CISG has a number of gaps in areas which fall into the CISG's legal scope of application. How to deal with those gaps is of utmost importance. For such gaps, Article 7(2) CISG provides that they ought to be filled in accordance with the principles which are based within the CISG. Only if a gap cannot be filled in accordance with CISG based principles, can, according

---

[207] Compare in regard to this point Schlechtriem, *UN-Einheitliches Kaufrecht*, 25.

[208] Very clear in regard to the possibilities and explanations why the principle of good faith cannot only be seen as interpretation maximise for the CISG but also as part of contractual obligations between the parties: Farnsworth, Tul J Int'l and Comp L,47, 56.

[209] In regard to the latter in a case where the buyer slipped on a banana peel in the shop on her way to conclude the contract the Bundersgerichtshof held that the seller breached a (pre) contractual duty and damages based on contract law were awarded. The Court based its development of the duty on good faith – (BGH (26 Oct 1961) NJW 1962, 31).

[210] Printed in Bridge, *International Sale of Goods*, Appendix 2.

to Article 7(2) CISG, the domestic law which is applicable according to the private international law rules of the forum be used.[211]

46. However, gap-filling based on CISG principles is not allowed where the drafters of the CISG intentionally left a gap and, therefore, wanted the application of domestic law to prevail. An example is the incomplete regulation in Article 78 CISG which leaves the amount of interest and the law applicable to determine the amount open because no agreement could be reached in Vienna on either point. In this case it is not possible to substitute the "non-decision" of the CISG drafters, which is also a "non-decision" of the ratifying domestic legislature and either to develop a CISG private international law rule or even to develop a CISG substance norm to fill the gap.[212]

47. Article 7(2) CISG allows in other cases the development of supplementary, that means gap-filling, rules by way of analogy,[213] whereby the differentiation between gap-filling and analogy is theoretically possible but practically of no great importance.[214] Also the generous interpretation of certain provisions can be the solution in regard to particular issues. Firstly, therefore, it has to be determined, whether, a real gap exists. It is important to resist the temptation to circumvent the consequence which a certain provision provides for by finding that a rule is an exception and that, therefore, a gap exists and to fill that gap with a favourable principle.

Example: The buyer has not given notice in regard to the non-conformity of the goods in time. Seller and buyer have initially negotiated how they should proceed. However, they cannot agree. The seller claims the purchase price. The buyer pleads the non-conformity of the goods. The seller defends his claim with the lack of timely notice. Can the consequences of Article 39 CISG, the non-timely notice of lack of conformity, be ignored because the seller has waived his right to rely on the lack of notice? Article 40 CISG provides explicitly the circumstances under which the seller is not entitled to rely on the lack of notice of non-conformity. Additionally, Article 44 CISG guarantees that, under certain circumstances the buyer has certain rights despite his or her lack of timely notice. Next to those provisions can a gap exist, in regard to the seller waiving his right to rely on the lack of notice? And can that gap be filled by reverting to the general principles set out in Articles 40 and 44 CISG? In the authors' view no gap can exist.[215]

---

[211] See comprehensively (also to the history) Frigge, *Externe Lücken und Internationales Privatrecht*, 33 et seq, 50 et seq, 71 et seq; Magnus, RabelsZ 59 (1995) 473, 474; van Alstine, (1998) 146 U Pa L Rev, 687, 726, et seq, 733.

[212] Compare Diedrich, RIW 1995, 353, 363; Arbitral Award of the International Arbitral Tribunal of the Bundeskammer der gewerblichen Wirtschaft in Österreich (15 Jun 1994) CISG-online 120, 121 = RIW 1995, 590 et seq with commentary by Schlechtriem in RIW 1995, 590, 591.

[213] See para 52.

[214] See Schlechtriem in Schlechtriem/Schwenzer, *Commentary*, Art 7 para 30.

[215] See Arbitral Award of the International Arbitral Tribunal of the Bundeskammer der gewerblichen Wirtschaft in Österreich (15 Jun 1994) CISG-online 120, 121 = RIW 1995, 590 et seq with

48.   Not only do gaps exist insofar as the CISG does not contain general rules which are applicable for all contracts – including for sales contracts – but also in regard to some substantial sale of goods issues.[216] Explicitly formulated principles can only rarely be found in the CISG, for example, in Article 7(1) CISG.[217] Other general principles which are based on specific provisions can be determined even though caution has to be used in regard to the long list of such general principles collected in the literature.[218] One of the general principles is the obligation of the parties to observe good faith in regard to the contract which is a generally acknowledged principle by the jurisprudence to the CISG and the literature (despite the fact that the drafters could not agree to include such a requirement in Article 7(1) CISG. In the authors' view the parties' obligation to observe good faith can be based on the reference to the "reasonable man" standard to which the parties have to achieve which can be found in the provisions of the CISG.[219] A concretisation of good faith principle is the protection of a party's reasonable reliance caused by the other party (based on Article 16(2)(b), Article 29(2)(2nd s) CISG).[220] With the help of the principle of the protection of a party's reasonable reliance, the requirements of which are determined in accordance with Articles 16(2)(b) and 29(2)(2nd s) CISG, gaps can be filled: for example, the open question whether and for how long declarations according to Articles 26, 27 CISG (which do not have to reach the other party) can be revoked. Furthermore, the principle of reliance protection is also helpful when determining whether a buyer's claim to performance can be rejected because he or she has already claimed damages because of non-performance.

---

commentary by Schlechtriem in RIW 1995, 590, 592–594, compare OLG Oldenburg (5 Dec 2000) CISG-online 618.

[216] See para 41 et seq.

[217] See para 43.

[218] Compare, for example, Magnus, RabelsZ 59 (1995) 467 et seq who lists the following principles or questions which can be determined by using the existing principles embodied in the CISG (480 et seq): party-autonomy, pacta sunt servanda, freedom of form (Art 11 CISG), estoppel or the prohibition of a venire contra factum proprium, the protection of a party's reasonable reliance, caused by the other party (principle based on Artt 16(2)(b), 29(2) (2nd s) CISG), a general duty to avoid or mitigate losses and disadvantages (based in Artt 77 and 80) and generally to co-operate, ancillary duties of buyer and seller to achieve full performance of their main obligations or to inform about details of the process of formation of the contract such as inclusion of standard terms by reference; the seller's place of business as the place of performance for payments (based on Art 57 CISG); the unwinding of contracts terminated by agreement under Art 29 (based on Art 81 et seq), claims falling due without additional notice of demand (based on Art 59 CISG), general right to withhold performance (based mainly on Art 58 and 71); general burden of proof rule that every party has to prove the facts on which his or her claim, right or defence is based (based on wording of Artt 79 and 2(a)); see also Schlechtriem in Schlechtriem/Schwenzer, *Commentary*, Art 7 para 30; in regard to gap-filling, analogy and principles: Schlechtriem in *Symposium Frank Vischer*, II.

[219] See, for example CISG, Art 8(3), Art 25; compare paras 44, 54; see also Magnus in *Staudinger*, Art 7 para 43.

[220] Insofar correct the International Arbitral Tribunal of the Bundeskammer der gewerblichen Wirtschaft in Österreich (15 Jun 1994) CISG-online 120, 121 = RIW 1995, 590 et seq with commentary by Schlechtriem in RIW 1995, 592–594.

49. The priority of party-autonomy is a general principle that can also be used for gap filling.

Example: A has sold goods to B which she herself wants to buy from C. B contacts C directly in the course of the performance of the contract who then delivers directly to B. Later a dispute arises whether C's delivery is based on the contract A – B and, therefore, performed, or whether C performed in accordance with his own contract with B. The CISG itself does not contain any rules on third-party performance of a contract. Determinative has to be in light of the general principle of party autonomy if the parties have not come to any agreement the intention for the performing party. Articles 32(1) and 67(2) CISG, for example contemplate the possibility of a one-sided stipulation of the goods to a contract.

Another general principle is the freedom of form (Articles 11, 29 CISG). Further, the obligation to make restitution as set out in Article 84(2) CISG can be used to allow for restitution for received services in case of the avoidance of a contract.[221] In the authors' view the right to claim restitution for the use of nonconforming goods, which have to be returned after the delivery of the substitute goods (Article 46(2) CISG) can be based on the restitution principle as well.

50. Who bears the burden of proof is uncertain. At the Vienna Conference delegates clearly did not want to regulate the burden of proof in the Convention because they feared that they would regulate procedural questions with it for which they lacked the mandate.[222] As a result of the undecisiveness, the CISG contains some provisions which deal with the burden of proof in regard to certain issues whereas in regard to other question the CISG is silent in relation to the burden of proof question: sometimes it was said in regard to specific provisions that the burden of proof should be left to the courts. In specific provisions, however, the burden of proof has been clearly allocated, so for example, in Article 79(1) CISG or impliedly in Article 2(1) CISG. The longer the time elapsed since Vienna Conference, the less fresh the memory of the fear will be, the more confident about the warnings of the CISG judges, lawyers, and arbitrators will become, and the easier it should be to develop a unified approach to burden of proof in the interest of a uniform application and interpretation of the CISG which will make a fall back on domestic law unnecessary.[223] From the abovementioned provisions, however, the general principle can be extracted that each party has to prove the facts which are beneficial for them or the factual requirements of the provision they involve.[224] The fall back on domestic law should be avoided through gapfilling by using developed principles.[225]

---

[221] See para 333.

[222] See Müller, *Beweislastverteilung*, 30, 31.

[223] Müller, *Beweislastverteilung*, 33; see also BGH (9 Jan 2002) CISG-online 651 = NJW 2002, 1651 et seq para I.2.6; Appellationshof des Kantons Bern (11 Feb 2004) CISG-online 1191 = IHR 2006, 149 et seq para II 3.

[224] Compare Magnus in *Staudinger*, Art 4 paras 63–69, Art 7 para 57. Comprehensive in regard to burden of proof Henninger in *Die Frage der Beweislast* who first convincingly argues that and why

51. From Article 18(1)(2) CISG one can deduce the principle that silence or inactivity themselves do not constitute acceptance. Therefore, for example, one cannot assume a gap in regard to the question of what happens if a merchant's acceptance including his or her (standard) terms is met by silence from the other merchant. Under German law a merchant's silence after receiving a merchant's acceptance with his or her (standard) terms is viewed as acceptance of a (modified) offer. The principle deduced from Article 18(1)(2) CISG, however, means that German law in regard to a merchant's acceptance with (standard) terms cannot be followed if the contract falls within the ambit of the CISG unless that practice fulfils the requirements of Article 9(2) CISG, being a usage known in international trade or the conduct of the addressee has the meaning of acceptance.[226]

52. Comparable with using an analogy is the gap-filling in terms of Article 7(2) CISG if the drafters of the CISG did not and could not anticipate issues, for example, because of technical advancements. Such gaps have to be filled by analogy in regard to individual provisions. For example, Article 13 CISG can be used by analogy in regard to declarations via fax or email (if the addressee can print the email out).[227] If no principles from the CISG can be determined and therefore, gap-filling is not possible.[228]

However, in the authors' view the UNIDROIT Principles can only be used as far as the Principles can also be found in the CISG.[229] Insofar as the Principles deal with issues which the drafters of the CISG did not address explicitly, for example, the question of the applicable international law rule to determine the interest rate (see para 318), it is reasonable to suggest that the Principles should not be used to inform interpretation. Unless the parties' intention is clearly to the contrary, the issue should be determined by domestic law which is applicable through the private international law rules of the forum. The CISG itself does not contain private international law rules, except for Article 28 CISG.[230] In New Zealand, Canada,

---

the objective burden of proof is an issue falling in the ambit of the CISG (153 et seq) and lastly comments in regard to individual provision in regard to burden of proof (201 et seq); similar Müller, *Beweislastverteilung*, 31 et seq and also Jung, *Beweislastverteilung*, both with numerous suggestions in regard to the burden of proof in regard to the burden of proof in regard to individual provisions.

[225] Contrast, however, the Arbitral Awards of the ICC Paris (1 Jan 1993) CISG-online 71 = JDI 1993, 1040 which applied in regard to a German-Syrian steel contract for which the parties had chosen French law as the proper law of the contract, the CISG as the applicable French law. However, the Chamber then fell back on the Code Civil in regard to questions of burden of proof.

[226] See in regard to common law position which is similar to the German position, for example, *Thomson v Burrows* [1916] NZLR 223; Burrows/Todd, *Contract Law*, para 3.3.9.

[227] See para 67.

[228] Very doubtful and controversial is the possibility of determining the principles through a comparative analysis regardless of the CISG. Firstly, the drafters of the CISG meant in Art 7(2) CISG only principles based on the CISG; secondly, the practical difficulty of determining general principles through a comparative analysis is enormous in Schlechtriem's view insurmountable, unless the analysis is narrowed to the easy accessible European and North-American legal systems. Magnus suggests using the UNIDROIT "Principles of International Commercial Contracts" (which make a claim in regard to its use for the CISG in its preamble).

[229] Similar Huber/Mullis, *The CISG*, 36.

[230] See para 119.

and Australia the private international law rules developed by common law are applicable to determine the proper law of the contract,[231] in member states of the European Union the Rome Convention[232] will be applicable, in the member states of the Hague Uniform Sales Law[233] the private international law rules of that Convention are applicable. Whether in addition to the proper law of the contract for individual issues, a separate private international law inquiry has to be done is controversial, but, for example, should be considered in regard to the issue of interest.[234] In the authors' view it is not possible to develop general private international law rules through the principles embodied in the CISG, so, for example in regard the issue of a missing stipulation of the interest rate in the CISG a general private international law rule that the interest rate is always determined by the domestic law of the creator is not possible.[235]

2 General Provisions

53. Articles 7–13 C ISG contain general provisions which are applicable not only in regard to contract formation but also in regard to all other provisions of the CISG. Article 10 CISG has already been dealt with since the place of business is an important requirement to determine whether the CISG is applicable at all according to Article 1(1) CISG.[236] Also Article 7 CISG, which is an addition to the provisions dealing with the ambit of the CISG, has already been examined since the interpretation of the CISG, according to Article 7(1) CISG can lead to a change in the limits of the ambit. Furthermore, Article 7 CISG has been dealt with in the previous part because the limits have to always be determined anew if gapfilling is undertaken because of the evaluative decision-making whether to find general principles by gap-filling or whether to revert to domestic law.[237]

2.1 Interpretation of Party Statements and Conduct

54. The interpretation of party statements and the party's legally relevant conduct is governed by Article 8 CISG. In the first instance the real (subjective) intention of the parties and/or the parties' conduct which has legal relevance is determinative. However, the subjective intention of the party needs to be known or at least ought to have been known (to the other party). Otherwise statements made

---

[231] *The Laws of New Zealand*, part VII, para 357.

[232] "Convention on the Law Applicable to Contractual Obligations" (19 Jun 1980) (80/934/EEC).

[233] "Uniform Law on International Sale of Goods (ULIS) (1 Jul 1964) and "Uniform Law on the Formation of Contracts for International Sale of Goods" (ULF) (1 Jul 1964).

[234] Para 318.

[235] However, compare the Arbitral Award of the International Arbitral Tribunal of the Bundeskammer der gewerblichen Wirtschaft in Österreich (15 Jun 1994) CISG-online 120, 121 = RIW 1995, 590 et seq with commentary by Schlechtriem in RIW 1995, 592–594.

[236] Paras 9–11.

[237] Paras 45 et seq.

by and/or other conduct of a party are to be interpreted according to the under-standing that a reasonable person of the same kind as the other party would have had in the same circumstances (Article 8(2) CISG). Determinative is the under-standing of "a reasonable person of the same kind as the other ... in the same circumstances". Since the term "reasonable person" has to be interpreted in light of Article 7(1) CISG can good faith in international trade be determinative in regard to its interpretation?[238] The place of Article 8 CISG in Part I of the CISG, the general provisions, but also the wording of 8(1) CISG clearly indicates that Article 8 CISG is not only applicable in regard to statements concerning contract formation – and therefore, for the interpretation of contracts – and their revocation (Article 16 CISG) but for all legally relevant statements and conduct in Part II and III as well as conduct with legal effect, such as the setting of deadlines, declaration of avoidance, statement of specification (Article 65 CISG), notice of non-conformity, deduction of price, and the withholding of performance. Also party statements which lead to legal consequences or agreements with a content to which the CISG is not applicable, (like, for example, statements in regard to set-off which lead to the retention of title, or the agreement of a penalty clause) should be gov-erned in the authors' view by Article 8 CISG and not by the subsidiary proper law of the contract.

The interpretation of statements in regard to the formation of the contract is important in regard to the inclusion of trade clauses.[239]

55. The CISG does not stipulate the legal consequences of a discrepancy between the actual but not discernible intention of the party making a statement and the objective meaning of that statement as determined through an Article 8(2) CISG analysis. The consequences of incompatibility between the statements of the parties are incompatible are also not laid down in the CISG. Domestic law decides upon the consequences of such defects of intention. For example, if German law is applicable, parties can challenge the contract according to § 119 BGB[240], or the rules in regard to (express or hidden) intentions in accordance with §§ 154, 155 BGB[241] are applicable. Standard terms and conditions do not form part of the

---

[238] For example, the party's understanding can be determined according to the requirements of § 157 BGB which states that contracts have to be interpreted in light of good faith and ordinary usage: Huber, RabelsZ 43 (1979) 413-526 in regard to the UNCITRAL draft; critical Schmidt-Kessel in Schlechtriem/Schwenzer, *Commentary*, Art 8 para 30 with further references.

[239] Compare OGH (22 Oct 2001) CISG-online 614 = IHR 2002, 24 et seq: Notice to Incoterms in offer; see also OGH (13 Sep 2001) CISG-online 644 = IHR 2002, 74, 76 and standard forms, referred to in the acceptance and, or the offer. See para 58.

[240] BGB, § 119: "(1) A person who, when making a declaration of intent, was mistaken about its con-tents or had no itention whatsoever of making a declaration with this content, may avoid the decla-ration if it is so be assumed that he would not have made the declaration with knowledge of the factual position and with a sensible understanding of the case.
(2)   A mistake about such characteristics of a person or a thing as are customarily regarded as essential is also regarded as a mistake about the content of the declaration."

[241] BGB, § 154: "(1) As long as the parties have not yet agreed on all points of a contract on which an agreement was required to be reached according to the declaration even if only one party, the con-tract is, in case of doubt, not entered into. An agreement on individual points is not legally binding even if they have been recorded.

contract unless they have clearly been incorporated during contract formation.[242] In exceptional circumstances the CISG classifies, what according to German law, would be a defect of intention on a matter of interpretation. An example is the discrepancy between (internal) intention and incorrect formulation of that intention which results in an avoidable misunderstanding of the addressee in accordance with Article 8(1) CISG.[243] Articles 8(1) and 8(2) CISG should exclude a heavy reliance on the (internal) intention (secret reservations) and its defects and, therefore sham transactions should be valid. Furthermore, Article 27 CISG takes precedence over domestic law in regard to errors or delay in the transmission of the communication and Article 19(2) CISG regulates what constitutes an irrelevant defect in regard to a consensus between parties.[244]

56.   Article 8(3) CISG is concerned with determining the intent of a party by allowing the contract negotiations, that is the circumstances of the formation of the contract, to be taken into account and usages among the parties to be considered. The latter, however, includes, in contrast to Article 9(2) CISG,[245] traditions and practices which only exist locally, regional, nationally or among a certain group of people. Article 8(3) CISG does have another function than Article 9(2) CISG. Article 8(3) CISG is not concerned with the supplementation of the contract or the content of usage, but rather with the interpretation of party statements. In regard to the latter, the specific circumstances which are relevant are those important for the interpretation of behaviour of the parties or for determining what a reasonable person in the shoes of the addressee would have understood the other party's statement meant.

57.   That also the subsequent behaviour of the parties can be relevant for the determination of their intent at the time of contract formation is rational but logically hard to justify because the meaning of a statement has to be certain when it becomes effective. That in Article 8(3) CISG "subsequent behaviour" is, therefore, to be understood as behaviour which allows for evaluating the party's intent at the time of making the statement. Where the subsequent behaviour stipulates a changed intent Article 29 CISG might be fulfilled.

Example: The Nigerian seller delivered tropical wood to the German buyer who refused to pay the purchase price. In dispute between the parties was, inter alia, whether the parties had concluded a contract for the sale of the wood or whether the German party only wanted to hold the wood

---

(2) If notarial recording of the contract contemplated has been arranged, the contract is, in case of doubt, not entered into until the recording has taken place.

BGB, § 155: "If the parties to a contract which they consider to have been entered into have, in fact, not agreed on a point on which an agreement was required to be reached, whatever is agreed is applicable if it is to be assmed that the contract would have been entered into even without a provision concerning this point."

[242] See BGH (31 Oct 2001) CISG-online 617 = NJW 2002, 370, 371; see as well para 58.

[243] See Schmidt-Kessel in Schlechtriem/Schwenzer, *Commentary*, Art 8 para 6.

[244] In regard to the prevalence of the CISG to domestic law in regard to material defects and the regulation of the rights of suspension and stoppage see para 36a.

[245] See para 61.

on commission. After a first inquiry by the German party the seller had responded that a Dutch company would sell the wood. This latter behaviour of the seller could have been relevant to ascertain whether there was a contract between the parties. However, the evidence showed that the German buyer had concluded the contract. Therefore, the subsequent conduct of the Nigerian seller had to be interpreted as the offer to terminate the contract which the German party agreed upon.[246]

58. Whether standard terms and conditions have been incorporated into a contract has to be determined according to Article 8 CISG which in that way fulfils a certain control function.

Example: A German seller sold to a Spanish buyer a machine incorporating its standard terms and conditions in the sales agreement which included an exemption from liability clause which was not included in the offer. The German BGH held that the possibility the buyer could inform itself about the seller's standard terms and conditions was not sufficient in cross-border sale of goods to make the standard terms and conditions "for a reasonable person in the shoes of the buyer" (Article 8(2) CISG) part of the offer. That suggests that the BGH expects that the standard terms and conditions have to be sent to the other party.[247]

The control of the content of standard terms and conditions in regard to prohibited or improper terms and conditions proceeds only through the applicable domestic law in accordance with Article 4 (2nd s(a)) CISG.[248]

Jurisdiction and arbitration clauses are interpreted first and foremost according to domestic law, the Brussels Regulation or Lugano Convention or, the New York Convention on the Recognition and Enforcement of Foreign Arbitral Awards since procedural questions lie generally outside the ambit of the CISG. Furthermore, international provisions in regard to the jurisdiction have precedence because of international conventions precedent according to Article 90 CISG.[249] As far as such procedural Conventions or rules do not contain any provision(s) in regard to the formation of the jurisdiction or arbitration clause, the CISG is applicable if the clause is part of a contract which falls in the ambit of the CISG or has been drafted

---

[246] Compare OLG Köln (26 Aug 1994) CISG-online 132 = RIW 1994, 972.

[247] BGH (31 Oct 2001) CISG-online 617 = NJW 2002, 370, 371; critical Schmidt-Kessel, NJW 2002, 3444–3446; see also Hoge Raad (28 Jan 2005) CISG-online 1002 (gap-filling in accordance with Art 7(2) CISG); (Belgian) Rechtbank van Koophandel (8 Dec 2004) IHR 2005, 114 = CISG-online 980 (copy of standard terms and conditions on invoice is not sufficient); OGH (6 Feb 1996) CISG-online 224 = öst ZfRV 1996, 248 et seq; OGH (31 Aug 2005) CISG-online 1093 (additional incorporation of standard terms through "usage" between the parties (Art 9(1) CISG) lower courts approved, also to the question of (language); the issue is further discussed in: Janssen, IHR 2004, 194–200 with further references; Janssen, IHR 2005, 155 et seq (discussing Hoge Raad (28 Jan 2005) CISG-online 1002).

[248] CISG, Art 4(a) states that the CISG is not concerned with, inter alia, the validity of the contract – see para 34.

[249] In regard to jurisdiction and arbitration clauses as well as in regard to the precedent of international conventions in general and in regard to the Brussels Convention in particular see above para 41; and Magnus in *Staudinger*, Art 90 paras 10, 11.

in close connection with such a "CISG contract", for example, as a post-contract amendment according to Article 29 CISG.

2.2   Trade Usages and Usages/Practices of the Parties (Article 9 CISG)

59.   Under Article 9(1) CISG, trade usages or party practices are binding on the parties if the parties agreed upon them.[250] Article 9(1) CISG is a manifestation of the autonomy of the parties to determine the content of their contract and the formation of the contract. Nevertheless, party autonomy is not complete: Article 4 (2nd s(a)) CISG[251] stipulates that domestic prohibitions in regard to particular usages qualify party autonomy.

60.   "Practices" refers to conduct which has been established between the particular parties.[252] It is necessary that the particular conduct of the parties be of sufficient intensity and duration that it can be assumed that a practice mutually accepted by the parties exists. For example, particular practices can develop in regard to payment (such as the sending of cheques, the use of a particular bank account or Skonti[253]) or to the giving of leeway or tolerance in respect of conforming to delivery times.[254]

61.   The method for establishing existing usages was very controversial. Trade usages, other than in accordance with Article 9(2) CISG, can only exist by agreement between the parties. The agreement can also be implicit or silent.[255] The possibility of an implied agreement between the parties according to Article 9(2) CISG has been accepted only for a small number of usages. First, the usage has to be acknowledged and widely observed by parties to contracts of the type involved in the particular trade concerned.[256] Secondly, the parties must have known or ought to have known of the international usages. Article 9(2)(2nd half s) CISG in other words requires: actual exercise of the practice, agreement in regard to the specific

---

[250] Compare UCC where under the revised s 1–303 the express words of the contract pre-empt all other interpretations. Therefore, trade usages and course of dealings between the parties are only interpretation tools when the express language of the agreement does not indicate the parties' intent; see Gabriel, *Contracts for the Sale of Goods*, 58.

[251] See para 34.

[252] See contrast to majority view: Holl/Keßler, RIW 1995, 457–460.

[253] Compare Magnus in *Staudinger*, Art 9 para 13.

[254] Compare Schlechtriem/Junge, *Kommentar zum Einheitlichen UN-Kaufrecht*, Art 9 para 7.

[255] For a different view, see Holl/Keßler, RIW 1995, 457–460. However, the authors base their view on the German law which was rejected during the Vienna Conference.

[256] The US Court of Appeal (5th Cir) in *BP International, Ltd and BP Exploration & Oil, Inc v Empresa Estatal Petroleos de Ecuador, et al., US Ct Appeal* (5th Cir) (11 Jun 2003) CISG-online 730, 332 F3d 333 incorporated Incoterms according to Art 9(2) CISG because they are widely acknowledged in international trade: *BP International, Ltd and BP Exploration and Oil, Inc v Empresa Estatae Petroleos de Ecuador et al.*, (Fed 3rd, 322 = CISG-online 730).

usage in question in the particular trade and some duration of the practice.[257] Domestic, regional or local usages, which have only been used in domestic sales of goods and have not been used in cross-border sales cannot therefore, be taken into account as usages according to Article 9(2) CISG. They do not become "international" just because a foreign party knew of them or ought to have known that they used in the local domestic or regional system of the other party. However, if they have been used in cross-border sales, then they are applicable even if they are only known in a few countries.[258]

Because of the narrow requirements for "international usage" in Article 9(2) CISG, jurisprudence on what constitutes an international usage under Article 9(2) CISG is scarce. An Argentine Court, for example, has accepted an international usage in regard to the calculation of interest commencing from the time when performance is due and thereby filled a gap left by Article 78 CISG.[259]

The party relying on a usage has to prove its content and its applicability.[260]

62.   Usages can also play a role in the formation of the contract. In Germany, for example, usage has developed in regard to commercial letters of confirmation. However, the usage can only be taken into account if the particular parties have complied with the usage and the usage has become an "individual usage" of the parties, or if the usage has been established among parties similarly positioned in the industry.[261] It is not sufficient that in the countries in which the parties have their seats of business a similar or parallel usage exists. The usage has to be known in the particular industry and be used regularly and has to be recognisable by the parties in question. The existence of parallel usage in countries where the parties are located, however, is a good indication that the requirements are met.

Example: The formation of a contract for the sale of goods between a German party and a Swiss party was in dispute. In Switzerland, as in Germany, silence in answer to a commercial letter of confirmation is regarded as accep-

---

[257] The requirements stipulated in Art 9(2) (2nd half s) are an international version of the German requirements for the establishment of a trade usage: Schmidt-Kessel in Schlechtriem/Schwenzer, *Commentary,* Art 9 para 61.

[258] See, for example, the usages in regard to the sale of wood between Austria and Germany – the "Tegenseer Gebräuche" OGH (21 Mar 2000) CISG-online 641 = IHR 2001, 40.

[259] Juzgado Nacional de Primera Instancia en lo Comercial (20 May 1991) CISG-online 461; for further references see Schmidt-Kessel in Schlechtriem/Schwenzer, *Commentary*, Art 9 para 21.

[260] Compare OLG Dresden (9 Jul 1998) CISG-online 559 = IHR 2001, 18, 19.

[261] See in regard to the application of the UNIDROIT – Principles – int 2.12: Schilf, (1999) Uniform L Rev, 1004 et seq (approving).

tance.[262] Prima facie silence to a commercial letter of confirmation is a known (or ought to be a usage known to both parties) and practised.[263]

63. The existence of a trade usage is a matter of fact and has to be proven should the other party dispute its existence. The courts often take advice from the relevant locality's Chamber of Commerce on whether a particular trade usage exists.[264] If an international trade usage has been established then its interpretation should follow according to Article 7(1) CISG.[265]

2.3 Freedom of Form

2.3.1 Principle

64. Article 11 CISG lays down the principle that contracts do not have to conform to any particular form. Article 11 CISG is placed in Part I of the CISG which shows that despite the fact that the wording of Article 11 CISG is only concerned with the formation of a sale of goods contract the principle of freedom of form is applicable to all legally binding acts within the CISG. The principle is especially applicable to modifications and additions to and termination of contracts according to Article 29 CISG. The wording "subject to any other requirement as to form" makes clear that requirements which could be considered as requirements of form (in the sense of formation of the contract), such as consideration, and which can be especially problematic in regard to unilateral binding contracts, are rejected. Form requirements in domestic legislation are also excluded by Article 11 CISG. Statute(s) of Frauds are not applicable.[266] The parol evidence rule, as

---

[262] Compare, however, the case decided by the Zivilgericht Basel, BJM 1993, 310: contract between Austrian and Swiss parties. The Court mistakenly held that in Austria mere silence to a commercial letter of confirmation is an acceptance of the terms and conditions stipulated in the letter and concludes the contract formation. The Court held that if the legal systems of the countries in question concur in regard to the legal analysis of particular question according to their domestic law, once can conclude that in regard to sale of goods between Austria and Switzerland the same rules are applicable. A usage according to Art 9(2) CISG has, therefore, to be approved.

[263] See critical quote in Schlechtriem, *Internationales UN-Kaufrecht* (4 ed, 2007) fn 161; Compare to the contrary GGIA, öst JBl 1993, 783 – acceptance in regard silence to a commercial letter of confirmation only if the silence can be understood as acceptance of an offer [original quotation in Schlechtriem, *Internationales UN-Kaufrecht* (4 ed, 2007) fn 161, compare to the contrary OGH, öst JBl 1993, 782: acceptance in regard to silence to a commercial letter of confirmation only if the silence can be understood as acceptance to an offer (original quote in Schlechtriem, *Internationales UN-Kaufrecht* (4 ed, 2007) fn 161, and (critical) in regard to Swiss decision: Kramer, BJM 1995, 1–27, 7: "This decision is not triable" (original quote Schlechtriem, *Internationales UN-Kaufrecht* (4 ed, 2007) fn 161).

[264] Compare Junge in Schlechtriem, *Einheitliches Kaufrecht und nationales Obligationenrecht*, Art 9 para 13.

[265] Controversial see Junge in Schlechtriem, *Einheitliches Kaufrecht und nationales Obligationenrecht*, Art 9 para 6 differently Schmidt-Kessel in Schlechtriem/Schwenzer, *Commentary*, Art 9 para 20 pointing out the contractual nature of the usages.

[266] Compare *GPL Treatment Ltd v Louisiana-Pacific Corp* Sup Ct Oregon (11 Apr 1996) CISG-online 202.

provided for in section 2-202 UCC, which does not allow for evidence of the terms of any oral agreement to be considered alongside the written agreement does not apply to CISG contracts.[267] The discussion whether procedural provisions which prohibit witness evidence for certain claims and, therefore, indirectly impose a certain form should be qualified as substantive law for Article 11(2nd s) CISG clearly allows for every kind of evidence.[268] The principle of freedom of form postpones (for a moment) the decision whether statements sent electronically and contracts formed by them are formally valid.[269]

2.3.2 Reservation

65. The principle of freedom of form for legally binding statements in regard to the formation of the contract and in connection with a sale of goods contract was one of the most controversial issues during the drafting of the CISG.[270] As a compromise for the countries which were adamant in insisting on form requirements, Article 96 CISG allows for member states to make a reservation in respect of Article 11. The reservation has the effect that the principle of freedom of form allowing for the informal conclusion, modification, or termination of the contract stipulated in Article 11 CISG does not apply where any party has its place of business in a reservation state (Article 12 CISG).[271] Article 12 CISG is mandatory. The parties can neither deviate for it nor vary it.[272] However, what effect the reservation according to Article 96 CISG and the application of Article 12 CISG have is controversial. The majority view contends that courts must apply the conflict rules of the forum in order to determine which law governs requirements as to form.[273] The minority view holds that the rules as to form of a reservation state in which one of the parties has its place of business always prevail and, therefore, become international uniform law.[274] In the author's view, the minority view fails to appreciate that the reservation state's universal claim to the validity of its formal requirements which would then exclude the private international law rules of other Contracting States could make those requirements internationally applicable uniform law. Accordingly, in a German-Hungarian case, a Hungarian court

---

[267] Compare *Filanto SpA v Chilewich International Corp* District Court (SD NY) (14 Apr 1992) CISG-online 45 = 789 F Supp 1229, 1239. The US jurisprudence, however, is not uniform. See in regard to parole evidence rule and CISG AC-CISG Opinion No 3 (by Hyland) headnote 1 and comments 2.1 et seq, Butler, "Doctrine of Parole Evidence Rule and Consideration", 54, 56 et seq.

[268] Domestic procedural rules in regard to the means by which evidence can be brought and their limits, for example, in regard to the action on the basis of a document or in regard to the examination of a party, are not affected and depend on the lex fori see Schlechtriem in Schlechtriem/Schwenzer, *Commentary*, Art 11 para 12.

[269] However, see para 66: if oral statements are sufficient a fortiori electronic communication, too.

[270] Compare Schlechtriem, *Einheitliches UN-Kaufrecht*, 30. See also Schlechtriem in Schlechtriem/Schwenzer, *Commentary*, Art 12 para 5: the legislative history of Art 12.

[271] Declarations have been made by, for example, China, Russia, Ukraine, Hungary.

[272] CISG, Art 12 (2nd s). Note that Art 6 CISG makes particular reference to Art 12 CISG excluding it from party autonomy set out in Art 6 CISG.

[273] Bridge, *International Sale of Goods*, para 31 (English courts), Fenge in Soergel, Art 12 para 2; Witz in Witz/Salger/Lorenz, Art 12 para 12 with further references.

[274] See, for example, Reinhart, IPRax 1995, 365, Art 12 para 3.

was, in the author's view, correct in applying German law as the law governing matters of form and in holding that a contract concluded by telephone was effective even though Hungary was a reservation state.[275] Furthermore, the use of German law led in this case to the application of Article 11 CISG, and not domestic German law.[276] A mandatory form, therefore, only applies if the private international law of the forum state points towards a reservation state which in regard to sales contracts or statements in respect of the formation, modification or performance of the contract requires a certain form.

2.3.3 Agreed Form

66.   Article 11 CISG does not prevent the parties, unless Article 12 CISG is applicable, to agree on a particular form. Also, in regard to form, party autonomy is paramount according to Article 6 CISG.

2.3.4 Writing Requirement

67.   If the parties have agreed on a writing requirement, the question arises whether, for example, it requires a handwritten signature at the foot of the document (as § 126(1) BGB requires) or whether an electronic signature[277] or text form suffices.[278] The interpretation of the parties' agreement will be determinative (Article 8 CISG).[279] Whether, when agreeing on a form of electronic communication the possibility of saving or printing out at any time is sufficient to fulfil the agreed writing requirement is a matter of interpretation of the agreement as to form. When interpretation is necessary it is in particular pertinent to have regard to the practices which the parties have established between themselves practices between the parties in accordance with Article 8(3) CISG, for example, the use of fax or e-mail to exchange statements. If such an interpretation is not possible, then the domestic law of the party suggesting or demanding the writing requirement can be important in determining whether the parties have agreed on a particular form which is derived from a domestic law. It is also a question of interpretation what significance an agreed form requirement should have. A form requirement can be a validity requirement or can have significance as the means by which evidence can be brought. It also can be used as a refutable or irrefutable presumption of completeness so that oral collateral agreements either have to be specifically proven or are not valid at all. Even though the CISG does not contain the parole

---

[275] Fövarosi Biróság (24 Mar 1992) CISG-online 61, Vida, IPRax 1993, 263, 264, who also sets out Hungary's reason for its reservation.

[276] Witz in Witz/Salger/Lorenz, Art 12 para 12 controversial; differently the Hungarian Court in the mentioned case; Fövarosi Biróság (24 Mar 1992) CISG-online 61, Vida, IPRax 1993, 263.

[277] See §§ 126 (3), 126a BGB accordingly. § 126 BGB deals with the writing requirement. § 126 BGB (3) BGB states that the writing requirement can be substituted by electronic form unless the law states otherwise. § 126a BGB stipulates what requirements the electronic form has.

[278] See, for example, § 126b BGB which stipulates the legal requirements for text form.

[279] See paras 57 et seq.

evidence rule[280] party autonomy in regard to form requirements allows the parties to agree on, for example, the parole evidence rule if they so wish.

The possibility of using telegram or telex to satisfy a writing requirement (Article 13 CISG) was only incorporated at the Vienna Conference following a proposal by the Federal Republic of Germany.[281] The stipulation that telegram and telex are sufficient to fulfil a writing requirement means that these forms of communication are sufficient if writing is not required by the parties and a reservation according to Article 12 CISG is in place.[282] The latter, however, is highly controversial and many authors take the view that Article 13 CISG is only applicable where the CISG itself lays down the need for writing (Articles 21(2) and 29(2) CISG).[283]

68.   Article 13 CISG is, because of the technical and electronic development, antiquated. German Telecom, for example, has not processed international telegrams since (the end of) 2000. Facsimile had not been considered when drafting Article 13 CISG. According to majority opinion facsimile is also acceptable under Article 13 CISG, albeit via an interpretation of Art 13 through Article 7(2) CISG.[284] However, that can only be the case, if the fax has been printed off and, therefore, like a telegram or telex represents the legal statement. Electronic statements may equally (if they can be printed) fall under Article 13 CISG.[285] However, the agreement of the parties is determinative.[286]

---

[280] See para 64.

[281] Official Report, p 74, Art 9 No 3; with respect to the proposal see A/Conf 97/CI/L18, Official Report, p. 90, Art 9 No 2 et seq.

[282] See para 65.

[283] Compare the controversy in Schlechtriem in Schlechtriem/Schwenzer, *Commentary,* Art 13 para 4.

[284] Compare instead to everybody else, Magnus in *Staudinger,* Art 13 para 5.

[285] Magnus in *Staudinger,* Art 13 para 5; Ferrari, (2000) European L Forum, 301, 305; Schroeter, (2002) 6 VJ, 267 et seq, 273; in regard to electronic datpa exchange von Bernstorff, RIW 2000, 181, 19.

[286] See para 67.

Part II of the CISG

1 Introduction

69. The second part of the Convention governs the conclusion of sale of goods contracts through offer and acceptance.[1] However, Articles 14 et seq CISG are in danger of becoming antiquated since important questions of substance, which should have been regulated in regard to contract formation (as can be seen when comparing Part 2 of the UNIDROIT – Principles), have been left open. Examples are: the questions whether a contract can be concluded despite difficulties to identify statements as "offer" and "acceptance" or, the inclusion of conflicting[2] standard terms.[3]

70a. The CISG broadly adopts common law principles to ascertain whether a contract has been concluded:[4] two statements following each other in time (offer and acceptance) are the building blocks for the conclusion of a contract. The Convention works on the assumption that these statements have been made and can be ascertained even if these statements were made during long negotiations in which the parties only came to an agreement by a gradual process. Taking into account the external indicators (offer and acceptance) to find a consensus does not fit situations where there is no controversy in regard to the agreement of the parties; but the agreement has been reached other than by two clearly identifiable and congruent statements following each other. Under the CISG, it must be possible to form a contract via conduct where only an implicit intention is present.[5] In the authors' view, if it can be proven that the parties agreed then domestic law need not be invoked as Article 6 CISG allows the parties to decide the way in which they reach consensus. Their agreement is determinative; while proof is required, this can be determined through their conduct, for example, the unchallenged implementation of the contract.[6] In the majority of cross-border contracts it should be possible to ascertain offer and acceptance. The possibility to take into account the reasonable

---

[1] See in regard to form above paras 64 et seq; in regard to validity of contracts paras 34 et seq; 41 seq.

[2] See below para 92.

[3] See above para 58.

[4] Bridge, *International Sale of Goods,* 12.03.

[5] Compare BG (5 Apr 2005) CISG-online 1012 = IHR 2005, 204-206: contractual obligations through implicit conduct which had to be interpreted in accordance with Art 8 CISG as an intention to be bound.

[6] Compare CISG, Art 18(3).

understanding the parties could have from the conduct of the other party,[7] makes it possible that unclear verbal statements may be clarified if conduct of the parties clearly indicates a mutual intent.[8] The absence of regulation of open or hidden dissent[9] can be dealt with through gap-filling in accordance with Article 7(2) CISG using the principle of party autonomy: if the parties did not reach agreement on parts of the contract it is decisive whether the parties would have concluded the contract also without those parts in question. Domestic law should be invoked to determine the validity of the contract only where it is not possible to determine that the parties formed a mutual intention to be bound despite some issues remaining to be agreed.[10] Questions of consensus which clearly belong in the ambit of the Convention should be dealt with through additional interpretation in accordance with Article 7 CISG instead of relying on domestic law.

70b. Electronic means of communication were not taken into account because their use was in its infancy when the CISG was drafted. UNCITRAL drafted a Model Law on Electronic Commerce in 1996[11] and has presented a Draft Convention on the use of Electronic Communications in International Contracts in 2004. In the authors' view questions of substance in regard to electronic means of communication can be dealt with adequately by the CISG: the first issue is the localisation of the party's place of business which is important in regard to the applicability of the CISG. This is not necessarily identical with the place of the equipment and technology supporting an information system.[12] The starting point for the enquiry where the place of business of the respective parties are Articles 1 and 10 CISG. Accordingly, a stable and autonomous character of the place of

---

[7]   See CISG, Artt 8(1), 8(2) as well as for acceptance Art 18(1).

[8]   Compare BG (5 Apr 2005) CISG-online 1012 = IHR 2005, 204–206.

[9]   Hidden dissent (mutual mistake) occurs where an agreement is objectively ambiguous and the parties each attach a different meaning to it, that is the parties are at cross-purposes (Burrows/Finn/Todd, *Law of Contract*, 10.1.1). Open dissent (common mistake) occurs where the parties' actions are governed by the same mistake, (Burrows/Finn/Todd, *Law of Contract*, 10.1.1), for example, A agrees to sell to B a boat that both believe is safely in dry dock, neither knowing that it had been destroyed by fire. A common mistake may also arise in respect of the legal meaning of a provision. In common law open and hidden dissent are dealt with under the doctrine of mistake. A mutual mistake may mean the agreement between the parties is insufficient to conclude a legally binding agreement (see, for example, *Falck v Williams* [1900] AC 176 (PC); *Van Praagh v Everidge* [1903] 1 Ch 434 (CA); *Parkes v Parkes* [1971] 3 All ER 870 (CA)). A common mistake as to the existence of the subject matter means the contract is void, (see, for example, *Couturier v Hastie* (1856) 5 HL Cas 673 (HL). See also *Bell v Lever Brothers Ltd* [1932] AC 161 (HL); and *Halsbury's Laws of England*, Mistake, paras 17–19) but a common mistake as to quality of the subject matter or other material fact, or the parties' rights and obligations, unless it is sufficient to render the contract void at common law, does not justify rescission of a contract that is otherwise valid and enforceable on ordinary principles of contract law (see, for example, *Great Peace Shipping Ltd v Tsavliris Salvage (International) Ltd* [*The Great Peace*][2002] 4 All ER 689 (CA)).

[10]   CISG, Art 4 (2nd s (a)).

[11]   www.uncitral.org; see also von Bernstorff, RIW 2002, 179, 181, 182; Ramberg, (2001) European L Rev, 429 et seq in regard to the UNCITRAL Model Law for E-Commerce.

[12]   See above para 9.

business is required.[13] In regard to e-commerce Article 10(a) CISG which deals with the situation where a party has multiple places of business and provides that the place of business is the one "which has the closest relationship to the contract and its performance" is particularly relevant. Based on Article 10(a) CISG and the requirements of a stable and autonomous character of the place of business the place of the server, which the business uses is not by itself determinative since the server lacks the required autonomous character. Since it is possible that the information system is located in a place different from the one where a party carries out its business, the server would have to solely meet the requirement of autonomy to be able to fulfil the requirement of a place of business. The inquiry where the place of business is an e-commerce situation should be made on a case-by-case basis. The place of business of a party will be where the party pursues its economic activity on a permanent basis and where it has autonomy to conclude the sales contract.[14] The second issue is the (agreed) form and the compliance with it if electronic means are used when concluding the contract.[15] Questions of "receipt" and "sending" are the third issue but can satisfactorily dealt with Articles 24 and 27 CISG.[16] The especially high failure rate of electronic communication devices which in Europe led to Articles 10 and 11 of the E-Commerce Regulation stipulating particular duties of a business, which uses electronic means of communication, is a matter of validity in regard to which accordance with Article 4 (2nd s(a)) CISG the domestic law according to the private international law of the forum is applicable.[17]

70c. The CISG does not generally regulate pre-contractual obligations.[18] These duties only belong partially to the regulatory ambit of sales law: as far as pre-contractual duties protect the assets of legal importance to the other party they are part of tort law.[19] As far as duties to inform protect the transparency of the electronic contract conclusion, there is a gap in the CISG which can only be filled through the use of the applicable domestic law.[20] On the other hand pre-contractual duties may protect the conclusion of the contract, for example, against the stopping of contract negotiations; or protect the legal position of (one of) the parties; or take into account the characteristics of the goods or whether a party will perform (information about characteristics, credit worthiness, etc). In the authors' view, those pre-contractual duties are provisions in regard to breach of contract, liability for the goods being in conformity with the contract or the avoidance of the contract

---

[13] See Bianca in Bianca/Bonell, *Commentary*, Art 1 paras 27, 30; OLG Stuttgart (28 Feb 2000) CISG-online 583; Ferrari, (2003) 22 J L & Com, 57, 69;
Asante Technologies Inc v PMC-Sierra Inc (27 Jul 2001) US District Court (Northern District Court of California) CISG-online 616; ICC Paris (1 Jan 1994) CISG-online 565.

[14] See for a very detailed discussion: Verzoni, Nordic J Comm L, 2 paras II.1.2 to II 1.2.2.3.

[15] See above paras 67, 68.

[16] See below paras 94, 95.

[17] EU-Regulation 2000/31/EG of the European Parliament and the Council of 3 Jun 2000. ABR.2 178/1. See above paras 42a, 42b, 42c.

[18] See para 42.

[19] Compare ECJ (17 Sep 2002) NJW 2002, 3159: jurisdiction determined according to where the tort was committed in regard to claims arising out the breach of pre-contractual duties.

[20] Above already para 42b.

according to Article 72 CISG, and are ones for which the solution has to be found within the CISG and should not be superseded by domestic law rules in regards to the breach of pre-contractual duties.[21] In general, common law jurisdictions do not impose pre-contractual obligations on parties.[22] In particular, agreements to negotiate in good faith, even those supported by consideration, are not justiciable.[23] A claim for restitution-based damages will usually only lie where there was a joint assumption that a binding contract would be entered into.[24] An option only gives rise to a binding contract where its precise terms are met.[25] A right of pre-emption or first refusal is a contractual obligation in its own right, a breach of which may give rise to a claim for damages.[26] In regard to statements which constitute the conclusion as a contract the rules are conclusive. Articles 14 et seq CISG are not fragmented rules which can be interpreted and complemented by domestic law, for example, in regard to rules in respect of the conclusion of the contract in case of standard terms of business.[27]

71.   The statements which constitute the conclusion of a contract, offer and acceptance, as well as the revocation of such a statement and the rejection of an offer have generally to reach the other party. Bridge[28] argues that in treating all acceptances alike, in that they are effective upon receipt, departs from the common law as no exception is made regarding the postal acceptance rule.[29] In regard to what constitutes "reaching", Article 24 CISG stipulates that it is decisive whether and when the statement reaches the sphere of the other party. Article 24 CISG distinguishes between declarations made orally and those made by other means. In the first instance the statement has to reach the addressee directly. In case of statements, a written statement can be delivered to the addressee's place of business or mailing address or, if the addressee has neither, to his/her habitual residence.[30] Electronic statements have generally reached the addressee when it has entered the addressee's server in such a way that it can be retrieved, read, and

---

[21]   See *Schmid, Zusammenspiel von Einheitlichem UN-Kaufrecht und nationalem Recht*, 262 et seq.

[22]   *Sabemo Pty Ltd v North Sydney Municipal Council* [1977] 2 NSWLR 880, 900 Sheppard J: "It has long been the law that parties are free to negotiate such contract as they may choose to enter into. Until such contract comes about, they are in negotiation only. Each is at liberty, no matter how capricious his reason, to break off the negotiations at any time. If that occurs that is the end of the matter and, generally speaking, neither party will be under any liability to the other."

[23]   *Wellington City Council v Body Corporate 51702 (Wellington)* [2002] 3 NZLR 486 (CA). For an in-depth discussion of this issue see McLauchlan, (2005) 11 NZBLQ, 454.

[24]   *Leading Edge Events Australia Pty Ltd v Kiri Te Kanawa* [2007] NSWC 228, para 256, Bergin J. See also *Pavey & Matthews Pty Ltd v Paul* (1987) 69 ALR 577 (HCA); and *Angelopoulos v Sabatino* (1995) 65 SASR 1.

[25]   Burrows/Finn/Todd, *Law of Contract*, 3.7.4.

[26]   Burrows/Finn/Todd, *Law of Contract*. The authors refer the reader to Flannigan, (1997) 76 Canadian Bar Rev 1, for an in-depth discussion of the issues.

[27]   Compare, however, previously Huber, RabelsZ 43 (1979) 413, 447.

[28]   Bridge, *International Sale of Goods*, 12.05.

[29]   *Adams v Lindsell* (1818) 1 B & Ald 681, 106 ER 250.

[30]   "Mailing address" refers to a letter box or PO Box but not to an address which does no longer exists for the addressee because he/she has moved.

understood by the addressee.[31] However, a requirement is that the addressee agreed to this form of communication and the use of it in the chosen form; this may be implicit in the addressee's own use of electronic communications. Oral declarations or statements reach the addressee when the addressee can hear them.[32]

72. Whether a declaration to a third person or the passing of a written statement to a third person constitutes "reaching" the addressee depends on the authority of the third person which has to be determined according to the applicable domestic law.[33] If a statement has been recorded on voice mail or an answering machine the statement reaches the addressee when the statement gets saved on the voice mail or answering machine, since having an answering machine, a voice mail or an email in-box is like having a post box.[34]

2   Offer

2.1   Criteria for an Offer

73. Article 14(1) CISG defines "offer" and stipulates the requirements which differentiates an offer from other statements before or in relation with the contract negotiations and conclusion; it especially differentiates an offer from an invitatio ad offerendum.[35] Requirements of an offer are: sufficiently definite goods[36] and an intention to be bound, that means the intention if the addressee accepts the offer to be contractually bound (this is different from the problem of being bound by an offer).[37] These basic requirements correspond generally with the requirements which the common law stipulates for an offer except for the doctrine of consideration. During the deliberations a decision was made not to adopt the doctrine of consideration for the CISG.[38]

If the intention to be bound is absent from a statement it can mean that the other party is invited to make an offer (invitatio ad offerendum). An invitatio ad offerendum is generally assumed if the "offer" is directed towards an unspecified number of people, for example, posted on a website.[39] The intention to be bound

---

[31] In regards to the common law position see Coote, (1971) 4 NZULR, 331.
[32] Compare below paras 94 et seq, in regard to the details see Schlechtriem in Schlechtriem/Schwenzer, *Commentary*, Art 24 para 6.7.
[33] See comprehensive Schlechtriem in Schlechtriem/Schwenzer, *Commentary*, Art 24 para 5.
[34] Compare Schlechtriem in Schlechtriem/Schwenzer, *Commentary*, Art 24 para 12; the mentioning of an electronic address means the agreement with receiving statement under that address and in electronic form.
[35] CISG, Art 14(2) sets out the invitation to make an offer.
[36] See paras 74 et seq.
[37] See in regard to bound by an offer below paras 77 et seq.
[38] See a discussion Butler, "Doctrine of Parole Evidence Rule and Consideration", 54, 63, 66.
[39] CISG, Art 14(2); compare von Bernstorff, RIW 2000, 181 (in regard to the UNCITRAL Model Law on Electronic Commerce) but see also BGH (7 Dec 2001) NJW 2002, 363 et seq in regard to the launching of a website for an internet auction as offer (not a CISG case).

can also be missing if a suggestion is made to a particular person. Whether the "offeror" had an intention to be bound has to be ascertained by interpreting his or her declaration in accordance with Article 8 CISG, whereby Articles 8(2) and 8(3) CISG play an important role ascertaining the objective meaning of the statement made.[40]

2.2   Offer has to be Sufficiently Definite

74.   To be 'sufficiently definite' a statement has to fulfil the strict requirements set out in Article 14(1) CISG: the offer has, according to Article 14(1)(2nd s) CISG, to indicate the nature of the goods, the quantity has to be determinable and the offeror has to name the price, or the device by which the price will be determined. The determination of the goods is also according to common law an essentialia negotii.[41] The determination of goods is also a necessary minimum requirement in common law. The subject of the contract may be existing goods or future goods, including goods to be manufactured or acquired by the seller and fructus industrials, and can include goods whose acquisition by the seller depends on an uncertain contingency.[42] A contract for sale of unascertained goods does not become unconditional until the goods have been unconditionally appropriated to the contract.[43] If that requires some act to be done, for example, measuring, weighing, testing, or counting the goods, the goods are not ascertained until that occurs.[44] In regard to the quantity of the goods it is sufficient that the parties devise a mechanism which makes the quantity of the goods determinable. It is sufficient that one party has sole responsibility for determining the quantity.[45] Since the CISG was applicable, the question arose whether according to Article 14(1) CISG the offer had been sufficient even though the time of delivery had been left open. The Court relied on the offeror's intention to be bound and an industry custom according to which the offer and, therefore, the contract were sufficiently definite; the exact quantity of the goods was determinable because of commercially

---

[40]   In regard to Art 8 CISG see above paras 54 et seq.

[41]   *Halsbury's Laws of England*, paras 47, 124. Hawes et al., *Butterworths Introduction to Commercial Law*, para 11.4.2; see, for example, *Wait and James v Midland Bank Ltd* (1926) 31 ComCas 172; *Re Ellis Son & Vidler Ltd* [1995] 1 All ER 192 (ChD, HC).

[42]   *Halsbury's Laws of England*, para 47.

[43]   Hawes et al., *Butterworths Introduction to Commercial Law*, para 11.4.2.

[44]   *Halsbury's Laws of England*, para 124. See, for example, *Wait and James v Midland Bank Ltd* (1926) 31 Com Cas 172; *Re Goldcorp Exchange Ltd* (in receivership) [1994] 3 NZLR 385 (PC); *Re Ellis Son & Vidler Ltd* (in administrative receivership) [1995] 1 All ER 192 (Ch D, HC).

[45]   Included are therefore requirement contracts or output contracts, that means contracts which the quantity in the former case depends on the needs of the buyer and in later case depends on the production volume of the seller. In *Geneva Pharmaceutical Technology Corp v Barr Laboratories Inc, Brantford Chemicals Inc and others*, US District Ct (SD NY) (10 May 2002) CISG-online 653 = 201 F Supp 2d 236 it was controversial whether the parties had concluded a contract and whether the contracts had been breached (it needs to be noted that the case mainly concerned merger questions (sub VI); also see Honnold, *Uniform Law for International Sales*, § 137.3.

reasonable notices to deliver. The measurement and other characteristics of the goods by one party can be enough to sufficiently determine the form.[46]

75.   There was considerable controversy during the preparatory meetings, continuing at the Vienna Conference concerning the requirement that the price had to be sufficiently definite or at least had to be determinable. Suggestions to eliminate this requirement failed because of the resistance of the delegates of the Soviet Union, a number of developing countries, France and other states.[47] Section 9(1) of the Sale of Goods Act 1979 (UK) allows the contract to be avoided if a third party valuation of price does not take place so long as the goods have not been delivered.[48]

The motives for the tremendous resistance against a provision which would have allowed for the seller to determine the price or to allow the price determination through objective criteria have often been reported.[49] It should be noted that Article 14(1)(2nd s) is slightly contradictory to Article 55 CISG since the latter provision requires that contracts without a sufficiently definite price can be concluded validly.[50] Indeed Article 14(1)(2nd s) CISG does not prohibit a silent determination of the price or a solely implicit determination,[51] so that negotiations or trade practices between the parties may often open the possibility of amending the offer by a definite price or at least a determinable price. The Austrian Oberster Gerichtshof has held:[52]

> For the assessment whether an offer can be accepted it is sufficient if the required minimum content can be understood by a reasonable person of the same kind as the addressee in the same circumstance (Article 8(2) CISG). According to Article 8(3) CISG are all considerable circumstances have to be taken into account to ascertain the intention of a reasonable person would have had. Negotiations between the parties, the trade practices between them, the trade usages

---

[46] See CISG, Art 65.

[47] See in regard to the applications OR 74, 75, 79, 92, 93, 120, 121 and in regard to the discussion OR 275 et seq, 292 et seq, 363 et seq, 367. In France which at the beginning advocated for a pretium certum (in accordance with Art 1591 Code Civile) at the UN-Conference in 1980 the Cour de Cassation has more or less abandoned the requirement of a sufficiently definite price for domestic law but also in regard to Art 14(1) CISG, see judgment of 4 Jan 1995 CISG-online 138; Witz/Wolter, ZEuP 1996, 648 et seq (in regard to the plenary decision of the Cour de Cassation of 1 Dec 1995).

[48] See Bridge, International Sale of Goods, 12.09.

[49] Compare Kramer in *FS Welser*, 539-558, 542 et seq; Schlechtriem in Schlechtriem/ Schwenzer, *Commentary*, Art 14 paras 9–11.

[50] Compare in regard to a solution of this contraction Art 14(1) (2nd s) and Art 55 CISG especially Bucher, *FS Piotet*, 390 et seq; Kramer in *FS Welser*, 539-558, 542 et seq; as well as Schlechtriem in Schlechtriem/Schwenzer, *Commentary*, Art 25 para 11; also see Honnold, *Uniform Law for International Sales*, § 137.3.

[51] Compare the example LG Neubrandenburg (3 Aug 2005) CISG-online 1190: German-Belgian sale of goods contract in regard to cherries in glasses; future determination of the price to be fixed during the season sufficient because of the seasonal price of the seller was implicitly agreed in accordance with Art 55 CISG.

[52] OGH (10 Nov 1994) CISG-online 117 = JBl 1995, 253, 254 with comment by Karollus.

and the conduct of the parties after the conclusion of the contract have to be taken into account. In summary an implicit determination of the price or quantity as well as an agreement which allows to determine the price or the quantity are possible....

The following facts were the basis for the decision: in a sale of goods contract between an Austrian and a German party about Chinchilla furs, the price range was stipulated between DM35 and DM65 per fur. The claim that the contract was invalid because the price was not sufficiently definite was unsuccessful: the price has to be explicitly stated or has to at least determinable. Article 14(1)(2nd s) CISG also allows for an implicit determination. This means that circumstances have to be taken into account which allows an interpretation that leads to a sufficiently definite price. However, it is sufficient if the price is determinable:

> "This requirement is fulfilled if the parties without explicitly determining the price agree implicitly on factors which at least make the determination of the price possible... By agreeing on a price range of DM35 to DM65 for furs of average to good quality the parties have specified enough factors from which depended on the quality of the furs a price can be determined. This price agreement is sufficiently definite according to Article 14 CISG. The contract has been, therefore, concluded with a determinable price. The applicability of Article 55 CISG does not have to be determined".[53]

76.   If the parties have performed the contract despite no definite price having been agreed, or have in other way made clear that they wanted to perform the contract, the requirement of a sufficiently definite or determinable price can be seen as having been excluded by the parties. Accordingly, a valid contract has been concluded and the price has to be determined according to Article 55 CISG.

If Article 14(1)(2nd s) CISG is interpreted narrowly, there is a danger that contracts will not be enforced by the courts. The case of *Pratt & Whitney v Malev Airlines*[54] illustrates this danger. The American manufacturer of aircraft engines Pratt & Whitney offered the Hungarian airline Malev engines and engine systems for the renewal of older aeroplanes and for newly purchased Airbuses. In the documents which had been sent by Pratt & Whitney, the different prices for different engines and different engine systems (that means engines plus spare parts, suspension devices etc) were specified to a large extent but not completely. Malev sent a telex at the last day of the offer indicating that they had chosen a particular engine for the first fittings of the aircrafts and they were looking forward working together. Subsequently, Malev let Pratt & Whitney know that they had decided to get Rolls Royce turbines. The Court of first instance found that a contract between

---

[53] OGH (10 Nov 1994) CISG-online 117 = JBl 1995, 253, 254 with comment by Karollus. The judgment is written in German and here translated: Schlechtriem, *Internationales UN-Kaufrecht*, para 75 at the end.

[54] Supreme Court of Hungary (25 Sep 1992) CISG-online 63, see also Vida, IPRax 1995, 261 et seq.

the parties had been concluded. The Supreme Court of Hungary held inter alia, that for the engine which Malev had chosen no sufficiently definite price or determinable price could be ascertained and the price could not be determined in accordance with Article 55 CISG. The authors cannot determine whether the negotiations between the parties would or would not have allowed for the Court to determine a price. An American commentator who analysed the case called it "hometown justice"[55] and formulated therewith the concern that domestic courts could favour domestic parties and that Article 14(1)(2nd s) CISG gave the Courts the opportunity to do so.

2.3   Withdrawal of an Offer

77.   Articles 15 and 16 CISG distinguish between a withdrawal of an offer and a revocation of an offer. Article 15(1) CISG emphasises again that for offer and acceptance to become effective they have to reach the other party.[56] Until the offer reaches the offeree the offer can be withdrawn if the withdrawal reaches the offeree before or at the same time as the offer.[57] The withdrawal is a statement; it is implicit in Article 15(2) CISG that it has to reach the other party.

79.   Whether an offer becomes binding when it reaches the addressee, or whether it can be revoked once it has reached the addressee had been one of the most controversial issues even during the drafting of the Hague Sales Conclusion Law (EAG), and again during the preparatory work and meetings for the CISG. One option is to treat the offeror as bound by his or her offer for a reasonable time or a set time.[58] This proved unacceptable, especially for common law jurists, since in the common law an offer which is limited to a particular period is not binding. A time period only means that the offer is valid for the time period. However, the speed of modern forms of communication means that the uncertainties arising from earlier, much slower forms of communication, are largely a thing of the past. In regard to the EAG and the CISG the issue has not been of practical concern.

80.   In Vienna a compromise was reached allowing the offer to be revoked after it had become valid upon reaching the offeree according to Article 16(1) CISG. However, the offeror cannot revoke his or her offer once the addressee has sent the acceptance according to Article 16(1) CISG. The termination of the right to revoke under Article 16(1) CISG is more far-reaching than the common law postal acceptance rule[59] since not only does the dispatch of an acceptance by letter

---

[55]   Amato, (1993) 13 J L & Comm, 1, 16 et seq.

[56]   In regard to the definition of "reaching" see Art 24 CISG and paras 94 et seq below.

[57]   CISG, Art 15(2).

[58]   Compare BGB, § 145 in conjunction with §§ 147(2), 148, BGB.

[59]   But see Bridge, *International Sale of Goods*, 12.03, 12.05, 12.06. "Much of the postal rule is preserved." and acknowledging that the English law is far more reaching by allowing the revocation of a contractual offer at any time (12.03). See general to the postal acceptance rule: Burrows/Finn/ Todd,

or telegram suffice for that purpose, but also other means of communication, like telex, telefax, or email. To accommodate the other view[60] Article 16(2) CISG states that an offer cannot be revoked if the offer indicates either a fixed time for acceptance or that the offer was irrevocable. It ought, therefore, to follow that an attempted revocation in breach of Article 16 will be ineffectual. This conclusion accords with the treatment in Article 46 of the CISG of the requirement of performance as the primary remedy for non-performance. An unequivocal intention, to be bound, is especially evident in an offer tied to a specific time-period. However, it is uncertain, whether a deadline set by the offeror is already a non-rebuttable assumption for the offeror's intention to be bound, or just a rebuttable assumption arrived at through interpretation.[61] In using the interpretation rules of the Articles 8(2), (3), CISG, the addressee of an offer formulated by an offeror from a legal system that does not treat such deadlines as binding, but "only" as the time of its validity can, if there are no additional indicators, assume that the offeror wants to be bound for the length of the time period set.

Another possibility that the offer is binding is stated in Article 16(2)(b) CISG namely that the offeror is bound if the addressee reasonably could rely on the offer's irrevocability and already acted in reliance of the offer. The provision contains the general principle of estoppel. Therefore, Article 16(2)(b) CISG embodies an important principle which can be important for gap-filling accuracy in relation to Article 7(2) CISG.[62] To act according to Article 16(2)(b) CISG also means to refrain, for example, not to seek more offers.

81.   Revocation of the offer despite the offer being deemed irrevocable by Article 16(2) CISG can be counter-acted by the addressee by accepting the offer. The refusal of the offeror to perform that contract is a breach of contract and leads to the legal consequence stipulated in Part III. Therefore, there is no need for additional damages.[63] However, if a revocation is permissible under the CISG the domestic law in regards to liability for failed contracts should not be invoked

---

Law of Contract, 3.4.6 – which draws attention to the difference between the postal acceptance rule and the regime under the CISG.

[60] Compare Schlechtriem, Einheitlichem UN-Kaufrecht, 39, 40.

[61] See in regard to references of the different views Schlechtriem in Schlechtriem/Schwenzer, Commentary, Art 16 para 9, 10.

[62] Compare Arbitral Award of the International Arbitral Tribunal of the Bundeskammer der gewerblichen Wirtschaft in Österreich (15 Jun 1994) CISG-online 120, 121 = RIW 1995, 590 et seq with commentary by Schlechtriem in RIW 1995, 590 and above para 48.

[63] Note that, for example, according to German law a situation where the party could reasonably rely on the conclusion of a contract where at the end the other party revokes an offer (or acceptance) the party can get damages according to the doctrine of culpa in contrahendo see RGZ 78, 239 since 2002 codified in §§ 311 (2), (3) BGB; compare Magnus in Staudinger, Art 16 para 15. There is no common law equivalent of the culpa in contrahendo doctrine (obligation to act in good faith during negotiations). As noted in para 70 above, even specific agreements to negotiate in good faith are not justiciable. Relief for bad faith during negotiations, for example fraud or misrepresentation, is only possible after a contract has been formed. Possible remedies include voiding of or rectification of the contract, or damages.[63] Many common law jurisdictions have codified aspects of pre-contractual obligations and remedies, for example in New Zealand relevant statutes include the Contractual Mistakes Act 1977, the Contractual Remedies Act 1979, and the Fair Trading Act 1986.

because to do so would disregard the compromise of Article 16 CISG and the evaluation of the parties' interest intended by the drafters of the convention.[64] The issue surrounding pre-contractual duties was acknowledged during the drafting of the CISG, however, an application by former East-Germany to include a doctrine like culpa in contrahendo in the Convention was rejected because such a doctrine would make it difficult to assess consequences for substantial questions in regard to which the CISG had stipulated solutions.[65]

2.4   Termination of Offer

82.   An offer is terminated if it is withdrawn or has been validly revoked as well as when the addressee rejects the offer.[66] That applies also for an irrevocable offer which is rejected during the set time period.[67] Whether an offer ends with the end of the set time period depends on why a time period was set: the time period might only be set to bind the offeror according to Article 16(2)(a) CISG, but after that time period has ended the offer should be left in place until the offeror decides to withdraw it. In general, however, a set time period for an offer means that the offer expires when the period ends.

3   Acceptance of an Offer

83.   Articles 18 to 22 CISG regulate the requirements for the acceptance to an offer which concludes the contract as well as the delayed acceptance and the acceptance which differs in substance from the offer. The common law position in regard to acceptance is similar, but not identical, to that expressed in the CISG. Under common law, acceptance requires an "external manifestation".[68] An offeror cannot deem silence to be consent,[69] but in some circumstances silence may amount to conduct conveying assent, for example if the offer is accompanied by some benefit that the offeree accepts.[70] However, unlike Article 19(2) CISG which allows "modified acceptances" that do not materially alter the terms of the offer, the common law requires the acceptance to be complete and unconditional.[71] Any alteration amounts to a counter-offer. For example, an acceptance of a purchase

---

[64]   See already paras 42, 77a.
[65]   Compare Köhler, *Haftung nach UN-Kaufrecht*, 212 et seq, Schlechtriem, *Einheitliches UN-Kaufrecht*, 45.
[66]   CISG, Art 17.
[67]   Compare Herber/Czerwenka, *Internationales Kaufrecht*, Art 17 para 7.
[68]   Burrows/Finn/Todd, *Law of Contract*, 3.4.
[69]   *Felthouse v Bindley* (1862) 11 CB(NS) 869; 142 ER 1037.
[70]   Burrows/Finn/Todd, *Law of Contract*, 3.4.1, citing at fn 142: *Empirnall Holdings Pty Ltd v Machon Paull Partners Pty Ltd* (1988) 14 NSWLR 523; *Rust v Abbey Life Assurance Co Ltd* [1979] 2 Lloyd's Rep 334. Compare *Lundberg v Royal Exchange Assurance Corp* [1933] NZLR 605 at 614-615.
[71]   Burrows/Finn/Todd, *Law of Contract*, 3.3.6; see also English Law: Bridge, *International Sale of Goods*, 12.05.

option in a lease which specified a settlement date that did not conform to the terms of the option was not an acceptance, but a counter-offer.[72] Even "commercially insignificant" alterations that do not effect the substance of a bargain will amount to a counter-offer.[73] As regards time, common law rules differ somewhat from those in Articles 20 and 21 CISG. An offer that specifies an absolute time limit, either by reference to a specific date and time, or by reference to specified period from the making of or the receipt of the offer, expires at the end of that time.[74] Referential time limits do not automatically run from the time of dispatch; the courts' approach has been to treat time as running from the time of receipt (or constructive receipt),[75] so in the case of a misdirected letter (offer) requiring a response by "return post", an acceptance posted on the actual date of receipt complied with the terms of the offer.[76] The common law also differs from Article 22 CISG in that the strict application of the postal acceptance rule precludes withdrawal of an acceptance once the letter has been posted.[77] There is no English decision directly on point;[78] but in New Zealand[79] and South Africa[80] the Courts have ruled against altering an acceptance once the letter has been posted.[81] In other situations the prima facie rule is that an acceptance may be revoked before it becomes effective, but there is an exception where an offeror in a bilateral contract has explicitly dispensed with the need to communicate acceptance.[82]

3.1   Acceptance by Declaration

84.   The acceptance to an offer to conclude a contract can be made orally or it can be implied.[83] Whether certain acts can be classified as acceptance has to be considered according to Article 8 CISG; it is, therefore, dependent on the interpretation of the conduct. Examples of conduct which imply acceptance are: delivery

---

[72] *Reporoa Stores Ltd v Trealor* [1958] NZLR 177 (CA). See also *Frampton v McCully* [1976] 1 NZLR 270 (CA).

[73] Burrows/Finn/Todd, *Law of Contract*, 3.3.6. See *Gulf Corporation Ltd v Gulf Harbour Investments Ltd* [2006] 1 NZLR 21. As Burrows, Finn and Todd note: "The majority view has been forcefully criticised by McLauchlan, [2005] NZLJ 300. The issue may well be revisited by the Courts." The position in English law is the same as in New Zealand – see *Halsbury's Laws of England*, Contract, para 661; see also *Haugland Tankers AS v RMK Marine* [2005] 1 All ER (Comm) 679.

[74] *The Laws of New Zealand*, Contract, para 51 (last updated 1 Mar 2007). For English Law, see *Halsbury's Laws of England*, Contract, para 666; for Australian law, see *Halsbury's Laws of Australia* (last updated 31 May 2003) 110 Contract, paras 110–295.

[75] *The Laws of New Zealand*, Contract, para 51 (last updated 1 Mar 2007).

[76] *Adams v Lindsell* (1818) 1 B & Ald 681, 106 ER 250.

[77] Burrows/Finn/Todd, *Law of Contract*, 3.4.8.

[78] *Halsbury's Laws of England*, Contract, para 680.

[79] *Wenkhei v Arndt* (1873) 1 NZ Jurist 73.

[80] A to Z Bazaars (Pty) Ltd v Minister of Agriculture (1974 (4) SA 392).

[81] Burrows/Finn/Todd, *Law of Contract*, 3.4.8.

[82] *Halsbury's Laws of England* (Reissue, LexisNexis, Bath) vol 9(1), Contract, paras 659, 666.

[83] CISG, Art 18(1)1, SOGA, s 4(1) allows contracts to be made in writing, orally or by conduct.

of goods[84] – also partial delivery,[85] payment,[86] even the signing off or the handing in of a bill to the credit institution financing the buyer's purchase or a promissory note.[87]

Example:	In *Magellan International Corp v Salzgitter Handels Gmbh* the steel trading business which has its seat in the US negotiated with German company in regard to the delivery of Ukrainian steel. In regard to the claimant's offer the respondent originally sent an acceptance including its standard terms of delivery which differed from those of the claimant. This resulted in further negotiations in which the claimant relented and established a line of credit in favour of the respondent for the payment of the goods. After that the respondent wanted further amendments to the contract which the claimant refused. The respondent refused delivery of the Ukrainian steel and the claimant sued for damages because of breach of contract. The issue was whether the issuing of the line of credit would be interpreted as acceptance and, therefore, the contract was concluded. The Court affirmed that the issuing of the line of credit was an acceptance according to Article 18(1)1 CISG "other conduct of the offeree in indicating assent to an offer".[88]

85.   An acceptance is generally only valid if it reaches the offeror according to Article 18(2)(1st s) CISG; it can be withdrawn until it reaches offeror.

86.   In exceptional circumstances the offeree may indicate assent by performing an act. If the offeror renounced his or her right to receive the acceptance, or if trade usage between the parties indicates the performing act is accepted as acceptance, the acceptance is effective at the moment the act is performed.[89] The sending off of goods or of the purchase price can, therefore, be a valid acceptance before they impliedly reached the other party.

Example:	The buyer signed off on a bill, which had been sent to the buyer in advance and had presented it to their financial institution. An Argentinean Court saw therein an implied acceptance.[90]

87.   Silence by itself or no reaction at all to the offer does not have, according to Article 18(1)(2nd s) CISG, constitute acceptance. The aim is to prevent the ambushing of the addressee of the offer (for example by sending unsolicited goods with a purchase offer, stipulating that retaining the goods amounts to acceptance). The

---

[84] Compare Farnsworth in Bianca/Bonell, Art 18 para 2,2.
[85] Compare in regard to the EAG: LG Dortmund, RIW 1981, 854, 855.
[86] Farnsworth in Bianca/Bonell, Art 18 para 2.2; Karollus, *UN-Kaufrecht*, 68.
[87] OLG Frankfurt (30 Aug 2000) www.unilex.info.
[88] *Magellan International Corp v Salzgitter Handels Gmbh* US District Court (ND Illinois) (7 Dec 1999) CISG-online 439 = 76 F Supp 2d 919.
[89] CISG, Art 18(3).
[90] *Inta SA v MCS Officina Meccanica*, SpA (1 Apr 1993) CISG-online 543 = El Derecho (25 Apr 1994) 3-7 with commentary from Martorell.

phrasing "in itself", however, makes clear that in conjunction with other circumstances silence can amount to acceptance – especially according to Article 8(3) CISG. Furthermore, because trade usages and practices between the parties have to be taken into account according to Article 9 CISG, silence can amount to acceptance as an exception. The necessary interpretation, however, is only valid in regard to the individual case and cannot be generalised.[91]

Example 1:   The parties had in the past already conducted numerous business transactions. The American buyer then in another offer pointed the Italian (shoe) seller to a contract it had with its Russian buyer and the arbitration clause in that contract. The Court found that the Italian seller's silence in conjunction with the certain other manifestations stipulated clearly that the seller accepted the offer (including the arbitration clause).[92]

Example 2:   The German buyer of tropical wood had objected to the non-conformity of the wood to the Nigerian seller. The seller informed the buyer that the seller wanted to advertise and sell the wood which was stored in Hamburg itself or through a Dutch company. Later the seller (or rather the assignee) claimed the purchase price. The Court found that the statement that the sellers wanted to advertise and sell the wood itself was a termination of the contract which the buyer silently accepted.[93]

3.2   Deadline for Acceptance

88.   So far as the offeror has not stipulated a deadline or such deadline cannot be determined by the circumstances, a verbal offer has to be accepted immediately according to Article 18(2)(3rd s) CISG in other circumstances a reasonable time is enough, Article 18(2)2 CISG.[94] Relevant factors in determining what a reasonable period of time is include the circumstances of the deal and the means of communication chosen by the offeror. Article 20 CISG stipulates extensive rules in regard to the period of time which depend on the choice of the means of communication. Public holidays or statutory non-business days occurring during the period for acceptance are included in calculating the period.[95] In international cross-border

---

[91] More examples can be found in Honnold, *Uniform Law for International Sales*, § 160.

[92] *Filanto SpA v Chilewich International Corp*, District Court (SD NY) (14 Apr 1992) CISG-online 45 = 789 F Supp 1229, 1239, above, para 64; see in regards to the details of the facts Schlechtriem in Schlechtriem/Schwenzer, *Commentary*, Intro to Artt 14-24 fn 16.

[93] OLG Köln (22 Feb 1994) CISG-online 127 = RIW 1994, 972 annotation by Schlechtriem, EWiR 1994, 867.

[94] The CISG is more specific than English law in dating the period from which the time for acceptance begins to run, see Bridge, *International Sale of Goods*, 12.06.

[95] CISG, Art 20(2)1. The common law rule in regard to time is similar to Art 20(2)(1) CISG. In general, Sundays and holidays are treated the same as any other day, and it makes no difference if the last day falls on a Sunday (*Halsbury's Laws of England*, Time, para 241). That general rule might be derived from if custom shows only working days are intended to be included (see *Nielsen v Wait* (1885) 16 QBD 67 (CA); *Alvion SS Corpn Panama v Galban Lobo Trading Co SA of Havana*

trade the parties cannot be expected to know and to adjust to the numerous, national, regional, and local public holidays. This ratio, however, is not applicable in regard to the timely receipt of the acceptance of the offeror: the offeror knows "his or her" public holidays and non-business days unlike the acceptor. Article 20(2) CISG therefore "extends" the time period for the offer to the next working day. However, that refers to public statutory non-business days and not, for example, to the day of a works outing or of a strike.[96]

89.   A late acceptance is one which reaches the offeror after the set time period. In general, a late acceptance will not conclude a contract.[97] However, despite a late acceptance a contract can be concluded according to Article 21 CISG if certain requirements are met. The CISG differentiates between an acceptance sent late and an acceptance sent on time but has been delayed in transit to the offeror. Unlike the common law, the latter type of acceptance is effective provided the offeror either informs the offeree without delay or disputes a notice to the effect that the contract is concluded.[98] A late acceptance can be remedied through the statement of the offeror even if the statement is lost or if that statement reaches the offeree late. Determinative for the point in time for the conclusion of the contract is, therefore, the time when the late acceptance leaves the offeror and not when the offeror's declaration of conclusion of the contract reaches the offeree.

If the acceptance is late because it was delayed in transit the contract will be concluded when the acceptance reaches the offeror unless the offeror orally protests or dispatches a notice that the offeror considers the offer lapsed.[99]

90.   In the authors' view Article 21 CISG does not prevent the addressee of a late acceptance terminating the acceptance according to Article 17 CISG by expressly rejecting the acceptance and responding with a counter-offer which initiates a new contract.[100]

3.3   Divergence Between Offer and Acceptance

91.   The problem of divergence between offer and acceptance is regulated similarly to the common law:[101] Firstly, Article 19(1) CISG stipulates that an

---

[1955] 1 All ER 457 (CA)). Further, the general rule does not apply where the effect would be to render performance impossible, for example where the whole period consists of holidays; in such cases time is extended until the next possible day (*Halsbury's Laws of England*, Time, para 239. See *Mayer v Harding* (1867) LR 2 QB 410; *Waterton v Baker* (1868) LR 3 QB 173).

[96] See in regard to more comprehensive discussion Schlechtriem in Schlechtriem/ Schwenzer, *Commentary*, Art 20 para 6.

[97] CISG, Art 18(2) as well as Art 18(3) CISG at the end.

[98] See in regard to common law: Hawes et al., *Butterworths Introduction to Commercial Law*, para 3.1.7.

[99] CISG, Art 21(1).

[100] See competing theories in Honnold, *Uniform Law for International Sales*, § 162.

[101] See above para 83; The only significant difference is that common law does not admit any alterations to an offer – this constitutes a counter offer. *Reporoa Stores Ltd v Treloar* [1958] NZLR 177 (CA). Burrows/Finn/Todd, *Law of Contract*, 3.3.6.

acceptance which contains additions, limitations or modifications is a rejection of an offer but constitutes a counter-offer.[102] The counter-offer has to be accepted for a contract to be concluded but the acceptance can be silent, for example, when accepting the goods.[103] If the acceptance contains modifications which do not alter the conditions of the offer significantly, the conclusion of the contract is made easier according to Article 19(2) CISG. A contract is concluded incorporating the conditions of the offer modified by the insignificant modifications of the acceptance[104] so far as the offeror does not orally object, or dispatch a notice in which he or she objects to the discrepancy.[105] Article 19(3) CISG stipulates a presumption by listing contract issues which are seen as significant to ease the difficulties surrounding the differentiation between significant and insignificant modifications. The wording of Article 19(3) CISG which was kept despite proposals in Vienna to modify Article 19(3) CISG[106] makes it possible to draw clear lines for the majority of contractual clauses that are found in practice.

The list means that additions, limitations or other modifications of a contract are always significant in practice since Article 19(3) CISG does not leave room for any insignificant modifications unless the interpretation rule is in concrete refuted.[107] The demand of pre-payment,[108] arbitration or jurisdiction clauses which the acceptor suggests are, therefore, significant modifications of the contract.[109] In regard to contract issues which are outside the Article 19(3) CISG list, the differentiation between significant and insignificant modifications depends on the circumstances in the individual case. For example, in the case of demanding securities (for example, a performance bond), rights of withdrawal, revocation or termination, or the manner of packing and dispatching the goods the importance must be weighed in each individual case.

Example: A German company bought tiles from the manufacturer which had its business in Italy. In its acceptance the seller pointed to its standard form delivery conditions which allowed a 30 day period from the day of issuing the bill to inform the seller of any non-conformity with the contract. The Court saw in this modification no significant differentiation from the offer so that the notice and its time period (which the buyer had failed to observe) became part of the contract since the buyer had not protested against the modification.[110] Clauses which declare oral agreements to be invalid or exclude oral amendments to a written contract[111] will have to be regarded as material

---

[102] See in general to Art 19 CISG and its history van Alstine, *Fehlender Konsens*, 195 et seq.
[103] Compare Kantonsgericht Zug (2 Dec 2004) CISG-online 1194 = IHR 2006, 158 et seq para 3.3.
[104] CISG, Art 19(2)2.
[105] CISG, Art 19(2)1, (2nd half s).
[106] Compare Schlechtriem, *Einheitliches UN-Kaufrecht*, 43 fn 181; Schlechtriem in Schlechtriem/Schwenzer, *Commentary*, Art 19 para 8.
[107] In regard to the question of the character of Art 19(3) as a refutable assumption rather than a closed rule see van Alstine, *Fehlender Konsens*, 200, 201 (controversial).
[108] OLG Hamm (21 Mar 1979 in regard to the EAG) in Magnus in Schlechtriem, Art 7 EAG No 4.
[109] Also see Honnold, *Uniform Law for International Sales*, § 169.
[110] Compare LG Baden-Baden (14 Aug 1991) CISG-online 24 = RIW 1992, 62.
[111] See CISG, Art 29(2).

alternations;[112] the same is true for choice of law clauses (assuming that it is not already a matter covered by the term "settlement of disputes" in the list in Article 19(3) CISG.[113]

3.4   Battle of Forms

92.   In regard to what is in practice the most important issue of a divergence between offer and acceptance, no special provision was made in Vienna despite several attempts regarding the "battle of forms".[114] In most cases the battle of forms can, therefore, only be solved on the basis of Article 19 CISG which deals in a modest way with some of the counter-offer issues that typically arise where there is a "battle of forms". A congruence in standard forms is a rarity in the international sale of goods. As any divergence between these standard forms will often be significant for the purpose of Article 19(2) CISG, any acceptance which refers to its own standard form will generally be termed a counter-offer. If the offeror through his or her acts, especially through performance or at least the start of his or her performance, or through acceptance of the performance of the other party, has impliedly accepted the counter-offer, then the acceptor has asserted his or her standard forms. However, if the offeror protests again with reference to his or her own standard forms and the acceptor is silent, the performance of the contract rather than the standard forms of the offeror are determinative for the contract between the parties.

Example: A German Company ordered 200t bacon from an Italian seller. The offer to purchase stipulated in it its standard business terms that the bacon was to be delivered tightly packaged. The acceptance containing the seller's standard business terms on the other hand contained a notice that the bacon was to be delivered unpackaged. The German buyer did not contradict that notice and accepted the first four instalments. Thereafter the buyer, however, refused the acceptance of the remaining instalments. The Court held that the divergence between offer and acceptance was material, that, therefore the acceptance of the Italian buyer had to be seen as a counter-offer that had been accepted by the German buyer.[115]

For the Court it was, therefore, material which party "had the last word". The "last word" approach which favours the party which has last referred to its standard

---

[112] Compare Farnsworth in Bianca/Bonell, Art 19 para 3.1.

[113] Compare *Société Les Verreries de Saint Gobain, SA v Martinswerk GmbH* (Cour de Cassation) (16 Jul 1998) CISG-online 344.

[114] Compare van Alstine, *Fehlender Konsens*, 207 et seq; Perales, (1998) 10 Pace Int'l L Rev 97, 101; as well as Schlechtriem, *Einheitlichem UN-Kaufrecht* 43, 44.

[115] Compare OLG Hamm (22 Sep 1992) CISG-online 57, OLG Köln (24 May 2006) CISG-online 1232 = IHR 2006, 147 et seq, para 2; see also Schwenzer/Mohs, IHR 2006, 239 III.

terms without those terms being rejected to is also favoured by same authors.[116] Some courts and authors favour the conclusion of the contract without the contradictory (standard) terms. The contradictory terms are to be substituted by the law applicable to the contract, for example, the relevant CISG provision.[117] The German Supreme Court also favours the "knock-out" approach. The claimant, the buyer, which had its business in the Netherlands, bought milk powder from the defendant, the seller, which had its business in Germany. The milk powder was on sold to a purchaser in Algeria. That purchaser complained about the quality of the milk powder (a rancid taste due to a fungal contamination) and the buyer paid damages. The buyer claimed the damages paid from the seller which defended the claim based on the liability provisions in its standard terms and conditions. The buyer on the other hand relied on its standard terms and conditions and the guarantees contained in them. The German Supreme Court firstly held that the two standard forms in regard to the issue contained contradictory provisions and neither party had accepted the provision of the other party. This, however, was not contrary to finding that both parties intended to conclude a binding contract since the parties had not perceived the contradictory standard term provisions as an obstacle to the performance of the contract. It held further that the provisions were invalid and according to the *Rechtsgültigkeitstheorie* ("knock-out" approach) the applicable law provided the solution to the issue. Furthermore, the Court stated that the application of the "last word" approach would have not made a difference in this case since the defendant could not in good faith (Article 7(1) CISG) rely on the application of the claimant's standard terms which were favourable for the defendant because of its missing objection.[118]

The basis for the "knock out" approach is party autonomy, as stipulated in Article 6 CISG, which allows parties to divert from Article 19(1), (3) CISG. Parties can conclude a legally binding contract although they have not reached agreement in regard to the binding standard terms, or in regard to the contradictory provisions in the contract as long as they are in agreement in regard to the essentialia negotii.[119]

If the negotiation between the parties took place over a long period of time during which both parties have several times referred to their standard terms and negotiations clearly show that the parties wanted to conclude the contract even if that meant that they had to forgo their standard terms, then the "knock-out" approach is especially appropriate to satisfy the principle of party autonomy.

---

[116] Among others, for example: Farnsworth in Bianca/Bonell, Art 19, note 2.5; Blodgett, (1989) 18 Col Law 423, 426; Kelso, (1983) 21 Colum J Transnat'l L, 529, 553; Honsell et al., (eds) *Kommentar zum UN-Kaufrecht*, Art 19 paras 37, 38.

[117] Honnold, *Uniform Law for International Sales*, § 170.4; von Mehren, (1990) 38 Am J Comp L, 265, 275 et seq); Magnus in *Staudinger*, Art 19 para 24; Schlechtriem, *FS Herber*, 36-49.

[118] BGH (9 Jan 2002) CISG-online 651 = NJW 2002, 1651 et seq.

[119] See CISG, Art 14 para 74; and commentary on Art 14 in Schlechtriem in Schlechtriem/Schwenzer, *Commentary*, Art 14 paras 2 et seq. Compare BG (5 Apr 2005) CISG-online 1012 = IHR 2005, 204, 205 et seq where the Court found, despite contradictory statements, an intention to be bound by interpreting the conduct of the parties in accordance with Art 8 CISG.

The performance of the contractual obligations in particular is evidence that the parties did not want the contract to fail because of their contradictory standard terms.[120]

3.5   Commercial Letter of Confirmation

93.   Similar problems to those in regard to standard terms arise in regard to commercial letters of confirmation in relation to the formation of the contract, especially the issue of whether silence in regard to such a letter of confirmation can amount to acceptance. The formation of a contract through silence after a commercial letter of confirmation can only be brought about if the silence is in accordance with the parties' usual practices or if the silence is in accordance with international practices or usages;[121] only in exceptional circumstances will one party's commercial letter followed by silence of the other party amount to a contract formation.[122]

4   Effectiveness of Statements in Regard to Contract Conclusion

94.   Part II of the Convention stipulates that for the conclusion of a contract the parties' statements have to generally reach the other party to be effective. Offer and acceptance as well as other statements (for example, withdrawal of an offer (Article 15(2) CISG); revocation of an offer (Article 16(1) CISG); rejection of an offer (Article 17 CISG); fixing of a time period for acceptance (Article 20(1) CISG), and withdrawal of the acceptance (Article 22 CISG)) will only become effective if and when they reach the other party. However, in some instances the CISG does not demand that a statement reach the other party to be effective: for example, Article 19(2)(1st s) CISG only requires that the offeror objects to an

---

[120] See also van Alstine, *Fehlender Konsens*, 213, 214, 216, 217, 220 et seq: "if the parties agreeably perform the contract without having reached agreement in regard to specific issues one has to proceed from the premise that the parties do not want to fail in the conclusion of the contract only because they could not agree upon some secondary issues – unless there is some actual proof of a supposition to the contrary." – original quote see: Schlechtriem, *Internationales UN-Kaufrecht*, para 92 fn 49; as well as Kramer in *FS Welser*, 539, 553-557 ("superiority of party autonomy"); furthermore, with additional sources Schlechtriem in Schlechtriem/Schwenzer, *Commentary*, Art 19 paras 19–21.

[121] See above para 62.

[122] Compare, para 87; compare BGH (22 Mar 1995) NJW 1995, 1671; Kramer in *FS Welser*, 546, 547 – the sending of a commercial letter of confirmation has to be interpreted constructively also in regard to the CISG as the application of a contract modification which can perhaps be accepted by silence); similarly van Alstine, *Fehlender Konsens*, 241, 242: "That means that according to the CISG, silence in regard to a commercial letter of confirmation can generally only be seen as agreement to the provisions in the letter of confirmation which supplement and concretise the oral agreement between the parties." (Original quote in German in Schlechtriem, *Internationales UN-Kaufrecht*, para 93 fn 50).

immaterial alteration of the offeror by the accepter "without undue delay" but does not require that the objection reaches the accepter; it merely has to be dispatched.[123] Furthermore, in the case of a late acceptance, the offeror's "acceptance of the late acceptance" does not have to reach the offeree (Article 21(1) CISG) and the protest of the offeror according to Article 21(2) CISG also does not generally have to reach the offeree.[124]

95.   Article 24 CISG stipulates when a statement "reaches" the addressee. The CISG differentiates between orally made statements and statements which the addressee receives "by any other means." Oral statements are statements between parties who are in each others' presence at the time of their statements, including statements made via the telephone or radio. It will not include, for example, a message on an answering machine.[125] Whether the addressee has to actually hear the statement, "recognised theory", or whether an objective standard applies, that is addressee ought to have heard the statement, is uncertain.[126] In regard to all recorded statements (that means all statements recorded electronically, in writing, or by other means) the statement has to reach the addressee's "sphere of control" so that he or she has the unhindered opportunity to get knowledge of the statement. The addressee's actual awareness of the statement is irrelevant.[127] The opportunity to take notice of the statement requires that the statement is delivered in a language that addressee is able to understand, that means either in the language of the addressee, or the language the parties used during the negotiations or a language of which the sender could reasonably assume that addressee would be able to understand.

Example: The German buyer bought some batches of socks from the Italian seller. The contracts were formed orally in Italy whereby the buyer had been represented by its Italian agent. The Italian seller informed the German buyer (via registered mail) that its claims in regard to the purchase price had been assigned to an Italian bank. The notice of assignment was written, as standard form, in English as well as in French. The German buyer paid the purchase price to the Italian seller which shortly afterwards was declared bankrupt. The Italian bank claimed the assigned purchase price from the buyer. Determinative of its claim was whether the notice of assignment had reached the German buyer. The Court decided that questions of assignment were not regulated by the otherwise applicable CISG, rather, that the

---

[123] See in regard to the history of the provision Schlechtriem in Schlechtriem/Schwenzer, *Commentary*, Art 19 paras 1, 15 et seq.

[124] CISG, Art 21(2): "If a letter or other writing containing a late acceptance shows that it has been sent and reached the offerer in due time, the late acceptance is effective as an acceptance unless, without delay, the offerer orally informs the offeree that he considers his offer as having lapsed or dispatched a notice to that effect." See in regard to a history of the Art 21 CISG: Schlechtriem in Schlechtriem/Schwenzer, *Commentary*, Art 21 para 1 and see also paras 7–9; 16, 20, 21.

[125] See Schlechtriem in Schlechtriem/Schwenzer, *Commentary*, Art 24 paras 4, 8.

[126] Compare Schlechtriem in Schlechtriem/Schwenzer, *Commentary*, Art 24 paras 6, 7.

[127] See in regard to examples when different means of communication are "delivered" Schlechtriem in Schlechtriem/Schwenzer, *Commentary*, Art 24 paras 12–14.

question whether a notice of assignment effectively reached the addressee had to be interpreted in accordance with Article 24 CISG. In regard to the case before the Court, the Court held that the buyer had the opportunity to gain reliable knowledge of the content of the notice of assignment in English.[128]

An electronically transmitted statement reaches the addressee when it arrives at the receiver (for example, the addressee's fax machine) and is able to be retrieved from there. The addressee must have stipulated the receiving equipment or the receiver has to be in his or her sphere of control.[129] However, depending on the means of transmission, the opportunity to retrieve the statement may require that the addressee has a programme available which allows the conversion of data to readable text. In regard to central mail servers, the possibility that they might be turned off for certain periods, sometimes suppress data (for example, spam mail), or cannot be accessed for reasons outside the control of the user, so that the addressee has no opportunity to retrieve the information must be taken into account. The requirement that it must be possible for the addressee to be aware of the statement has to be interpreted in light of Article 7(1) CISG.[130] "The possibility of awareness" does not extend to situations where the access to the statement was rendered more difficult if the increased difficulty does not comply with the uniform application of the Convention and good faith in international trade.[131] The issue of whether a statement, conveyed via an intermediary reached the addressee (including reached statements) is decided in accordance with standards applicable in domestic law.

95a. Article 16(1) CISG states that an offer may be withdrawn at any time before the contract is concluded, but the offeree must receive notice of the revocation before she or he accepts the offer. This is anomalous as an acceptance that does not reach the offeror is only effective in exceptional circumstances (Article 18(3) CISG) and that means, generally, that revocation should only be precluded by the conclusion of the contract. However, Article 16(1) CISG implies that revocation is not possible in any circumstances after an acceptance has been dispatched, even if it has not reached the offeror. Under common law, revocation of an offer is possible at any time before acceptance because until this time, no legal obligation exists.[132] This is so even if the offer is stated to be open for a specified

---

[128] OLG Hamm (8 Feb 1995) CISG-online 141 with commentary from Schlechtriem, IPRax 1996, 197.

[129] See already above para 70b as well as UNCITRAL Draft Convention on the Use of Electronic Communications in International Contracts (CA/CN 91577) Art 10(2): "A statement reaches the addressee at the time... when it becomes capable of being retrieved by the addressee at an electronic address designated by the addressee."

[130] See generally to Art 7 CISG paras 43 et seq.

[131] Compare Schlechtriem in Schlechtriem/Schwenzer, *Commentary*, Art 24 paras 13–15.

[132] *Payne v Cave* (1789) 3 Term Rep 148; 100 ER 502. See also *Dickinson v Dodds* (1876) 2 ChD 463 (CA); *Financings Ltd v Stimson* [1962] 3 All ER 386 (CA); *Goldsbrough Mort & Co Ltd v Quinn* (1910) 10 CLR 674; *Veivers v Cordingley* [1989] 2 Qd R 278 at 296; (1988) 67 LGRA 61 at 79 per McPherson J (Andrews CJ and Demack J concurring) (SC (QLD), Full Court).

period.[133] Like the CISG, under the common law, notice of the revocation must reach the offeree (or her or his agent) before it is effective. Under the CISG an offer is accepted when the acceptance reaches the offeror.[134] Common law also requires an acceptance to be communicated to the offeror, but the postal acceptance rule is an exception. Under the postal acceptance rule, the contract is formed upon the dispatch of the letter confirming acceptance; a prior revocation of an offer that does not reach the offeree before she or he confirms acceptance is ineffective.[135] The revocation of an offer must reach the offeree.

5   Modification of the Contract

96.   The possibility of contract modification according to Article 29 CISG is materially a matter of Part I of the Convention, the Application and the Ambit of the Convention, and only in regard to how a contract can be modified a matter of Part II of the Convention, Contract Formation. Despite Article 29 CISG being placed in Part III, Chapter 1 of the CISG Article 29 will be discussed at this point. Article 29 CISG which had no forerunner in the ULF and the ULIS was contentious until the end at the Vienna Conference.[136] For the common law juris-dictions where the doctrine of consideration, at least in theory, is a serious hurdle to the modifications of contracts[137] meant an important political decision for the common law states.[138] However, an exception, and in one sense "a good example" has been the United States where a similar rule to Article 29 CISG has long existed in domestic law[139] and where section 2-209 (1) UCC unequivocally states that "[a]n agreement modifying a contract... needs no consideration to be binding." However, accuracy to the Official Comment 2 to the UCC stipulates that a modi-fication must meet the test of good faith,[140] and also adds an undesirable extra requirement.[141]

---

[133] *Routledge v Grant* (1828) 4 Bing 653; 130 ER 920.

[134] See also Bridge, *International Sale of Goods*, 12.05 with comparison to English Law.

[135] Burrows/Finn/Todd, *Law of Contract*, 3.5.2. See *Sommerville v Rice* [1912] 31 NZLR 370; com-pare *Byrne v Van Tienhoven* (1880) 5 CPD 344. See also *Stevenson v McLean* (1880) 5 QBD 346; and *Henthorn v Fraser* [1892] 2 Ch 27.

[136] See Geldsetzer, *Einvernehmliche Änderung*, 26 et seq.

[137] See Butler, "Doctrine of Parole Evidence Rule and Consideration", 54, 56 et seq, who shows that in practice courts have been rather creative in finding "consideration" if there was clear intention to modify. See also Bridge, *International Sale of Goods*, 12.11.

[138] See, as an example where the Court especially mentioned the missing consideration requirement in Art 29 CISG: *Shuttle Packaging Systems v Tsonakis INA SA et al.*, US DC Michigan (17 Dec 2001) CISG-online 773; non-competition clause valid even without special consideration.

[139] Gabriel, *Contracts for the Sale of Goods*, 03 fn 452.

[140] Gabriel, *Contracts for the Sale of Goods*, 105 fn 467.

[141] See Hillman, (1988) 21 Cornell Int'l L J, 449

97.   Articles 8 and 14 to 24 CISG apply to the modification or the termination of a contract.[142] Statements and conduct of the parties have to be interpreted according to Article 8 CISG. Modifications can be made through implicit conduct.[143]

Example: A German dealer ordered textiles from an Italian company for a German company and in its name. Later, a bill of exchange was drawn on the buyer and accepted by the buyer. The Court concluded from the later bill of exchange that the parties modified the contract according to Article 29(1) CISG so that payment of the purchase price was delayed until the bill of exchange matured.[144]

Often new provisions are introduced to the contract (only) with the invoice. The question arises whether the statement contained in the invoice is a legally binding offer to modify contract. That has to be ascertained by interpretation of the invoice in accordance with Article 8 CISG. If the statement is interpreted as legally binding the next question is whether an uncontradicted payment of the invoice is an implicit acceptance according to Article 18(1) CISG – "by or other conduct".

Example: The Canadian buyer bought 11 batches of wine bottle corks from the seller which had its business in the United States and France. The buyer alleged that the corks were faulty. The seller which was sued in the United States asserted the jurisdiction clause of the contract stipulated Perpignan, France. The jurisdiction clause was printed on all of the seller's invoices which the buyer paid uncontested. A key consideration for the Court was (in the authors' view) whether the invoices with the jurisdiction clause could be interpreted as an offer to modify the contract and whether the buyer had accepted that offer by contested paying the invoices.[145]

Subsequently added jurisdiction or arbitration clauses, however, might have to conform generally to domestic or international procedural rules. The only role the

---

[142] Uncontested, compare Strohbach in Enderlein/Maskow/Strohbach, *Internationales Kaufrecht*, Art 29 para 1.2; Herber/Czerwenka, *Internationales Kaufrecht*, Art 29 para 3; OLG Köln (22 Feb 1994) CISG-online 127 = RIW 1994, 972 annotation by Schlechtriem, EWiR 1994, 867 see in regard to the facts of this case above para 87.

[143] There are numerous decisions in regard to the question whether an offer was implicitly accepted by conduct: OLG Düsseldorf (12 Mar 1993) CISG-online 82; OLG Köln (22 Feb 1994) CISG-online 127 = RIW 1994, 972 annotation by Schlechtriem, EWiR 1994, 867 and Reinhart, IPRax 1995, 365 et seq; Cour d'appel de Grenoble (29 Mar 1995) CISG-online 156.

[144] LG Hamburg (26 Sep 1991) CISG-online 21 = IPRax 1991, 400 annotation from Reinhart, *UN-Kaufrecht*, 376.

[145] *Chateau des Charmes Wines Ltd v Sabate, USA Inc* US Ct of Appeals (9th Cir) (5 May 2003) CISG-online 767: the Court, however, mixed Artt 29 and 19(3) CISG together but decided justifiably that the parties did not incorporated the jurisdiction clause into the contract through modification of the contract. The Ontario Superior Court, in a continuation of the case before the Canadian Courts, indicated that for the first delivery a modification of the contract in regard to the jurisdiction clause had to be denied; but that for the later deliveries the question of modification had to be seen differently since the buyer had been aware of the jurisdiction clause (Ontario Superior Court of Justice (28 Oct 2005) CISG-online 1139).

CISG only plays is the establishing of an agreement between the parties (or rules as lex specialis) are not applicable.[146]

Generally, the alteration, modification, and termination of a contract does not need to comply with any form requirement (Article 11 CISG). However, Article 12, CISG which in effect requires that all legally binding statements in regard to a contract have to be in writing has to be taken into account if the member states have made a declaration under Article 96 CISG.[147]

98.   Another exception to the general rule that no particular form is required for the modification, alteration, or termination of a contract is Article 29(2)(1st s) CISG which requires that the modifications, alteration, or termination have to be in writing if the parties have agreed in the original contract to a "no oral modification" clause. What the parties meant by "writing" in a "no oral modification" clause has to be interpreted according to Article 8 CISG. However, the forms stipulated in Article 13 CISG will suffice.

99.   However, Article 29(2)(2nd s) CISG establishes a defence where one party justifiably relied on the conduct of the other party which gave rise to or expressed a modification of the contract. Examples of such reliance inducing conduct are the performance of the contract without objection, following an oral modification,[148] or the manufacture of contractually-agreed goods to an (orally) amended specification.[149]

The ability "to circumvent" Article 29(2)(1st s) CISG, even though Article 29 (2)(2nd s) CISG is a sensible and common rule, gives rise to the difficulty that a "no oral modification" clause seeks to prevent: that is, the difficulty of proving a modification, alteration or termination of the contract, the waiver and the fear of false claims.[150]

Article 29(2) CISG is also applicable in regard to merger clauses[151] which exclude oral ancillary agreements. However, in light of Article 29(2)(1st s) CISG, it is doubtful whether an oral agreement (provided that that an oral agreement can be proved and is interpreted in accordance with Article 8 CISG) can have an invalidating effect.[152] That means merger clauses with a clause requiring amendments to be in writing can be more easily overturned than no oral modification clauses for the subsequent alteration, modification or termination of a contract

---

[146] See above para 41; compare in regard to the doctrine of facture accepteé, that means the generous inclusion of arbitration clauses on invoices: Schlosser/Pirrung, *Schiedsgerichtsbarkeit*, paras 380, 382; but also BGH (21 Sep 2005) NJW 2005, 3499 et seq: invoices which recognisably (only) settle the given service cannot be interpreted as a commercial letter of confirmation of an oral agreement with the possible consequence, that an arbitration clause containing standard terms has any effect.

[147] See above para 65.

[148] Secretariat's Commentary OR 28, example 27A in No 9 on Art 29.

[149] Honnold, *Uniform Law for International Sales*, § 204; further examples in Geldsetzer, *Einvernehmliche Änderung*, 160, 161 analysing United States' case law.

[150] See Gabriel, *Contracts for the Sale of Goods*, 104.

[151] See AC-CISG Opinion No 3 (Oct 2004) (by Hyland), comments sub 4.

[152] See *TeeVee Tunes, Inc et al., v Gerhard Schubert GmbH* (US DC, NY SD) (23 Aug 2006) CISG-online 1272.

in contract. In the authors' view Article 29(2)(1st s) CISG can be derogated from in accordance with Article 6 CISG in regard to merger clauses.[153]

However, the purpose behind Article 29(2)(1st s) CISG, namely to preserve the parties' chosen protection writing, should prevent a hasty assumption that the parties had an implicit intention to derogate from Article 29(2)(2nd s) CISG in accordance with Article 6 CISG by allowing the oral modification of a merger clause.[154] The defence of reliance has to be taken into account ex officio.[155] The principle behind Article 29(2)2 CISG is a general one which can be used for gap-filling in accordance with Article 7(2) CISG as it prohibits a party invoking a contractual requirement where they are guilty of flouting that rule and the other party relies on that conduct.

---

[153] Affirmative the Court in *TeeVee Tunes, Inc et al., v Gerhard Schubert GmbH* (US DC, NY SD) (23 Aug 2006) CISG-online 1272.

[154] Schlechtriem in Schlechtriem/Schwenzer, *Commentary*, Art 29 para 5.

[155] Schlechtriem in Schlechtriem/Schwenzer, *Commentary*, Art 29 para 12.

Part III of the CISG

1 General

1.1 Content of Part III

100. Part III of the Convention contains the provisions of the substantive sale of goods law, that means the rights and obligations of the parties as well as the consequences of the disruption or interference in regard to the performance of the contract, especially the parties' remedies in regard to the failure of the other party to perform her or his obligations. Part III is set out in five chapters. The core provisions are contained in chapters 2 and 3. Chapter 2 of the CISG regulates firstly the obligations of the seller (Sections 1 and 2, Articles 31–44 CISG), followed by the remedies available to the buyer because of the seller's breach of contract (Section 3, Articles 45–52 CISG).[1] Chapter 3, mirrors Chapter 2 by setting out firstly, the obligations of the buyer, in Sections 1 and 2, (Articles 53–60 CISG) and then, in Section 3, the remedies of the seller in regard to a buyer's breach of contract (Articles 61–65 CISG). In substance, part of the buyer's duty to pay the purchase price also regulates the passing of the risk in chapter 4 (Articles 66–70 CISG), since the regulation of the passing of the risk stipulates whether the buyer has to pay the purchase price even if the buyer did not receive the goods, or the goods received were damaged.

101. The specific provisions in chapters 2 to 4 in regard to the obligations of seller and buyer, the remedies available in case of a breach of those obligations, and the passing of the risk are supplemented by general provisions, that means provisions applicable to the buyer as well as to the seller. However, these general provisions are spread between chapter 1 (Articles 25–29 CISG) and chapter 5 (Articles 71–88 CISG).[2] Under the heading *General Provisions* chapter 1 contains quite diverse provisions, whereas chapter 5 has six Sections regulating *Common Obligations of Seller and Buyer*. If the CISG had followed, the division of general and subject matter specific provisions in a strictly systematic manner, the provisions of chapters 1 and 5 should have preceded chapters 2 to 4. The following

---

[1] See above para 5.
[2] See above para 6.

discussion of Part III follows the structure of the CISG. However, to be able to fully appreciate Articles 25 to 28 CISG in chapter 1, it is necessary to first give a summary about the remedies available in the CISG.

1.2   Preliminary Remarks to Chapter I: Basic Remedies

102. Chapter 1 regulates several very different problems: Article 29 CISG, the alteration, modification, and termination of contracts and the related issue of a writing requirement belong to the questions of "party autonomy" and "contract formation" and was discussed in conjunction with Articles 14 to 24 CISG.[3] Articles 26 and 27 CISG regulate declarations which have to be made in relation to the performance of a contract and/or the exercise of a remedy in case of a disruption or interference while performing a contract, especially in regard to the risk of delay, of error in the transmission, or the non-arrival of the declaration. Articles 25 and 28 CISG contain specific remedies, namely the remedy "to require specific performance", "to demand subsequent delivery", and "to avoid the contract". The significance of those remedies can only fully ascertained if, as mentioned above in para 101, the system of the CISG's remedies, which are, so to speak, the backbone of the CISG and define the legal status of the parties, is elucidated beforehand. The CISG contains four basic remedies. In addition to those four remedies, the buyer has the remedy of a reduction in the purchase price (Article 50 CISG) should the goods not conform to the contract.

The basic remedies are:

1.2.1   Right to "Specific Performance" and to "Subsequent Performance"

103. Unlike the common law, the CISG starts from the premise that every obligation of a party corresponds with the right to specific performance of the obligee. However, to bridge the gap between the Continental European legal system, for which specific performance as contained in Article 28 (1st half s) CISG is the primary contractual remedy,[4] and the common law-derived legal systems, Article 28 (2nd half s) CISG stipulates a limitation to the right to specific performance. According to Article 28 (2nd half s) CISG, a court is free not to enter a judgment for specific performance if it would not do so under its own law in respect of similar contracts. In principle, the buyer can also demand performance in the form of further delivery when the goods received do not conform to the contract.

In regard to non-conforming goods in particular the buyer can demand delivery of substitute goods, or the buyer can require the seller to remedy the non-conformity by repair according to Articles 46(2) and 46(3) CISG respectively. However, if the buyer requests a replacement delivery, the seller's demand for

---

[3]   See above paras 96 et seq.

[4]   See an interesting analysis in regard to specific performance and common law: Cuncannon, (2004) 35 VUWLR, 657.

the return of the non-conforming goods has the effect of terminating the original contract. A termination of the contract due to a replacement delivery has the same requirements as the termination of a contract.[5]

1.2.2 Right to Withhold Performance

104. The impairment of performance allows the obligee at first to withhold his or her own performance as far it had to match that of the other party.[6] Further, under Article 71 CISG each party can withhold performance if it becomes apparent that the other party is unable to perform her or his obligations under the contract. Under Article 71(3) CISG the party suspending performance must give immediate notice to the other party; the suspension must be lifted if adequate guarantees of performance are available. This right to withhold is of practical importance for the party which has to perform first. Further rights to withhold can be found in Articles 81(1)(2nd s), 85(2nd s) and 86(1)(2nd s) CISG. Whether, in light of the rights to withhold stipulated in the CISG, the conclusion can be drawn that a general right to withhold exists is controversial but in the authors' view has to be supported through gap-filling under the CISG in application of Article 7(2) CISG.[7]

1.2.3 Damages

105. The most important remedy in practical terms is the right to claim damages which the CISG grants the buyer in principle in Article 45(1)(b) CISG and the seller in Article 61(1)(b) CISG. Those rights are supplemented by Articles 79 and 80 CISG which contain certain exemptions of the obligor who should otherwise be liable for damages in regard to the breach of a contractual duty. In effect they stipulate additional requirements which have to be met before the obligee can realise his or her right to claim damages. Articles 74 to 77 CISG provide the general rules in regard to the extent of damages and its calculation.

1.2.4 Avoidance of the Contract

106. The underlying basis for the avoidance of a contract under the CISG is that the breach of the other party is a "fundamental breach" of the contractual obligations.[8] The obligor can, in certain cases of a breach, clarify whether a breach is fundamental by fixing an additional time period. In those cases the CISG allows the obligor to avoid the contract if the obligee does not comply within the additional time allowed. In numerous cases, however, the concept of "fundamental breach" is of central importance. In anticipating the importance, the drafters of the CISG have already attempted a definition of fundamental breach in Article 25

---

[5] See below para 106.
[6] Compare to begin with Art 58 (1) CISG, which is construed as a provision setting out when performance is due.
[7] See para 42d.
[8] See CISG, Artt 49(1), 64(1)(a).

CISG. Common law jurisdictions originally developed a concept of "fundamental breach" to deal with the problem of excessively wide exclusion clauses,[9] however, today, the term connotes any breach that goes to the root of the contract, entitling the innocent party to treat the contract as at an end.[10] In this context, common law jurisdictions more often talk about repudiation or repudiatory breach, that is a refusal or failure to perform an obligation that has the effect of frustrating the contract. There must be a substantial failure of performance.[11] Delay in performing an obligation will, by itself, not necessarily amount to repudiation. Each case is treated on a case by case basis. An election by the innocent party to affirm the contract, notwithstanding a repudiatory breach, does not relieve the party in breach from liability for damages.[12]

1.3   Statements and Declarations in Accordance with Articles 26, 27 CISG

1.3.1 Declaration of Avoidance

108. Article 26 CISG provides that the avoidance of a contract is only effective if there is notice to the other party. The provision is a reaction to the regulation of avoidance in the ULIS where the declaration of avoidance had been dealt with separately in connection with each ground for avoidance, particularly where an ipso facto avoidance in accordance with certain requirements was possible.[13] The drafters of the CISG explicitly rejected the possibility of an ipso facto avoidance; this is reflected in Article 26 CISG.[14] A declaration of avoidance releases the parties from their remaining contractual obligations, and all parties have to restitute to each other what they have received.[15] Further, the avoidance of the contract is often accompanied by a damages claim. Because of the consequences of avoidance, the statement avoiding the contract has to be unmistakably clear and precise

---

[9] See, for example, *Mallet v Great Eastern Railway Company* [1899] 1 QB 309; *Hain SS Co Ltd v Tate & Lyle Ltd* [1936] 2 All ER 597 (HL(E)); *Chandris v Isbrandsten Moller Co Inc* [1950] 1 All ER 768 (CA); *UGS Finance v National Mortgage Bank of Greece and National Bank of Greece, SA* [1964] 1 Lloyd's Rep (CA). See, generally, McManus, *The Law of Contracts*, 754–764.

[10] *Halsbury's Laws of England*, Contract, paras 805, 996; for *Australian law*, see *Halsbury's Laws of Australia* (last updated 31 May 2003) 110 Contract, paras 110-2480 et seq. See also *Suisse Atlantique Société D'armement Maritime S A v N V Rotterdamsche Kolen Centrale* [1966] 2 All ER 61, 70 (HL) Lord Reid: "General use of the term "fundamental breach" is of recent origin, and I can find nothing to indicate that it means either more or less than the well known type of breach which entitles the innocent party to treat it as repudiatory and to rescind the contract." See generally to avoidance fundamental breach and the similarties between common law and the CISG: Bridge, *International Sales Law*, 12.24, 12.25.

[11] Waddams, *The Law of Contracts*, para 581 et seq.

[12] McManus, *The Law of Contracts*, 641.

[13] See Hornung in Schlechtriem/Schwenzer, *Commentary*, Art 26, paras 1, 2.

[14] See Hornung in Schlechtriem/Schwenzer, *Commentary*, Art 26, para 2.

[15] Compare Art 81 CISG. See in regard to the different theoretical models which kind of legal relationship results from the avoidance of a contract-contractual restitutionary relationship (Germanic writers); unique or no dogmatic explanation (Anglo-American writers): See Hornung in Schlechtriem/Schwenzer, *Commentary*, Art 26, paras 4–6, Art 81, paras 9–9d.

and has to convey the party's intention to avoid the contract.[16] The importance of notifying the other party of the avoidance is also implicit in the UCC even though the UCC does not have a specific provision requiring notice for the avoidance of a contract.[17] Generally, at common law, the innocent party must communicate her or his decision to disaffirm the contract to the repudiating party.[18] As noted by Asquith L J in *Howard v Pickford Tool Co Ltd*:[19] "An unaccepted repudiation is a thing writ in water and of no value to anybody; it affords no legal rights of any sort or any kind." The innocent party does not need to give the defaulting party notice, and time to rectify a breach, before exercising her or his right to terminate the contract,[20] but a failure to give notice of termination may, depending on the circumstances, amount to an affirmation of the contract.[21]

Article 11 CISG does not require that the statement comply with a particular form.[22] While the parties are generally free to agree on the form of the statement, trade usages and party practices can demand a certain form. In regard to the interpretation of such statements, especially of implicit conduct can amount to a statement, Article 8 CISG, and Articles 8(2) and (3) CISG in particular, have to be applied.[23] In regard to the validity of the "avoidance statement", especially its timing and the legal consequences in regard to the loss or error during transmission, Article 27 CISG has to be applied.[24] The risk for the recipient is diminished because an "avoidance statement" is not valid unless it has been dispatched according to Article 27 CISG in a way that the other party can receive it.[25]

1.3.2 Other Notices and Communications

109. Notices, requests and other communications which are detailed in provisions in Part III but also in Part II of the Convention, have to be dispatched to be valid unless the CISG explicitly provides differently, for example in regard to the declarations concerning the formation of the contract where special rules are laid down as regards whether the statement must reach the addressee or whether dispatch is sufficient.[26] The addressee carries the risk of the loss or error in transmission of a notice, request, or communication. That the addressee takes the risk

---

[16] Compare OLG Frankfurt (16 Sep 1991) CISG-online 26 = RIW 1991, 952, 953; OGH (6 Feb 1996) CISG-online 224.

[17] See Gabriel, *Contracts for the Sale of Goods*, 95.

[18] McManus, *The Law of Contracts*, 641.

[19] [1951] 1 KB 417, 421 (CA).

[20] *British & Beningtons Ltd v North Western Cachar Tea Ltd* [1923] AC 48 (HL); *Connaught Laboratories Ltd v Canada* (1983) 49 NR 332 (FCA); *Scandinavian Trading Co A/B v Zodiac Petroleum SA and William Hudson Ltd* (The Al Hofuf) [1981] 1 Lloyd's Rep 81 (QB).

[21] *Howard v Pickford Tool Co Ltd* [1951] 1 KB 417 (CA). See, generally, McManus, *The Law of Contracts*, 641–642.

[22] See OGH (5 Jul 2001) CISG-online 652 = IHR 2002, 73 (possibly implicit through filing a statement of claim).

[23] Compare Schmidt-Kessel in Schlechtriem/Schwenzer, *Commentary*, Art 8 para 1.

[24] Controversial see Hornung in Schlechtriem/Schwenzer, *Commentary*, Art 26 paras 11, 12.

[25] See below para 110.

[26] See above para 94.

seems reasonable in situations where the statement is a reaction to the addressee's breach of contract, for example, the notice of lack of conformity of the goods in Article 39 CISG.[27] Delay, error in transmission or the loss do not affect the validity of the statement. However, some authors are of the opinion that the statement is only effective when it reaches the addressee.[28] Those authors have to assume the timing of the hypothetical receipt of the statement in case a statement is lost. Where the CISG explicitly requires the occurrence of the event which the statement was meant to achieve the event has to occur for the statement to be effective. However, the wording of Article 27 CISG, as well as Article 26 CISG, and the intention of the drafters of the CISG leaves no doubt that the statements which fall in the realm of Article 27 CISG are valid upon their dispatch.[29]

Another controversial question is the question when a statement becomes effective. However, because the clear regulation of the transmission risk means that the question of the point of time of effectiveness is only relevant in regard to two scenarios. Firstly, the question whether, for example, the "avoidance declaration" is effective upon dispatch or only when it has been received (that means in case the declaration is lost, at the hypothetical time when it would have been received) could be relevant in regard to "secondary" claims such as interest or damages.[30] Article 84(1) CISG states, in case of an avoidance of the contract, that interest on the purchase price is calculated from the date of payment. The same has to be true in regard to a sum which has to be paid back because of reduction in price. Therefore, in those important cases, the effectiveness of the "avoidance statement" or the "statement in regard to the reduction of price" is not important. Since Article 84(1) CISG stipulates that if the seller has to refund the purchase price the seller has to pay interest on it, from the date on which the price was paid, the same must be true for a buyer's damages claim due to the refinancing of his or her refund claim. Again, the time of the effectiveness of the notice of avoidance is not significant.

Only the second question, that is from which point in time the declarator is bound by his or her declaration has practical significance. In regard to this question one can take the view that the effectiveness of the declaration (at the moment of dispatch) and the question whether the declarator is bound by the declaration have to be separated. That means declarator can revoke or charge his or her declaration, as long as the addressee does not know the declaration has been made and has not acted on it. If there is doubt it has to be assumed that the addressee has knowledge upon the receipt of the declaration and has acted on it so that it is binding on the declarer.[31]

---

[27] Compare Schlechtriem in Schlechtriem/Schwenzer, *Commentary*, Art 27 para 1.

[28] Compare Stern, *Erklärungen*, para 454 (summary); Leser in Schlechtriem (ed) *Einheitliches Kaufrecht*, 237, 238; Neumayer/Ming, Art 27 para 2.

[29] Neumayer's argument (Neumayer/Ming, Art 27 para 2) that statements which alter the parties' legal situations (Gestaltungserklärungen) cannot be effective unless the addressee has received them has weight de lege ferenda. However, the CISG has explicitly regulated the risk of loss of a statement and, therefore, the de lege ferenda argument cannot prevail.

[30] Affirmative Schlechtriem in Schlechtriem/Schwenzer, *Commentary*, Art 27 para 1.

[31] See Schlechtriem, *Bindung an Erklärungen*, 259, 271 et seq.

110. Declarations according to Articles 26 and 27 CISG do not have to reach the addressee, but have to be able to reach the addressee, that means, they have to be made using the means appropriate in the circumstances to be effective. The declarer generally has free choice concerning the means of communication. He or she cannot invoke Article 27 CISG if a means of communication inappropriate in the circumstances was chosen and because of that delivery of the declaration was delayed, or contained an error did not eventuate or the transmission of the declaration was incomplete at all.

Example: The buyer sends a declaration of avoidance via airmail to the seller in country X. A strike of the air traffic controllers which is known by both parties in country X prevents a transportation of the letter for several weeks so that the declaration of the avoidance does not reach the addressee within a reasonable time, according to Article 49(2)(a) CISG. The declaration is late since the declarer chose an inappropriate means of communication in light of the known strike. He or she cannot rely on the mitigating effect of Article 27 CISG.

1.4   Fundamental Breach

111. A fundamental breach of contract is required before a contract can be avoided. Such a breach can be committed by either the buyer or the seller.[32] There was agreement among the delegates of the Vienna Conference in regard to the core principle that the avoidance of a contract should be dependent on a serious breach of a duty, however, the formulation of the principle created difficulties.[33] The compromise which was worked out by a small ad hoc working group still leaves some doubt. Two points were particularly controversial: firstly, what constitutes the "fundamentality" of the breach and secondly, what significance "forseeability" has in regard to a fundamental breach.

1.4.1 Fundamentality

Article 25 CISG measures the fundamentality of a breach by reference to the effect on the creditor. The breach is significant if the creditor does not get substantially what he or she could have expected according to the contract. The German delegation in Vienna had pressed the subjective interest of the creditor as determinative factor and not the objective extent of the resulting (or threatened) damage. The ad hoc working group and later the plenum followed the view of the German delegation.[34] Therefore, it is not the objective weight of the breach of contract, and

---

[32] See above paras 106, 107 in regard to subsequent delivery because of non-conforming goods which, in practical terms, is nearly as significant as an avoidance of the contract (see above para 103); see in regard to passing of the risk: Art 70 CISG in first instance.

[33] Compare in regard to the history Schlechtriem in Schlechtriem/Schwenzer, *Commentary*, Art 25 para 2.

[34] Some academic writers, however, still persist that the disadvantage has to be determined according to objective criteria: compare Magnus in *Staudinger*, Art 25 paras 9, 11, 13 who categorises the

not the extent of the damage, that determines whether a breach is fundamental, rather the significance for the creditor is the key consideration. Of course, the creditor must suffer a disadvantage. The creditor does not need to prove how much damage occurred or will occur as a result of the breach, although this could be achieved by "opening the books" to show, for example, the creditor's purchases and the agreed purchase price.

1.4.2 Foreseeability

112. Often foreseeability is mistaken as a subjective fault requirement. The drafting history of the CISG is instructive as regards the function of foreseeability. The misunderstanding what the element of foreseeability in Article 25 CISG entails is evidenced in the debates to Article 25 CISG.[35] The timing of when the fundamental nature of the breach of contract has to be foreseeable is especially controversial, that is it when the contract is formed, or when the actual breach of contract occurs?[36] If the core principle of the provision is that the contracting parties' interests crystallise at the time of contract formation, as does the extent of their respective duties then foreseeability is a matter to be determined from the point of contract formation.[37]

Since it is, strictly speaking, an issue of contract interpretation and an agreement on duties, the main issues are the degree of proof and the burden of proof in regard to the significance of the breach. In other words, the party who avoids the contract has to prove that the particular duty was decisive in their decision to enter into the contract and whether the other party knew or ought to have known that. In general, the party who relies on the particular duty has to prove it. It is, therefore, desirable to explicitly regulate those duties in the contract.[38]

1.4.3 Fundamental Breach in Case of Non-performance

General Introduction

113. A fundamental breach in terms of Article 25 CISG will generally exist if, subjectively or objectively, circumstances make it impossible for the delivery of the goods to be completed. If performance is still possible and the performance is "just" delayed, then the importance of the agreed delivery date determines

---

"objective disadvantage" as a requirement additional to the subjective interest of the creditor; against this view correctly: Lurger, IHR 2001, 91.

[35] Schlechtriem in Schlechtriem/Schwenzer, *Commentary*, Art 25 para 3.

[36] See, Will in Bianca-Bonell, Art 25 para 2.2; see also Lurger, IHR 2001, 91, 92; Salger in Witz/Salger/Lorenz, Art 25 para 14.

[37] UNCITRAL CLOUT Case No 275 (24 Apr 1997) Germany *Oberlandesgericht* [Appellate Court] Düsseldorf; Gabriel, *Contracts for the Sale of Goods*, 89, 90. Huber, RabelsZ 43 (1979) 413, 463 (on the New York draft 1978), Magnus in *Staudinger*, Art 25 para 19; Schlechtriem in Schlechtriem/Schwenzer, *Commentary*, Art 25 para 15 see in regard to discussion Honnold, *Uniform Law for International Sales*, § 183; Nicholas, (1989) 105 LQR 201, 219.

[38] Salger in Witz/Salger/Lorenz, Art 25 para 14.

whether the breach is fundamental or not. If the contract is a fixed-time transaction, or if the goods are seasonal goods, a delay will generally result in a fundamental breach so that the contract can immediately be avoided (without additional time for delivery).

Example 1:   A German buyer had ordered clothes for the autumn season from an Italian seller. The delivery was supposed to occur in a number of part-deliveries between July to September. The seller failed to meet the deadline for the first delivery and only offered the last delivery on 10 November. The buyer refused to accept the late deliveries. The Court found that the buyer specifically wanted fashion for the autumn season which the Italian seller knew. The seller should have known that the buyer would not have entered the contract if she or he knew at the time of contract formation that the clothes would only arrive near the end of the autumn season. The Court, therefore, found a fundamental breach and a valid declaration of avoidance.[39]

Example 2:   A Swiss firm ordered a variety of bags, including backpacks and wallet carry-on bags, from an Italian manufacturer. The delivery was supposed to occur within 10–15 days. However, the delivery was delayed considerably. Two months after the goods had been paid for they had not been delivered and the buyer avoided the contract. The seller then made a partial delivery of one-third of the goods which the buyer refused to accept. The Court held that the parties' agreement and their conduct made it clear that the prompt delivery was a fundamental aspect of the contract. Delivery of one-third of the goods two months after contract formation and payment of the full contract price was a fundamental breach which allowed the buyer to avoid the contract as provided for in Article 51 (part performance) and Article 73 CISG (instalment contracts of part performance).[40]

114. Whether the duties were at the core of the contract or "merely" ancillary is not important: ancillary duties can also be so important for the creditor that the contract is dependent on performance of those duties. However, the importance attached to such a duty has to be proven by the creditor.[41]

Example 1:   A German shoe seller ordered shoes from an Italian manufacturer which were supposed to have the trademark, 'Marlboro', for which the German buyer had an exclusive trademark. Therefore the parties had clearly agreed (which was confirmed by witnesses at trial) that, for the buyer, the protection of the trademark was an important part of the contractual agreement. There was a prohibition on the seller

---

[39] Compare OLG Hamm (8 Dec 1980) in Magnus in Schlechtriem, Art 26 EKG No 3.

[40] Pretura di Parma-Fidenza (24 Nov 1989) CISG-online 316. More specific regulations govern cases where the question arises if and under which requirements such a partial performance has such weight that the entire contract can be avoided (see in regard to those cases below paras 191 et seq).

[41] Compare: Koch, 35, 36 et seq. The author would like to keep the distinction between primary and ancilliary duties but the author rightly recognises that the dividing line has to be drawn according to the fundamentality of a duty according to Art 25 CISG.

distributing goods with that trademark which the buyer wanted to distribute itself. The seller displayed shoes with the buyer's trademark at a shoe fair. The Court saw the display as an infringement of the ancillary duty to respect the buyer's exclusive trademark and found a fundamental breach which allowed the buyer to avoid the contract.[42]

Example 2:   A French company and a US-American buyer formed an instalment contract for 'Bonaventure' trademarked jeans which the seller was supposed to sell directly to the buyer's purchaser in South-America. The contract explicitly stipulated that the goods were not to be reimported because the seller had exclusive distribution contracts with European traders. However, the seller's jeans appeared on the Spanish market, reducing the sales of the Spanish traders. The Court held that during the contract negotiations the essential importance of the distinction between the seller's distribution areas had been made clear to the buyer so that the infringement of this agreement was a fundamental breach which allowed an avoidance of the contract for future deliveries according to Article 73(2) CISG in conjunction with Article 25 CISG.[43]

Defective Performance

115. Cases where the goods do not conform to the stipulation in the contract, particularly in regard to quality, are very difficult. To the extent that the defect can be rectified and where the seller has offered to remedy the defect within reasonable time, avoidance because of fundamental breach will rarely be a remedy available to the buyer.[44] Even if the defects cannot be rectified, the buyer may not be able to avoid the contract rather she or he may have to keep the goods and to claim damages for the disadvantage caused by the non-conformity where, for example, the defect means the goods can only be sold at a giveaway and a considerable loss results. Therefore, before the contract can be avoided, the defect has to be so severe that it cannot be rectified within a reasonable time nor can the goods be useable (or saleable) even if at a loss.[45]

Of course, despite the attempt to consolidate the principle of fundamental breach through Article 25 CISG, there is still room for the national courts and arbitral tribunals to assess the concept of fundamental breach according to the particular domestic understanding of fundamental breach, its significance in the particular national legal system, and the particular traditions which necessarily leads to slightly different approaches by different courts and tribunals. The German and the Swiss

---

[42]   OLG Frankfurt (17 Sep 1991) CISG-online 28 = NJW 1992, 633, 634.

[43]   Cour d'appel de Grenoble (22 Feb 1995) CISG-online 151 = D1995 IR 100 as well as summary in Witz/Wolter, RIW 1995, 810 et seq.

[44]   Compare Lurger, IHR 2001, 91; Magnus, *FS Schlechtriem*, 599, 602–605.

[45]   Compare instead of all the other commentators: Magnus in *Staudinger*, Art 49 para 14; Magnus, ZEuP 1995, 202, 210, 211 with references.

Supreme courts take a strict approach on fundamental breach whereas the French, Austrian, and United States courts are more flexible in finding a fundamental breach and allowing avoidance of the contract.

Example 1:   A German buyer bought a large quantity of British cobalt sulphate of specific quality from a Dutch seller. The contract required the seller to supply certificates confirming the origin and quality of the cobalt sulphate with delivery of the goods. The seller, however, supplied cobalt sulphate originating from South Africa which was not of the agreed quality. The accompanying documents were partly falsified. However, the German Supreme Court (BGH) did not find a fundamental breach by the delivery which was different from what the parties had agreed on according to Article 35 CISG. The Court held the buyer had remedies in damages and reduction in value. The buyer could sell the non-conforming goods albeit at a loss. "Avoidance" and "restitution" found the Court were last resorts under the CISG. However, the Court pointed out that the buyer could have stipulated the particular characteristics of the goods as fundamental in the contract.[46]

Example 2:   The Italian seller added sugar to wine delivered to the French buyer. According to French wine law that wine could not be sold as wine for human consumption but only as industrial alcohol. The Cour de Cassation approved the decision of the Appeal Court allowing avoidance of the contract since wine was not in conformity with the contract according to Article 35 CISG.[47]

Example 3:   A New York company delivered a portable air conditioning compressor which had a smaller cooling capacity and was using more electricity than agreed to an Italian buyer. The attempt to remedy the compressors' defects was unsuccessful. The District Court and the Court of Appeal (2nd Circuit) held that the non-conformity of the goods meant the buyer did not get what she or he could have fundamentally expected under the contract according to Article 25 CISG. Therefore, the buyer could avoid the contract due to fundamental breach.[48]

In general, as already mentioned, the defect in or the non-conformity of the goods will not be a fundamental breach if the non-conformity can be remedied. However, even if the defect can be remedied, the non-conformity of goods can be a fundamental breach if the defect cannot immediately be rectified and the time of delivery had been of essence, for example if the buyer is contractually bound to certain delivery times to his or her purchasers and the goods cannot be used for any

---

[46] BGH (3 Apr 1996) CISG-online 135 = NJW 1996, 2364.

[47] Nota bene: The Court based the avoidance of the contract on the Code Civile and not on the CISG; Cour de Cassation (23 Jan 1996) CISG-online 159 = JCP 1996 II 2234 with comment by Muir Watt; see also Witz/Wolter, RIW 1998, 278, 279.

[48] *Delchi Carrier SpA v Rotorex Corp* (6 Dec 1995) US Court of Appeals (2nd Circ) CISG-online 140 = 10 F 3rd 1024.

other purpose. By not remedying the non-conformity in a reasonable time (substitute delivery or fixing of the defect) a fundamental breach can occur. However, the emphasis is on "can". A fundamental breach does not automatically arise simply because an extension had been granted and the other party had not acted upon it.[49]

116. The question of whether the degree of non-conformity of the goods is significant also depends on the purpose the buyer has purchased the goods for and whether the seller could reasonably be aware of that purpose. The agreement between the parties is of utmost significance. The agreement ideally is evinced in the contract. However, pre-contractual negotiations and other circumstances also can play an important role in ascertaining the content of the parties' agreement.[50] The following example illustrates the importance of agreement between the parties according to the CISG. A "defect" according to product liability laws is, therefore, not the same as a "defect" or "non-conformity" which constitutes a fundamental breach according to the CISG even though it can have significant consequences.[51]

117. Common law jurisdictions, including Canada, Australia, and New Zealand have largely codified the law relating to the sale of goods, based on the original Sale of Goods Act 1893 (UK).[52] The caveat emptor rule still applies,[53] however, except where specifically modified by each jurisdiction's Sale of Goods Act(s), or other legislation. The buyer may, within a reasonable time, reject non-conforming goods, but if the contract is not severable and the buyer accepts all or part of the goods, she or he can only claim damages.[54] Common law does not provide a remedy for a buyer who acts under a mistaken assumption regarding the quality of the goods being contracted for, unless both buyer and seller act under the same mistake, and that mistake is sufficient to vitiate the parties' consent.[55] Increasingly,

---

[49] In Art 44(2) ULIS there is a possibility that allowing a reasonable time to remedy the non-conformity of the goods set up the possibility of avoidance of the contract; and in the discussion in regard to the drafting of the CISG and in the literature to its interpretation one finds the suggestion that the timing of the seller's failure to remedy the defect is of significance. This question needs further discussion and ultimately a solution. Compare foremost AC-CISG Opinion No 5 (by Schwenzer); further Schlechtriem, *FS Huber*, 565, 569 et seq. See: Tribunal of International Commercial Arbitration at the Russian Federation Chamber of Commerce and Industry (4 Apr 1998) CISG-online 1334; *Downs Investments Pty Ltd v Perjawa Steel SDN BHD* (17 Nov 2000) (SC, Queensland) CISG-online 859; *Shuttle Packaging Systems v Tsonakis INA SA et al*, US DC Michigan (17 Dec 2001) CISG-online 773; CIETAC (10 May 2005) CISG-online 1022.

[50] See paras 54 et seq in regard to the application of Art 8 CISG.

[51] Compare Hornung in Schlechtriem/Schwenzer, *Commentary*, Art 25 para 21.

[52] Repealed and replaced by the Sale of Goods Act 1979 (UK).

[53] See, for example, *Harlington & Leinster Enterprises Ltd v Christopher Hull Fine Art Ltd* [1990] 1 All ER 737 (CA).

[54] See, for example, *Sale of Goods Act 1979*, s 35(4) (UK); *Taylor v Combined Buyers Ltd* [1924] NZLR 627 (SC); *Clegg and Anor v Olle Andersson (trading as Nordic Marine)* [2003] 1 All ER (Comm) 721 (CA).

[55] McManus, *The Law of Contracts*, 531–535. See also *Lord Kennedy v Panama, New Zealand and Australian Royal Mail Co (Ltd)* (1867) LR 2 QB 580 (QB); *Bell v Lever Brothers Ltd* [1932] AC 161 (HL).

Sale of Goods Acts have been supplemented by consumer protection legislation[56] which give buyers additional remedies including the right to require the supplier to rectify the defect within a reasonable time (this may be through repair or replacement depending on the nature of the defect), and if the supplier fails to comply, the buyer may have the defect rectified elsewhere and claim damages from the supplier.[57] However, unlike Sale of Goods Acts, this type of consumer protection legislation does not apply to goods supplied for trade or commercial purposes.

1.4.4 Breach of Buyer's Obligations

117a. The buyer generally has two obligations towards the seller: first, he or she has to pay the purchase price and second, the buyer has to accept delivery of the goods.

In regard to the payment of the purchase price literature and case law suggest that a delay in payment will, by itself, only be a fundamental breach of contract in exceptional circumstances.[58] The buyer's insolvency is generally such an exceptional circumstance and should give the seller the right to avoid the contract.[59] If the buyer refuses to pay the purchase price at all, the seller must be allowed to cancel the contract.[60] The seller can fix an additional time period for the buyer to pay (Article 64(1)(b) CISG) and when that period ends the seller can avoid the contract.[61]

The buyer's definite refusal to accept delivery or the impossibility of taking delivery will, in the authors' view, generally constitute a fundamental breach of the contract. The seller must be able to free himself or herself from the contract, to on-sell the goods, and to claim damages incurred on the basis of Article 75 CISG.[62] It will depend on the agreement between the parties whether a late acceptance of delivery has such significance that the seller can avoid the contract.[63]

---

[56] See, for example, Consumer Guarantees Act 1993 (NZ). The drafting of the Act was influenced by similar legislation from other common law jurisdictions, for example: Supply of Goods and Services Act 1982 (UK); Trade Practices Act 1974 (Aus); Consumer Products Warranties Act 1977 (Sask).

[57] Hawes et al., *Butterworths Introduction to Commercial Law*, para 18.4.

[58] Compare Hager in Schlechtriem/Schwenzer, *Commentary*, Art 64 para 5; OLG Düsseldorf (17 Nov 1983) in Magnus in Schlechtriem, Art 26 EKG No 6: mere failure to observe payment dates is not a fundamental breach for the purposes of Art 10 ULIS; von Caemmerer in Dölle, Art 62 EKG para 6: an obligation to pay the purchase price with time of the essence for the contract is very rare.

[59] *Roder Zelt-und Hallen Konstruktionen GmbH v Rosedown Park Pty Ltd* and *Reginald Eustace van Doussa J 57*, FCA (Sth Australia) (28 Apr 1995) 216 et seq CISG-online 218.

[60] See von Caemmerer in Dölle, Art 62 EKG para 16; Scheifele, *Rechtsbehelfe*, 121; Schlechtriem in Schlechtriem/Schwenzer, *Commentary*, Art 25 para 22.

[61] See Schlechtriem in Schlechtriem/Schwenzer, *Commentary*, Art 64 para 8.

[62] See paras 310 et seq.

[63] Hager, *Rechtsbehelfe des Verkäufers*, 207; Schlechtriem in Schlechtriem/Schwenzer, *Commentary*, Art 25 para 23.

1.5   Specific Performance

118. Article 28 CISG allows a court or arbitral tribunal[64] to decline award to a remedy of specific performance if the court would not award specific performance under its own domestic law in respect of similar contracts of sale where governed by the CISG. Article 28 CISG is a compromise concerning the possibility of claiming specific performance and is aimed at accommodating the continental European legal systems as well as common law based legal system.[65] Specific performance is the "general" or "normal" remedy in continental European legal systems for breach of contract. It is seen as the natural consequence of the principle of pacta sunt servanda[66] that a party can demand the contractually agreed performance in case of breach of contract instead of having to rely on damages. In common law based legal systems, however, the primary remedy for breach of contract is damages.[67] The remedy of specific performance is granted only in exceptional cases, for example in the case of "commercial uniqueness" or if monetary compensation is inadequate.[68]

---

[64] General opinion is that arbitral tribunals are included in Art 28 CISG: see Müller-Chen in Schlechtriem/Schwenzer, *Commentary*, Art 28 para 8 with fn 33 for further references.

[65] See in regard to the historical background: Secretariat's Commentary OR Art 26 Nos 2, 43, 49, 51; Lando in Bianca/Bonell, Art 28 note 1.1 et seq.

[66] Müller-Chen in Schlechtriem/Schwenzer, *Commentary*, Art 28 para 1 with fn 2; see also Cuncannon, (2004) 35 VUWLR, 657.

[67] See Beatson, *Anson's Law of Contract*, 589 et seq; Paterson et al., *Principles of Contract Law*, para 26.05 et seq; Waddams, *The Law of Contracts*, paras 695 et seq; Burrows/ Finn/Todd, *Law of Contract*, 21.1 et seq; see for a good summary of the English position: Zahraa/Ghith, (2000) 15 Arab L Q, 304, 312 et seq.

[68] Compare Zweigert/Kötz, *Einführung*, 190, 480, et seq; Cuncannon, (2004) 35 VUWLR, 657; See Beatson, *Anson's Law of Contract*, 632 et seq; Paterson et al., *Principles of Contract Law*, paras 30.10 et seq; Waddams, *The Law of Contracts*, paras 665 et seq; Burrows/Finn/Todd, *Law of Contract*, 21.4.1 et seq. See also UCC § 2-716 which states that "a promise can demand performance if the parties have agreed to it, if the Court finds that the goods are unique", or "in other proper circumstances". See also in regard to the Sale of Goods Act 1979, s 52(1): Piliounis, (2000) 12 Pace Int'l L Rev 1, 10 et seq: "Section 52(1) limits specific performance to those circumstances involving 'specific' or 'ascertained' goods. In other words, section 52(1) only clearly applies to goods 'identified and agreed on at the time a contract of sale is made' or 'identified in accordance with the agreement after the time a contract of sale is made'. On its face then, section 52(1) is only meant to apply in limited circumstances involving limited types of goods. However, the mere fact that specific or ascertained goods are involved is no guarantee that the court will exercise its discretion and order specific performance, including instances where the buyer was put to significant hardship in obtaining any sort of replacement good, such as custom machinery or a ship. This discretionary approach to specific performance is, by its very nature, uncertain. A plaintiff seeking specific performance has no means of knowing whether the remedy will be granted even if successful on the merits of the case where either a unique or semi-unique good is involved." The lack of consensus over whether the SGA codifies common law, or whether remedies available under the SGA are additional to those available at common law or equity adds to the uncertainty. The potential ambiguity concerning section 52(1) SGA (it appears under the heading "Buyer's remedies", but the section itself refers to "plaintiff" and "defendant", not "buyer" and "seller") is, in practice, not an issue because the circumstances when a seller would seek specific performance will be rare. However, while it is possible to conceive of circumstances where a seller may seek specific performance, such as where changes in the market price for the goods may render a damages award speculative, it is uncertain whether the Courts are able to make such an order."

119. Article 28 CISG fulfils two functions: firstly it allows courts and tribunals to limit the enforcement of specific performance and secondly it allows the application of the foreign law alongside the CISG.

The question arises what Article 28 CISG means in practice. First, it has to be noted that Article 28 CISG is only relevant if one of the parties has a claim for which the CISG gives the party a right to claim specific performance, for example,[69] the buyer's right to delivery of the goods (Article 31 CISG), to handing over the documents (Article 34 CISG), and to transfer the property in the goods (Article 30 CISG), or the seller's right to be paid the purchase price (Article 53 CISG),[70] for the buyer to take delivery (Articles 53, 60 CISG), or for the buyer open a letter of credit.[71] Second, according to the wording of Article 28 CISG a court or tribunal can still give judgment for specific performance even though the domestic law or the lex arbitri would not recognise a claim for specific performance in the particular circumstances. However, if a court or tribunal decided not to give judgment for specific performance in cases where the CISG stipulates it, the court or tribunal can only do so in the same manner its domestic courts would do.[72]

2   Seller's Obligations

2.1   Overview

120. The seller's obligations and the buyer's interdependent obligations are outlined in Articles 30 to 44 CISG. Undoubtedly, the seller's obligations are the cornerstone of any sales contract.[73] Article 35 CISG in particular has attracted a great deal of academic and jurisprudential attention.[74] Articles 30–35 CISG state the seller's duties in regard to the time and place of delivery as well as what the seller needs to deliver (in terms of the conformity of the goods with the contract). The next four articles (Articles 37–40 CISG) describe the procedures which apply when goods are defective: the seller's right to cure defects in the goods (Article 37

---

[69] See for a more comprehensive list of examples: Müller-Chen in Schlechtriem/Schwenzer, *Commentary*, Art 28 para 6.

[70] Secretariat's Commentary OR Art 28 Nos 2, 3, Art 58 No 6; Honnold, *Uniform Law for International Sales*, § 195 et seq as well as § 348, Kastely, (1988) 63 Wash L Rev, 607, 634.

[71] Achilles, *Kommentar*, Art 28 para 2.

[72] See in regard to some of the controversy and limitations in regard to the application of Art 28 CISG: Müller-Chen in Schlechtriem/Schwenzer, *Commentary*, Art 28 paras 9–20.

[73] This is evidenced by the generally accepted rule in private international law that the seller furnishes the characteristic performance; see: *Bonaldo v AF* (29 Jun 1994) Kantonsgericht Valais, Switzerland http://cisgw3.law.pace.edu/cases; *In-line skates* case OLG Hamm (5 Nov 1997) http://cisgw3.law.pace.edu/cases/; *Paint mist vacuuming machine* case OGH (29 Mar 2004) http://cisgw3.law.pace.edu/cases; Kegel/Schurig, *Internationales Privatrecht*, 577, 578.

[74] See, for example, Schlechtriem in Schlechtriem/Schwenzer, *Commentary*, Art 35; Hyland in Schlechtriem (ed), *Einheitliches Kaufrecht*, 305–341; see further Annotated Text of CISG, Art 35 on www.cisg.law.pace.edu with further overview of case law, commentary, books and journals articles; Winship, (1995) 29 Int'l Lawyer, 525–554.

CISG) as well as the buyer's obligation to examine the goods and notify the seller of any non-conformity (Articles 38–40 CISG). Articles 41 and 43 CISG define the buyer's rights if the seller does not deliver the goods free from third party claims or intellectual property rights, and the buyer's duty to notify the seller. Article 44 CISG provides an exception to the buyer's duty to give the seller notice of the goods' non-conformity with contract.

2.2   Duty to Deliver

121. Article 30 outlines the seller's main obligations and contains "the beginnings of an obligation to cooperate"[75] with the buyer. It stipulates that the seller has to: (a) deliver the purchased goods; (b) transfer the property in the goods; and (c) hand over the documents relating to the goods.[76] Importantly, Article 30 CISG emphasises that the scope and substance of the seller's obligation are determined by the contract between the parties. That can mean, for example, that the seller's duty to transfer the property is modified and a retention of title agreed between the parties specifying how and when the transfer is to be made. How property passes from the seller to the buyer is an issue which is determined by the private international law of the forum (Article 4 (2nd s(b)) CISG), generally the lex rei sitae.[77] In general, property in the goods passes when the parties intend it to pass.[78] Unless the parties have agreed to the contrary, where there is an unconditional contract for the sale of goods in a deliverable state, property passes to the buyer when the contract is concluded, irrespective of whether payment or delivery or both are delayed.[79] This means a buyer can transfer good title to a third party, even if she or he has not paid for the goods and the goods remain in the seller's possession. For unascertained goods, property is not transferred until the act(s) required to appropriate the goods to the contract have been completed.

The substance of the seller's duty to delivery and the place of delivery are set out in more detail in Article 31 CISG.[80] Article 31 CISG is supplemented by Article

---

[75]   Enderlein/Maskow, *International Sales Law*, 127.

[76]   It has to be noted that according to the Secretariat's Commentary to the UNCITRAL draft 1978 p 40 subpara 8 (UNICTRAL, Report on Eleventh Session (1978) 10–30; the resolution of the UN General Assembly is at A/Res/33/93 (16 Dec 1978)): the purchase of documents does not fall under Art 2(d) CISG (see in regard to Art 2 CISG paras 29 et seq) and is, therefore, within the ambit of the CISG; see in regard to document trade Schlechtriem in *Symposium Frank Vischer*, www.cisg-online.ch/ publications/html.

[77]   The applicable domestic law also determines the validity of a retention of title clause. See in regard further issues in relation to retention of the clauses: Huber & Widmer in Schlechtriem/Schwenzer, *Commentary*, Art 30 para 8. See also para 37.

[78]   NZSGA 1908, s 19(1).

[79]   NZSGA 1908, s 20.

[80]   Art 31 CISG reads: "If the seller is not bound to deliver the goods at any other particular place, his obligation to deliver consists:
if the contract of sale involves carriage of the goods – in handing the goods over to the first carrier for transmission to the buyer;
if, in cases not within the preceding subparagraph, the contract relates to specific goods, or unidentified goods to be drawn from a specific stock or to be manufactured or produced, and at the time of

32 CISG which outlines the seller's additional obligations should she or he use an independent carrier for delivery.[81]

122. Article 30 CISG obliges the seller to hand over documents associated with the goods unless the parties agreed otherwise. Remarkably, the leading common law texts are relatively silent on the issue of documentation accompanying goods – this is probably because documents of title (and even transfer of possession) have little to do with delivery or transfer of property under common law or the respective Sale of Goods Acts in the UK, Canada, New Zealand, and Australia.

What documents have to be handed over is determined first and foremost by the contract itself. Furthermore, any usage applicable in accordance with Article 9 CISG, and the principle of good faith can be determinative if there is a question concerning which documents need to be handed over.[82] A contract may also contain Incoterms which include detailed rules specifying which documents have to be handed over.[83] The most important documents in practice are: bills of lading, duplicate consignment notes, delivery notes, delivery orders, transport insurance policies, and the invoices. How the property in the documents is transferred to the buyer is again a question of the applicable domestic law. Article 34 CISG sets out the time and place at which the documents are to be handed over.[84]

123. The goods delivered must conform to the contract (Article 35(1) CISG). A discrepancy between the goods delivered and the goods contracted for – peius or aliud delivery can be cured if the buyer does not give notice of the non-conformity within a reasonable time.[85] Attempts to distinguish between a delivery of defective goods and an aliud delivery are, therefore, inconsequential and should be rejected.[86] Irrespective of the objective degree of discrepancy between the goods delivered and the goods contracted for goods have been "delivered" in terms of Article 31 CISG if the requirements of Article 31 CISG are fulfilled. The buyer loses his or her remedies if he or she does not give notice to the seller within a reasonable time.

---

the conclusion of the contract the parties knew that the goods were at, or were to be manufactured or produced at a particular place – in placing the goods at the buyer's disposal at that place;

in other cases – in placing the goods at the buyer's disposal at the place where the seller had his place of business at the time of the conclusion of the contract."

[81]   The applicable domestic law will be in general determined by the lex rei sitae, see Dicey, *The Conflict of Laws,* paras 22.001–22.022.

[82]   See paras 53 et seq and 43 et seq respectively; compare Huber in Schlechtriem/ Schwenzer, *Commentary*, Art 30 para 6.

[83]   See for a list of incoterms www.iccwbo.org.

[84]   CISG, Art 34 states: "If the seller is bound to hand over documents relating to the goods, he must hand them over at the time and place and in the form required by the contract. If the seller has handed over documents before that time, he may, up to that time, cure any lack of conformity in the documents, if the exercise of this right does not cause the buyer unreasonable inconvenience or unreasonable expense. However, the buyer retains any right to claim damages as provided for in this Convention."

[85]   See paras 158 et seq.

[86]   Secretariat's Commentary OR 29 Art 29 No 3 which is slightly confusing on that point: delivery of potatoes instead of corn is non-delivery; Hyland in Schlechtriem (ed), *Einheitliches Kaufrecht,* 305; Huber & Widmer in Schlechtriem/Schwenzer, *Commentary*, Art 31 para 34.

2.3   Place of Delivery

2.3.1 Introduction

124. The place of delivery is firstly a question of an agreement between the parties. If the contract does not expressly or impliedly stipulate a place of delivery, Article 31 CISG provides for where delivery has to occur. Article 31 CISG distinguishes between carriage of goods and where the buyer is required to collect the goods. The issue of the seller's obligation to deliver are important not only in practice as regards where and how the buyer gets possession of the goods, but is also important in regard to passing of the risk for the goods. Articles 67, 68, and 69 CISG which set out the rules in regard to the passing of the risk go hand in hand with Article 31 CISG in that they also distinguish between the different categories of delivery when allocating the passing of the risk.[87]

2.3.2 Seller Hands Over Goods to Carrier

124a. Where the carriage of goods is agreed upon, the seller fulfils his or her obligation by handing the goods over to the first carrier for transmission to the buyer (Article 31(a) CISG). When the risk passes in carriage of goods contracts is set out in Article 67(1).[88] Where the goods are to be handed over to the first carrier may be set out in the contract, otherwise it is at the seller's option.[89]

2.3.3 Seller Him/Herself has to Deliver to the Buyer

124b. If the transportation of the goods is necessary, as will generally be the case, the parties can also agree on that the seller has "to perform" at the place of the buyer (or a third place). Such an agreement might be evidenced by a provision in the contract such as "delivery free to business"[90] or that the seller is supposed to use its own staff to complete delivery.[91]

---

[87] See in regard to CISG, Artt 67–69 paras 225 et seq.

[88] CISG, Art 67(1) reads: "If the contract of sale involves carriage of the goods and the seller is not bound to hand them over at a particular place, the risk passes to the buyer when the goods are handed over to the first carrier for transmission to the buyer in accordance with the contract of sale. If the seller is bound to hand the goods over to a carrier at a particular place, the risk does not pass to the buyer until the goods are handed over to the carrier at that place. The fact that the seller is authorized to retain documents controlling the disposition of the goods does not affect the passage of the risk."

[89] Compare Huber & Widmer in Schlechtriem/Schwenzer, *Commentary*, Art 31 para 5.

[90] Compare in regard to German clause "Lieferung frei Haus" ("delivery free to residence") OLG Köln (16 Jul 2001) CISG-online 609 = IHR 2001, 66 where the Court took a narrower view and held that clause only meant that the buyer did not have to bear the cost of the delivery.

[91] Compare LG Freiburg (13 May 2005) CISG-online 1199 (interpretation of Art 5 EuGVO and Art 31 CISG); compare also UCC §§ 2–503, 2–504, which sets out the seller's obligations in regard to the delivery of the goods. According to the UCC party agreement in regard to delivery is paramount. In the absence of a party agreement, normal commercial practice requires the buyer to take delivery of the goods at the seller's place of business. See for a more detailed discussion: Gabriel, *Contracts for the Sale of Goods*, 111 et seq.

2.3.4 Buyer has to Collect

If the contract for the sale of goods does not require the carriage of goods, and the parties have not agreed on a specific place of delivery, the place of delivery is where the seller makes the goods available to the buyer to collect.[92]

125. Articles 31(b) and (c) CISG set out in what way the seller has to make to the goods available. Article 31(b) CISG provides for four different scenarios:[93]

1. The contract of sales concerns specific goods and, at the time of the conclusion of the contract, both parties are aware of the location of those goods.[94]

2. The contract for sale of goods concerns a specific stock, for example, a tun of wine, the content of an oil tank, or the cargo of a ship which has berthed; a specific quantity has been sold from that stock; both parties are aware, when the contract is concluded, where the stock is located.

3. The sales contract concerns goods which have yet to be manufactured by the seller or a third party and both parties know at the time of contracting where the manufacturing will take place.

4. The sales contract concerns items yet to be produced and both parties know at the time of contracting where the production will take place, for example, cotton from a plantation, timber from a forest, or gravel from a quarry. Article 31(b) CISG is also applicable in regard to floating goods.

126. If the requirements of Article 31(b) CISG are not fulfilled and if the contract does not require the goods to be transported, and if no particular place of delivery has been agreed upon, Article 31(c) CISG stipulates that the seller has to make the goods available at his or her place of business. If the seller has more than one place of business, the place of business is the one which has the "closest relationship" to the contract (Article 10(a) CISG) at the time of the conclusion of the contract.[95] The buyer's habitual residence at the time of the conclusion of the contract is determinative if the seller has no place of business (Article 10(b) CISG). "Making the goods available" means that the goods have to be available in such a manner that the buyer merely has to take possession of them.

127. "Making available" generally encompasses that the seller, for example, has separated the goods from the bulk stock or has at least identified the goods in a way which links the goods to the buyer, as well as preparing the goods for collection, for example by wrapping them, and informing the buyer that the goods are ready. If the separation of the goods from a bulk stock is possible at the time the buyer or a person authorised by the buyer arrives at the seller's business the goods

---

[92] Compare CISG, Art 31(c).
[93] See Huber & Widmer in Schlechtriem/Schwenzer, *Commentary*, Art 31 para 46.
[94] Cases where the seller will be unaware where the goods are will be rare. In practice, it is buyer's awareness or knowledge which will be significant.
[95] See CISG, Art 10 paras 9, 10.

need to be separated from the bulk at that point.[96] If the goods are securely stored (deposited), the seller might have to order their release.[97]

128. If Incoterms apply to the contract, the place of delivery might differ from the one required under Article 31 CISG.[98] The suggestion that interpretation guidelines for the Incoterms be drafted was not well received in Vienna.[99] Issues in regard to the interpretation of Incoterms, however, can be solved by applying Article 8 CISG.[100]

2.3.5 Seller's Obligations during Transport

129. If the seller has to transport the goods in accordance with Article 31(a) CISG ("carriage of goods") then Article 32 CISG sets out the seller's further obligations unless the parties agreed on alternative terms. First, the seller has to conclude all the contracts necessary for the carriage of the goods. What contracts are necessary depends on the individual circumstances (Article 32(2) CISG). Whether the seller has to insure the goods depends on the terms of the contract and normal trade usage concerning transport requirements.[101] The seller has to provide the buyer with all information if the buyer needs, so that the buyer can insure the goods himself or herself (Article 32(3) CISG). If the goods sold or their packaging are not marked distinctively at the time they are handed over to the carrier, for example, by way of carrier documents, seals, stamps or signs, and their attribution to the sales contract could be difficult, the seller has to make the good identifiable by notice of consignment when handing them over to the carrier (Article 32(1) CISG). A breach of that duty prevents the passing of the risk at that time (Article 67(2) CISG). It can also mean that the buyer has remedies for breach of contract. Contracts, standard forms, and standard contracts used in the trade often contain notice requirements which are far more extensive than Article 32(1) CISG.[102]

2.3.6 Jurisdiction of the Courts and Place of Performance

129a. The place of performance under Article 31 CISG is not only of significance as part of the contractual matrix set out in the CISG but it also establishes

---

[96] Huber & Widmer in Schlechtriem/Schwenzer, *Commentary*, Art 31 para 50; Piltz, *Internationales Kaufrecht*, § 4 para 26; Karollus in Honsell, Art 31 para 34; but see Secretariat's Commentary OR Art 29 No 16 ("normally" the case).

[97] It has to be noted though that frequently documents handed to the buyer will contain the release claims for the goods already. Another example is that the seller has agreed to store the goods for the buyers. The delivery takes place in those circumstances where the buyer could have taken possession and the storage agreement becomes effective; Huber & Widmer in Schlechtriem/ Schwenzer, *Commentary*, Art 31 para 50.

[98] See in detail Huber & Widmer in Schlechtriem/Schwenzer, *Commentary*, Art 31 paras 72–75.

[99] Schlechtriem, *Einheitliches UN-Kaufrecht*, 53, 54.

[100] See in regard to Art 8 CISG paras 54 et seq.

[101] Compare Huber & Widmer in Schlechtriem/Schwenzer, *Commentary*, Art 32 paras 26, 27 for further discussion of Incoterms.

[102] Compare Huber & Widmer in Schlechtriem/Schwenzer, *Commentary*, Art 32 paras 7, 13.

jurisdiction in certain circumstances. If the jurisdiction of a court is determined by the place of performance and if such a place is determined in accordance with the law applicable to the contract, the procedural question of jurisdiction is determined by the CISG's substantive rules on the place of performance (if the CISG is applicable to the contract). Examples, where the place of performance can determine jurisdiction are: Article 5(1) of the Brussels Regulation[103] and Article 5(1) of the Lugano Convention[104] as well as § 29 ZPO (Germany) and Article 113 IPRG (Switzerland).

2.4 Time of Delivery

130. The seller must deliver the goods within a reasonable time period after the conclusion of the contract (Article 33(c) CISG) unless the parties have agreed otherwise (Article 33(a) CISG). Article 33(b) CISG contemplates that a time period has been agreed upon between seller and buyer. Within that period either the buyer or the seller can choose the time of delivery.

Example: The German buyer ordered clothes from the Italian seller which were to be delivered in July, August, and September. The seller made the first delivery at the end of September. An interpretation of the time of delivery in accordance with Article 8 CISG foun'd that a third of the goods had to be delivered each month at a time determined by the seller in July, August and September but not the entire goods at the end of September.[105]

The time at which the goods have to be delivered is either determined by the parties' agreement on a specific date, by an agreement which allows the time at which the goods have to be delivered to be determined, or by the buyer who, according to the contract, has the right within an agreed time to determine the time of delivery of the goods. If the seller then does not perform by the agreed time the buyer can demand immediate delivery. Furthermore, the buyer can also claim damages for the loss she or he has incurred because of the late delivery without prior warning. The buyer does not have to accept early delivery (Article 52(7) CISG). However, if the buyer accepts early delivery then this constitutes performance of the contract.

130a. The contract can also allow the seller to determine the time of delivery or collection after the contract has been concluded. Generally, the seller will have a specified period within which the delivery time must be determined. If the seller does not determine the delivery date within that agreed time period, the seller

---

[103] Former Convention on Jurisdiction and the Enforcement of Judgments in Civil and Commercial Matters (27 Sep 1968); Council Regulation (EC) 44/2001 on the Jurisdiction and the Recognition and Enforcement of Judgments in Civil and Commercial Matters.

[104] Convention on Jurisdiction and the Enforcement of Judgments in Civil and Commercial Matters (16 Sep 1988) [1988] OJ L 319, 9–48.

[105] Compare AG Oldenburg (24 Apr 1990) CISG-online 20 = IPRax 1991, 313. The Court did not find a fundamental breach since the buyer had not set an additional time period.

breaches one of his or her contractual obligations and the buyer can withhold the purchase price.[106] If the seller does not determine the delivery date, this may be the first step towards the seller's breach of contract.[107] If the parties have not agreed on a delivery time, the seller has to deliver within a reasonable time after the conclusion of the contract (Article 33(c) CISG). If that time has passed a breach of the seller's obligation to deliver may have occurred.

2.5   Handing Over of Documents

131. Article 34(1st s) CISG provides that the contract between the parties is determinative in regard to the place, the time, and the method of delivery of the documents related to the goods sold. Trade practices and usage have to be taken into account. If the seller hands over the documents before the agreed time of delivery the seller can remedy any defect in the documents, such as the handing over of a ship owner's bill of lading instead of the required shipped bill of lading, or generally incomplete documents, unless that would cause the buyer unreasonable inconvenience and/or expense (Article 34(2nd s) CISG).[108] The buyer retains his or her right to claim damages from the seller who fixes the defects in the documents (Article 34(3rd s) CISG). Article 34(3rd s) CISG corresponds with Article 37 CISG (early delivery of goods which do not conform to the contract). After the delivery deadline has passed the seller only has a right to remedy any failure to perform his or her obligation or to hand over the documents if the requirements of Article 48 CISG are met.[109]

---

[106] Above para 42d.

[107] See paras 269 et seq.

[108] Examples of defects in documents are discussed in Huber & Widmer in Schlechtriem/ Schwenzer, *Commentary*, Art 34 para 8: a discrepancy between the invoice and the price under the contract (compare Comisíon para la Protección del Comercio Exterior de Mexico (29 Apr 1996) CISG-online 350 = (1998) 17 J Law & Comm, 427).

[109] CISG, Art 48 reads:
"(1) Subject to article 49, the seller may, even after the date for delivery, remedy at his own expense any failure to perform his obligations, if he can do so without unreasonable delay and without causing the buyer unreasonable inconvenience or uncertainty of reimbursement by the seller of expenses advanced by the buyer. However, the buyer retains any right to claim damages as provided for in this Convention.
(2) If the seller requests the buyer to make known whether he will accept performance and the buyer does not comply with the request within a reasonable time, the seller may perform within the time indicated in his request. The buyer may not, during that period of time, resort to any remedy which is inconsistent with performance by the seller.
(3) A notice by the seller that he will perform within a specified period of time is assumed to include a request, under the preceding paragraph, that the buyer make known his decision.
(4) A request or notice by the seller under paragraph (2) or (3) of this article is not effective unless received by the buyer."
Compare Huber & Widmer in Schlechtriem/Schwenzer, *Commentary*, Art 34 para 6.

2.6   Conformity of the Goods

132. Chapter 2 Section 2 is entitled "Conformity of the Goods and Third Party Claims". This Section is probably the most frequently referred to in any commentary or text book on the CISG since it contains Article 35 CISG which sets out when goods are deemed to conform to the contract. It is one of the key provisions of the CISG. Section 2 also contains the obligations the buyer needs to comply with to be able to claim his or her rights under the CISG, for example the buyer's obligation to give notice about the non-conformity (Article 39 CISG). Further, Section 2 specifies the seller's obligation to deliver goods free from defects in title or third party claims based on intellectual property rights.[110]

The key concept of "lack of conformity" includes differences in quality, quantity, delivery of an aliud, and packaging. The CISG differs from most domestic laws which make more subtle distinctions between the different kinds of defects. Swiss law, for example, differentiates between the ordinary characteristics of goods (Sacheigenschaft) and a specific warranty that particular characteristics exist (Zusicherung);[111] the Austrian law distinguish between peius and aliud[112] English law differentiates between conditions and warranties[113] and the UCC acknowledges express and implied warranties:[114] It is important to be aware of the different approaches in domestic law and not to succumb to the danger of interpreting "conformity" in line with the domestic law instead of in accordance with the CISG.[115]

2.6.1   *Conformity of Goods due to Contractual Requirements*

133. Defects in regard to either quality or quantity can form the basis of the goods' non-conformity with the contract.[116] The agreement between parties in regard to the goods, ie the contract, is decisive if questions arise over whether the goods conform or not. Article 35(1) CISG states:

> The seller must deliver goods which are of the quantity, quality, and description required by the contract and which are contained or packaged in the manner required by the contract.

The conformity of the goods with the contract is not determined objectively but depends first and foremost on the "subjective" description of the goods in the

---

[110] See CISG, Artt 41 and 42 respectively, see paras 163 et seq.

[111] See OR, Art 197.

[112] Schwenzer in Schlechtriem/Schwenzer, *Commentary*, Art 35 para 4.

[113] Sale of Goods Act 1979 (UK), ss 14, 15.

[114] UCC, §§ 2-313 et seq; note that some US academic literature sees Art 35(1) CISG corresponding with express warranties whereas Art 35(2) is seen to correspond with implied warranties: Hyland in Schlechtriem (ed), *Einheitliches Kaufrecht*, 308, 312.

[115] Schwenzer in Schlechtriem/Schwenzer, *Commentary*, Art 35 para 4.

[116] See in regard to the fact that also defects in regard to quantity can constitute "non-conformity": Schlechtriem, *Internationales UN-Kaufrecht*, para 132; Schwenzer in Schlechtriem/Schwenzer, *Commentary*, Art 35 para 8 who notes that a defect in regard to quantity might not be seen as a lack of conformity if such a discrepancy is permitted in the particular trade sector and usual in that particular trade sector.

contract. The same is true in regard to packaging. The CISG, therefore, unequivocally adheres to the concept of "subjective defect".[117]

Example: The buyer agreed to purchase from the seller 200 tons of Pre
                  Suspension Resin ("F622") produced by US Formosa Plastics Corp
                  at a unit price of RMB 790/ton CFR Huangpu Port, China. The total
                  price of the goods is RMB 158000. Three percent more or less in
                  quantity and total price is allowed, subject to the seller's discretion.
                  When the goods arrived the buyer discovered that the goods that
                  were delivered were compliant to "H622" instead of "F622",
                  however, was not suitable for what the buyer wanted to use the PVC
                  suspension resin for. (However, objectively they conformed to a
                  resin of "H622" standard.)[118]

The use of the concept of "subjective defect" is not exclusive to the CISG but
also used in various domestic legal systems.[119] The agreement between the parties
means the seller's contractual obligations can include the requirement to supply
goods with characteristics, which at the time of the agreement, cannot be manufactured because the "know how" is missing.

Example: A Swedish building business bought from a German manufacturer
                  of chemical products pink batts which according to the contract
                  were supposed to have a certain insulation capacity. It was techni-
                  cally not possible to manufacture the agreed insulation capacity at
                  the time of contract conclusion. The seller breached the contract since
                  if the seller promises something which is impossible he or she has to
                  take responsibility for it.

134. Agreements in regard to the characteristics of the goods do not need a special emphasis. However, special emphasis on the characteristics or particular aspects
of the characteristics of the goods could be beneficial in lowering the threshold for
a fundamental breach and assist in fulfilling the requirements for the avoidance of
the contract in accordance with Article 49(1)(a) CISG and the requirements for a
substitute delivery (Article 46(2) CISG).[120] Often the agreement between the
parties will have to be interpreted in accordance with Article 8 CISG in order to
ascertain what characteristics the parties have agreed upon. When interpreting the
agreement between the parties, the seller's public statements or third party
statements in regard to the quality of the goods, as well as the seller's advertising,
also have to be taken into account. Those can potentially become part of the
agreed characteristics of the goods.

---

[117] Schwenzer in Schlechtriem/Schwenzer, *Commentary*, Art 35 para 6 with fn 16a.

[118] Compare CIETAC (7 Apr 1997) http://cisg3.law.pace.edu.

[119] For example see § 434 BGB (Germany) Schlechtriem, *Schuldrecht BT*, para 33; for French law
Abderrahmane, *Droit et Pratique Du Commerce International*, 1989, 551, 553; for Switzerland:
Honsell, *OR BT*, 74; for Austria: Koziol/Welser, *Grundriß des bürgerlichen Rechts*, 253.

[120] See para 117.

Goods do not conform to the contract if they are an aliud (that is different goods from what was agreed upon), however material the discrepancy might be.[121] The wording of Article 35(1) CISG makes it clear that any divergence from the quantity constitutes a lack of conformity with the contract; so the delivery of too great a quantity is, therefore, a "defective" delivery.[122] It has to be noted that the CISG also does not draw a distinction between lacks of conformity resulting from the ordinary characteristics of the goods and because of a defect in title.[123] However, the difference becomes important in regard to the exclusion of liability on account of the buyer's awareness of lack of conformity. Under Article 35(3) CISG the seller is not liable for the non-conformity of the goods if the buyer could not have been unaware of a lack of conformity. If the goods have a defect in their title, however, the seller is not liable for the defect only if the buyer consented to take the goods subject to a third party claim.[124]

2.6.2 CISG's Standard of Conforming Goods

135. Parties rarely agree in detail on all characteristics of the goods in a contract. The CISG, therefore, sets out ancillary objective rules and standards which apply if the parties have neither explicitly nor impliedly agreed on the characteristic in question, that is the intention of the parties cannot be ascertained in accordance with Article 8 CISG. Paragraphs (a)–(d) of Article 35(2) CISG contain five "objective" standards: the goods have to be fit for the purpose for which the goods would ordinarily be used (Article 35(2)(a) CISG) fit for a particular purpose (Article 35(2)(b) CISG) resemble a sample or model (Article 35(2)(c) CISG) to be packaged in a usual or adequate way (Article 35(d) CISG).

Article 35(2) CISG should be seen as a continuum of the parties' presumed intention. Article 35(2) CISG sets out what reasonable parties would have agreed upon had they put their mind to it. This is important since it means that the first inquiry has to be what the parties agreed upon and only if that inquiry is not satisfactory is Article 35(2) CISG applicable.

136. The "ordinary purpose" of goods of the same description (Article 35(2)(a) CISG) is ascertained in accordance with the objective view of a person in the trade sector concerned. A first, very superficial, division can be drawn from the type of goods and the buyer himself or herself. The ordinary purpose, for example, might be determinable depending on whether the goods are supposed to be consumed by the buyer (such as commodities, materials, parts), or to be used by the buyer (for example, machines), or whether the goods are supposed to be sold on. Market

---

[121] Compare in regard to aliud delivery and the explicit mentioning in Art 33(1)(b) ULIS and BGH (2 Jun 1982) NJW 1982, 2730; Schwenzer in Schlechtriem/Schwenzer, *Commentary*, Art 35 paras 2, 32.

[122] Compare in regard to a delivery which exceeded the agreed quality the wrong decision of the Cour de Cassation, Witz/Wolter, RIW 1995, 810, 813.

[123] Compare BGH (15 Feb 1995) CISG-online 149 = NJW 1995, 2101 (translated in parts http://www.iuscomp.org); see Schwenzer in Schlechtriem/Schwenzer, *Commentary*, Art 35 para 5.

[124] See CISG, Art 41 and paras 163 et seq.

expectation concerning the way in which the goods can be (ordinarily) be used is dependent on various factors such as traditions, culture, economic circumstances, or legal requirements. Public law provisions, such as the regulatory approval for machines, permitted or prohibited additives in food or cosmetics controlling the usage of the goods in the particular market are directly relevant. Whether the public law provisions in question have been validly implemented or could be challenged is not decisive – what is important is whether in practice the public law provisions do influence market expectation concerning how the goods will be ordinarily used.

Example: A public authority issues a ban on the consumption and the sale of certain foods because the authority mistakenly assumes that unhealthy additives are added to the foods. The authority issues the ban without having any legal basis. As they cannot be sold, it is not fit for purpose for which goods are ordinarily used.

137. The standard "fit for ordinary use" criterion will be often difficult to apply in international markets or markets which are not homogenous: what is a delicacy in one country might be considered inedible in another and, therefore, will not be able to be sold in that country. Manuals and safety instructions for technical goods might be in one country the norm but in another country that might be very expensive or a luxury.[125] If such differences exist, then an objective measure for deciding whether the goods are fit for ordinary use is required. If one interprets Articles 35(2)(a) and (b) CISG only as a stipulation of implied party intention, then this might lead to the result that the parties agreed on the ordinary use of the goods in a particular country.

137a. Article 35(2)(a) CISG does not stipulate whether the goods have to be of average quality to be fit for average purpose which many domestic legal systems require.[126] The Canadian proposal to include a reference to "average" in Article 35 CISG, was dropped after consultation with representatives of the other common law countries.[127] Differences in interpretation over what standard the goods have to meet are likely. English courts will probably use "merchantability"[128] (whether the goods can be resold) as a benchmark, whereas Continental European and the US American courts will probably interpret Article 35(2)(a) CISG as requiring goods to be of average quality.

In 2002, a Netherlands Arbitration Institute arbitral award held that the quality required to be delivered under Article 35(2)(a) CISG was "reasonable" quality. "Reasonable" quality is defined as what the buyer could justifiably expect.[129]

---

[125] See in regard to a discussion of the methodoly of Art 35(2)(a) CISG in regard to what should be taken into account: DiMatteo/Dhooge/Greene/Maurer/Pagnattaro, *International Sales Law*, 116–118.

[126] Germany § 243(1) BGB, § 360 HGB; Switzerland Art 71(2) OR; France Art 1246 Cc; USA §§ 2–314(2)(b) UCC.

[127] Schwenzer in Schlechtriem/Schwenzer, *Commentary*, Art 35 para 15.

[128] *Cehave NV v Bremer Handelsgesellschaft mbH, The Hansa Nord* [1976] QB 44 but see also SSGA 1994 (UK), s 14(2) which replaced "merchantability" with "satisfactory condition" in the SGA 1979 (UK) which is based on the buyer's reasonable expectation. See in regard to a comparison between English sales law and the CISG: Bridge, *International Sale of Goods*, 12.15.

[129] Netherlands Arbitration Institute (15 Oct 2002) CISG-online 780 paras 71, 108.

138. The seller only has to deliver goods for a purpose other than the purpose for which they would ordinarily be used if that purpose was expressly or impliedly made known to the seller at the time of the conclusion of the contract, the buyer relied on the seller's skill and judgment, and if it was reasonable for the buyer to do so. Article 35(2)(b) CISG is modelled on section 14(3) Sale of Goods Act 1979 (UK) and § 2–135 UCC.[130] But, if the parties expressly or impliedly agreed upon a particular purpose, that purpose has become part of the characteristics of the goods in accordance with Article 35(1) CISG. In practice, however, the classification of the purpose under Articles 35(1) or 35(2)(b) CISG is irrelevant. It illustrates the function of Article 35(2) CISG as an interpretation tool which comes to play if the intention of the parties cannot be ascertained from the contract itself, with or without the help of the interpretation tools provided for in Article 8 CISG.[131]

A particular purpose can derive from the buyer's individual circumstances and the way in which the goods will be used. Examples are: special production requirements in the buyer's factory; particular climate conditions where the goods will be used (high humidity, very cold temperatures, unsealed roads etc); or public law requirements in the country where the goods will be used.[132] How explicit the buyer has to be in making the seller aware of the particular purpose is uncertain.[133] In the authors' view it should be enough that the seller could reasonably have derived the goods' particular purpose from the circumstances.[134]

139. As has been mentioned earlier,[135] the use of goods for an ordinary purpose or a particular purpose can depend on public law provisions, especially safety regulations or cultural traditions and the general world view which can be different in the seller's and buyer's country.

Example 1:   A Swiss export company sold New Zealand mussels to a German company. The mussels had a cadmium level. The German company claimed that the cadmium level was too high and unlawful under the German Good Safety laws. The buyer, therefore, avoided the contract. The seller claimed that the cadmium level of the mussels was within the allowed levels of the Swiss law. The BGH held that the adherence to particular public law provisions in the buyer's country

---

[130] See in regard to a discussion about similarities and differences to the UK SGA 1979 Bridge, *International Sale of Goods*, 12.14, 12.15; in regard to the US Gabriel, *Contracts for the Sale of Goods*, 121–128.

[131] See paras 54 et seq for Art 8 CISG.

[132] Schwenzer in Schlechtriem/Schwenzer, *Commentary*, Art 35 para 19; see also in regard to public law requirements para 139.

[133] Magnus in *Staudinger*, Art 35 para 28 with further references; in detail see also Schwenzer in Schlechtriem/Schwenzer, *Commentary*, Art 35 para 21.

[134] Magnus in *Staudinger*, Art 35 para 28; Karollus, *UN-Kaufrecht*, 117; Strohbach in Enderlein/Maskow/Strohbach, *Internationales Kaufrecht*, Art 35 note 11; Schwenzer in Schlechtriem/Schwenzer, *Commentary*, Art 35 para 21.

[135] See paras 137, 138.

or the country where the goods were to be used cannot generally be expected from the seller.[136]

Example 2:   The buyer which had its business in Louisiana/USA bought from the Italian seller mammogram machines which did not comply with the American safety standards (but the Italian standards). The machines were seized in the USA. The buyer avoided the contract and claimed damages. The US District Court which had to decide the arbitral award expressly approved of the decision of the BGH in the New Zealand mussels case (example No 1). It also noted with approval the special circumstances the BGH laid out in the judgment. The Court held that the machines did not conform to the American safety standard (and that the non-conformity was a fundamental breach in accordance with Article 25 CISG).[137]

Example 3:   The German company, V, sold juice which contained alcohol to the company, K, which has its business in an Islamic country. In that country no state indorsed but a religious alcohol prohibition exists. The buyer avoids the contract because the juice was not fit for being sold because of its alcohol content. The seller points out the German standards in regard to fruit drinks with alcohol content. Since in the example the prohibition is a religious one and not a state one the BGH's decision in the New Zealand mussels case that the seller cannot be held accountable for the public law prohibitions in the buyer's country has to apply in this case.

Example 4:   The Belgian seller supplied pork to the German buyer; the pork was delivered to a client of the buyer. That client on-sold the pork to another purchaser in Bosnia-Herzegovina. It was not until when the pork arrived in Bosnia-Herzegovina Germany issued a regulation which basically prohibited the trade with Belgian pork because of suspicions concerning dioxin contamination of Belgian pork. Belgian subsequently issued an equivalent regulation. At the time the risk in the pork passed, however, there was no restriction on the trade in pork in Belgium. The seller claimed the unpaid balance of the purchase price. The buyer defended the claim, arguing that the pork was defective since it may have been contaminated by dioxin. The Court held that not withstanding the absence of public law restrictions in the export country at the time the risk in the pork passed, a reasonable suspicion that the pork was contaminated by dioxin existed and that was enough, held the Court, to constitute non-conformity with the contract.[138]

---

[136] BGH (8 Mar 1995) CISG-online 144 = NJW 1995, 2099 (NZ mussels case); also OGH (13 Apr 2000) CISG-online 576; OGH (25 Jan 2001) CISG-online 1223 = IHR 2006, 110 et seq; Schlechtriem, IPRax 1999, 388 et seq; Lurger, IHR 2001, 91, 99 et seq.

[137] *Medical Marketing International, Inc v Internazionale Medico Scientifico SRL* US District Court (ED Louisiana) (17 May 1999) CISG-online 387; case note of that judgment by Schlechtriem, IPRax 1999, 388.

[138] Compare BGH (2 Mar 2005) CISG-online 999 = IHR 2005, 158 et seq = JZ 2005, 844 et seq with discussion by Schlechtriem at JZ 2005 846–848.

How to answer the question which standard applies where the seller's country and the buyer's country have public law regulations which impact differently on the goods is difficult from a legal-political point of view.[139] A solution cannot be found by giving preference to either the seller's standards or the buyer's standards. Unless the parties have agreed on the applicable standard, the purpose for which the goods will be used is decisive. The purpose will depend significantly on the country where the goods will be used and its standards. That country can be the buyer's country or a third country to which goods are supposed to be exported. The seller, however, has to have knowledge of the third country.[140] This solution draws on the one stipulated in Article 42(1) CISG concerning goods which may be subject to intellectual property restrictions. The solution stipulated in Article 42(1) CISG is an evaluation of the issue.[141] In regard to intellectual property restrictions the seller, as the BGH held in the mussels case, cannot know the public law prohibitions of the buyer's country, or the country where the goods will be used, and that has to be acknowledged (Article 42(1) CISG), but only insofar as the buyer cannot claim that he or she relied on the seller's skill and judgment (Article 35(2)(b) CISG).[142] If the public law provisions are particularly unusual and are unknown in the buyer's country, or in the country in which the goods are to be used, it cannot be assumed that the buyer relied on the seller's skill and judgment. The buyer can only rely on the seller's skill and judgment in those circumstances if the buyer has notified the seller of the special conditions of use of the goods before the conclusion of the contract. Otherwise large export companies could be required to get information on, or to expressly include in their contracts the standards of the export country (which often happens in practice). The seller is protected if the seller informs the buyer about the permitted characteristics and usual characteristics of his/her goods before the contract was concluded, or the buyer could not have been unaware of them (Article 35(3) CISG).[143] Cases such as example 3 can be solved with the help of rules set out in this paragraph, notwithstanding whether the alcohol content in food is unlawful in the buyer's country or whether the fruit juice (with alcohol) cannot be sold because of the immanent religious prohibition.

140. The buyer's specification of the goods' particular purpose puts the seller's duties in more concrete terms. The seller's non-fault liability is determined by those duties (Article 79(1) CISG).[144] This is hard for those sellers who do not have the necessary skill and judgment to assess whether the goods are fit for the particular purpose the buyer wants to use them for. Despite that "unfair" risk, the seller

---

[139] Compare in addition to fn 553 Koller/Stalder, *FS Gauch*, 477–492 especially 487 et seq with multiple further references; Koller/Stadler, recht 2004, 10–21.

[140] OGH (25 Jan 2006) CISG-online 1223 circumvents this issue on the facts.

[141] It has to be noted that the BGH in the pork case, (example 4); decided in the proposed manner. The BGH has verbally followed its decision in the New Zealand mussels case, that only the public law of the export country is determinative despite the fact that in the particular case this was unnecessary since in the exporting country as well as the buyer's country a suspicion that the meat was contaminated with dioxin existed which made the meat not tradeable.

[142] See also para 140.

[143] See paras 143, 144.

[144] See para 288 et seq.

is liable. Article 35(2)(b) CISG intends a modification of the seller's liability only in cases where the buyer has not relied on the seller's skill and judgement or it was unreasonable for the buyer to do so. Article 35(2)(b) CISG, therefore, carefully delineates the seller's liability and allows the circumstances in each individual case to be taken into account. The doctrinal justification for the differentiation can be found in the fact that Article 35(2) CISG articulates assumed party agreement.

141. If the seller uses a model or a sample of the goods during contract negotiations, the parties impliedly agree that the goods will possess the qualities of that sample or model (Article 35(2)(c) CISG). However, the presentation of the sample or model "without any obligation" allows the seller to avoid liability.[145] Also, the requirement concerns the seller's use of a model or a sample, and not the buyer's. Article 35(2)(c) CISG is not applicable if the buyer refers to an order sample. If the buyer uses an order sample it has to be ascertained whether the characteristics of that sample have been agreed upon impliedly and if the requirements of Article 35(1) CISG have been met.

142. According to Article 35(2)(d) CISG, the packaging is part of the characteristic of the goods. The goods have to be packaged in the way typical for the particular kind of goods, and/or by the packaging typical in the particular trade. The purpose of packaging, the protection of the goods, need to be taken into account.[146] If objective standards are not in place in regard to the packaging then the packaging, has to be adequate. For example, the kind of goods, the time and kind of transport, the climate are all factors which have to be taken into account.[147]

2.6.3 The Buyer Knows or Ought to have Known (Article 35(3) CISG)

143. The seller is not liable for the implied characteristics in accordance with Article 35(2) CISG if the buyer knew or could not have been unaware of the lack of conformity of the goods (Article 35(3) CISG). "Could not have been unaware" is generally understood to mean gross negligence.[148] However, a duty on the buyer to inspect the goods at the time of contract conclusion cannot be implied from Article 35(3) CISG.[149]

144. The caveat in Article 35(3) CISG only applies to cases of lack of conformity under Article 35(2) CISG, not to contractually-agreed qualities of the goods

---

[145] Compare Schwenzer in Schlechtriem/Schwenzer, *Commentary*, Art 35 para 26.

[146] Compare Schwenzer in Schlechtriem/Schwenzer, *Commentary*, Art 35 para 29.

[147] See Schwenzer in Schlechtriem/Schwenzer, *Commentary*, Art 35 para 31.

[148] Compare Magnus in *Staudinger*, Art 35 para 48; Schwenzer in Schlechtriem/Schwenzer, *Commentary*, Art 35 para 34 "denotes more than gross negligence"; Honnold, *Uniform Law for International Sales*, § 229; Huber, RabelsZ 43 (1979) 413, 479.

[149] General opinion in the literature: Magnus in *Staudinger*, Art 35 para 48; Honnold, *Uniform Law for International Sales*, § 229; Hyland in Schlechtriem (ed), *Einheitliches Kaufrecht*, 325.

or their packaging under Article 35(1) CISG.[150] In the literature this is sometimes disputed.[151] The interpretation of Article 35(3) CISG favoured by the authors is appropriate since if the buyer and seller agree on the goods' characteristics, the buyer can rely on the seller to rectify any non-conformity in the goods before the passing of the risk even if the buyer knew about the lack of conformity at the time of the conclusion of the contract. Also, the lack of knowledge based on gross negligence does not remove the buyer's rights since the buyer must be able to rely on the agreement between the parties as to the characteristics of the goods. It has to be determined on a case by case basis whether the characteristics of the goods delivered were agreed upon for the purposes of Article 35(1) CISG.[152] Where the lack of conformity cannot be rectified and the buyer knew or could not have been unaware of an insistence on compliance with the contract, only in this case does the doctrine of venire contra factum proprium.[153]

It has to be noted that in practical terms Article 35(3) CISG is not applicable to Article 35(2)(c) CISG. If the buyer buys goods according to a sample or a model the buyer cannot be unaware of any defects.

2.6.4 Determinative Time for the Characteristic

145. The determinative period of time when the characteristics of the goods have to be present for Article 35 CISG is the passing of the risk (Article 36(1) CISG). Once the risk is passed, and the buyer has not given notice of the lack of conformity, the buyer has the burden of proof that the goods lacked conformity before the passing of the risk.[154] When the lack of conformity was noticeable is of no importance. Difficulties arise in regard to guarantees[155] and their interpretation, especially warranties in regard to the durability of the goods. Two questions have to be differentiated: first, the meaning of guarantee and, second, the issue of the period of time for which the goods have to be fit for their purpose.[156]

146. First, it has to be determined through interpretation what the parties meant by the word "guarantee" or "warranty". For example, in case of an ordinary guarantee, the seller (only) wants to assume liability in regard to the durability of the goods for a specified length of time during which the goods (should) have the

---

[150] Secretariat's Commentary OR Art 33 No 14; Bianca in Bianca/Bonell, Art 35 note 2.9.2.

[151] See, for example, Schwenzer in Schlechtriem/Schwenzer, *Commentary*, Art 35 para 38, with further references in regard to the different opinion Magnus in *Staudinger*, who himself differentiates, Art 35 paras 50, 51.

[152] Schwenzer in Schlechtriem/Schwenzer, *Commentary*, Art 35 para 38.

[153] Schwenzer in Schlechtriem/Schwenzer, *Commentary*, Art 35 para 38, "[T]he characteristics of the goods that were actually agreed for the purpose of Article 35(1) must be determined in each case by way of interpretation."

[154] Compare BG (7 Jul 2004) CISG-online 848 = IHR 2004, 252, 253; *Chicago Prime Packers Inc v Northarn Food Trading Co* (23 May 2005) (US Court of Appeal (7th Circ)) CISG-online 1026; Appellationshof des Kantons Bern (11 Feb 2004) CISG-online 1191 = IHR 2006, 149 et seq sub III.3; Schwenzer in Schlechtriem/Schwenzer, *Commentary*, Art 35 para 49 differentiates.

[155] CISG, Art 36(2).

[156] Below para 147.

characteristics agreed at the time of the passing of the risk and which are necessary for the goods' ordinary use until the end of the guarantee period. The seller does not commit himself or herself to remedy defects free of charge while the goods are under guarantee, where the defects are caused by improper use or external influences. A durability guarantee shifts the burden of proof from the buyer to the seller in regard to proving that defects which occur during the time of the guarantee have their origin in the characteristics of the goods in existence when the risk passed, albeit unrecognised.[157] Of course more extensive guarantees can be given, for example, the seller may assume a duty to maintain the goods in a usable condition for a certain time and to remedy any defect irrespective of its cause. However, such guarantees are not widespread. What kind of guarantee is intended has to be ascertained through interpretation (Article 8 CISG).[158]

147. Another issue is for how long the goods have to be fit for their ordinary purpose or fit for their particular purpose.[159] If an express guarantee has been given, the period for which the goods have to be fit for their ordinary or particular purpose will also be stipulated. Ascertaining the durability period in the case of an implied guarantee poses on issues. The question arises whether the period of time has to be determined by the contract or at least determinable from the contract, or whether the time is one which is to be determined by the courts. Applications which wanted to insert a "reasonable period as the case may be" have been unsuccessful, so that the period of the guarantee has to be determined by interpretation of the contract (at the Diplomatic Conference in Vienna).[160]

However, the practical difference between this view and the alternative which stipulates that the period of time has to be determined by the courts is, in regard to implied guarantees, generally non-existent. Following the contract-based determination in the case of an implied guarantee, a court must also have regard to what a reasonable person would have agreed to in the particular circumstances.[161] On the other hand, courts (because Article 6 CISG gives party agreement priority) have to take the parties' intention into account.[162] The real issue, determining durability period for particular goods in the circumstances, is neither resolved nor resolvable by the CISG. As Schwenzer points out it is only possible to lay down general criteria to a limited extent.[163] Perishable goods should have a reasonable shelf life. Other goods should remain fit for their purpose for almost the length of their relevant life expectancy. It is advisable for the parties to expressly agree on the

---

[157] Schwenzer in Schlechtreim/Schwenzer, *Commentary*, Art 36 para 7.

[158] See paras 54 et seq.

[159] See CISG, Art 36(2).

[160] Secretariat's Commentary OR 105 No 3 para (2)(ii).

[161] Compare CISG, Art 8(2).

[162] Schwenzer in Schlechtriem/Schwenzer, *Commentary*, Art 36 para 9. See in regard to party autonomy (Art 6 CISG) paras 19 et seq.

[163] Schwenzer in Schlechtriem/Schwenzer, *Commentary*, Art 36 para 10; Aue, *Mängelgewährleistung*, 142 et seq with examples from English case law.

terms of a guarantee and its length. National prohibitions in regard to the standard clauses have to be taken into account however.[164]

The use of the term "guarantee" in a contract to which the CISG is applicable poses the question whether the parties strengthen the position of the buyer in some areas but weaken it in others as the buyer is limited to the CISG remedies.[165]

Example: The German machine manufacturer V-AG sold a paper mill to the Swedish buyer. In the contract V-AG guaranteed particular characteristics of the paper mill, for example, a certain electricity and water consumption, a certain amount of emissions, production capacity etc. The parties chose German law. The liability for damages was capped at $2.5 million. Because the paper mill exceeded the allowed emission standard their Swedish environment protection agency shuts it down. The additional modernisation of the mill to fulfil the emission standards took eleven months. The buyer claims damages (costs of the modernisation, loss of earnings during the time of the closure) of $4 million. The seller claimed the limited liability stipulated in the contract. The buyer pointed out § 444 BGB and claimed full damages under Article 74 CISG.[166]

Article 6 CISG[167] affords the parties autonomy in how they regulate their dealings, including limitations on liability. However, domestic law poses also a limit in regard to that kind and whether liability can be limited (Article 4 2nd s(a)).[168] In the given example, the question arises whether the buyer can invoke § 444 BGB. § 444 BGB does not render the contract or a provision of a contract void but "only" prevents the seller from relying on a limited liability clause. The BGB intentionally avoided the sanction of "voidability" to ensure the entire contract was not voided. Further, it needs to be remembered that the seller's liability for the good's conformity with the contract, and the limits on prohibited standard terms or abuse provisions, are at the core of the CISG. A national legislature cannot interfere without infringing its public international law obligations. The drafters of § 444 BGB could not have intended to infringe those obligations, so § 444 BGB is not applicable if the CISG is applicable.[169]

2.6.5 Seller's Right to Cure Lack of Conformity

148. Article 37 CISG gives the seller the right to cure any lack of conformity in the goods until the agreed time of the delivery if the goods were delivered early.[170] The seller can chose how to cure the lack of conformity. The buyer has to

---

[164] See para 34.

[165] Schlechtriem, *Internationales UN-Kaufrecht*, para 147.

[166] BGB, § 444 reads: "The seller may not rely on an agreement excluding or restricting the buyer's rights in respect of defects if the seller fraudulently concealed the defect or if he has guaranteed the quality of the goods." (translation from www.iuscomp.org).

[167] See para 22.

[168] Paras 34 et seq.

[169] Convincing: Piltz, IHR 2002, 1–5.

[170] Compare also UCC, § 2-508(1) which makes the same distinction as the CISG.

be compensated for damages suffered or expenditure incurred because the goods were delivered before the due date. The option of delivering substitute goods has no impact on the buyer's rights. The buyer also can claim any damages which he or she incurs as a result of the seller curing the lack of conformity.[171] The buyer can only refuse the seller's attempt to remedy the defect, or the seller's choice of remedying the lack of conformity, if the associated costs or difficulties this causes for the buyer are unreasonable; in such cases the buyer can invoke the remedies for breach of contract.[172] Once the date of delivery has passed the seller can only remedy the defect in accordance with Article 48 CISG.[173]

2.7   Examination and Notice

2.7.1 Introduction

149. Articles 38 to 40 and Article 44 CISG set out the buyer's responsibilities in regard to the timely clarification of lack of conformity issues and winding-up of the contract. The buyer's obligations to inspect the goods and to notify the seller of potential non-conformity as well as sanctions, that means the loss of rights if the buyer does not realise those are the CISG's focal points to ascertain the lack of conformity issues. The UCC, on the other hand, does not set out an affirmative duty for the buyer to inspect the goods.[174] However, in practice the buyer has to inspect the goods under the UCC, too, since the buyer only has a remedy for the non-conformity of the goods if the buyer notifies the seller of the non-conformity – which the buyer generally can only do if he or she has inspected the goods. At common law, the rules on acceptance are subject to the buyer's reasonable opportunity to examine the goods to ensure they are in conformity with the contract. What constitutes a reasonable opportunity to examine the goods is considered on a case by case basis, and includes the nature of the goods and the nature of alleged defects.[175] The buyer can waive the right of inspection, expressly or impliedly. Rejection of non-conforming goods implies an obligation to notify the seller. Goods are deemed to be accepted where (a) that intimation is given to the seller, or (b) the goods have been delivered and the buyer acts in a way that is inconsistent with the seller's rights in the goods, or (c) the buyer retains the goods for a reasonable time without indicating that the goods have been rejected. If the buyer rejects the goods, she or he must do so unequivocally.[176] Unlike German law, under the CISG the buyer only has to give notice within a reasonable time and not immediately.[177]

---

[171] CISG, Art 37 (2nd s).

[172] Compare the comparable solution in regard to documents, para 131.

[173] Para 179.

[174] Gabriel, *Contracts for the Sale of Goods*, 134.

[175] Sale of Goods Act 1908 (NZ), s 36; Sale of Goods Act 1954 (ACT), s 38; Sale of Goods Act 1979 (UK), s 34. See generally, Burrows/Finn/Todd, *Law of Contract*, 14.4.2; Sutton, *Sales and Consumer Law*, paras 20.1–20.18.

[176] Sale of Goods Act 1908 (NZ), s 37; Sale of Goods Act 1954 (ACT), s 39; Sale of Goods Act 1979 (UK), s 35. See generally, Burrows/Finn/Todd, *Law of Contract*, 14.4.1, 14.4.3; Sutton, *Sales and Consumer Law*.

150. How to formulate the notice requirement and what sanction a late notice or a lack of notice would have been one of the most difficult issues faced when drafting the CISG. Early drafts of the CISG substituted the requirement of "promptly" giving notice under Article 39 ULIS with a provision allowing the buyer a "reasonable" time to fulfil the notice requirement. Two issues remained controversial in Vienna: the loss of all remedies by the buyer if the buyer did not give notice, and the complete exclusion of buyer's remedies after two years independent of whether the defect was discernible. The supporters of the strict standard were successful in pushing through the two year exclusion rule. The supporters of the more lenient view succeeded in preserving the buyer's remedies of reduction in price and damages claim (except for loss of profit) within the two year rule, as long as the buyer has a reasonable excuse for his or her failure to give the required notice (Article 44 CISG).[178]

The provisions which set out the buyer's examination requirements and the notice requirement, as well as the consequences if the buyer fails to give notice, are of significant practical importance. Numerous decisions concerning the CISG deal with those requirements.[179]

2.7.2 Examination

151. Article 38 CISG provides for buyer's obligation to examine the goods and the timeframes within which the examination has to be done. The phrasing of the time limit "within as short a period as it is practicable" recognises that there may be significant differences in the factors influencing the conduct of an examination, for example, the characteristics of the goods, the special circumstances of the buyer, and how the goods can be examined in situ.

Example: A Dutch company contracted with an Italian company for the delivery of deep frozen cheese. The buyer argued that the cheese was infested with maggots. Since the examination only took place some time after the cheese had been delivered and consequently notice had been given late, the decisive factor was whether the examination had been done in a period as short as practicable. The buyer claimed that an earlier examination had not been possible because the cheese was delivered frozen. The Court did not accept this argument: The buyer could have examined part of the cheese delivery and could have examined these cheeses immediately.[180]

---

[177] See in regard to German law § 377(1) HGB.

[178] Compare in regard to the history of that provision: Schlechtriem, *Einheitliches UN-Kaufrecht*, 60 et seq.

[179] Compare Eric Bergsten, AC-CISG Opinion No 2 with comprehensive references to the jurisprudence in its Annex.

[180] Rechtbank Roermond (19 Dec 1991) CISG-online 29 = 10 NIPR (1992) No 394. The CISG did not embody the Art 38(4) ULIS which stated that trade and trade usage at the place of examination had to be taken into account.

Considerable weight has to be given to the type of goods when determining the length of time practicable for examination. If the goods are perishable a shorter examination period is reasonable than, for example, if the goods are highly technical, complex, or of a considerable size, such as an industrial plant. Whether defects can be discovered during a test run is a factor to be taken into account, as is whether the goods (the machines) have to run for a certain amount of time before any defects can be discovered.[181] In certain circumstances experts might have to assess whether the goods were defective or whether the buyer made a mistake in operating the machine. The time needed for the expert to make his or her findings has to be taken into account.[182]

152. If the goods are transported the examination may be deferred until after the goods have arrived at their destination (Article 38(2) CISG). In cases where the goods are sent on or the buyer redirects them, Article 38(3) CISG stipulates that if the buyer did not have a reasonable opportunity for examination and at the time of the conclusion of the contract the seller knew or ought to have known of the possibility of a redirection or redispatch, the examination can be deferred until after the goods have arrived at the new destination. The rationale behind Article 38(3) CISG is to avoid the need to open the goods' packaging before the goods arrive at their new destination.

Example: A steel merchant situated in Germany bought steel sheets from an Austrian manufacturer. Those sheets were to be delivered to Rostock but were to be redispatched immediately to the German steel merchant's Portuguese customer. The steel sheets were rolled up, so that an examination was only economically viable by the end purchaser once the sheets had reached their final destination. The Court held that the examination period only started from the time the sheets had reached the Portuguese purchaser.[183]

2.7.3 Notice

153. If the buyer discovers a defect, or could have discovered the defect, the buyer has "a reasonable time" from the time of detection to give notice to the seller. The buyer has to object to any non-conforming delivery[184] or quantity (including not only delivery less than agreed but also more than agreed).[185] If the buyer does not give notice he or she loses his or her right to claim remedies.[186] The notice travels at the addressee's risk. Under Article 27 CISG the seller carries the risk that

---

[181] Compare in regard to details Schwenzer in Schlechtriem/Schwenzer, *Commentary,* Art 38 paras 15–18.

[182] Magnus in *Staudinger*, Art 38 paras 355, 40–45.

[183] Compare Arbitral Award of the International Arbitral Tribunal of the Bundeskammer der gewerblichen Wirtschaft in Österreich (15 Jun 1994) CISG-online 120, 121 = RIW 1995, 590 et seq with commentary by Schlechtriem in RIW 1995, 590, 591.

[184] See above para 149.

[185] Compare Witz/Wolter, RIW 1995, 813.

[186] See para 158.

the notice gets lost.[187] However, the buyer must give notice in a way either agreed by the parties or which is warranted in the circumstances.[188] The notice needs to be specific enough to inform the seller of the nature of the non-conformity.[189]

154. The determination of a "reasonable time" depends on the circumstances in the particular case, especially the characteristics of the goods in question (for example, whether they are seasonal goods or perishable goods). As the Tribunale di Rimini held:[190]

> "Reasonableness under Article 39(1) contains both objective and subjective components. To determine whether the objective component of "reasonableness" is met in a given case, one should refer to available case law to gauge the varying periods of time other Courts applying Article 39(1) have found to be timely or untimely. On the other hand, the subjective component of "reasonableness" should be analysed by taking into account factors specific to the case including the terms of the contract, the characteristics of the goods, and the purpose for which the goods are used."

In the German literature the tendency is towards shorter notice periods;[191] the BGH tends to find four weeks an appropriate notice period.[192] The OGH on the other hand found a period of 14 days appropriate.[193]

The buyer's examination obligation and the obligation to give notice have to be strictly separated. They cannot be combined to one time period. However, they can influence each other: if the examination was very time intensive, for example because an expert had to be consulted, then the buyer can decide during that time what he or she should do once the examination is complete: if the examination reveals defects, a quick reaction from the buyer might be reasonably expected.[194]

---

[187] Compare para 109.

[188] See para 110; The issue under Art 27 CISG whether a declaration is only affective when it reaches the addressee cannot be controversial under Art 39 CISG because of the drafting history of Art 39(1) CISG and its predecessor Art 39(3) ULIS.

[189] LG Erfurt (29 Jul 1998) CISG-online 561; BGH (4 Dec 1996) CISG-online 260 = NJW – RR 1997, 690; Handelsgericht des Kantons Zürich (21 Sep 1998) CISG-online 416.

[190] *Al Palazzo Srl v Bernardaud di Limoges SA* Tribunale di Rimini (26 Nov 2002) CISG-online 737.

[191] Compare Salger in Witz/Salger/Lorenz, Art 39 para 6; for a more generous approach see Schwenzer in Schlechtriem/Schwenzer, Art 39 para 17: medium notice period: 1 month.

[192] BGH (3 Nov 1999) CISG-online 475 = RIW 2000, 381, 382; also OG Luzern (8 Jan 1997) CISG-online 228 = SZIER 1997, 132, 133.

[193] OGH (27 Aug 1999) CISG-online 485 = IHR 2001, 81; further jurisprudence Magnus, ZEuP 2002, 523, 534 et seq; Magnus, TranspR 1999, 29 et seq; Ferrari, IHR 2001, 179, 185 (Italy); note that virtually all of the case law cited is either of German, Swiss, or Austrian origin: compare Gabriel, *Contracts for the Sale of Goods* 134, 135 with fn 606, 607; Schwenzer in Schlechtriem/Schwenzer, *Commentary*, Art 39 paras 15–18; compare also Eric Bergsten, AC-CISG Opinion No 2, para 3 zu Art 39; Magnus in *Staudinger*, Art 39 paras 42 et seq; Soergel, Art 39 para 3; Saenger in Bamberger/Roth (eds) *Kommentar*, Art 39 para 8.

[194] In BGH (3 Nov 1999) CISG-online 475, after the machine was a total write off, the buyer was given one week to check and to evaluate whether a mistake in the operation had caused the damage and how to proceed further; a further 2 weeks were set aside for the expert and at the end the buyer

155. The requirement for a valid notice is that the defects have been substanti-ated ("specifying the nature"). After receiving the notice, the seller has to be able to judge the kind of defect and how (or if) it can be remedied.

Example: The buyer who was situated in Germany bought shoes from the Italian seller. The buyer refused the payment of the purchase price for the delivered shoes and declared avoidance of the contracts. When giving notice the buyer had stated that shoes were defective in all aspects, the material was defective and finish was different for each pair of shoes – sometimes the shoes were stepped sometimes folded. The Court held that these notices were deficient since it was not possible to ascertain from them the exact nature of the defects and the degree of non-conformity.[195]

The buyer's demand that the seller examine the goods himself of herself is no longer needed. Article 39(2) ULIS set out that requirement and caused enormous difficulties.

The buyer needs to substantiate the notice in light of its function – it needs to make it possible for the seller to examine and to remedy (if necessary) the claimed defects. The buyer has to describe the defects as precisely as possible. However, the buyer does not have to stipulate the exact cause of the defect unless the buyer becomes aware of this when examining the defect.[196]

Valid notices, that means notices on time and substantiated, allows the buyer to claim damages under Article 45(1)(b) CISG: the right to require delivery of substitute goods under Article 46(2) CISG; the right to obtain repair of defective goods under Article 46(3) CISG; to reduce the price (Article 50 CISG); to avoid the contract (Article 49 CISG); and to fix an additional time for performance under Article 47 CISG. Whether the notice has merit is to be proven by the buyer. The buyer has to prove after the risk has passed that the goods at that time lacked con-formity.[197]

2.7.4 Seller's Knowledge

156. The seller is not entitled to rely on the lack of examination and/or notice if that lack relates to facts of which the seller knew or could not have been unaware and which the seller did not disclose to the buyer (Article 40 CISG). Article 40

---

was given an additional (normal) 4 weeks so that a notice 7 weeks after the defect had occurred was held to be reasonable. This seems to be slightly excessive since the buyer had the time during the examination period to evaluate what to do; see for a well reasoned judgment OLG Oldenburg (5 Dec 2000) CISG-online 618 = RIW 2001, 381.

[195] OLG Frankfurt (18 Jan 1994) CISG-online 123 = NJW 1994, 1013, 1014: the requirements the Court had on the notices was very strict; see also Lookofsky, *Understanding the CISG*, paras 4–9, 49.

[196] Compare BGH (4 Dec 1996) CISG-online 260 = NJW – RR 1997, 690, 691; BGH (3 Nov 1999) CISG-online 475.

[197] This is very controversial: for an alternative view see Appellationshof des Kantons Bern (11 Feb 2004) CISG-online 1191 = IHR 2006, 149 et seq sub III 3 with discussion by Piltz, IHR 2006, 53, 154 et seq; like here burden of proof shifts with passing of the risk: BG (13 Nov 2003) CISG-online 840; for an overview of the different views see Piltz, IHR 2006, 53, 154 et seq.

CISG covers gross negligence as well as fraudulent deception.[198] However, a detailed examination, such as the opening of the original packaging by a merchant who on-sells the goods, is not necessary.[199] The facts which the seller has to disclose are not only the characteristics of the goods but also facts which are outside the seller's responsibility but which can effect the goods and which can change their characteristics or otherwise affect them.

2.7.5 Forfeiture

157. It is unclear whether the principle of forfeiture should be available next to Article 40 CISG.

Example: Both parties had, after the buyer gave a late notice, negotiated further and waited for the reaction of the buyer's end-purchaser. When the negotiation stalled and the buyer claimed remedies, the seller objected drawing attention to the late notice. The buyer replied, pointing out the further negotiations, arguing that the seller had waived his or her right to a lack of notice defence.[200]

Negotiations which the parties later continue might be understood as a modification of the contract (Article 29(1) CISG) in which the seller agrees to waive his or her right to receive a timely notice. The parties' negotiations might have to be interpreted in accordance with Article 8 CISG to determine whether the parties intended to modify the contract accordingly. To allow a forfeiture of the defence of late notification of the lack of conformity with the aim of giving the buyer at least some remedies is judicial contract formation which leads to legal uncertainty.

2.7.6 Consequence of Failure to Give Notice

158. The buyer who fails to give notice forfeits his or her right to refer to the non-conformity of the goods. However, under Article 44 CISG the buyer retains the right of purchase price reduction and a limited claim to damages (except for loss of profit) there is a reasonable excuse for the lack of notice or inadequate substantiated notice.[201] The interpretation of the concept of "reasonable excuse" should not be guided by dogmatic concepts of domestic law. However, the requirement for the buyer to have a "reasonable excuse" suggests more than just fairness

---

[198] The burden of proof generally lies with the buyer: compare BGH (30 Jun 2004) CISG-online 847 = IHR 2004, 201, 202.

[199] See OLG Oldenburg (28 Apr 2000) CISG-online 683 = IHR 2001, 159.

[200] Compare Arbitral Award of the International Arbitral Tribunal of the Bundeskammer der gewerblichen Wirtschaft in Österreich (15 Jun 1994) CISG-online 120, 121 = RIW 1995, 590 with commentary by Schlechtriem in RIW 1995, 590, 591; BGH (25 Nov 1998) CISG-online 353 = NJW 1999, 1259 sub III. 2a: loss of right to a lack of notice defence through further negotiations; see also Schlechtriem/Schmidt-Kessel, EWiR 1997, 1097 discussing BGH (25 Jun 1997) CISG-online 277 = NJW 1997, 3311.

[201] Gruber in *MünchKomm*, Art 44 para 1.

balancing but rather elements such as negligence, fault, and fauté.[202] What "reasonable excuse" means depends on the circumstances in the individual case, especially the buyer's particular situation: objective obstacles (such as a strike or breakdown of all means of communication), and some subjective obstacles (for example, the concept of notice is unknown in the buyer's country) can both excuse the failure to give notice.[203]

2.7.7 Loss of Competing Claims Through Failure to Give Notice

159. The formulation "the buyer loses the right to rely on a lack of conformity" does not clarify whether the buyer whose property is damaged because of the defective goods is precluded from claiming damages because he or she failed to give notice. For example, if the seller supplies defective corks which result in the ruin of the buyer's wine, but the buyer has failed to give notice of the corks' defect then it is questionable whether the buyer's tort claims deriving from the property damage are precluded. Article 39 CISG takes away the buyer's right to rely on a breach of contract (because of the goods' lack of conformity) but Article 39 CISG does not prevent the buyer asserting his or her rights in regard to a "defect" under product liability laws. This means the seller has to observe the general duty of care not to supply dangerous goods.[204] In contrast, tort claims, which according to domestic law aim to compensate for the decreased value of the goods because of the defect, are excluded since these are intended primarily to compensate for the buyer's interests embodied in the contract.[205]

2.7.8 Time Limit (Article 39(2) CISG)

160. The buyer finally loses his or her rights due to the goods' lack of conformity two years after the goods were actually handed over (Article 39(2) CISG). The two year time limit is an absolute exclusionary limit; it cannot be suspended or interrupted and has to be observed ex officio.[206] The time limit does not apply if the parties agreed on a guarantee period in their contract which is incompatible with the absolute exclusionary limit. That can be the case if the parties agree to a shorter than two year guarantee period, or if they agree to a longer than two year guarantee time period.[207] But even if the parties agreed on a guarantee, the buyer will generally have to notify the seller of any open or hidden defects.

---

[202] Compare Schwenzer/Huber in Schlechtriem/Schwenzer, *Commentary*, Art 44 paras 4, 5; see Neumayer/Ming, Art 44 para 2.

[203] See Huber in Schlechtriem (ed) Art 44 para 8 who, in his analysis of case law to Art 39 ULIS, shows that Art 44 CISG has also relevance to merchants from developed countries.

[204] Compare also BGHZ 101, 337, 341 et seq; see also para 40.

[205] See para 40.

[206] Compare Schwenzer in Schlechtriem/Schwenzer, *Commentary*, Art 39 para 23.

[207] Schwenzer in Schlechtriem/Schwenzer, *Commentary*, Art 39 para 26.

2.7.9 Contrary Agreement

161. Articles 38, 39, and 44 CISG are dispositive. Parties can vary their content. In addition to modifying Article 39 CISG by agreeing on a guarantee period, the parties can agree on a different format in regard to the examinations of the goods, or agree on a particular form of the notice. For example, the parties can agree that part of the examination process of a machine includes test runs in the presence of the seller or an impartial third party, and that all discrepancies from the characteristics agreed upon have to be recorded in the minutes of the test run which both parties have to sign.[208] The validity of the agreements is governed by domestic law (Article 4(a) CISG).[209]

2.7.10 Limitation Periods

162. Other than the absolute exclusionary time period stipulated in Article 39(2) CISG general limitation periods must also be taken into account. If the requirements for the United Nations Convention on the Limitation Period in the International Sale of Goods[210] are met, the limitation period is generally four years (Articles 8 et seq). Since the Limitation Period Convention has been ratified in its amended form by only 19 countries[211] most often domestic law will provide for limitation periods since the CISG itself is void of any regulation of limitation periods. Common law countries (like New Zealand, Canada, Australia, UK) have statutory provisions governing limitation periods. The usual period for a simple contract is six years.[212] The limitation period runs from the time the cause of action accrues, which, usually, is when the breach of contract occurs even if the putative plaintiff is unaware of the breach. However, the courts normally apply a "reasonable discovery" test: time starts to run once all material facts which make up the ingredient parts of the cause of action have become reasonably discoverable.[213] In contract cases where tortious liability is alleged, there is some debate whether the law should extend the "reasonable discoverability rule" (as is typically the case with latent defects in buildings, personal injury, and sexual assault). In New Zealand, the Court of Appeal has recently said that this would require legislative change.[214]

---

[208] See Schlechtriem, *Einheitliches UN-Kaufrecht*, para 161, for the relationship between German law and CISG in the case of shorter periods of giving notice in standard form contracts.

[209] Compare Schwenzer in Schlechtriem/Schwenzer, *Commentary*, Art 39 paras 34, 35.

[210] (14 Jun 1974) as agreed in the Protocol of 11 Apr 1980 (1511 UNTS 171) see appendix.

[211] See UNCITRAL website: www.uncitral.org; 27 countries signed the original Convention; see for a commentary of the Limitation Period Convention: Müller-Chen in Schlechtriem/Schwenzer, *Commentary*, 941 et seq.

[212] See, for example, Limitation Act 1950, s 4(1)(a) (NZ); Limitation Act 1980, s 5 (UK); Each Australian state and each Canadian province has its own Act, but the terms of the state/provincial legislation is consistent in – see, for example, Limitation Act 1985 (ACT), s 11; Limitation Act 1969 (NSW), s 14; Limitations of Actions Act 1989 (NS), s 2(1)(e); Limitations of Actions Act (Man), CCSM cl 150, s 2(1)(i).

[213] See generally, Beatson, *Anson's Law of Contract*, 656-57; Burrows/Finn/Todd, *Law of Contract*, 21.6.1.

[214] *Murray v Morel & Co* [2006] 2 NZLR 366 (CA) Chambers J for the Court. The case involved a failed forestry investment partnership.

In cases where fraud by the defendant is alleged, or where the defendant deliberately conceals the right of action from the claimant, or where relief is sought for the consequences of a mistake, the various Limitation Acts provide that time does not start to run until the fraud, misrepresentation, or mistake is discovered.[215]

2.8 Defects in Title

2.8.1 Requirements of a Defect in Title

163. The CISG differentiates between the "normal" rights of third parties (Article 41 CISG) and industrial and intellectual property rights (Article 42 CISG) which can be asserted by third parties in regard to the goods. The delivery of goods which are not free from third party rights is a breach of seller's obligation to deliver goods free from legal obligations (unless the parties agreed on the sale of such goods). This corresponds with the sales law in most domestic legal systems.[216] The provisions are understood to apply also in regard to rights that are claimed by third parties which, while not proven, give rise to the seller's liability.[217] In contrast to the liability for defective goods, the seller is only discharged from his or her liability if the buyer consents to take the goods subject to that right or claim. Consent requires more than mere knowledge, however, it can also be given impliedly.[218]

164. Third parties' rights can be rights in rem but also rights in personam. The specific classification of such rights is governed by the lex rei sitae. In case of a third party's property right, the lex rei sitae will decide the legal consequences (in practice, the seller's creditors' security interests are particularly important).[219] In personam rights against the seller will generally not effect the buyer's rights in the goods since they are personal rights against the seller (for example, claims resulting from selling the same goods twice, or if goods are under a right of retention). They may only lead to liability under Article 41 CISG if the third party brings a claim against the buyer under the earlier contract with the seller (perhaps because the seller is bankrupt).[220]

---

[215] Limitation Act 1950 (NZ), s 28; Limitation Act 1980 (UK), s 32; Limitation Act 1985 (ACT), ss 33-34; Limitations of Actions Act (Man), CCSM cl 150, s 5.

[216] Compare BGB, §§ 433(1), (2), 435; SGA 1979, s 12, UCC §§ 192–196. Sale of Goods Act 1908, s 14 (NZ); Canada and Australia do not have federal legislation, but the provinces (Canada) and the states (Australia) have separate but consistent legislation. See for example: Sale of Goods Act 2000, s 14 (Alta); Sale of Goods Act 1978, s 14 (Sask). These Acts do not distinguish "normal" third party rights (such as mortgages) and industrial and intellectual property rights. See generally, Burrows/Finn/Todd, *Law of Contract*, 13.3; Beatson, *Anson's Law of Contract*, 153–54.

[217] See para 165.

[218] Magnus in *Staudinger*, Art 41 para 22; Karollus, *UN-Kaufrecht*, 123.

[219] See especially Schwenzer in Schlechtriem/Schwenzer, *Commentary*, Art 41 para 4 with fn 11.

[220] Schwenzer in Schlechtriem/Schwenzer, *Commentary*, Art 41 para 4.

165. The seller's liability under the CISG arises if a third party claims a right[221] even if later the claim turns out to be unfounded. The defence of such claims is the seller's responsibility. A decisive factor is whether the third party's claims can hinder the buyer's enjoyment of the goods. If the third party's claims are not very well substantiated then it is unlikely that the seller committed a fundamental breach. However, the seller might have to reimburse costs the buyer incurs in warding off the third party's claims. Whether the seller's liability is excluded if the third party's claim is frivolous, or if the buyer and the third party collude, is uncertain but probably only a theoretical issue.[222]

166. Encumbrances under public law which limit the use of the goods, for example, because of national safety laws, work health and safety regulation or environmental protection standards do not fall under Article 41 CISG but are dealt with under Article 35 CISG.[223] A seizure of the goods by a public authority before delivery has taken place breaches the duty to deliver under Article 30 CISG. Only such public law provisions and acts which not only limit the use of the goods but also impact on the legal position of the buyer as owner amount to a defect in title under Article 41 CISG.[224] The differentiation between defect and defect of title is, therefore, important for the application of the CISG[225] especially as the liability because of defect of title is only eliminated if the buyer consents. If the goods lack conformity the seller is not liable if the buyer's gross negligence means she or he does become aware of the non-conformity (see Article 35(3) CISG). Further, the absolute exclusionary time limit of Article 39(2) CISG does not apply to defects of title.[226]

---

[221] See BGH (11 Jan 2006) CISG-online 1200 = NJW 2006, 1348, IHR 2006, 84 with discussion by Schroeter, EWiR Art 43 CISG, 427, 488.

[222] Compare in regard to that issue Schwenzer in Schlechtriem/Schwenzer, *Commentary*, Art 41 para 10; Magnus in *Staudinger*, Art 41 paras 15–17.

[223] See para 136.

[224] Compare Schwenzer in Schlechtriem/Schwenzer, *Commentary,* Art 41 paras 5–7.

[225] The position re a defect in the goods and a defect in title resulting from government/ public law requirements is dissimilar under common law. The key is that the seller has control over/responsibility for delivery of goods whose quality/conformity is in accordance with *known* public law requirements. Goods that are seized before delivery because of non-compliance with *known* statutory obligations will, arguably, result in *wrongful* neglect to deliver under s 52 of the Sale of Goods Act 1908, rendering the seller liable for damages. Unforeseen government intervention may frustrate the contract, or makes its continuance illegal – see generally Burrows/Finn/Todd, *Law of Contract*, 20.2.1(c); Beatson, *Anson's Law of Contract*, 541-46. See – Sale of Goods Act 1908 (NZ): (Note: These provisions are mirrored in the equivalent Australian (state) and Canadian (provincial) legislation which are based on the same UK model:
s 14 – Implied undertakings as to title etc (see Art 41 CISG)
s 16 – Implied conditions as to quality of fitness (see Art 35 CISG)
s 29 – It is the duty of the seller to deliver the goods …
s 52(1) – Where the seller *wrongfully* neglects or refuses to deliver the goods to the buyer

[226] Schwenzer points out that the limitation periods for defects and defects of title are different in many domestic laws: Schwenzer in Schlechtriem/Schwenzer, *Commenary*, Art 41 para 5.

2.8.2 Notice

168. As with a defect because of non-conformity of the goods, a defect of title has to be objected to within a reasonable time after the buyer gained the knowledge or ought to have become aware of the right or claim. The buyer has to specify the nature of the right or claim (Article 43(1) CISG). The reasonableness of the time to give notice depends on the circumstances in the individual case.[227] It has to be taken into account, however, that the seller is also liable for claimed but not substantiated third party rights: the buyer faced with a third party claim does not need to clarify its merits, but only needs to notify the seller of the nature of the right or the claim the third party has made to fulfil his or her substantiating duties under Article 43(1) CISG. This justifies a shorter notice period in most cases than in regard to defects due to lack of conformity because of the more complicated nature of the enquiry.[228] Because Articles 41 et seq CISG do not contain an Article 39(2) CISG equivalent, the seller has to be prepared for claims because of defects of title until the limitation period is reached.

169. If the buyer has a reasonable excuse for failure to give notice then the exception as set out in Article 44 CISG applies. Article 44 CISG allows the buyer to claim damages (except for loss of profit). The right to reduce the purchase price is not applicable in regard to defects of title.[229] The seller cannot rely on the lack of notice if he or she knew the nature of the right or the third party claim (Article 43(2) CISG). In contrast to the seller's liability for defects because of lack of conformity, in regard to defects of title the seller must have positive knowledge. That the seller could have been aware of a defect in title is not sufficient. The decisive time for the seller's knowledge should be the hypothetical moment in which the notice, had it been given, would have reached the seller. At that point the seller would have acquired knowledge. If the seller had acquired knowledge at that point a notice is not necessary.

170. In regard to limitation periods, the proper law of the contract applies if the Convention on Limitation Periods is not applicable. If German law applies § 438 I No 1(a) or perhaps (3)[230] apply so that in regard to a third party claim of return the seller has to take responsibility for 30 years. Common law rules concerning the indefeasible title of the original owner of goods are typically modified by statutory limitation periods, for example, in New Zealand the time limit on causes of action resulting from the conversion or wrongful detention of chattels is six years.[231] If an action is not commenced within that time, the title of the person claiming ownership is extinguished.[232] However, these general rules do not affect

---

[227] Compare BGH (11 Jan 2006) CISG-online 1200 = IHR 2006, 84 et seq: 2 months was no longer sufficient.

[228] See Benicke in Lindenmayer/Möhring, 1822 et seq; Schroeter, EWiR, Art 43 CISG 1106, 428 sub 3.

[229] See further paras 202 et seq.

[230] See para 162.

[231] Limitation Act 1950 (NZ), s 5(1).

[232] Limitation Act 1950 (NZ), s 5(2).

the provisions of the Sale of Goods Act 1908 (NZ).[233] Under section 26(1) of the Sale of Goods Act 1908 (NZ), where goods have been stolen and the offender convicted, the original owner retains the title indefinitely.[234] This means a seller cannot pass good title, and there is no time limit on the buyer's claim for breach of contract if the goods are reclaimed by the original owner.

Section 26(1) of the Sale of Goods Act 1908 (NZ) applies only where the goods have been stolen; section 26(2) provides:[235]

> ... where goods have been obtained by fraud or other wrongful means not amounting to theft, the property in such goods shall not revest in the person who was the owner of the goods, or his personal representative, by reason only of the conviction of the offender.

Further, section 26(1) of the 1908 Act will not apply where the seller is a mercantile agent in possession of the goods with the owner's permission, even if the subsequent sale to an unsuspecting buyer is without the owner's permission, or contrary to the owner's instructions.[236] Section 23(2) of the Sale of Goods Act 1908 preserves the provisions in the Mercantile Law Act 1908 and the Personal Property Securities Act 1999 which enable a purchaser who acquires goods from a seller in the ordinary course of the seller's business to get good title.[237] Section 23(1) of the 1908 Act[238] is a statutory embodiment of the common law nemo dat rule: where the sale is not completed via a mercantile agent, the original owner's prior rights remain extant.[239]

2.9 Industrial Property or Intellectual Property Rights

171. Like other third party rights or defects because of lack of conformity, industrial property rights and intellectual property rights can impact on the usability of the purchased goods. Third party rights based on industrial property right or intellectual property rights are classified in domestic law either as rights stemming from a defect of title[240] or rights stemming from a defect because of lack of conformity with the contract.[241] The Convention establishing the World Intellectual Property Organisation defines intellectual property as: "all... rights resulting from

---

[233] Limitation Act 1950 (NZ), s 5(3).

[234] See also, Sale of Goods Act 1954 (ACT), s 28(1).

[235] See also, Sale of Goods Act 1954 (ACT), s 28(2).

[236] See Burrows/Finn/Todd, *Law of Contract*, 12.3.

[237] See also, Sale of Goods Act 1979, s 21(2) (UK); Sale of Goods Act 1954 (ACT), s 26(2).

[238] "Subject to the provisions of this Act, where goods are sold by a person who is not the owner thereof, and who does not sell them under the authority or with the consent of the owner, the buyer acquires no better title to the goods than the seller had, unless the owner of the goods is by his conduct precluded from denying the seller's authority to sell."

[239] See also, Sale of Goods Act 1979 (UK), s 21(1); Sale of Goods Act 1954 (ACT), s 26(1).

[240] For example, the German law, compare BGHZ 110, 97.

[241] Compare in regard to Swiss law BGE 82 II 238; further Schwenzer in Schlechtriem/Schwenzer, *Commentary*, Art 42 para 1 fn 3.

intellectual activity in the industrial, scientific, literary or artistic fields".[242] This definition is in line with other intellectual property Conventions and should be taken as the basis for the CISG.[243] The definition of intellectual property encompasses "industrial property". The explicit reference to "industrial property" is included to avoid doubt.[244] Rights of personality or rights to bear a name should be treated like intellectual property right under the CISG.[245] Such rights can impact on the buyer if the goods are tainted with such third party rights. On the one hand, the third parties might obtain restraining orders or they may even seize the goods[246] and the goods cannot be resold. On the other hand, a machine might not have be patented but is supposed to work according to a protected process or to produce goods which are subject to some intellectual property right of a third party.[247]

172. The notification requirement in Articles 42 and 43 CISG is set out in regard to the consequences, if the buyer fails to notify, similar to the consequences in regard to a failure to notify in regard to the liability for a defect in title (Article 43(1) CISG). Also, the treatment in regard to the seller's knowledge and in regard to a "reasonable excuse" for the failure to give notice is parallel to that of the defect of title.[248] However, the provisions of Article 42 CISG show that intellectual property rights are a special category of inadequate performance for which the liability of the seller is curbed. Two additional requirements have to be met before the seller is liable: first, the seller is only liable for third party rights affecting the goods in those States where, according to the contract, the goods were to be used (para 173). Second, the seller's liability is further restricted by a subjective requirement: the seller is only liable for such rights and claims of which she or he knew or could not have been unaware of at the time of the conclusion of the contract (para 174).

2.9.1 Technical Limitations

173. What the parties have agreed in regard to where and how the goods were to be used helps determine the seller's liability. The seller is not liable to deliver goods which are free from intellectual property rights in a global sense but only in regard to countries where the goods are to be used. If the parties have not specifically agreed on such countries, Article 42(1)(b) CISG stipulates it to be the country in which the buyer has his or her place of business which will be determined by reference to Article 10 CISG. If the goods are resold or used in a country other than the one where the buyer has his or her place of business, then the use of the

---

[242] Convention Establishing the World Intellectual Property Organisation (Stockholm, 14 Jul 1967; amended 28 Sep1979) Art 2(viii).

[243] Schwenzer in Schlechtriem/Schwenzer, *Commentary*, Art 42 para 4.

[244] Secretariat's Commentary OR Art 40 No 1 fn 1.

[245] Schwenzer in Schlechtriem/Schwenzer, *Commentary*, Art 42 para 5 who notes that intellectual property rights are often said to be derived from the right to personality (fn 19).

[246] Compare Ahrens, BB 1997, 902 et seq.

[247] Schwenzer in Schlechtriem/Schwenzer, *Commentary*, Art 42 para 4.

[248] See CISG, Art 44.

goods can be impaired because of that country's laws (Article 42(1)(a) CISG).[249] The use in that country (or countries) must have been contemplated at the time of the conclusion of the contract.

2.9.2 Seller's Knowledge or Culpable Lack of Knowledge

174. An additional requirement for the seller's liability is that the seller knew or could not have been unaware at the time of the conclusion of the contract of the intellectual property right. Whether the seller had actual knowledge should not pose too many difficulties in practice. However, when the seller cannot be unaware of an intellectual property right is less certain. The Secretariat's Commentary states that the seller could not have been unaware if the intellectual property right in question had been published in the destination State.[250] If one considers that intellectual property rights are territorial and legal effects only arise in the State which acknowledges them and/or awards them, and that only intellectual property rights in the State where the goods are used can be considered,[251] then the circle of States where the intellectual property rights can be claimed and lead to the seller's liability will be very small. The seller's State can generally be eliminated, as can any State through which the goods transit.[252]

2.9.3 Exclusion of Seller's Liability

175. The seller is not liable if the buyer knew or could not have been unaware at the time of the conclusion of the contract about the intellectual property right (Article 42(2)(a) CISG). This corresponds with the regulation of the liability for a defect because of the lack of conformity in Article 35(3) CISG, and differs from the regulation of the defect of title.[253] The seller is also not liable under Article 42(1) CISG if he or she has used technical drawings, designs, formulae, or other such specifications furnished by the buyer to manufacture the goods for the buyer (Article 42(2)(b) CISG).

3 Buyer's Remedies for the Seller's Breach of Contract

176. The parties' remedies are summarised in respective chapters.[254] However, in regard to buyer's remedies, the consolidation of the remedies as the consequence of the unified concept "breach of contract" was not totally successful. For some forms of the seller's breach of contract special rules apply in regard to the legal consequences of such a breach, for example, the reduction in price for

---

[249] See in regard to Art 10 CISG paras 9 et seq.
[250] Secretariat's Commentary OR Art 40 No 6.
[251] See para 173.
[252] Compare Schwenzer in Schlechtriem/Schwenzer, *Commentary*, Art 42 paras 13, 13a.
[253] See CISG, Art 41 (1st s).
[254] See in regard to buyer's remedies paras 179 et seq; in regard to seller's remedies paras 235 et seq.

defects in the quality and quantity of the goods.[255] Further, the CISG specifies additional requirements for substitute goods (because of lack of conformity of the goods) which are dependent on whether the buyer makes a special request within a reasonable time (Article 46(2) CISG); or the ability to claim repair of the defective goods is dependent on whether it is reasonable to claim that right (Article 46(3) CISG). Furthermore, Article 73 CISG which regulates the disruption of a contract for delivery of goods by instalments belongs in the chapter of buyer's remedies (and not Chapter V which covers provision common to the seller and buyer) since it is closely related to the regulation of part delivery in Article 51 CISG and generally only breached by the seller.

177. Article 45 CISG contains an overview of the buyer's remedies in the event of the seller's failure to perform any of the seller's contractual obligations: that is, right to performance, right to avoid the contract, right to claim damages, and the right to reduce the price. Except for the right to reduce the price, all other rights require that the seller has breached only one of his or her obligations under the contract or the CISG.[256] Article 45(2) CISG explicitly states that claims can be cumulative.

178. Domestic laws which allow domestic courts and arbitral tribunals to extend the seller's deadline for performance are expressly excluded by Article 45(3) CISG since such reprieves are inappropriate in international trade and judicial discretion could lead to the domestic party receiving preferential treatment. Other domestic provisions intended to give the buyer the advantage, such as additional remedies, and particularly remedies in regard to mistakes resulting from lack of conformity, must be excluded. A challenge due to a mistake in the contract leads to a void contract and, therefore, the possibility of challenge is formally a question of the validity of the contract under Article 4 (2nd s(a)) CISG. However, since the core structure of the CISG for example, in regard to notice and the lack of notice, would otherwise be undermined in regard to mistake due to lack of conformity, the CISG has to have precedence over the domestic law in this area.[257]

---

[255] See paras 202 et seq.

[256] Compare § 235 Restatement 2nd Contracts: "When performance of a duty under a contract is due any non-performance is a breach." See also Handelsgericht des Kantons Zürich (10 Feb 1999) CISG-online 488; therefore, not correct ICC Paris (1 Mar 1999) CISG-online 708: "Art 45(1) CISG... only entitled the buyer to damages for breach of primary obligations by the seller."; see in regard to a list of primary and ancillary obligations of the seller: Müller-Chen in Schlechtriem/ Schwenzer, *Commentary*, Art 45 para 3.

[257] Compare already para 36; as well as Schwenzer, NJW 1990, 602, 603; Strohbach in Enderlein/ Maskow/Strohbach, *Internationales Kaufrecht*, Art 4 para 3.1; LG Aachen (14 May 1993) RIW 1993, 760, 761; contrary view Neumayer, RIW 1994, 99, 102; Bydlinski, *Allgemeines Vertragsrecht*, 57, 85, 86; Lessiak, öst JBl 1989, 487 et seq; extensive discussion in Schluchter, *Gültigkeit von Kaufverträgen*, 98 et seq. In regard to discussion of this issue at the Vienna Conference see Schlechtriem, *Einheitliches UN-Kaufrecht*, 66. Another remedy in common law which might arise from duress, which arises from illegitimate pressure which does not need to be unlawful. The pressure can be physical to a person or to goods or property or it can be purely economic. See Beatson, *Anson's Law of Contract*, 277 et seq.

3.1   The Seller's Right to Substitute Performance

179. As long as the buyer has not validly avoided the contract the seller can generally still perform the contract after the delivery deadline. That means, deliver, remedy the lack of conformity, remedy any defect of title, defend third party claims to the goods, or deliver substitute goods. However, the seller has to do this without unreasonable delay and without causing the buyer unreasonable inconvenience or uncertainty of reimbursement (Article 48(1) CISG).

180. Whether and how the seller's right to substitute performance is threatened by the buyer's right to avoid the contract was a controversial issue in Vienna and remains so to a degree in the literature.[258] In practice, this controversy does not carry a lot of weight because if substitute performance without reasonable delay is possible and can be expected from the seller, the requirements of a fundamental breach are generally not met and the buyer has no right to avoid the contract (yet).[259] Immediate avoidance of the contract will only be possible if the delivery has become impossible or the seller refuses performance (compare Articles 72(1)(3) CISG), as well as if the defects cannot be remedied or are so grave that the goods cannot be used by the buyer. Further, the requirements for a fundamental breach are fulfilled if the delivery deadline is fundamental to the contract. Such a contract can be avoided immediately. If the contract is for a fixed-time transaction the substitute delivery of goods or the remedying of defects would be too late.

3.2   Setting of Time Limits

181. Unlike in the common law, the buyer has first and foremost a claim for specific performance (Articles 28, 46 CISG). However, Article 28 CISG recognises the differences between the civil and common law legal systems in regard to specific performance by placing a caveat on the buyer's right to specific performance: the courts are not bound to enter a judgment for specific performance unless the court would do so under its own law.[260] The right to claim performance encompasses the right that the substitute performance, even if a specific good has to be delivered, has to adhere to the agreed characteristics.[261] Uncertainty about rights of performance and possible legal remedies in the context of impaired performance can be reduced or eliminated by a system that links the deadlines for the buyer's right to performance and the seller's right to substitute performance or remedy defects. Linking the deadlines should achieve clarity: first, the buyer can give the seller a reasonable deadline to perform his or her duties (Article 47(1) CISG). The buyer cannot during this time resort to any remedies for breach of

---

[258] Compare Magnus in *FS Schlechtriem*, 599, 602 et seq; Magnus in *Staudinger*, Art 48 paras 18–23.

[259] Müller-Chen in Schlechtriem/Schwenzer, *Commentary*, Art 48 para 18; Salger in Witz/Salger/Lorenz, Art 48 para 2; Magnus in *FS Schlechtriem*, 599, 611, 612.

[260] See paras 118, 119.

[261] See in regard to this issue below paras 184 et seq.

contract unless it is a claim for damages that have already accrued (Article 47(2)(1) and (2) CISG). The significance of fixing an additional period of time is that if the seller does not perform within the additional time allowed, it gives the buyer the option of avoiding the contract in accordance with Article 49(1)(b) CISG.[262] On the other hand, the seller who wants to perform can give notice to the buyer and require the buyer to declare whether the buyer will accept performance during a certain period of time (Article 48(2) CISG). During that period the buyer cannot declare any remedies (especially not avoidance) which would be inconsistent with the seller's right to late performance or to reduce the price in regard to defects the seller promises to remedy (Article 48(3) CISG). The request under Article 48(2) CISG as well as the notice under Article 48(3) CISG is in contrast to Article 27 CISG,[263] only effective if they are received by the buyer (Article 48(4) CISG).

182. In practice, the interaction between the different deadlines and the resultant closing off of remedies for the buyer is not easy to follow. It is, therefore, important to emphasise that neither a duty nor an obligation exists to set a further time period.[264] In particular, the buyer does not have to grant an additional time period before he or she can claim remedies. Only if there is doubt over whether a late delivery amounts to a fundamental breach should the buyer attempt to better his or her legal position by granting the seller an additional period.

3.3   Right of Performance and Substitute Performance, Articles 46, 47 CISG

183. The buyer can demand performance as long as she or he did not choose a remedy which excludes performance (Article 46(1) CISG) or as long as the buyer did not lose his or her rights because of their failure to give notice. The right to claim performance however, might not be enforceable (Article 28 CISG).[265] The right to claim performance is excluded if the buyer has validly avoided the contract, but also if the buyer reduced the purchase price where the buyer could have demanded either substitute delivery because of the lack of conformity of the goods, or that the seller remedy the defect. The right to claim performance should also be excluded if the buyer claims damages because of non-performance and the seller has acted in reliance on the claim, especially if damages have been paid. This results from the principle of venire contra factum proprium which can be found in Articles 16(2)(b), 29(2)(2) CISG as well as based on Articles 46(1) and 62 CISG and which comes to play through gap-filling (Article 7(2) CISG).[266]

184. Articles 46(2) and (3) CISG contains important restrictions in regard to late performance in form of substitute performance or in the form of remedying the

---

[262] See para 190.

[263] See in regard to Art 27 CISG para 109.

[264] Compare Schlechtriem, *Fristsetzungen*, 321, 321 et seq.

[265] See paras 118, 119.

[266] Müller-Chen in Schlechtriem/Schwenzer, *Commentary*, Art 46 para 7; in more detail: Schlechtriem in *FS Georgiades*, 383–402.

defect. It is questionable whether the term "goods do not conform to the contract" in Articles 46(2) and (3) CISG includes defects of titles as well as defects due to lack of conformity (a similar question arises in regard to the reduction of price). It would have been prudent to include in the term "goods do not conform to the contract" both defects due to the lack of conformity as well as defects of title to avoid the sometimes difficult distinction between the two. In the literature, numerous authors already advocate this solution for the CISG,[267] however, the opposite view probably better reflects the opinion of the drafter of the CISG.[268] Articles 46(2) and (3) CISG, therefore, are only applicable in regard to defects due to lack of conformity.[269]

185. Performance in regard to defects of title means that the buyer has a right of performance under Article 46(1) CISG and can demand from the seller the removal of third party rights on the goods or the defence of third party claims. Whether the defect of title amounts to a fundamental breach of contract or whether remedying of the defect is difficult is generally not important.[270] That Article 46(2) CISG is not applicable is also justified because of the nature of the defect.[271]

186. Performance in regard to defects due to lack of conformity means either substitute performance (Article 46(2) CISG) or repair of the defect. The buyer can generally choose between these two forms of performance. In practice that right to choose is, however, very limited. The seller can curtail that right by performance under Article 48(1) CISG or through setting a deadline and can, through his or her choice, subject to the limits of Article 48(1)(1) CISG, perform. Furthermore, the requirements for the two performance alternatives in Articles 46(2) and 46(3) CISG are so different that a free choice would hardly ever be possible for the buyer. The buyer can only demand delivery under Article 46(2) CISG if the lack of conformity of the goods amounts to a fundamental breach. As already stated (para 115), the requirements for fundamental breach will only be fulfilled in exceptional circumstances, for example, if the defect cannot be remedied or the goods are unable to be used for any purpose. "Unable to be used" includes not even being able to be sold to give away prices, and where it would be unreasonable to ask the buyer to keep the goods and (only) to claim damages.[272] If a claim for delivery is justified, the buyer has to give back the defective goods under Article 81(2)(1) CISG.[273]

---

[267] Compare Will in Bianca/Bonell, Art 46 para 3.1., Strohbach in Enderlein/Maskow/ Strohbach, *Internationales Kaufrecht*, Art 46 para 3; Herber/Czerwenka, *Internationales Kaufrecht*, Art 46 para 6; Audit, *Vente internationale*, para 128; Neumayer/Ming, Art 46 para 8; Mohs, IHR 2002, 59, 63, 64 with numerous sources in regard to the controversy.

[268] Compare P Huber in *MünchKomm* Art 46 para 9; Secretariat's Commentary OR p 36 Art 39 Nos 7, 8; Karollus, *UN-Kaufrecht*, 136; Piltz, *Internationales Kaufrecht*, § 5, para 147.

[269] In regard to defects due to the delivery of the wrong quantity see, however, Art 35(1) CISG, above para 134.

[270] Compare Schwenzer in Schlechtriem/Schwenzer, *Commentary*, Art 41 para 21.

[271] Huber in Schlechtriem (3 ed), Art 46 para 27.

[272] See examples in para 115 – delivery of something totally different – aliud.

[273] See para 322.

187. The seller can refuse to remedy the goods' defect if the remedying of the defect is unreasonable, taking all circumstances into account (Article 46(3)(1st s) CISG). The threshold for a claim to remedy a defect is different from the right to delivery under Article 46(2) CISG (for which it is not a requirement that the remedy has to be reasonable for the seller). The threshold is in most cases lower for Article 46(3) CISG than Article 46(2) CISG since it should be generally reasonable for the seller to repair the goods. However, there may be circumstances where a repair is unreasonable because of technical difficulties in regard to the repair or because of the costs involved. The claim to repair the goods requires that the spare parts have to be delivered. The threshold for the delivery of those spare parts is Article 46(3) CISG and not Article 46(2) CISG. That means the seller cannot claim that extensive delivery of spare parts which are needed to repair the defect of the goods requires a fundamental breach of the contract under Article 46(2) CISG.

> Example: The German buyer ordered window elements from an Italian seller. The windows had to be repaired because of the defects in the insulation glass. To repair the windows new glass had to be ordered by the seller. The seller was required to order the new glass under Article 46(3) CISG, even though the defect did not meet the threshold of fundamental breach.[274]

The seller has to bear the costs of the repair. The seller must complete the contract, that is, deliver conforming goods, within the agreed purchase price. If the substitute delivery or the repaired goods still do not conform to the agreed characteristics agreed on the contract then the buyer has to again give notice in regard to the lack of conformity.

> Example: A German company bought six foldout beds from an Italian company. Since five of those beds had defects they went back to the seller for repair. In regard to the seller's claim for payment of the purchase price, the buyer claimed that the beds still were defective. The repair had been not successful. The buyer, however, had only notified the seller about the unsuccessful repair four weeks after the "repaired" beds had been given back to the buyer. The buyer had, because of the late notice, lost all his or her rights under Article 39(1) CISG.[275]

If the buyer has to remedy the defect partly or completely himself or herself, then the buyer can claim damages for the costs involved.[276]

---

[274] Compare OLG Hamm (9 Jun 1995) CISG-online 146 = IPRax 1996, 269.
[275] LG Oldenburg (9 Nov 1994) CISG-online 114 = NJW – RR 1995, 438.
[276] Compare OLG Hamm (9 Jun 1995) CISG-online 146 = IPRax 1996, 269.

3.4 Avoidance of the Contract

188. The remedy of "avoidance" is similar to avoidance in common law.[277] The CISG is based on the principle that avoidance is generally only possible if the breach of contract is so fundamental that the at fault party at least ought to have known that the other party would not have any further interest in being bound by the contract. The CISG, therefore, requires a fundamental breach before the buyer can avoid the contract (Article 49(1)(a) CISG).[278] In addition, the CISG enables a contract to be avoided if an additional time for delivery does not lead to performance of the contract. However, this avenue is only open if the seller did not deliver at all (Article 49(1)(b) CISG). Unlike Article 44(2) ULIS, the CISG does not allow avoidance if the buyer unsuccessfully grants an additional time period to remedy any defects of the goods. There were two main reasons for this. First, opportunities to avoid the contract were to be minimised generally; and second, the granting of an additional time period should not be able to be used to elevate minor breaches of the contract to the level of fundamental breaches.[279] However, if the seller does not fulfil his or her obligations under Articles 46(2) or 46(3) CISG in the agreed time period, that can amount to a fundamental breach.[280] The requirements for a fundamental breach might also be met if the buyer is entitled to reject delivery because of defects and this results in a breach of a fixed delivery time.[281]

The right to avoid the contract, however, can be lost under the circumstances set out in Article 49(2) CISG. This is where, to put it simply, the goods have been delivered and the buyer unreasonably delayed the attempt to exercise her or his right to avoid the contract.[282]

3.4.1 Non-delivery

189. "Non-delivery" means that the goods do not reach the buyer, that means the goods never come into the direct or into the indirect possession of the buyer.[283]

---

[277] However, there is no single test in common law what constitutes avoidance. The different tests, all of which overlap to a greater or lesser extent, comprise factors, such as was there: a failure of condition present? a failure of consideration? a breach of condition or of a warranty? a "fundamental" breach? The effect of the breach may also be relevant. *Halsbury's Laws of England*, Contract, para 990 et seq. See generally Burrows/ Finn/Todd, *Law of Contract*, 18.2 et seq; McManus, *The Law of Contract*, 615 et seq; Waddams, *The Law of Contracts*, para 579 et seq. See for a comparison between CISG and English law: Bridge, *International Sales Law*, 12.25.

[278] Compare to "fundamental breach" paras 111 et seq.

[279] Compare discussion at the 22nd session of the 1st Committee ORS 351 et seq.

[280] Compare the US case of *Delchi Carrier SpA v Rotorex Corp* (6 Dec 1995) US Court of Appeals (2nd Circ) CISG-online 140 = 10 F 3rd 1024 and paras 115, 180.

[281] Schlechtriem, *FS Huber*, 563, 571.

[282] See para 200.

[283] Although common law does not use the term "indirect possession" it does recognise the concept, in the sense that goods can be "delivered" to the buyer, without the buyer taking physical possession or any physical transfer taking place. "Possession" is not defined in the UK Sale of Goods 1979, or any of the other like common law Sale of Goods Acts. The actual terms of the contract, express or implied will be determinative for what constitutes "possession", direct or indirect, or what action is sufficient to constitute delivery. For example, bulk goods can be appropriated to a contract

A delivery of non-conforming goods is not dependent on whether the "non-conformity" stems from a non-conformity in quality or whether the goods are an aliud[284] unless the buyer rejects the delivery.[285] However, as Article 49(1)(b) CISG demonstrates, not even the non-delivery as such always meets the requirements for the avoidance of contract. Article 49(1)(a) CISG states that the non-delivery has to meet the requirements of a fundamental breach. Since the delivery of the goods is generally the buyer's core expectation, whether the seller intends to deliver or can still deliver will be decisive when determining whether the non-delivery is a fundamental breach. If the contract is a time limited transaction, exceeding of the fixed date for delivery already constitutes a fundamental breach. Impossibility of delivery, irrespective of whether the impossibility was likely from the outset, or arose after conclusion of the agreement, and irrespective of whether the impossibility was due to the fault of the seller, is most likely always a fundamental breach. The same is true if the seller declines performance at the time performance is due[286] so that it is irrelevant why the seller does not want to deliver. Further, a fundamental breach generally occurs if the seller does not hand over the documents accompanying the goods which represent the possession of the goods; similarly with document of title to goods.[287] The reasons for the non-delivery do not affect whether the contract can be avoided. Even in cases of hardship or other grave

---

such that "property", ie risk, passes to the buyer before physical delivery takes place. (*Halsbury's Laws of England,* para 163). Further, the seller can complete delivery by doing any act or thing by which the goods are put into the custody or under the control of the buyer or the buyer's agent, (*Halsbury's Laws of England,* para 164) or by which the buyer or the buyer's agent is able to obtain custody or control of the goods. For example, delivery of a key to the place where the goods are stored can be sufficient to constitute delivery. (See *Ellis v Hunt* (1789) 3 Term Rep 464 at 468 per Lord Kenyon CJ; *Chaplin v Rogers* (1801) 1 East 192 at 195 per Lord Kenyon CJ; *Gough v Everard* (1863) 2 H & C 1; *Ancona v Rogers* (1876) 1 Ex D 285, (CA); *Hilton v Tucker* (1888) 39 Ch D 669. *Cf Milgate v Kebble* (1841) 3 Man & G 100; *Lloyds Bank Ltd v Swiss Bankverein, Union of London and Smith's Bank Ltd v Swiss Bankverein* (1913) 108 LT 143 at 146, CA, per Farwell LJ). Where the seller is authorised to send the goods to the carrier, delivery to the carrier (whether named by the buyer or not) is deemed to be delivery to the buyer (Sale of Goods Act 1908, s 34(1)) (and presumably amounts to indirect possession). Constructive delivery is also possible, such as in a sale and leaseback agreement where the goods never leave the seller's possession but where the seller acknowledges the buyer's right to possession. The consequence of the "transfer of possession" is delivery to the buyer followed by immediate redelivery to the seller as bailee (Fawcett/ Harris/ Bridge, *International Sale of Goods,* para 3.218). It is worth noting also that negotiable instruments such as bills of lading can transfer possession – transfer of the bill of lading is a form of symbolic delivery – but the same is not the case in respect of documents such as delivery orders which (usually) constitute no more than a promise to deliver. Such documents are not transferable unless there is a general or local trade custom to that effect (*Halsbury's Laws of England,* para 163; *The Laws of New Zealand,* Sale of Goods, para 169 (last updated 15 Apr 2007). The legal consequences of physical (and deemed) and constructive delivery are not tied to the physical possession of the goods, although obviously that may be relevant for determining whether the seller has complied with his or her obligations. Of more importance is who has the property in the goods and, therefore, who bears the risk of loss.

[284] General opinion, Huber in Schlechtriem (3 ed) Art 49 para 19.

[285] Schlechtriem, *Symposium Frank Vischer,* sub II.5.c

[286] In regard to the deciding of performance before the time performance was due see Art 72 CISG and paras 269 et seq.

[287] Compare Huber in Schlechtriem (3 ed) Art 49 para 16: non-delivery of the duty to hand over is always an objective fundamental breach of contract.

changes in the basis of the contract only the result of non-delivery and its significance is important, and not why the seller cannot perform. Unfortunately, a provision which would give the seller the right in hardship cases to newly negotiate the contract or to demand an adaptation of the contract like that set out in Article 6.2.3 UNIDROIT-Principles.[288]

190. The buyer does not need to clarify whether the non-delivery of the goods fulfils the requirements of a fundamental breach if the buyer allows the seller an additional time period under Article 47(1) CISG and the period has passed without the goods being delivered (Article 49(1)(b) CISG).[289] The granting of an additional time period and its expiry means the clarification of the reasons of the non-delivery and therefore whether the non-delivery will be final which is normally significant for determining whether there has been a fundamental breach, is not necessary. Further, it avoids the argument whether the delivery date was so important for the parties that non-compliance amounts to a fundamental breach.[290]

Example: The seller told the buyer at the time of the agreed delivery that he or she thought the delivery time was non-binding and therefore asked for an additional two months to affect delivery. The buyer disagreed immediately and granted an additional appropriate time for delivery of four weeks. After the four weeks have passed, the buyer can avoid the contract without having to show why she or he has no interest on the performance after the time period has lapsed.

3.4.2 Part Performance and Delivery of Partly Non-conforming Goods

191. For contracts which have only been partly performed, or whose goods only partly conform to the contract, deciding what justifies part avoidance and in what circumstances can be problematic because of the impact on the rest of the contract, including the part of contract which has been fully performed. CISG Articles 51 and 73 provide for a special regime in regard to those contracts.[291] Both provisions work from the principle that the remedy of avoidance can only apply to the part which does not conform to the contract or has not been delivered at all

---

[288] UNIDROIT-Principle, Art 6.2.3 states:
  (1) In case of hardship the disadvantaged party is entitled to request renegotiations. The request shall be made without undue delay and shall indicate the grounds on which it is based.
  (2) The request for renegotiation does not in itself entitle the disadvantaged party to withhold performance.
  (3) Upon failure to reach agreement within a reasonable time either party may resort to the court.
  (4) If the court finds hardship it may, if reasonable,
    (a) Terminate the contract at a date and on terms to be fixed; or
    (b) Adapt the contract with a view to restoring its equilibrium.
[289] Compare to the setting of additional time period and its consequences paras 181, 182.
[290] The predecessor of the CISG, the ULIS, formulated it for cases where the additional time period was granted to rectify a non-fundamental disruption of the contract: "If the delivery is not achieved within this time period…, this will amount to a fundamental breach." (Art 27(2)(2), Art 31(2)(2) ULIS).
[291] Note that the delivery of less than the agreed amount is dealt with under Art 35(1) CISG, see para 134.

(Articles 51(1), 73(1) CISG). Therefore, the buyer can avoid the contract where the non-performance of part of the contract is a fundamental breach of the particular (part) obligation to perform the contract. That will be generally in the case where the performance is impossible, the seller refuses performance, or a fixed date for delivery passes. Further, the effect the part breach of contract has on the faultlessly performed parts is of considerable importance. Although non-delivery of part of the goods, or delivery of partly conforming goods, have a similar impact in terms of performance disruption, Articles 51 and 73 CISG have some significant differences.

192. The decisive characteristic of contracts for delivery of goods by installments is that the several deliveries (at least two deliveries are required for an instalment contract to exist) are separate from each other in time. In other words, there is a difference in time between the first and the later deliveries. Often the contract specifies different delivery dates or time periods or that a party has the right to determine those. In contrast, Article 51 CISG deals with contracts where delivery delegations are concurrent and contemporaneous, but which are dividable and where technical reasons, for example, the capacity of the transport, means deliveries are made in parts.[292]

Example: An Italian seller sells a conveyor belt consisting of three parts to a Czech buyer. One part was faulty. In regard to the other two parts, parts were missing. The Arbitral Tribunal decided that the buyer could avoid the contract in regard to the faulty part. In regard to Article 51(1) CISG it was decisive whether the faulty part was an independent part which could be changed to complete the delivery of the whole.[293]

192a. If the defect is that the seller has delivered less of the quantity than it was agreed between the parties, the question can arise whether the reduced quantity is a defect under Article 35(1) CISG or whether it amounts to part performance. The buyer can in any case demand an additional delivery. The limiting requirements of Article 46(3)(1st s) CISG are probably only applicable in exceptional circumstances, for example, in regard to less quantity in tinned food. The categorisation of the delivery of a lesser quantity as part performance or a defect under Article 35(1) CISG has some consequences in regard to the avoidance of the contract, for the obligation to give notice, and for the limitation period. In the authors' view, the delivery of less than the agreed quantity of the goods should be treated as a defect due to lack of conformity (Article 35(1) CISG). Article 51(1) CISG provides an easier way to avoid the contract, since in regard to the missing quantity an avoidance of the contract can be achieved by granting an additional time period (Articles 49(1)(b) in conjunction with Article 47(1) CISG). If the seller does not fulfil his or her obligation within the additional time period granted the buyer will be able to avoid the entire contract because this passing of the additional time period will

---

[292] Compare P Huber in *MünchKomm*, Art 51 para 5: Art 73 CISG takes precedence over Art 51 because it is the more specific Article.
[293] ICC Paris (23 Aug 1994) CISG-online 129.

generally amount to a fundamental breach (Article 51(2) CISG). In contrast, the passing of an additionally granted time period in regard to other defects generally does not meet the requirements of a fundamental breach.[294] However, Article 51(2) CISG requires that the buyer gives within notice a reasonable time.[295] In regard to the limitation period the proper law of the contract is applicable.

193. There are also differences between Articles 51 and 73 CISG in regard to the legal consequences of the breach. The failure to deliver the agreed quantity under Article 51(1) CISG is a part delivery and as such lacks conformity with the contract under Article 35(1) CISG. However, while Article 51(1) CISG allows the buyer to pursue remedies set out in Articles 46 to 50 CISG in regard to the goods not delivered, or delivered but defective goods which are only part of the performance required, Article 73(1) CISG, according to its wording, seems to allow only for avoidance of the instalment in regard to which the seller has failed to meet his or her obligations under the contract. However, the other remedies have to be applicable in regard to an instalment contract in regard to non-delivery of an instalment or in regard to instalments which do not conform with the contract.[296] Should the instalment be faulty, the buyer can claim damages or reduce the price. Further, if the seller does not comply with part of his or her obligations under Article 51(1) CISG, or if the seller does not deliver an instalment under Article 73(1) CISG, the buyer must have the opportunity to grant an additional time period for the seller to perform the obligations due under the contract. This forces a clarification in regard to the significance of the breach of contract and makes it possible to then avoid the contract. Under Article 72 CISG an anticipatory breach might allow the buyer to avoid the contract in regard to the partly performed parts.

194. In regard to instalment contracts, Article 73(2) CISG raises the possibility of future avoidance of the contract. If the breach of contract that has already occurred gives the party a reason to believe that further breaches of contract will occur in regard to future instalments, the buyer can avoid the entire contract. Insofar Article 73(2) CISG stipulates a type of an anticipated breach of contract (with slightly less stringent requirements for avoidance).[297]

195. In regard to instalments which have already been faultlessly performed Articles 51(2) and 73(3) CISG, even though they differ in their wording, have the same idea at their core: a breach due to the non-performance of all or part of the contract, or a performance which does not conform with the instalment contract must be a fundamental breach in regard to the contract **as a whole** for the buyer to be able to avoid the entire contract.

---

[294] See paras 115 and 197.
[295] Compare, Hirner, *Rechtsbehelf der Minderung,* 134 et seq but who rejects reduction in price, 136.
[296] Schlechtriem, *Internationales UN-Kaufrecht,* para 193; Hornung in Schlechtriem/Schwenzer, *Commentary,* Art 73 para 14.
[297] See para 196.

Example: A German company bought from the US-American manufacturer
                          eleven computer components to perform a contract it had with an
                          Austrian company. The seller, however, only delivered five parts
                          and denied that a contract about eleven (instead of five) components
                          had been concluded. The German buyer refused to pay for the deliv-
                          ered five components and claimed avoidance of the entire contract.
                          The Court assumed that the buyer would have been able to get sub-
                          stitutes for the non-delivered six components so that the require-
                          ments of a fundamental breach in regard to the entire contract had
                          not been met and, therefore, under Article 51(2) CISG the entire
                          contract could not be avoided.[298]

Article 73(3) CISG on the other hand depends on whether the instalments are
interdependent and the purpose of the contract can no longer be achieved using the
deliveries already made along with all future deliveries.[299]

3.4.3 Anticipated Breach of Contract

196. The situation where it is clear before the delivery is due that the seller will
fundamentally breach the contract is provided for in the CISG in the general provisions for seller and buyer (Article 72 CISG). Article 72 CISG allows the non-
offending party to avoid the contract so that the buyer can avoid the contract if it is
clear that the seller will breach the contract and the seller can avoid the contract if
it is clear that the buyer will breach the contract.[300]

3.4.4 Inadequate Performance

197. Even if the seller does perform the contract, but the performance is an
inadequate delivery of non-conforming goods, or goods whose titles are defective
or which are not free from third party industrial or intellectual property rights, the
breach still has to be fundamental for the buyer to avoid the contract.[301] Since one
of the core deals underlying the CISG are to keep the contract "alive" as long as
possible the threshold for a breach to be fundamental is relatively high.[302] The
buyer can only avoid the contract if she or he grants the seller an additional time
period to fulfil his or her obligations under the contract and that the time has
passed, or if the buyer refuses to accept the goods because of their lack of conformity and the resultant passing of a fixed time period in itself is a fundamental breach

---

[298] LG Heidelberg (3 Jul 1992) CISG-online 38.

[299] UNCITRAL, Case Law Digest on the CISG, Art 73 para 10, see Piltz, *Internationales Kaufrecht*,
§ 5, para 266.

[300] See paras 269 et seq.

[301] The doctrine of fundamental breach has developed in relation to exemption clauses used in standard form contracts. The clauses will be allowed only if the conduct of the person who asserts the
clause does not amount to a fundamental breach. In *Suisse Atlantique case* [1966] 2 All ER 61, the
breach must be of a high threshold and must go to root of the contract before exemption clauses are
denied; see also *Photo Productions Ltd Securior Transport Ltd* [1978] 1 WLR 856 per Lord
Denning.

[302] See in regard to what constitutes a fundamental breach paras 111–116, especially para 115.

of the contract.[303] Otherwise, the requirements of a fundamental breach are only met if the goods, due to their lack of conformity are of no use whatsoever to the buyer.[304]

198. In regard to defects of title, the decisive issue is the impact this has on the usability of the goods and if the buyer's interest in utilising the goods is interrupted, the time period within which the defect can be remedied.[305] If the buyer can discharge the third party right then it can be expected the buyer will keep the goods and claim the discharged sum including all associated costs as damages from the seller. If, however, the owner or the holder of a security right demands the goods to dispose of them, or if the holder of a trademark seizes the goods which have been manufactured by product pirates,[306] then the buyer can avoid the contract because of a fundamental breach of the contract by the seller.

3.4.5 Other Breaches of Contract by the Seller

199. As already set out in para 114, the CISG does not differentiate between primary and secondary obligations in determining whether a fundamental breach has occurred.

Also, the breach of a secondary or ancillary contractual obligation can lead to the buyer not receiving from the contract, what he or she could have expected from it. The breach of a secondary or ancillary contractual obligation can, in exceptional circumstances, amount to a fundamental breach.[307]

3.4.6 Loss of the Right to Avoid the Contract and Loss of the Right to Rescind the Contract

200. Under Article 49(2) CISG the buyer can lose the right to avoid the contract if the buyer does not declare avoidance within a reasonable time. The provision makes sure that any lack of clarity in regard the future of the contract is avoided. Three cases have to be distinguished:

a) The buyer can avoid the contract at any time if there was no delivery at all. An unreasonable delay in giving the seller notice of the avoidance of the contract does not prevent the avoidance as such but might influence the buyer's damages claim under Article 77 CISG.[308] Insofar there is also no gap in the CISG which

---

[303] See para 188.

[304] See case discussed in para 139 where the goods, because of safety concerns had been seized; the view expressed here follows the line of German decisions to Art 25 CISG which set out a high threshold for fundamental breach; see in regard to other jurisprudence which often finds fundamental breach earlier: Lurger, IHR 2001, 96 et seq; comprehensive AC-CISG Opinion No 5 (by Schwenzer); detailed also Conrad, *Die Lieferung mangelhafter Ware*, 53 et seq.

[305] Compare Schwenzer in Schlechtriem/Schwenzer, *Commentary*, Art 41 para 21.

[306] See para 171.

[307] See case law under para 114.

[308] Compare, with references to the history, especially with reference to the international decisions in regard to abstain from a ipso-facto avoidance of the contract Huber in Schlechtriem (3 ed) Art 49 para 36 fn 168.

needs to be filled in accordance with Article 7(2) CISG since the seller is protected enough by the possibility to get clarity under Article 48(2) CISG.[309]

b) If the seller has delivered but delivered late then the reasonable time period starts when the buyer has become aware that the delivery has been made (Article 49(2)(a) CISG).

> Example: The sales contract stated for the delivery of seasonal goods 2 May 1995. The goods were to be delivered to the storage place of company X in the place where the buyer had its seat. They were to be stored for the buyer. The delivery to the storage company only took place on 14 May 1995. The buyer is notified on 16 May 1995 that the goods have arrived. The reasonable time of Article 49(2)(a) CISG starts on 16 May.

The type of goods and the circumstances of the individual case, are inter alia, decisive in regard to the reasonableness of the time period. Generally the buyer should be expected to decide quickly.[310] The German Bundersgerichtshof held three weeks to be reasonable.[311] The OLG Oldenburg even five weeks.[312] However, time periods should not be established by precedent; the individual circumstances should always determine the period in each case.

c) In regard to other breaches of contract like the delivery of non-conform goods, goods which are subject to the rights of the third party, or the breach of ancillary duties the time period starts generally after the buyer knew the breach of contract or ought to have known (Article 49(2)(b) CISG). In the case of granting time periods in accordance with Articles 47(1) or 48(2) CISG,[313] generally after those periods have been passed (Articles 49(2)(b)(ii) and (iii)) unless the futility of granting a time period is obvious due to a declaration by the seller (in case of (ii)) or the buyer (in case of (iii)).

> Example 1:   The seller has, without an agreement in the contract, declared a retention of title on the goods when delivering the goods. The seller breached the contract since the goods have a defective title. If the retention of title amounts to a fundamental breach of the contract then the buyer has to declare avoidance within a reasonable time after he or she knew or ought to have known about the breach. In the case that it was questionable whether the seller's declaration of a retention of title amounted to a fundamental breach and, therefore, the buyer granted the seller an extension to completely perform his or her obligation, that means to pass the property fully to the buyer,

---

[309] See para 181.

[310] Huber in Schlechtriem (3 ed) Art 49 para 38 who generally expect the buyer to decide immediately.

[311] BGH (3 Apr 1996) CISG-online 135 = BGHZ 132, 290, NJW 1996, 2364 – see also para 115.

[312] OLG Oldenburg (1 Feb 1995) CISG-online 253.

[313] CISG, Art 47(1) reads: "The buyer may fix an additional period of time of reasonable length for performance by the seller of his obligations." CISG, Art 48(2) states: "If the seller requests the buyer to make known whether he will accept performance and the buyer does not comply with the request within a reasonable time, the seller may perform within the time indicated in his request. The buyer may not, during that period of time, resort to any remedy which is inconsistent with performance by the seller."

the expiry of the extension will be determinative for the start of the period in which the statement must be made. An exception exists if the seller declares right from the beginning that he or she will not change his or her mind in regard to the retention of title.

Example 2:   In the Marlboro case[314] the period to declare avoidance of the contract by the buyer only started after the buyer had knowledge or could have had knowledge that the seller itself, in breach of the contract, had offered shoes at a shoe fare under the protected trade mark.

It is noteworthy that the buyer's right to avoid the contract can be blocked by Article 82(1) CISG if the buyer cannot give the goods back at all or not in essentially the condition in which the buyer received them.[315]

3.5   Damages

201. If the seller breaches his or her contractual duties or duties which are imposed by the CISG the buyer has a right to damages (Article 45(1)(b) CISG). Whether the breach is due to non-performance, part performance, not timely performance, or defective performance is irrelevant as is whether the duty is the main duty under the contract, that means the delivery of the goods, or whether it is an additional (secondary or ancillary) duty agreed on with the seller. Neither is the "fault" of the seller a relevant consideration. However, the CISG makes provision for exempting the seller in certain circumstances (Articles 79, 80 CISG).[316] The CISG also stipulates that the buyer has a duty to minimise the damage (Article 77 CISG). A breach of that duty can influence the amount of damages. In regard to putting the reasons to exempt the seller in more concrete terms, as for example the duty to minimise the damage, the reasons for the breach of the contract like the obstacle which occurred during the formation of the contract or later occurrences can be of relevance. Articles 74–77 CISG which contain general provisions in regard to damages[317] also set the parameters how to calculate damages.

3.6   Reduction in Price

202. The buyer has the right to reduce the price (Article 50 CISG) if the delivered goods do not conform to the contract.[318] The purchase price can in certain circumstances even be reduced to zero.[319] The non-conformity of the contract

---

[314] See above para 114 – infringement of the buyer's exclusive trademark by the seller/manufacturer.

[315] See also paras 324 et seq.

[316] See paras 287 et seq.

[317] See paras 299 et seq.

[318] See similarly s 48c(1)(a) SOGA which allows buyer to require seller to reduce purchase price by an appropriate amount.

[319] Compare BGH (2 Mar 2005) CISG-online 999 = IHR 2005, 158, 159; see also OGH (23 May 2005) CISG-online 1041 = IHR 2005, 165, 166, 167: reduction of price to zero despite the loss of the right to avoid the contract because of the lapse of the notice period (Art 49(2)(b) CISG). In the literature the

applies according to Article 35(1) CISG to defects of the goods, delivery of an aliud, and defects in regard to the agreed quantity of the goods.[320] It is controversial in the literature whether a reduction of price is also possible in the case of the non-conformity of good due to a defect in title.[321]

It would be desirable to allow a reduction in price for defects in regard to the legal status of the goods to avoid also in regard to this remedy the difficult demarcation between defects in regard to the quality of the goods and defects in regard to their legal status. The genesis of the provision and the reluctance of the common law countries to fully embrace this remedy which is based on the Roman actio quanti minoris and which from the common law point of view is superfluous speak against the analogous use of Article 50 CISG to defects in regard to the legal status of the goods. Also a unified approach will in practice not eventuate. A solution offers (in the case of a defect in regard to the legal status of the goods) a set-off with a damages claim because of a defect in the legal status, which of course can be different from a reduction in price and which can be subject to a defence by the buyer according to Articles 79(1) and 79(2) CISG.[322]

203. The function of a reduction in price is to re-adjust the contractual party which has been disturbed due to the non-conformity of the goods. It, therefore, follows that the adjustment has to be made in relation to the purchase price and not in regard to the absolute amount of the damages occurring due to the lesser value of the goods.[323] Further, the costs to remedy the non-conformity of the goods should also not be taken into account. The buyer can reduce the purchase price comparatively to the value of the defect less goods to the goods which do not conform to the contract.

| Example: | The buyer bought sulphur free fuel oil for €32 per 100 l. The seller delivered fuel oil containing sulphur. Sulphur free fuel oil had a value of €30 per 100 l (the buyer had bought disadvantageously); fuel oil containing sulphur on the other hand had only a value of €15 per 100 l and was, therefore, only worth half of the sulphur free fuel oil. The purchase price gets reduced to half, that means €16, and not in accordance with the about difference of the value of sulphur free |

---

price reduction to zero has been likened to avoidance and has, therefore, been denied because it would circumvent the requirements, like the notice period, of avoidance (see the discussion of the literature in the OGH judgment). However since the right to seek damages is not relinquished if the right to avoid the contract has lapsed it is no contrary to the principles of the CISG to allow a price reduction to zero.

[320] See in regard to defects in regard to quantity para 192a; see also Hirner, *Rechtsbehelf der Minderung,* 132 et seq (no reduction in price – p 136); as well as Huber in Schlechtriem (3 ed) Art 51 para 2 (defect in quantity is "normal" defect), Art 50 para 4 (of subsidianty of Art 50 CISG to Art 51 CISG); a defect in regard to the quantity of the goods actually is irrelevant: Müller-Chen in Schlechtriem/Schwenzer, *Commentary* Art 51 para 6.

[321] Against a reduction: Schwenzer in Schlechtriem/Schwenzer, *Commentary,* Art 41 para 20; Art 42 paras 25, 26; in regard to the contrary view: Reinhart, *UN-Kaufrecht,* Art 50 para 2; Herber/Czerwenka, *Internationales Kaufrecht,* Art 50 para 3; probably too Magnus in Staudinger Art 50 para 9. Very detailed Hirner, *Rechtsbehelf der Minderung,* 191 et seq (against a reduction) 214, 215.

[322] See para 203.

[323] See Honnold, *Uniform Law for International Sales,* §§ 312, 337.

and sulphur containing fuel oil, that means from €15 to €17 per 100 l: The reduction in price is comparatively high because the purchase price was above the objective value of the defectless goods. Had the buyer bought the fuel oil at a bargain price of €28 per 100 l; then the reduction in price would be (calculated on the comparative value of sulphur free and sulphur containing fuel oil 15:30 = ½) also half of the agreed price, therefore €14 per 100 l and not €13 per 100 l – the subtraction of the absolute difference: the cheaper purchase price in relation to the value of the good reduces also the reduction quota.

The relative calculation of the price reduction shows that the reduction of price is not a kind of damages "under relieved requirements", as some common law jurists at the Vienna Conference thought.[324] The seller cannot exonerate himself or herself in accordance with Article 79 CISG, in contrast to a claim of damages, when the buyer invokes his or her right of the reduction in price:[325] have the goods been damaged due to an impediment beyond the party's control the buyer can reduce the purchase price accordingly but cannot claim damages.

In practice it can be difficult to ascertain the value of the contract conform goods and the non-conforming goods necessary for the comparison. This is especially so if no market for the goods exists. The reform of the German law of obligations includes a provision which allows judges to estimate the value of the goods if the value cannot be ascertained any other way (§ 441(3) BGB). If one qualifies § 441(3) BGB as a procedural norm then § 441(3) BGB can be used even if the CISG is applicable.

Example: A Swiss buyer bought furniture from the Italian manufacturer. The buyer stated that certain living room furniture had been not conform to the contract. In regard to the delivered furniture the buyer's right to reduction of price was recognised. The Court calculated the price reduction in accordance with Article 50 CISG so that, unless proven to the contrary, the value of the contract conforming goods equals the value of the agreed purchase price.[326]

204. Article 50 CISG stipulates the time of delivery of the goods as the point in time to calculate the value of the non-conform goods.[327] The buyer, therefore, might lose the advantages of a bargain purchase if in the time between contract formation and date of delivery the price for the goods of the delivered, but not contract conforming, goods which conform with the contract.[328] The reduction of price is brought about by the buyer's statement which according to Article 27

---

[324] Compare: Bergsten/Miller, (1979) 27 Am J Comp L, 255 et seq; see in regard to the genesis of the reduction of price in the CISG, pp. 266 et seq.

[325] See CISG, Art 79(5).

[326] Compare Pretura di Locarno-Campagna (27 Apr 1992) CISG-online 68 = SZER1993, 665; unfortunately the Court did not stipulate how it calculated the value of the defective furniture; the decision only contains a comment that the Court did not equate the value of the defective furniture with damages calculated in relation to the necessary costs for repair.

[327] Bergsten/Miller, (1979) 27 Am J Comp L, 255, 260, 274, 275.

[328] See Hirner, *Rechtsbehelf der Minderung,* 364 et seq, 374–377.

CISG only needs to be dispatched but does not need to reach the addressee.[329] In case that the buyer has paid too much he or she has a restitutionary claim is in regard to the overpaid purchase price. This restitutionary claim is based on Article 81(2) CISG applicable by gap-filling in accordance with Article 7(2) CISG. To revert to domestic law of unjust enrichment is not necessary.[330] Accordingly, the seller has to pay interest on the overpaid purchase price (Articles 84(1) CISG).

3.7   The Buyer's Right to Withhold Performance

3.7.1 The Right to Withhold at the Time Performance was Due

205. The CISG does not contain an explicit general right to withhold performance.[331] Also the defence that a contract had not been performed (exceptio non admipleti contractus) is not provided for in detail in the CISG. Articles 58(1) (2nd s) and Article 58(2) CISG, however, stipulate specific rights to withhold – albeit casted as provisions regarding the time performance is due in regard to delivery and payment:[332] the buyer can withhold the purchase price until the seller has delivered the goods or the documents which entitle the buyer to dispose over the goods, especially document of title to goods.[333] On the other hand, the seller can make the delivery of the goods or the documents dependent on the buyer paying the purchase price controlling their disposition even if it is a distant sale (Article 58(2) CISG), from being paid the purchase price. Articles 58(1)(2nd s), 58(2) CISG are based upon the principle of step-by-step performance[334] which albeit only comes to bear if the parties have not agreed something else like a duty of advance performance by one party.

206. It is questionable whether a general right to withhold performance in accordance with Article 7(2) CISG[335] can be distilled from Article 58(1) CISG and other provisions like Article 85(1st s) CISG, which requires the principle of step-by-step performance, or Article 86(1)(2nd s) CISG which gives the buyer a specific right to withhold payment[336] so that reverting back to domestic law is not necessary.

Example: The seller agrees to the delivery of the machine and to set up the machine at the buyer's premises as well as to instruct the buyer's

---

[329] Compare paras 109 et seq.

[330] Hirner, *Rechtsbehelf der Minderung*, 411, 412: Hirner bases the payback claim directly on Art 50 CISG.

[331] German law has a general right to withhold performance (§ 273(1) BGB).

[332] See para 219.

[333] "Documents" in Art 58 (1) CISG refers not only to real document of title to goods but all documents which enable the seller to perform his or her obligations according to Artt 30, 34 CISG; Hager in Schlechtriem/Schwenzer, *Commentary*, Art 58 para 10; Schlechtriem, *Einheitliches UN-Kaufrecht*, 74 fn 327.

[334] CISG, Art 85 (1st s) also requires the principle of step-by-step performance for the payment of the purchase price and the delivery of the goods.

[335] See paras 45 et seq.

[336] See in regard to Art 86(1)(2nd s) CISG para 336.

employees in the handling of the machine. The delivery and the set up have been successfully completed, however, the promised instructions do not take place. Can the buyer withhold part or the entire purchase price?

It is desirable, as already discussed in para 42d, to distil a general principle from the CISG itself, Articles 58(1), 85(1st s), Article 86(1)(2nd s) CISG as well as Article 71(1) CISG suggest a general principle that the party's own performance can be withheld if the other party does not fulfil its obligations under the contract.[337] The acknowledgment of a general right to withhold and the therewith exclusion of reverting to domestic law is also advisable because a general right to withhold developed within the structure of the CISG allows limitations not known by domestic law. For example, under a CISG right to withhold the buyer should be able to withhold the entire purchase price if the seller's non-fulfilment of his or her obligations amounts to a fundamental breach of the contract. If the seller's breach does not amount to a fundamental breach and the buyer cannot avoid the contract the buyer should only be able to withhold the purchase price as much as the buyer can claim as damages or as reduction of price because of the seller's breach of contract. Further, the way the CISG has set out the party's right to suspend the performance of its obligation when after the conclusion of the contract, it becomes apparent that the other party will not perform a substantial part of its obligation (Article 71 CISG)[338] shows that only a breach of contract which breaches fundamental parts of the seller's obligations allows to withhold the party's own entire performance. Therefore, the buyer can only withhold the purchase price for the amount of a possible damages claim where the defeat is in regard to unimportant qualities at legal status' of the goods.

3.7.2 The Right to Suspended Performance when other Party will Apparently not Perform its Obligations

207. The buyer can withhold the purchase price because of the step-by-step principle if the counter-performance is mature and has not been furnished.[339] In addition, Article 71 CISG allows the parties to suspend performance when the other party will apparently not perform its obligations. This defence allows the party, especially in cases of advanced performance, to withhold its own performance if the other party's performance of fundamental obligations which are not matured yet is endangered. The CISG has set out this defence as general defence, that means, it is applicable to both parties and indeed in practice it is of equal importance for buyer and seller. Therefore, it will be dealt with later.[340]

---

[337] OGH (8 Nov 2005) CISG-online 1156 = IHR 2006, 87, 90 in regard to a contract of work and materials; see also footnotes in para 42d; Magnus in *Staudinger*, Art 4 para 47a.

[338] See paras 256 et seq.

[339] See para 205.

[340] See para 256 et seq.

3.7.3 Rejection of the Goods

208. The CISG does neither explicitly nor generally set out the buyer's possibility to reject the offered goods because the seller breached an obligation, that means to withhold acceptance of the goods. However, the CISG sets out some special circumstances: Article 51(1) CISG exemplifies that the buyer generally has to accept part-performance.[341] The buyer, however, can reject part-performance if the buyer could avoid the entire contract, that means the requirements of Article 51(2) CISG are met.[342] The buyer does not need to accept early delivery or delivery in excess of the quantity agreed upon (Articles 52(1), (2)(1st s) CISG).[343] The duties of the buyer in regard to possession and maintenance of the goods as set out in Article 86 CISG have to be observed in case of an early delivery or a delivery exceeding the agreed quantity, which even if the requirements of a right to refuse acceptance are met often will oblige the buyer to (at least) temporarily take care of the goods (Article 86(2)(1st s) CISG.[344] An effective rejection is, therefore, only possible if the buyer recognises the non-conformity with the contract when collecting the goods at the seller's.

Other than in cases of early delivery and excess quantity is it worth considering to give the buyer the right to withhold acceptance of the goods if the goods are not in conformity with the contract until the buyer can discern which remedies are available to him or her. However, the buyer should be obliged to take the goods and to store them for the seller in the meantime (Articles 86(1)(2), 87 CISG.[345]

208a. In case the seller delivers an excess quantity of the goods to be able to claim any remedies under the CISG,[346] the buyer only has to pay the agreed purchase price. If the buyer accepts the excess quantity or if the buyer fails to object to it, the purchase price will increase proportionally to the initially agreed quantity.[347]

4   Buyer's Duties

209. Chapter 3 of the CISG sets out firstly in Articles 53 to 60 CISG, Sections 1 and 2, the buyer's duty to pay the purchase price and to accept the purchased goods. In the following Section 3 (Articles 61-65 CISG) the seller's remedies in case of a buyer's breach of contract are set out.[348] Of special importance in relation to the buyer's duty to pay the purchase price are the provisions in regard to the allocation of risk, that means the risk in regard to the price which, therefore,

---

[341] Compare Huber in Schlechtriem (3 ed) Art 51 para 6.

[342] See paras 191, 192.

[343] See also CISG, Art 86(2) which assumes such a right to withhold.

[344] Compare Magnus in *Staudinger*, Art 86 para 14: duty to temporarily accept.

[345] See discussion Schlechtriem, *Symposium Frank Vischer*, sub II.5.c.

[346] See para 153.

[347] Instead of general opinion; P Huber in *MünchKomm*, Art 52 para 25 (with decision-making advice for the buyer).

[348] See paras 235 et seq.

will be discussed following a discussion of the buyer's duties.[349] When discussing the buyer's remedies, like when discussing the buyer's remedies, the general provisions (Articles 71 and 72 CISG) as well as special provisions in regard to the keeping of the goods (Articles 86 to 88 CISG) have to be considered.

The CISG explicitly sets out payment of the purchase price and acceptance of the goods as buyer's duties (Articles 53, 54 to 60 CISG). However, in its remedies available to seller in relation to a buyer's breach of a contractual obligation the CISG recognises that the contract can stipulate further duties for the buyer (compare Articles 61(1), 62 CISG "other obligations"); for example: to provide security, to obtain data, drawings, and technical specifications, to deliver certain materials or components, to comply with export or re-import prohibitions etc.[350] The agreement of Incoterms can constitute another ancillary duty. Article 54 CISG stipulates that necessary measures and formalities which are requirements for the payment are part of the duty to pay. Specification of the goods can be part of the duty to accept the goods. However, Article 65(1) CISG grants the seller a specific remedy in that regard.[351]

4.1   Payment of the Purchase Price

4.1.1 Requirements of the Payment

210. The buyer's duty to pay the purchase price encompasses, on the one hand, all arrangements stipulated in the contract, for example, payment per cheque, cash, advance payments, payment step-by-step against the delivery of documents,[352] and probably also the duty to provide a letter of credit. On the other hand, it compasses also the observation and compliance with relevant (domestic) law, for example, foreign exchange control regulations or transfer regulations, and, if applicable, the obtaining of foreign currency and the necessary money transfer and authorisations (Article 54 CISG).[353] "[F]ormalities as may be required under the contract or according to any laws and regulations" are not only the ones which apply due to the domestic law applicable to the contract in accordance with the private international law rules but also those rules which have to be observed on a practical level to be able to pay the purchase price like foreign exchange control regulations.[354] Since the duties imposed on the buyer by Article 54 CISG are part of the duty to pay the purchase price the breach of any of those obligations gives the seller the remedies in relation to the non-payment of the purchase price.

---

[349] See paras 222 et seq.
[350] See a comprehensive list of examples of such duties in Witz in Witz/Salger/Lorenz, *Internationales Einheitliches Kaufrech* Art 53 paras 11–17.
[351] See paras 252 et seq.
[352] See already CISG, Art 58(1) para 205.
[353] See Witz in Witz/Salger/Lorenz, *Internationales Einheitliches Kaufrecht*, Art 54 para 3; Hager in Schlechtriem/Schwenzer, Art 54 para 3.
[354] Compare Witz in Witz/Salger/Lorenz, *Internationales Einheitliches Kaufrecht*, Art 54 para 4; Hager in Schlechtriem/Schwenzer, Art 54 para 4. Therefore, an enquiry into the law applicable to the foreign exchange control regulations next to the proper law of the contract is not necessary.

4.1.2 Currency

211. A provision in which currency the purchase price has to be paid is absent in the CISG. First and foremost it is important what the parties have agreed. The party agreement or its interpretation, for example, decides upon whether the agreement of a particular currency means that the buyer only can pay the purchase price in that particular currency or whether the buyer can substitute that currency with another one.

> Example: A Hungarian company sold an Austrian company petrol and gas. The contract stipulates the payment of the purchase price in US$. The buyer set-off the seller's claim for payment of the purchase price with a claim against the seller in Forint (Hungarian currency). Austrian law which was applicable in regard to the set-off[355] required similarly of claim and counter-claim, that means the possibility of the buyer to substitute the agreed payment in US$ with Forint. The OGH denied the buyer that possibility because the right to domestic payments in this case the purchase price had to be paid in Hungary and due to the lack of any other agreement had to be paid in US$.[356]

If the parties have not specifically agreed upon a currency in which the purchase has to be paid often a particular usage between the parties or on an auxiliary basis due to usage in accordance with Article 9 CISG[357] will determine the currency. If the parties' intent cannot be ascertained by any means it is questionable whether the gap can be filled by using CISG principles or whether the domestic law determined by private international law rules is applicable to determine the currency.[358]

> Example: A contract between French manufacturer of printing machines and parts and a German company granted the German company the exclusive right to sell the products of the French manufacturer. Because of the delivery of a chip by the French manufacturer to a German client a legal dispute arose. In that legal dispute the issue arose, inter alia, whether the delivery of the chip was due to the sales contract with the German company and which currency the purchase price had to be paid. Since the parties had not agreed upon a currency in which the purchase price had to be paid the Court held that the purchase price had to be paid in the currency of the place of payment, that means, at the seller's place, therefore, (at that point in time) in French francs.[359]

---

[355] See para 42e in regard to which law is applicable to set-off.

[356] OGH (22 Oct 2001) CISG-online 614 = IHR 2002, 24 et seq.

[357] See for a discussion on CISG, Art 9 paras 59 et seq.

[358] See in regard to the question whether in relation to German law the proper law of the contract is applicable or whether a special determination has to be done: Hager in Schlechtriem/Schwenzer, Art 54 para 9; Witz in Witz/Salger/Lorenz, *Internationales Einheitliches Kaufrecht*, Art 53 para 5.

[359] OLG Koblenz (17 Sep 1993) CISG-online 91 = RIW 1993, 934; as well KG (24 Jan 1994) CISG-online 130 = RIW 1994, 683.

As a rule the buyer has to pay the purchase price in the currency of the seller's place of business (Article 57 CISG).[360] If the payment has to be made in a third country because of the delivery of the goods in that country or the handing over of documents, can another currency be considered. In the latter case it has to be carefully ascertained whether the usage or habit of the parties or a tacit agreement between them lead to a currency. A general authority of the buyer to substitute the agreed currency independent from the law applicable to the currency regulation with the currency of the place of payment has to be rejected.[361]

212. The differences in relation to the requirement of a "particular price" for the existence of an offer[362] amounted in Vienna to Article 14(1)(2nd s) CISG, since the majority in Vienna held on to the requirement that the purchase price had to be a "particular" price or at least a price which could be ascertained. Later the majority changed in regard to the rights and obligations of the parties in relation to an already concluded contract. A provision was agreed upon in Vienna which anticipates a contract where the purchase price was neither agreed upon nor being able be ascertained and where Article 55 CISG is filling the gap. Article 14(1)(2nd s) CISG and Article 55 CISG are in fact slightly contradictory which, as especially Bucher has proven,[363] in practice will only be relevant in the rare cases where the missing agreement in regard to the price is discovered before the contract is performed and it is doubtful whether the parties have agreed to a contract at all.[364] Article 55 CISG puts forward the assumption that the parties have silently agreed on the price of the goods which is the object of the contract and which in the relevant line of business would be charged in similar circumstances; the time of the contract formation is decisive in this case. The buyer is, therefore, quite well protected against

---

[360] See KG (24 Jan 1994) CISG-online 130 = RIW 1994, 683 different view Witz in Witz/Salger/Lorenz, *Internationales Einheitliches Kaufrecht*, Art 53 para 5 (determination according to Art 55 CISG).

[361] See OGH (22 Oct 2001) CISG-online 614 = IHR 2002, 24 et seq; further Hager in Schlechtriem/Schwenzer, Art 54 para 10 (but exceptions when "Treu und Glauben" (equity warrants it); see as well Schlechtriem, *Einheitliches UN-Kaufrecht*, 73 fn 320 in relation to the suggestions at the Vienna Conference which were not met with general approval. Different Art 6.1.9 which stipulates that:

(1) If a monetary obligation is expressed in a currency other than that of the place for payment, it may be paid by the obligor in the currency of the place for payment unless

(a) that currency is not freely convertible; or

(b) the parties have agreed that payment should be made only in the currency in which the monetary obligation is expressed.

(2) If it is impossible for the obligor to make payment in the currency in which the monetary obligation is expressed, the obligee may require payment in the currency of the place for payment, even in the case referred to in paragraph (1)(b).

(3) Payment in the currency of the place for payment is to be made according to the applicable rate of exchange prevailing there when payment is due.

(4) However, if the obligor has not paid at the time when payment is due, the obligee may require payment according to the applicable rate of exchange prevailing either when payment is due or at the time of actual payment.

[362] See para 75.

[363] Bucher, *FS Piotet*, 371 et seq; see also Bucher, *Preisvereinbarung*, 53 et seq.

[364] See for more details Schlechtriem in Schlechtriem/Schwenzer, *Commentary*, Art 14 para 11.

excessive prices; on the other hand, the buyer misses out on a bargain.[365] In a particular case it can be difficult to ascertain an objective price on special market for the goods in question. In the *Malev* case[366] the Supreme Court of Hungary assumed that there was no special market for jet power engines as required by Article 55 CISG.

213. The purchase price can also be determinable in accordance with Article 14(1)(2nd s) CISG if the price is to be fixed according to the weight of the goods even if the weight has still to be determined. Article 56 CISG contains a complementary rule according to which, if in doubt, the net weight (that means the total weight minus the packaging) is decisive.[367]

4.1.3 Place of Payment

214. Article 57(1) CISG stipulates that, as far as the contract does not require something different, the place of payment is the seller's place of business (Article 57(1)(a) CISG) or if the purchase price has to be paid bit-by-bit against the delivery of the goods or documents, the place of their handing over (Article 57(1)(b) CISG). According to Article 57(1)(a) CISG the buyer has to bear the risk and the cost of the money transfer. Only if the seller changes his or her place of business after the conclusion of the contract has the seller to bear the additional costs (Article 57(2) CISG). Of practical importance is the seller's place of business as place of payment especially if the buyer has to make an advanced payment or if the buyer got a credit for the purchase price, therefore, only has to pay after the delivery of the goods. The way the CISG has set out the place of payment as the seller's place of business accords with many domestic legal systems[368]

215. If the forum state provides for a jurisdiction dependent on the place of performance the regulation in Article 57 CISG can lead to a court's jurisdiction at the creditor's domicile or place of business which is from a legal-political point of view undesirable.[369] Suggestions of the delegation of the Federal Republic of Germany in Vienna to separate jurisdiction and place of performance were fruitless since it was decided that the Conference did not have the mandate to decide upon

---

[365] Compare Hager in Schlechtriem/Schwenzer, Art 55 para 8.

[366] See para 76.

[367] In regard to contractual provisions which contain a different regime and therefore refute Art 56 CISG see Hager in Schlechtriem/Schwenzer, Art 56 para 2.

[368] Note that, in contrast, the German law has set out the purchase price payment as (Hohlschuld – a dept to be discharged at the domicile of the debtor) see in regard to the genesis of the German provision: von Caemmerer in Flume (ed) 14: the drafters of the BGB wanted to avoid that, by making the place of payment the creditor's place of business, the court at the creditor's place of business would have jurisdiction. There is no suggestion that common law countries would be any different, although Honnold, *Uniform Law for International Sales*, § 332(2) argues that the place of payment may in some procedural systems also determine the place of jurisdiction. This may be problematic given that the seller often wants to sue in the buyer's country for the price.

[369] See ECJ (20 Jun 1994) NJW 1995, 183 in regard to the old Art 5 No 1 of the Brussels Convention.

procedural issues.[370] After the coming into force of the Brussels Regulations,[371] the successor to the Brussels Convention, Article 5 No 1(a) in conjunction with (b) (first bullet point) now stipulates the place of the delivery of the goods and also the court's jurisdiction for claims regarding the payment of the purchase price.[372] The place of delivery has to be determined in accordance with Article 31 CISG if the CISG is applicable to the contract.[373] If the contract of sale involves the carriage of goods the place where the goods are dispatched is decisive not the place where the buyer receives the goods.[374]

216. Article 5 No 1(b) Brussels Regulation sets out that the payment at the seller's place corresponds with the step-by-step principle embedded in Article 58(1)(2nd s) CISG.[375]

Example: An Austrian Company negotiated a contract with a company which had its place of business in Croatia. The contract was the installations and their fitting in a hotel. The payment was due bit-by-bit against the handing over of the goods at the place of the buyer's customer in the then Czechoslovakia. The Arbitral tribunal of the ICC, therefore, concluded that the payment had to be made in Czechoslovakia (Article 57(1)(b) CISG).[376]

The uses of Article 57(1)(b) CISG, however, are problematic in cases where the contract is for the carriage of goods or for the sale of goods in storage since in those cases the parties do not meet at a place to exchange their performances.[377] In such cases the principle of Article 57(1)(a) CISG is applicable.

---

[370] Compare: Schlechtriem, *Einheitliches UN-Kaufrecht*, 73 fn 325.

[371] Regulation Convention on Jurisdiction and the Enforcement of Judgments in Civil and Commercial Matters [2001] OJ L 12, 1–23.

[372] Therefore, decision of the ECJ in regard to the old Art 5(1) Brussels Convention are to some extent out-dated: see as well Magnus, ZEuP 2002, 523, 541; Magnus, IHR 2002, 45 et seq.

[373] See in regard to a discussion in regard to an autonomous determination of the place of delivery under Art 5 No 1 (a) in conjunction with (b) 1st bullet point versus a determination taking into account the relevant CISG provisions: Schroeter, *UN-Kaufrecht und Gemeinschaftsrecht*, 590 et seq; see also in regard to the provision of services BGH (2 Mar 2006) WM 2006, 980, 981 "has to be determined autonomously detached from the particular legal categories of the member states."

[374] Controversial: see discussion in Piltz, IHR 2006, 53, 56.

[375] Brussels Regulations, Art 5: "A person domiciled in a Member State may, in another Member State, be sued:
(a) in matters relating to a contract, in the courts for the place of performance of the obligation in question;
(b) for the purpose of this provision and unless otherwise agreed, the place of performance of the obligation in question shall be:
in the case of the sale of goods, the place in a Member State where, under the contract, the goods were delivered or should have been delivered,
in the case of the provision of services, the place in a Member State where, under the contract, the services were provided or should have been provided,
(c) if subparagraph (b) does not apply then subparagraph (a) applies;".

[376] ICC Paris (1 Jan 1992) CISG-online 36 = JDI 1993, 1028.

[377] Compare Hager in Schlechtriem/Schwenzer, *Commentary*, Art 57 paras 14–17.

Example: The seller, a mechanical engineering company with its place of business in Stuttgart, Germany had delivered an Italian company with its place of business in Geneva mining machines within a framework of a distribution contract. For the jurisdiction of the court it was decisive where the place of payment of the purchase price was which the German seller was claiming. The Italian buyer noted that contract for the carriage of goods had been agreed upon and, therefore the place of delivery of the machines in Geneva was also the place of payment of the purchase price. The BGH did not follow that argument: The Court first agreed that the contract was one for the carriage of goods. The principle of the step-by-step performance of the contractual obligations, however, was not compatible with a contract for the carriage of goods was that the seller with the dispatch of the goods to the carrier for transport to the buyer performed the seller's obligation of delivery of the goods. The spatial distance between the seller's place of business and the buyer is bridged by an independent third party, the carrier, and, therefore, the core requirement of a step-by-step performance, the immediate and simultaneous exchange by goods and purchase price payment between seller and buyer is not fulfilled. Article 57(1)(b) CISG is, therefore, not applicable if the contract is one for the carriage of goods.[378] The core principle that the seller's place of business determines the place of the payment of the purchase price remains.[379]

If the seller takes advantage of the possibility set out in Article 58(2) CISG, namely to agree that a carriage of goods contract the buyer will only be able to receive the goods if the buyer pays the purchase price then is the place where the goods are handed over also the place of payment of the purchase price.

4.1.4 Time of Payment

217. Article 58 CISG sets out the timeframes for the payment of the purchase price in case the parties have not agreed on a "specific" time of payment. At the same time Article 58 CISG contains the stipulation for the principle the "payment" means that the entire purchase price has to be paid incrementally against the handing over of the goods or the documents controlling the goods' disposition[380] (Articles 58(1)(2nd s), (2) CISG). In addition, Article 58(3) CISG allows the buyer to pay the purchase price only if the buyer had the opportunity to examine the goods unless the parties' agreement on delivery and payments arrangement do not exclude that. The buyer has the opportunity to detect the non-conformity of the goods before payment and to withhold the purchase in its entirety or in part.[381]

In particular, Article 58(1)(1st s) CISG stipulates that in case of the handing over the goods at the seller's place of business or at a third party the purchase price

---

[378] ULIS was still applicable in the circumstances: Art 59(1) ULIS corresponds with Art 57(1)(b) CISG.

[379] BGH (28 Mar 1979) NJW 1979, 1779.

[380] See para 205.

[381] See para 206.

becomes mature if the seller has done everything necessary so that the buyer can take over the goods (especially the selection of the goods and the notification of the buyer). If the seller has to offer the goods at the buyer's place of business or at a third party's place then the time the purchase price is due arises with the offer. In case of a purchase of stored goods are the goods offered to the buyer if the storekeeper at the instigation of the seller, acknowledges the buyer's right to possession as far as the buyer had the opportunity to inspect the goods (Article 58(3) CISG). In case the contract is for a carriage of goods the seller has to offer the goods at the agreed place. Simply to dispatch the goods with a third party is not enough to trigger the time performance was due.[382]

218. The time the purchase price payment is due arises at the time stipulated in the contract or under Article 58 CISG without that the seller is required to ask or to remind the buyer and without that particular formalities have to be observed (Article 59 CISG). Especially it does not need a reminder or a "mise en demeure" to bring about the time performance is due and in the case of non-payment to bring about a breach of an obligation. Exceptions are possible, for example, if the exact amount to pay needs further determination or notifications, like, for example, the weighing of goods or the delivery of the goods at a time the buyer did not need to expect them.[383]

219. The way Article 58 CISG provides for if the parties have not agreed on a time for the payment of the purchase price being due is slightly differently from the common law. First, in common law previous practices between the parties or established custom are used to assess an appropriate time for payment.[384] Failing this, payment is due when the seller informs the buyer that he is ready to deliver the goods.[385] The rules relating to time specified in the contract have usually been enforced strictly.[386] The unpaid seller has a right to rescind the contract or resell the goods where he gives reasonable notice of their intention to do so.[387] Whether this extends to the rejection of early payments or part payments is doubtful.

4.2   Duty to Accept Delivery

4.2.1 Content of the Duty to Accept

220. The duty to accept or the duty to take delivery is set out in Article 60 CISG and has two requirements. First, the buyer has to do all the acts which could

---

[382] Compare the case para 216.

[383] Magnus in Staudinger, Art 59 para 6.

[384] Benjamin, *Sale of Goods*, 9-056 citing s 55(l) Sale of Goods Act 1979 (UK), *King v Reedman* (1883) 49 LT 473, *R v Jones* [1898] 1 QB 119.

[385] Benjamin, *Sale of Goods*, 9-056, although s 28 of the Sale of Goods sees payment as being a concomitant of delivery which suggests a closer approach to Art 58 CISG than the approach in Benjamin.

[386] *Mardorf Peach & Co Ltd v Attica Sea Carriers Corp of Liberia* [1977] AC 850.

[387] Sale of Goods Act 1979 (UK), s 48(3).

reasonably be expected of the buyer in order to enable the seller to make delivery, for example, to procure necessary import permits or to prepare a site for the installation of a machine (Article 60(a) CISG). Part of the buyers' duty can also be to specify the goods.[388] Second, the buyer has to take over the goods (Article 60(b) CISG). If the seller can discharge his or her performance by making the goods available at his or her place of business or at a third place then the buyer has to transport them away. Not explicitly regulated is the question whether the buyer has a reasonable time period in which he or she can accept the goods. This question has to be solved in regard to Article 7(1) CISG. Generally, an immediate acceptance will be owed and will also need to be reasonable.[389] Part of taking delivery is that the buyer unloads the goods if they have been delivered and pays for the unloading.[390] By taking delivery, the buyer does not stipulate that the delivered goods are in conformity with the contract.[391]

4.2.2 Offer of Non-conforming Goods

221. The buyer has the choice to accept or to reject early delivery of the goods or the delivery of excess quantity (Articles 52(1), (2) CISG). The buyer has to accept a late delivery unless the buyer can avoid the contract under Article 49(1)(2nd s)(a) CISG.[392] Part performance has to be accepted by the buyer if the buyer cannot avoid the contract in its entirety (Article 51(2) CISG). Goods which do not conform with the contract can generally only be rejected by the buyer if the non-conformity amounts to a fundamental breach and the buyer requires the delivery of substitute goods (Article 46(2) CISG) or can avoid the contract (Article 49(1)(a) CISG). In case the buyer has a right to withhold[393] the buyer can refuse to take delivery for a certain amount of time. In those cases "to refuse" to take delivery does not necessarily mean a buyer's right to refuse to take possession of the goods for the seller in the limits outlined by Article 86(2) CISG[394] and to keep them.[395] In all other cases the buyer has to take delivery.[396]

4.3   Passing of Risk

222. The buyer's obligation to pay the purchase price depends on the performance of the seller's obligations. If the seller has performed his or her obligations in its entirety the buyer in general will have to pay the purchase price even if the

---

[388] See para 252.

[389] Magnus in *Staudinger*, Art 60 para 7.

[390] Magnus in *Staudinger*, Art 60 para 5.

[391] Magnus in *Staudinger*, Art 60 para 8.

[392] See para 188.

[393] See para 208.

[394] See para 337.

[395] See para 208.

[396] Compare para 208, as well as Hornung in Schlechtriem/Schwenzer, *Commentary*, Art 86 paras 8 et seq.

goods are destroyed or are damaged. In other words, the payment risk is passed on to the buyer once the seller has performed his or her obligations. If the seller does not perform his or her obligations, the buyer in general does not have to pay. Under the CISG, the seller's non-performance presents the due date for the buyer's payment to arise and gives the buyer the right if the requirements are met[397] to avoid the contract. If the buyer avoids the contract, the buyer's obligation to pay the purchase price is discharged (Article 81(1) CISG). The CISG does allow exemptions to that principle for certain cases in which the seller has not or only part performed and the buyer has to pay nonetheless, despite the fact that the buyer cannot claim complete performance anymore. The payment risk in such cases has already passed to the buyer before complete performance. Therefore, it is not the complete performance but the passing of the risk in regard to the buyer's obligations to pay the purchase price that is determinative.

4.3.1 General Rule

223. Article 66 CISG sets out the principle: The buyer has to pay the full purchase price, after the risk has passed even if the goods get lost or get damaged. The CISG makes an exemption in the case that the loss or damage is due to an act or omission of the seller (Article 66(2nd s) CISG). The terms loss and damage of the goods also cover other losses like theft, emergency unloading of the goods, or misdirection by the carrier.[398] However, rules on the bearing of the risk do not cover acts of state, such as confiscation of the goods or the adoption of export bans. Against the acts for state no insurance can be taken out; acts of state are legal measures which can be contested by the party concerned. Since this situation has nothing to do with risk and, therefore cannot be insured whether account should be taken of acts of state is a matter of international trade law. They do not fall under the passing of the risk rules.[399]

The passing of the risk requires that neither party is at fault in regard to the loss or the damage of the goods. Article 66(2nd s) CISG does not let the passing of risk occur if the loss or damage is due to an act or omission of the seller, for example, if the already delivered goods are damaged when they are offloaded.[400] Whether the seller breached a contract is not decisive. The seller's acts or omissions which later led to the loss or damage of the goods will often amount to a breach of contract, for example, if the goods are not properly packed, or when a defect transferred slowly into other goods and subsequently destroys the goods. The realm of the regulation when the risk passes, the distribution of the risk of the accidental loss of the goods has been left with these considerations.

---

[397] See para 189.
[398] Hager in Schlechtriem/Schwenzer, *Commentary*, Art 66 para 3.
[399] Hager in Schlechtriem/Schwenzer, *Commentary*, Art 66 para 4; Piltz, *Internationales Kaufrecht*, Art 66 para 4, para 186; very controversial – different view Magnus in *Staudinger*, Art 66 para 6. These cases can be liable cases where of course it has to be risk, whether the seller bears the risk or whether the seller can discharge his or her obligations under Art 79 CISG.
[400] Compare in regard examples Schlechtriem, *Einheitliches UN-Kaufrecht*, 78.

The "responsibility" of the seller under Articles 79(1) and (2) CISG[401] for acts or omissions which are the cause for loss or damage of the sold goods after the risk has passed can give the buyer additionally to the exemption to pay the purchase price damages claims due to a breach of contract (or non-contractual liability under domestic law) but is not a requirement for an exception to the passing of the risk. A mere causal connection between the seller's acts or omissions and the loss or damage of the goods cannot by itself prevent the passing of the risk. If the seller's conduct is completely lawful, for example if the seller stops the delivery of goods because of pending insolvency of the buyer (compare Article 71(2)(1st s) CISG)[402] which becomes the cause for the loss or damage of the goods (because had the seller delivered the goods they would have not been lost or damaged) the payment risk passes despite the causal connection between the seller's conduct and the loss or damage of the goods.[403] The conduct of the seller has to be not quite faultless and, therefore, attributable to and causal for the loss or damage of the goods.

224. The buyer can avoid the contract and therewith let the seller's right to claim the purchase price lapse if the seller's breach of the contract is fundamental. The risk passes back to the seller with the avoidance.[404] If the buyer has failed to object in time to the non-conformity of the goods (including to an aliud delivery) or any defect in title to the goods or the fact that the goods are not free from any right or claim of a third party based on industrial property or other intellectual property the buyer has to pay the purchase price even if the goods are lost and the buyer could have avoided the contract if the buyer had objected to the goods in time. If the buyer cannot give the goods back, for example, because of a consequential and insidious defect does not prevent the buyer to avoid the contract nor the passing back of the risk: the seller has to pay back the full purchase price even if the goods cannot be given back (Article 82(2)(a) CISG)[405].

224a. Hager is of the view that the seller's claim to the purchase price falls within the scope of Article 28 CISG.[406] That means that according to Hager the buyer does not need to pay the price if under the law of the forum the court would not order him to pay the price in a comparable situation. As Hager notes, his view is close to the American law. Under the UCC if the buyer of fungible goods breaches the contract by failing to take delivery of them, where upon the seller preserves the goods for him for an unreasonably long period and the goods are then accidentally destroyed, then despite the risk having passed to the buyer, the UCC prevents the seller from bringing an action for the price.[407] Behind Hager's

---

[401] See paras 288 et seq.

[402] See para 265.

[403] Compare Hager in Schlechtriem/Schwenzer, *Commentary*, Art 66 para 7.

[404] Compare Schlechtriem, *Einheitliches UN-Kaufrecht*, 79 fn 347.

[405] See paras 326 et seq.

[406] Hager in Schlechtriem/Schwenzer, *Commentary*, Art 66 para 7a.

[407] UCC §§ 2–510(3), 2–709 (1a)(b).

view and the approach under the UCC stands the idea that there must be a time limit during which the buyer in breach must bear the risk.[408] The drafting history and discussions surrounding Article 28 CISG, however, suggest that this was not what the drafters had in mind. Specific performance under Article 28 CISG has to be seen in contrast to damages which will always be monetary compensation. To extend Article 28 CISG to the purchase price payment would mean to substitute money for money which was not the aim of Article 28 CISG. Expectation damages are the cornerstone of contractual remedies. Therefore, limiting its possibility by calling it "specific performance" might go against this important concept.[409]

4.3.2 Sale Involving the Carriage of Goods

225. For sale of goods involving the carriage of the goods Article 67(1) CISG contains the regulation that the risk passes to the buyer when the goods are handed over to the carrier for transport to the buyer. The CISG does not distinguish between the transport by sea or over land. The primary case, as set out under Article 67(1)(1st s) CISG that the goods are handed over to the first carrier is often varied by special contractual agreements, like the use of Incoterms, that the goods have to be handed over to another carrier at a particular place. In that case, the risk does not pass to the buyer until the goods are handed over to the carrier at that place (Article 67(1)(1st s) CISG and not already when the goods are handed over to the first carrier.

Example:	If the goods have been sold FOB (free on board)[410] Hamburg the risk passes only to the buyer when the goods are loaded onto the ship at the Hamburg harbour.[411]

The passing of the risk, as set out in Article 67(1)(2nd s) CISG, by handing over "at a particular place" is applicable without any consideration for whether the first log of the transport has been carried out by the seller's employees or an independent carrier.

226. It is irrelevant in regard to the passing of the risk whether the transport documents have been withheld or whether they have been already handed over (Article 67(1)(3rd s) CISG. The retention of the documents, for example to secure payment, and the therewith remaining possibility for the seller to dispose over the goods does not prevent the passage of the risk. At the same time this makes it clear that the passage of the risk is independent from the passing or the remaining

---

[408] Note the UCC approach would be applicable under the CISG by virtue of Art 28 CISG, so that the buyer would be exempted from the obligation to pay the price even though the risk had passed to the buyer.

[409] See for further discussion Hager in Schlechtriem/Schwenzer, *Commentary*, Art 62 para 12 with fn 26.

[410] See in regard to an up-to-date list of Incoterms: http://www.iccwbo.org.

[411] The passing of the risk arises for the FOB-provision, see Hager in Schlechtriem/Schwenzer, *Commentary*, Art 67 para 6.

of the property in the goods at the seller. The documents or their handing over can be, of course, decisive for whether the property in the goods passes.[412]

227. The carrier is according to the general opinion only the independent carrier. If the seller transports the goods using his or her own employees the risk that the goods are lost, destroyed or damaged stays with the seller.[413] The handing over to an independent carrier results only then to a passing of the risk if the carrier charges a fee for the transportation of the goods to the buyer and therewith also in fact takes over the transport even if the carrier himself or herself uses a freight forwarder and does not transport the goods himself or herself.[414]

228. The passing of the risk when the contract is for the carriage of goods under Article 67(1) CISG in regard to generic goods requires that the lost, destroyed or damaged goods have been individualised, that means that the goods can be clearly assigned to a contract. Article 67(2) CISG requires, therefore, for the risk to pass to the buyer that the goods are clearly identified to the contract, whether, for example, by markings on the goods, by shipping documents or by notice given to the buyer. The latter, under Article 27 CISG, does not have to reach the buyer. The required identification of the goods can be effected by loading documents which are so precise that the identification of the goods is possible when the goods are unloaded at their destination.

229. Under Article 67 CISG it is possible that the question who bears the risk of the loss, destruction or damage of the goods is split between the buyer and the seller, for example, if the seller uses for part of the transport his or her own personnel, if the goods have to be handed over to the carrier or a particular place and the seller has to transport the goods to that place by himself or herself or if the seller only after the goods have been handed over to the carrier clearly identified the goods to the contract.[415]

4.3.3 The sale of Traveling Goods

230. The solution set out in para 225 in case of goods which have to be transported that the buyer has to pay the full purchase price of the goods which had been handed over get lost, destroyed or arrive damaged at the buyer requires that the point in time of the loss, destruction or damage be ascertained. Generally, that does not cause any problems since the point in time when the goods are handed over to the carrier is decisive: if the goods are lost or destroyed beforehand they

---

[412] Documents which entitle to dispose over the goods are, under Art 67(1)(3rd s) CISG, all paper which allow the disposal over the goods according to the transport contract, for example, securities which attest to the claims out of the transport contract: see Schlechtriem, *Einheitliches UN-Kaufrecht*, 80 fn 351.

[413] Hager in Schlechtriem/Schwenzer, *Commentary*, Art 67 para 5; Magnus in *Staudinger*, Art 67 para 11 respectively with more sources.

[414] Controversial: see Hager in Schlechtriem/Schwenzer, *Commentary*, Art 67 para 5.

[415] Compare Hager in Schlechtriem/Schwenzer, *Commentary*, Art 67 para 5.

cannot be handed over, if the goods were damaged before the handover generally reliable evidence exists about their condition at the time of handover.[416] However, if goods are being sold which are already in transit – by train, by plane, by ship, or by road – then it will often be difficult to ascertain later when exactly, before or after the conclusion of the contract, the goods were destroyed, lost, or damaged.

Example: A load of wheat was shipped from Rotterdam to Calcutta. The Indian trader had on sold the wheat on 15 October 2006 to a customer in Singapore. When the wheat arrives on 30 October 2006 it is established that water had been coming through a defective cargo hatch and the wheat had partially gone bad. However, it cannot be ascertained when exactly the damage has occurred – whether before the sale of Indian trader to the customer in Singapore or after. The question arises who in such case bears the risk for the damage to the goods.

Article 99(1) ULIS as well as the drafts to the CISG stipulated that the risk should pass already with the handover of the goods to the carrier, therefore, in the case scenario already before the conclusion of the contract since at the handover the condition of goods was more easily ascertained. This solution, however, also means that it is possible to conclude an effective contract for the sale of goods in regard to goods which at the time of contract conclusion are not existent anymore or already damaged and for which the buyer would have to pay. At the Vienna Conference this solution was not met with much favour[417] and the compromise set out in Article 68 CISG was found: the risk passes generally at the time of contract formation (Article 68(1st s) CISG). However the risk passes already with the hand-over of the goods to the carrier if it can be ascertained taking into all the circumstances that the buyer assumed the risk at that point in time already. Such an indication would be, for example, the existence of a transport insurance which in practice will generally be the case, so that the risk in the end in most cases will pass with the hand-over of the goods to the carrier who has issued the documents about the contract concerning the transport. The fact that a transport insurance has been taken out is seen in the literature as a sign that the buyer is unsure about when the risk passes; which means uncertainty when the damage occurs,[418] while the fact that transport insurance was taken out is interpreted that the seller has to deliver to the buyer that means the risk passes at the buyer's place and the seller has to bear the risk during the transport of the goods.[419]

231. As a rule, therefore, the risk will pass to the buyer at the time of the hand-over of the goods to the carrier. It follows from the analysis of Article 66 CISG that the CISG itself assumes that a contract can be validly formed although the

---

[416] For example, notes will have been made accordingly on the transport documents by the carrier; see in regard to the problems in relation to evidence in cases of container-traffic Hager in Schlechtriem/Schwenzer, *Commentary*, Art 67 para 11.

[417] Compare: Schlechtriem, *Einheitliches UN-Kaufrecht*, 81, 82.

[418] Compare Heuzé, *Traité des Contracts*, para 370.

[419] Neumayer/Ming, Art 68 para 3.

goods had been lost or destroyed at that point in time, that means a contract can oblige the seller to a performance which is from the start impossible to perform and the buyer to pay the purchase price for that impossible performance.[420] This, however, is only possible if documents verify the transport contract, if documents are missing then the rule is not applicable.[421] Documents are all certificates which evidence the transport contract they do not have to have securities character.[422] The increasing use of electronically recorded and sent transport or freight contracts through which documents have been trade redundant are not covered.[423] However, it has to be contemplated in those cases whether the parties' intention can be interpreted to the effect that the passing of the risk follows the same pattern as traditional documents.[424] However, if at the time of the conclusion of the contract of sale the seller knew or ought to have know that the goods had been lost or damaged and did not disclose this to the buyer, the loss or damage is at the risk of the seller (Article 68(3rd s) CISG). The seller's bad faith can only relate to the loss or damage of the goods at the time of contract formation not to a later occurring loss or damage.[425]

4.3.4 Purchase at the Seller's Place of Business and Purchase Inter Absentees

Purchase at the Seller's Place of Business (Article 69(1) CISG)

232. The sale of goods in transit (Article 68 CISG) and the sale involving the carriage of goods (Article 67 CISG) are so on the fore of the CISG that all other cases are dealt with in the "catch-all" provision of Article 69 CISG. If the goods are to be taken over at the seller's place of business (Hohlschuld), risk passes to the buyer when he or she takes over the goods, that means upon the change in control over them.[426] It is insufficient for the goods to have been merely placed at buyer's disposal ("…when he takes over the goods"). Placing the goods at the buyer's disposal, however, is sufficient for the risk to pass to the buyer if the buyer, by not taking delivery, breaches an obligation under the contract (Article 69(1) CISG). It is controversial whether only the failure to take delivery in time or also other breaches of the buyer's obligation which cause that the buyer cannot take over the goods are sufficient to lead to the passing of the risk, for example, the buyer's failure to

---

[420] The CISG has exclusively regulated this issue. Domestic provisions like Art 20(1) OR or the old § 306 BGB which declare a contract which is impossible to perform already at the point of contract formation for invalid cannot be fallen back on compare Art 4(2nd s(a)) CISG para 36).

[421] Herber/Czerwenka, *Internationales Kaufrecht*, Art 68 para 6.

[422] Herber/Czerwenka, *Internationales Kaufrecht*, Art 68 § 4 also to the genesis.

[423] See in regard to the history of the provision: Schlechtriem, *Einheitliches UN-Kaufrecht*, 83.

[424] Herber/Czerwenka, *Internationales Kaufrecht*, Art 68 para 6

[425] Compare Hager in Schlechtriem/Schwenzer, *Commentary*, Art 68 para 5.

[426] Compare the corresponding provisions of UCC, §§ 2–50 (3) and BGB, § 446 (1st s).

open a letter of credit for the seller contrary to the terms of the contract.[427] A case of a failure to take delivery contrary to the contract also exists if the buyer is ready to take over the goods but does refuse to pay the purchase price bit-by-bit and the seller withholds the goods because of the buyer's refusal.[428]

The buyer's reason why he or she cannot take over delivery is without consequences even if the buyer cannot fulfil his or her obligations under the contract due to circumstances covered by Article 79 CISG the risk passes to the buyer nevertheless once the seller has placed the goods at the buyer's disposal and has notified the buyer thereof.[429]

If the contract relates to goods which have to be identified the goods are only considered to be placed at the buyer's disposal once they have been clearly identified in the contract (Article 69(3) CISG).

Sale of Goods to Other Places of Delivery

233. According to Article 69(2) CISG the risk passes – in the event that the buyer has to take over the goods at another place other than the seller's place of business – at the time delivery is due (Article 33 CISG) and the buyer is aware of the fact that the goods are placed at his disposal at that place. That is, for example the case, if the goods have been stored and the buyer has been notified.[430] Like-wise agreements can be found in terms like "ex warehouse", "ex quay", or "ex works".[431] The notification requirement prevents the risk from passing to the buyer in the event that a mere delivery note (indicating the particulars of the transfer) has been sent to the buyer.[432] The seller, therefore, has to agree to a time with the buyer by which the goods must be collected. Otherwise the seller continues to bear the risk until the buyer contracts the warehouse keeper and the latter acknowledges the buyer's right to possession.[433] The warehouse keeper has to be independent from the seller.[434]

Buyer's Place of Business or Third Place

234. Article 69(2) CISG covers also the case where delivery is to be made by the seller at the buyer's place of business or at some other place than the seller's own place of business. Such contractual arrangements are evidenced by terms like

---

[427] The German literature affirms this view: compare Magnus in *Staudinger*, Art 69 para 16; see in regard to the German presentation in relation to this issue at the Vienna Conference its rejection and the discussion Schlechtriem, *Einheitliches UN-Kaufrecht*, 83.

[428] See paras 205, 250, 251.

[429] See CISG, Art 79(5); compare Magnus in *Staudinger*, Art 69 para 15.

[430] Compare Secretariat's Commentary OR p 65 Art 81 No 5; Magnus in *Staudinger*, Art 69 para 5.

[431] Hager in Schlechtriem/Schwenzer, *Commentary*, Art 69 para 6.

[432] Magnus in *Staudinger*, Art 69 para 22; Hager in Schlechtriem/Schwenzer, Art 69 para 7; Budzikiewicz in Soergel, Art 69 para 6.

[433] Note, however, that under the UCC §§ 2–509 (2)(c), 2–503(4)(b) the risk passes to the buyer after the expiry of a reasonable period.

[434] CISG, Art 69(1) applies if the warehouse is administered by the seller's personnel.

"free domicile", "ex ship", "FOB buyer's city".[435] In some cases problems in the interpretation of those terms can ensue:

Example: A company with its place of business in Germany had ordered via telephone goods from a company which had its place of business in France. The terms and conditions of the French seller were agreed according to which the delivery should have been "free ex domicile, duty paid and no tax paid". The seller had hired a freight company to transport the goods. According to the German buyer the goods never arrived. The High Court in Germany classified the contract as one which involves the carriage of the goods and, therefore, the risk passed to the buyer when the goods were handed over to the freight company (Article 67(1) CISG). The Court of Appeal, however, interpreted the term "free ex domicile" according to Article 8(2) CISG to mean that the seller should not only bear the costs but also the risk and that risk should only pass with the disposal of the goods at the buyer's place of business.[436]

As already set out in para 233: the risk passes at the earliest point at which the buyer can take delivery. The seller has to have offered the goods either at the place agreed between the parties or at the buyer's place of business. The seller has to offer the goods in such a way that the buyer is in a position to collect or to take delivery and that the buyer has knowledge that the goods are available (because of a document concerning the goods).

Article 69(2) CISG requires that the buyer is notified that the goods are at his or her disposal, often this will have occurred with the accompanying documents.

5   The Seller's Remedies in Regard to the Buyer's Breach of Contract

235. The seller's remedies are also set out together in the CISG and generally do not discriminate between types of breaches by the buyer (Article 61(1) CISG). However, Article 64 CISG sets out special provisions in regard to the breach of the duty to pay the purchase price or the duty to take delivery of the goods if the seller wants to avoid the contract. Article 65 CISG stipulates a special remedy – the seller's right to make the specifications himself or herself in case of a contract where the buyer has to specify the form, measurement or other features of the goods. In regard to the provisions in Chapter 5 which are applicable to the buyer and the seller Article 78 CISG has to be noted. Article 78 CISG sets out the entitlement to interest which allows the seller to claim interest should the buyer pay the purchase price in time. Also the right to a self-help sale under Article 88 CISG could be

---

[435] Compare Hager in Schlechtriem/Schwenzer, *Commentary*, Art 69 para 6; OLG Karlsruhe (20 Nov 1992) CISG-online 54 = NJW – RR 1993, 1316; UCC §2–319(1).

[436] OLG Karlsruhe (20 Nov 1992) CISG-online 54 = NJW – RR 1993, 1316, 1317; see also OLG Köln (16 Jul 2001) CISG-online 609 = IHR 2002, 66, 67.

important for the seller in case the buyer does not take delivery in time or refuses delivery altogether.

5.1 Right to Performance

5.1.1 Payment of the Purchase Price

236. The seller can require the payment of the purchase price under Article 62 CISG and has a legally enforceable remedy. Periods of grace, as known by the French based legal systems,[437] are not acceptable (Article 61(3) CISG) in international trade because of the insecurity they would bring to the contract. It would also expose the parties to broad judicial discretion.[438]

In regard to the purchase price claim under Article 62 CISG two issues are discussed: first, it is controversial whether the limitation in claiming specific performance under Article 28 CISG is also applicable in regard to the payment of the purchase price. The issue was controversial during the preparations of the CISG but the view seemed to be that the limitation of specific performance was only to be applicable in regard to the buyer's remedies and the seller's right to require the taking of the delivery. However, since Article 28 CISG sets out the issue generally it is now irrefutable that Article 28 CISG is also applicable to the seller's purchase price claim.[439] Consequently, the Secretariat's Commentary assumes that Article 28 CISG is also applicable to an action for the purchase price.[440]

The second issue is whether the buyer can hold the seller's duty to mitigate loss in its entirely or in parts against the seller.[441] Cases were anticipated in which the buyer notifies the seller early that he or she will not be able to take delivery of the ordered goods which still has to be manufactured by the seller and the seller nonetheless produces the goods and then tries to enforce the contract with an action for specific performance of the purchase price. As far as the enforcement of the specific performance action fails under Article 28 CISG the seller has to assert the purchase price as damages under Article 77 CISG. However, in the authors' view a breach of the seller's duty to mitigate the loss cannot be asserted directly against the action for the purchase price.[442] The principle, developed under Article 7(2) CISG, of forfeiture, venire contra factum proprium or a counter claim of the buyer based of the seller's breach of the duty, developed under Articles 7(2) and 77

---

[437] See Code Civile, Art 1184(3).

[438] Secretariat's Commentary OR p 39, Art 43, No 5.

[439] Compare Hager in Schlechtiem/Schwenzer, *Commentary,* Art 62 paras 10–12 with references in regard to the different opinions; see also Magnus in *Staudinger*, Art 62 para 12 who wants to leave it to the court whether the court sees the purchase price action under its domestic law an unenforceable request for specific performance.

[440] Secretariat's Commentary OR p 27, Art 26, No 3; p 48, Art 58, No 6.

[441] See in regard to the USA's attempts to make the bringing of an action for the price subject to the duty to mitigate loss during the preliminary work on the CISG Hager in Schlechtriem/Schwenzer, *Commentary*, Art 62 para 14. Under the UCC the seller is not entitled to continue production if it has become uneconomic to do so UCC § 2A-405(b).

[442] Compare P Huber in *MünchKomm*, Art 62 para 9.

CISG, to mitigate loss and to liquidate the contract in time can only be of help to the buyer in extreme cases.[443]

237. An action for performance is of course not available if the seller has executed a remedy which is not compatible with an action for the purchase price, especially if the seller has avoided the contract. If the seller fixed an additional time period under Article 63 CISG they cannot resort to an action for the purchase price during this additional time period. The seller can, parallel to an action for the purchase price, assert an action for damages for the delay as well as interest under Article 78 CISG.[444]

5.1.2 Acceptance of the Goods

238. The seller can require the acceptance of the goods. The duty to accept the goods has the same weight as the duty to apply the purchase price. Courts in common law countries do not need to impose specific performance in form of acceptance if the courts would not do it under their domestic law – Article 28 CISG is unquestionable applicable. Also in regard to acceptance, it has to be noted that the seller is restricted from executing a remedy which is not compatible with an action for specific performance (acceptance of the goods). The seller especially cannot avoid the contract or conduct a self-help sale under Article 88(1) CISG.

Actions for damages are compatible with an action for specific performance, for example, an action for substitution for additional transport costs.[445] Also expenses and expenditure due to the temporary storage of the goods (Articles 85, 87 CISG) can, despite the granting of an additional time period to perform, be claimed as damages.[446]

The seller can also make a cover sale and claim damages, instead of acceptance.[447] In some circumstances the seller might have to make a cover sale to mitigate loss. However, a damages claim then excludes a claim for specific performance.

5.1.3 Other Contractual Duties

239. "Other duties" of the buyer are ones which have been agreed on in addition to those stemming from the contract. For example, the buyer can agree not to re-export the goods into the country which they were exported from. The duty to

---

[443] Hager in Schlechtriem/Schwenzer, *Commentary*, who wants to help with Art 7(1) CISG, Art 62 para 14; Magnus in *Staudinger* who suggest to treat the specific performance claim as abuse but also depends on Art 7(1) CISG for his analysis. Stoll, RabelsZ 52 (1988) 617, 638 et seq: who wants to take into account the advantages onto the purchase price. The proper solution, in the authors' view is set out in para 651(3rd s) in conjunction with § 649 BGB: the customer has a right to resign the contract and a duty to partial compensation. That solution, however, is not transferable to the CISG since suggestions along these lines were rejected in Vienna (see para 26 fn 36).

[444] See paras 317 et seq.

[445] Compare CISG, Art 63(2)(2nd s).

[446] Compare Hager in Schlechtriem/Schwenzer, *Commentary*, Art 63 para 6.

[447] Compare Schlechtriem in *FS Georgiades*, 383, 384 et seq, also CISG-online.ch/publications/html.subl.

specify the goods is also an "other duty" for the purposes of Article 60. However, because of the special regulation of specification by the buyer in Article 65 CISG the seller cannot claim specific performance. At least the claim is required in the "request" of Article 65(1) CISG. Excluded from "other duties" but part of the duty to take delivery are acts of the buyer which the buyer has reasonably to undertake to allow the seller to deliver the goods (Article 60(1) CISG). Article 28 CISG is applicable to "other duties".

5.1.4 Fixing of an Additional Time Period

240. The seller can fix an additional period of time of reasonable length for performance by the buyer of his obligations (Article 63(1) CISG). The factions the additional time period fulfil similar to the mirror-image fixing of an additional time period by the buyer under Article 47 CISG.[448] Firstly, the fixing of an additional time period means that the seller is limited to certain remedies (Article 63(2) CISG). The seller cannot require specific performance or avoid the contract but the seller's right to claim damages because of late performance remains. Even before the additional time period the seller can resort again to all remedies if the buyer has notified the seller that he or she will not perform within the fixed period (Article 63(2)(1ˢᵗ s) CISG). For the breach of duty to pay the purchase price and to take delivery the fixing of an additional time period has an additional function, namely to open the possibility to avoid the contract in cases where the delay in paying the purchase price or taking delivery already fulfils the requirements of a fundamental breach (and would allow immediate avoidance any way) or the weight of the breach is doubtful.[449]

5.2 Avoidance of the Contract

241. Article 64 CISG sets out the seller's rights to avoid the contract should the buyer breach his or her duties instead of the possibilities of the buyer[450] to avoid the contract if the seller breaches his or her duties. If the buyer's breach amounts to a fundamental breach under Article 25 CISG the seller can immediately avoid the contract. If the buyer does not pay the purchase price or does not take delivery the seller can fix an additional time period under Article 63(1) CISG.[451] After that time period has expired, the seller can avoid the contract.

Although generally all duties of the buyer are equally important and, therefore, the breach of an ancillary duty entitles a seller to avoid the contract if the breach is a fundamental one. The duty to pay the purchase price is of special importance; if the buyer pays the purchase price the seller can lose the right to avoid the contract if the seller does not avoid in contract in time (Article 64(2) CISG).

---

[448] See para 181.
[449] See in regard to CISG, Art 64 para 241.
[450] See paras 188 et seq.
[451] See para 240.

5.2.1 Non-payment

242. The buyer's non-payment of the purchase price will rarely qualify as a fundamental breach.[452] Exceptions, however, are possible if the foreign exchange markets fluctuate or in cases in which the seller has to pay his supplier with the purchase price – perhaps where the seller is threatened with a penalty for breach of contract – because the seller has no money or credit.[453]

Example: The seller of crude oil has her business in a country in which the foreign exchange is tightly controlled. She sells some crude oil; the payment, as usual in the crude oil industry, was to be made in US dollar. The seller agreed with the buyer that the buyer should make a down payment on the oil to a Swiss bank account. This is necessary because the seller cannot get US dollars in her own country because the country has a foreign exchange control. The seller wants to use the down payment to pay her supplier. In the contract with the supplier high penalties ensue from delayed payments and it provides that the supplier can avoid the contract at any time should the seller not make payments in time. If the buyer does not pay the down payment in time to the Swiss bank account it has serious consequences for the seller since she cannot get the US dollars in her own country and outside her country will not have any money or be able to loan money. The delayed down payment would constitute a fundamental breach.

The refusal to pay the purchase price can amount to a fundamental breach. However, generally the avoidance of a contract due to the refusal to pay the purchase price can only be achieved by setting an additional time period first.

5.2.2 Breach of the Duty to Take Delivery

243. The breach of the duty to take delivery is generally also not a fundamental breach.[454] Expectations can exist, however, if, for example, the seller needs to clear his storage or needs to unload a transport; if no possibilities exist to store goods or if bulk goods are sold and the timely taking of delivery is vital for the seller to be able to operate his business.[455] The buyer's refusal to take delivery is generally a fundamental breach of the contact.

Example: Parties agreed on a contract for the sale of 200 t of bacon which had to be delivered in ten instalments. After the German buyer had accepted five instalments she refused to accept delivery of any more

---

[452] Hager in Schlechtriem/Schwenzer, *Commentary*, Art 64 para 5.

[453] Compare Hager in Schlechtriem/Schwenzer, *Commentary*, Art 64 para 5.

[454] Compare Hager in Schlechtriem/Schwenzer, *Commentary*, Art 64 para 6; Cour d'appel de Grenoble (4 Feb 1999) CISG-online 443.

[455] See in regard to these examples: Hager in Schlechtriem/Schwenzer, *Commentary*, Art 64 para 6; see also Witz in Witz/Salger/Lorenz, *Internationales Einheitliches Kaufrecht*, Art 64 para 9. The buyer's refusal to take delivery is generally a fundamental breach of the contact.

instalments. The buyer claims that the parties had agreed that the buyer could avoid the contract if the goods were complained about by the health and safety authorities and/or customs. The buyer could not prove such an additional oral agreement. The Court assumed that the refusal of the instalments was a fundamental breach.[456]

If the refusal to take delivery does not fulfil the requirements of a fundamental breach or is too doubtful, the seller has the possibility to avoid the contract by setting an additional time period (Article 64(1)(b) CISG).

Example: An Italian machine manufacture sold a French buyer a printing press. The buyer did not collect the machine at the time agreed upon with the seller. He also did not react in regard to any reminder or the setting of an additional time period. The seller avoided the contract and claimed damages. The buyer defended himself that the building in which the machine was to be installed had not been finished in time due to some building regulations problems. The seller's avoidance was not in good faith. The Milan Court allowed the claim because due to the setting of the additional time period for the payment and the acceptance of the delivery the avoidance requirements were fulfilled. The buyer had no defence. The use of the principle of good faith[457] could not come to a different result since international business deeply relied on legal certainty and contract stability.[458]

5.2.3 Breach of Ancillary Duties

244. The breach of ancillary duties by the buyer, for example, the duty to assist the seller in the manufacturing of the goods, to put to the seller's disposal plans and drawings, or the delivery of material (whose worth does not exceed the limits set by Article 3(1) CISG),[459] or particular limits in the use of the goods like a prohibition of re-exporting the goods to the seller's country[460] can only be a reason to avoid the contract if their breach meets the requirements of a fundamental breach. This can be the case in regard to ancillary duties if they have to be performed to a fixed deadline, for example, if the delivery of material or the putting off the plans to the seller's disposal was agreed upon to a fixed deadline. If the breach is not a fundamental one, the contract cannot be avoided. The seller can set an additional time period but the consequence flow from Article 63(2) CISG[461] the expiry of the time period does not result in the seller's right to avoid the contract.

---

[456] OLG Hamm (22 Sep 1994) CISG-online 57 = RIW 1994, 972, 973.

[457] See in regard to Art 7(1) CISG or Art 7(2) CISG paras 45 et seq.

[458] Appelate Court Milan (11 Dec 1998) CISG-online 430 = Riv. dir. int. priv. proc. 1999, 112; see also OGH (28 Apr 2000) CISG-online 581 = IHR 2001, 206.

[459] See paras 26 et seq.

[460] See para 285.

[461] See para 240.

5.2.4 Implementation and Effect of Avoidance

245. The avoidance of the contract is done by declaration in accordance with Article 26 CISG.[462] The effect of avoidance is set out in Articles 81 and 84 CISG.[463]

5.2.5 Loss of the Right to Avoid the Contract

246. For the seller the buyer's purchase price payment is the crucial performance because the seller agrees to the contract to be paid for his or her goods. Once the buyer has paid the purchase price, the seller's main interest is satisfied and a right to avoid the contract which has eventuated can lapse of certain requirements are met (Article 64(2) CISG). The CISG distinguishes between two scenarios whereby the purchase price payment is the underlying requirement.

247. If the breach fundamental because the buyer has performed a duty or duties late, for example, took delivery late, the seller can only avoid the contract as long as he or she has no knowledge of the performance which happened in the interim (Article 64(2)(a) CISG). That is also true if the right to avoid the contract came about by setting an additional time period (Article 64(1)(b) CISG).[464] Especially a right to avoid the contract which came about because of not paying the purchase price in time and the setting of an additional time period can lapse if the buyer does pay in the end and the seller only wants to exercise the seller's right to avoid the contract after he or she has got notice of the purchase price payment. The dispatch of the declaration of avoidance is decisive.[465]

Example: The German seller set an additional time period for the US buyer for the payment due on 1 October 2007 to 15 October 2007. The payment is received by the seller's Swiss bank on 16 October 2007 and is credited to the seller's account on 17 October 2007. The seller receives the bank statement stating the receipt of the money on 20 October. Has the seller sent his or her declaration of avoidance to the buyer on 19 October 2007 then the contract is effectively avoided. After the seller had notice of the late payment because of receiving the bank statement the seller's right to avoid the contract would have been lost if the seller only would have declared the contract avoided on 25 October 2007.

---

[462] In regard to the effect with dispatching of the declaration and in regard to the coming into the effect of the declaration see para 109; see also OLG Bamberg (13 Jan 1999) CISG-online 516 = TranspR – IHR 2000, 17, 18.

[463] See paras 330 et seq.

[464] Controversial: According to the Secretariat's Commentary is the performance which happens after the additionally set time period is lapsed not a "late performance" under Art 64(2)(a) CISG but is covered by Art 64(2)(b) CISG compare Hager in Schlechtriem/ Schwenzer, *Commentary*, Art 64 para 15.

[465] Controversial see paras 109, 110.

248. Is the breach of the buyer's duty not a late performance but a different kind of breach, for example, a complete non-performance or the refusal to perform other duties than the duty to pay the purchase price and is that breach a fundamental breach then the seller can avoid the contract if the seller declares the contract avoided

a) within a reasonable time after the seller knew or ought to have known about the breach (Article 64(2)(b)(i) CISG), or

b) within a reasonable time after an additional time period has lapsed through which a right to avoid the contract resulted (Article 64(2)(b)(ii) CISG), or

c) within a reasonable time offer the buyer refused to perform his or her part of the contract before the additional time period has lapsed (Article 64(2)(b)(ii) CISG).

A requirement in these scenarios is, however, that the buyer has paid the purchase price.

Example: The German buyer has paid the purchase price on time. However, the buyer disagrees with the French seller about the place and the time the buyer's duty to accept delivery of the goods. The French seller, stipulates its place of business as the place for the buyer to take delivery (Article 31(c) CISG) and gives the buyer additional time (Article 63(1) CISG). The seller has to declare the contract avoided within a reasonable time after setting the additional time period not to lose its right to avoid the contract.

5.3 The Seller's Damages Claim

249. If the buyer breaches his or her duties which are stipulated in the contract or in the CISG, especially the duty to pay the purchase price and to take delivery of the goods the seller has a damages claim (Article 61(1)(b) CISG). The kind of breach, whether it was complete non-performance, or part performance, or not timely performance[466] is as irrelevant as the buyer's fault. Since the CISG sets out the content and the extent of damages claim in general that means for buyer and seller equally (Article 74–77 CISG) they will be discussed separately.[467]

5.4 Rights of Retention

250. The seller can retain the right to trading over the goods or documents under Article 58(1)(2nd s) CISG and its step-by-step principle until the buyer has paid the purchase price. The seller has to raise the rights to retention as a defence

---

[466] The Directive "Late Payments in Commercial Transactions" (2000/35/EC) can overlap with the CISG, however according to the authors' opinion (see also para 345a) is the Directive not applicable when the CISG applies unless the Member States which have rectified the Directive made a declaration in accordance with Art 94 CISG; see in general to the relationship between the Directive "Late Payments in Commercial Transactions" and CISG: Meyer, *FS Otte*, 241 et seq, 262; and Schroeter, *UN-Kaufrecht und Gemeinschaftsrecht*), 229 et seq.

[467] See paras 299 et seq.

(as is suggested by the wording of Article 58(1)(2nd s) the seller "may"). The parties, can, of course, agree differently in the contract, for example, the seller's duty of advanced performance if the purchase price is created. However, even if the seller's advanced performance has been agreed upon the seller can retain his or her performance if it becomes apparent after the contract has been concluded that the buyer will not perform a major part of his or her duty under the contract, so for example, when the buyer will not pay the purchase price (Article 71(1) CISG).[468] The seller can even retain goods which have been sent already by ordering the carrier not to deliver the goods (Article 71(2)(1st s) CISG). It has to be noted that Article 71(2)(1st s) CISG does not contain a right against the carrier but only extends the seller's retention right against the buyer (Article 72(2)(2nd s) CISG). Therefore, if the carrier does not follow the seller's orders not to deliver the goods the seller does not have redress against the carrier under the CISG.

251. It is questionable whether the seller has a right to retention not only for delivery and payment but also for other obligations provided that they are of some significance, for example, an obligation to keep the origin of the goods secret. In the author's view generally a right to retention also exists in regard to other buyer's obligations than delivery and payment,[469] however, the same must be true as for the buyer's right to retention:[470] the retention of the goods should only be possible if either the buyer's breach of a fundamental breach or if after the seller set an additional time period the seller has a right to avoid the contract. Second, as far as the seller's performance is divisible and the seller has a damages claim in regard to a part of the buyer's performance the seller can exercise the right to retention in regard the value of the damages claim.

5.5   Specification by the Seller

252. Article 65(1) CISG sets out the seller's right to specify the form, measurement or other features of the goods if the buyer fails to make such specifications.[471] Article 65(1) CISG means that the seller has an additional remedy (Article 65(1)(2nd s) CISG) by being able to specify the goods himself or herself but it means also that the seller's offer can be sufficiently definite and a contract concluded on the basis of that offer if the goods contracted for still need such specification.[472] The fact that Article 65(1) CISG explicitly states that other remedies are not affected clarifies that the seller can claim damages and/or can avoid the contract should the omission of the specification by the buyer amount to a fundamental breach.[473]

---

[468] See in more detail paras 256 et seq.

[469] See para 42d.

[470] See para 206.

[471] See in regard to the reservations expressed in Vienna in relation to Art 65 CISG: Schlechtriem, *Einhetliches UN-Kaufrecht*, 77.

[472] Compare already para 74.

[473] Since the seller has the right to specify the goods himself or herself the breach of that obligation by the buyer will only in rare circumstances grant to a fundamental breach.

253. In the particular circumstances it depends first and foremost whether the specification had to have made at a certain point in time: if the buyer does not specify the goods at a certain point in time the seller can immediately specify himself or herself in other cases only after the seller has set an additional time period. If the seller exercises his or her right to specification the seller has to take into account the needs of the buyer as far as the seller is aware of them or ought to be aware of them.

254. The specification by the seller is not effective just by the act of specification the seller needs also to inform the buyer about the specification and its details and has to set a reasonable additional time period for the buyer to make a different specification (Article 26(2) CISG). The specification notice has to reach the buyer (in variation to Article 27 CISG) – the notice, therefore, travels at the seller's risk.[474] If, after the receipt of the notice, the buyer fails to make his or her own specification, the seller's specification is binding (Article 65(2)(2nd s) CISG).[475]

254a. It is questionable whether Article 65 CISG can be applicable analogously in other cases where the buyer does not exercise his or her obligation to participate and/or contribute the time of delivery and does not do that so that the seller is not able to deliver. In the authors' view the refined regulation set out in Article 65 CISG cannot be applied to other breaches of buyer's obligations to participate or to contribute. If, for example, the buyer omits to determine the time of delivery the seller can invoke Articles 63(1) (additional period) and 64(1)(b) (avoidance) CISG and or claim damages.

6   Provisions Common to the Obligations of the Seller and of the Buyer

255. Articles 71 to 88 CISG contain general rules about the obligations and the consequences of the breach of those obligations for both parties. Structurally it would have been more desirable to put those provisions into chapter 1.[476] Some provisions for example, Article 71(2) CISG – the seller's right to retention – do not affect both parties and would, therefore, would have been better put with the remedies of that party, in case of Article 71(2) CISG with the seller's remedies. After all, the important consideration is not the obligations of the parties but the remedies in case of a breach of an obligation or in case of an anticipatory breach.

---

[474] Hager in Schlechtriem/Schwenzer, *Commentary*, Art 65 para 6; as well as to the changes of the seller's specification for the seller para 7a.

[475] Note, that the rule stated in CISG, Art 65(2) is equivalent to the German law (§ 375(2) (2nd s) HGB.

[476] See para 101.

6.1   Right to Suspend Performance and Stoppage

256. Article 71 CISG allows a party to suspend its performance if the other party's economic situation deteriorates in a way that the performance of the contract is in jeopardy. In its core Article 71 CISG contains the idea of clausula rebus sic stantibus, that means the consequences of the cessation of or the change in contractual basis – accordingly the consultations in Vienna were very difficult.[477]

6.1.1   Requirements of the Right to Retention

257. Article 71(1) CISG differentiates three reasons for a possible jeopardising of the performance of contract by debtor which allows the creditor to suspend and/or retain his or her performance: the disruption of the debtor's creditworthiness might lead to the conclusion that the debtor cannot perform anymore (Article 71(1)(a) CISG). That is especially of course the debtor who has the obligation to pay the purchase price, the buyer. However, it might be also the case in regard to the seller if the seller's deficient creditworthiness results in, for example, that the seller is suppliers stop delivering the materials which are needed to manufacture the sold goods. Deficient credit worthiness exists, for example, the debtor is in bankruptcy, insolvent or other liquidation proceedings; if the debtor has ceased to pay bills; if the debtor's cheques have not been honoured. Why the creditworthiness of the debtor had diminished is not material, especially not whether it was the fault of the debtor.

Example: The company V which has its seat in Germany sold a company its with seat in the United Kingdom a machine. The machine was to be manufactured by the seller and to be delivered to the buyer within six months. The buyer was the subsidiary of the group of firms D to which another subsidiary belonged with the same name as the buyer. The latter company became insolvent which lead to doubts in regard to solvency of the entire group of firms D. The seller suspended the delivery as long as no letter of credit had been opened in regard to the purchase price and therewith payment would be secured. The Oberlandesgericht Hamm allowed the seller's right to retention because from the point of view of the reasonable creditor the fear that the debtor would not be able to pay the purchase price was justified.[478]

258. Not only the declining of the debtor's creditworthiness but also other circumstances which endanger the performance of the debtor allow the creditor under Article 71(1)(a) CISG to suspend the creditor's own performance, for example, a looming industrial action. Even if the financial situation is excellent

---

[477] Compare in regard to the consultations Schlechtriem, *Einheitliches UN-Kaufrecht,* 84–86; Schlechtriem was in Vienna the member of a small working group in which the ultimate version of the provision was drafted.

[478] Compare OLG Hamm (20 Jun 1983) NJW 1984, 1307, 1308 (decided in regard to Art 73 ULIS which mostly resembles Art 71 CISG).

can the performance be endangered,[479] for example, if an export prohibition for a certain type of technology exists in one of the supplier's country and, therefore, the manufacturing of the goods are in jeopardy. The reasons for jeopardising the performance are immaterial: if the seller's manufacturing facilities are destroyed due to a lighting strike, the buyer has the right to withhold an agreed advance payment since the chance that the seller will perform according to the contract is diminished.

Example: The buyer bought furniture from the seller. The contract stipulated that the seller would order the furniture from the manufacturer and then would store the furniture. The buyer was supposed to be able to get the furniture out of storage on demand. The seller's invoices were to be paid with the seller's notice that the furniture was stored. When the seller claimed the purchase price the buyer defended the claim by pointing out that no furniture was in storage (and that the furniture ostensibly had been lost) so that a delivery was not possible. The Oberlandesgericht Hamm agreed.[480]

259. The performance can also be endangered by the debtor's conduct when the debtor prepares performance or during the performance itself, for example, if the buyer does not obtain storage in time for the goods and it was part of the buyer's obligation to do so or if it is clear from the buyer's conduct that the buyer will not take delivery. The latter case is governed by Article 71(1)(b) CISG.

Example: The buyer ordered air conditioning units which he wants to install in a commercial building he is about to build. To install the air conditioning units, certain building code regulations apply, for example, in regard to the filtering of the units into the openings, in regard to the electrical corrections and the draw off of condensation. If the seller gains knowledge that the buyer has bought air conditioning units from another supplier and has specified the binding work to the requirements of those units which are not compatible with the first ordered unit from the seller, the buyer's preparations make it clear that the buyer will not take delivery at the time of delivery in regard to the seller's air-conditioning units.[481]

6.1.2 Time for the Diminishing of the Debtor's Performance Capacity

260. The diminishing of the capacity to perform can occur after the contract was concluded but also even before the conclusion of the contract coming to light later. That includes circumstances which already exist at the time of the conclusion of

---

[479] Compare Cohn, (1974) 23 Int'l & Comp L Q, 520, 522 zu Art 73 ULIS.

[480] See OLG H amm (23 Jun 1998) CISG-online 434 – facts simplified.

[481] See in regard to further examples: Hornung in Schlechtriem/Schwenzer, *Commentary*, Art 71 para 12 who quite rightly points out that the demarcation between "preparing to perform" and "to perform" is fluid.

the contract but whose impacts are only discernible after the conclusion.[482] The possibility for the creditor to rely on the diminished capacity to perform of the other party which already existed before the conclusion of the contract but which was not discernible for the creditor is important since it will often be nearly impossible to ascertain at what point in time the diminishing of the capacity to perform actually occurred. Especially in cases of financial difficulties it is for the creditor unsure and accidental whether the first bill of exchange or the cheque bounced before or after the conclusion of the contract. It would be odd if the "troubled" party could insist on the performance of the creditor despite not being able to perform arguing that it was already at the time of the conclusion of the contract not creditworthy or not able to perform for other reasons.

261. Article 71(1) CISG has special significance for the demarcation of the CISG: since Article 71(1) CISG also embraces situations before the conclusion of the contract which only came to light after the conclusion of the contract are such circumstances and their legal consequences "questions concerning matters governed by this Convention" under Article 7(2) CISG. Since the CISG has found for these "matters governed by this Convention" a special regulation the parties cannot invoke domestic law. Therefore, domestic remedies which allow the judiciary declared avoidance of a contract due to a subjective change of the contractual basis are excluded.[483] Further, the domestic law in regard to the avoidance of the contract due to mistake is also excluded even if a mistake would render the contract void which is generally under Article 4(2nd s) CISG a question of domestic law. An exclusion of the domestic law in regard to mistake in the case that only after the conclusion of the contract the diminished capacity to perform of a party becomes evident is in the interest of the "uniformity of application" of the CISG under Article 7(1) CISG since domestic laws govern contractual mistake very differently and often the laws are very complex. The question whether a contractual mistake exist or whether the contract is void can often only be ascertained after a close analysis of the jurisprudence. Would domestic law be applicable in this area insecurity would exists which CISG is supposed to negate. Therefore, mistakes in regard to the capacity to perform should generally only lead to a right to retention by the creditor under Article 71(1) CISG.[484] However, if the mistake is due to fraudulent misrepresentation domestic law is applicable since the conduct falls in the realm of tort law which is outside the CISG.[485]

---

[482] See in regard to the history and the debates in Vienna: Schlechtriem, *Einheitliches UN-Kaufrecht*, 85.

[483] See in regard to Art 4 CISG para 34.

[484] Controversial; like the authors: Magnus in *Staudinger*, Art 71 para 41; Hornung in Schlechtriem/Schwenzer, Art 71 para 16; Strohbach in Enderlein/Maskow/Strohbach, *Internationales Kaufrecht*, Art 71 para 2; Lüderitz/Dettmaier, Art 71 para 23; Neumayer/Ming, Art 71 para 1 (but see also para 3 fn 7); other view: Karollus, *UN-Kaufrecht*, 42; Lessiak, öst JBl 1989, 487, 493.

[485] One can the exclusion of fraudulent misrepresentation already derive from Art 4(1)(1st s) CISG; unfortunately a provision like Art 89 ULIS is missing in the CISG which in cases of intentional damage or fraudulent misrepresentation had an explicit reservation in favour of domestic law. The waiver of such a provision in the CISG, however, does not mean that a different decision should be made – see Schlechtriem, *Gemeinsame Bestimmungen*, 153.

6.1.3 Evidential Threshold

262. Another issue which has caused considerable problems at the Vienna Conference was the formulation of the evidential threshold, that means the degree of probability that the debtor will not perform.[486] On the one hand, the threshold was not to be determined solely by the creditor's subjective view but on the other hand the language of Article 71(1) CISG was to clearly signal that the threshold was not as high as for an anticipatory breach under Article 72(1) CISG ("becomes apparent" in contrast to "it is clear"). The language chosen in Vienna in the end is supposed to make clear that for an objective and reasonable person[487] in the shoes of the creditor, having regard to all circumstances, it is evident that the other party will not perform. To ascertain the knowledge the objective person from the same sphere as the creditors is decisive. The diminishing of the performance does not have to be objective is enough that it has the appearance that the other party will not perform.[488]

6.1.4 Weight of the Anticipated Breach of an Obligation

263. Not every obviously expected breach of contract justifies a right to withhold ones' own performance. Differently from the case of a general right of retention (which has been endorsed by the authors' para 42 d) in case of an already conducted breach of an obligation by the debtor Article 71(1) CISG requires that the non-performance relates to an essential part of the debtors duties which is not placed under insolvency or alike. Also the threatening breach of non-important and minor duties does not justify a right to retention.[489] It could be questionable whether the requirement that an essential part of the obligation meaning their performance has to be endangered is identical with the requirement of a "fundamental breach" for the avoidance of a contract. At the Vienna Conference this question was answered in the negative.[490] Since the remedy for an anticipatory "fundamental breach" is the avoidance of the contract under Article 72 CISG it is justified to allow the right to retention in case of less fundamental failures of the other party. In practice the difference, however, the difference will not matter greatly. Decisive is for the meaning of the obligation in question the concrete contract and the concrete interest of the creditor, therefore, object general rules cannot be stipulated. A particular packaging, an official certificate, the enclosure of instructions in a foreign language etc, can depending on the contract and the contract's purpose, be an essential part of the party's obligations. Whether their absence amounts to a

---

[486] Compare Schlechtriem, *Einhetliches UN-Kaufrecht*, 86, 87.

[487] Compare OLG Hamm (20 Jun 1983) NJW 1984, 1307, 1308 – example para 257.

[488] So, for example, in OLG Hamm (20 Jun 1983) NJW 1984, 1307, 1308 (para 257) where in actual fact the insolvency of a company which was part of a group of companies had no bearings on the other companies of that group. However, since the buyer in that case had the same name as the insolvent company and a justified cause to fear existed, that the entire group would be in difficulties the OLG Hamm held that the German seller could reasonably assume that it would not receive the purchase price.

[489] Compare to this issue paras 205, 206.

[490] Compare Schlechtriem, *Einheitliches UN-Kaufrecht*, 86.

"fundamental breach" in which case the creditor can avoid the contract (Article 72 CISG) has to be ascertained a separate inquiry since it can be of importance whether the creditor can be asked to keep the goods and to claim damages in regard to the absence of the performance of the other party's obligation(s).

6.1.5 "Suspension" of the Performance of the Obligation

264. "Suspension" of the performance of the obligation means first and foremost the retention of the creditor's own due performance, more exact: the retention of the performance which is necessary to fulfil the creditor's part of the contract, for example, the delivery, the dispatch of the goods, the transfer of ownership, the payment of the purchase price, the taking of delivery. If one takes the view, as stipulated in para 256, that the obligation and the possibility to perform of the other party is the basis for one's own obligation then it becomes clear that Article 71(1) CISG does not only let lapse the performance obligation and reinstates the step-by-step performance but that the endangerment of the other party's performance has generally lead to an adjustment of the performance deadlines. That means, that the party which invokes Article 71(1) CISG cannot only retain its performance at the due date but can already retain its preparatory work. The party can, once the factors leading to a diminished possibility of performance of the other party have lapsed and the other party will perform definitely at a later date. The time at which the performance is due is, therefore, suspended for the length of time in which it is not clear whether the other party will perform its obligations.

Example: The manufacturer of machine (V) with its seat in Switzerland sold special machines to the manufacturer of bicycles which had its seat in Germany on 1 October 2007 which were manufactured according to the buyer's plans. The machines were to be delivered on 1 February 2008. On 15 October 2007 the director of the buyer files for insolvency proceedings and notifies suppliers and customers. Since the endeavour to save the buyer seem hopeless at that time bankruptcy proceedings were likely. In the middle of December a Japanese company takes over the buyer, which supplied new capital and makes the buyer solvent again. The insolvency proceedings are stopped and the diminished capacity to perform is removed. The Swiss manufacturer was, after it had gained knowledge of insolvency proceedings, allowed under Article 71(1) CISG to step the production of the ordered machines. With the acknowledgment of the buyer's cash flow problem mid-December the manufacturer had to immediately start production again. The delivery date shifts for two months. The non-delivery of the machines on the original due date is not a breach of its obligation so that the buyer cannot claim damages for the delay. Also, the buyer cannot avoid the contact on 1 February 2008 or set an additional time period for performance with the aim to avoid the contract.[491]

---

[491] The possibility to retain only performance which is due but also to stop necessary preparations was contemplated by the drafters of the CISG: see Secretariat's Commentary OR p 52 Art 62 No 8;

6.1.6 The Right to Stoppage

265. Particularly for the seller who has already dispatched the goods Article 71(2)(1st) CISG sets out that the seller can prevent the delivery of the goods to the buyer if the requirements under Article 71(1) CISG are met. In that case the seller does not breach the contract. It is of course a requirement that the freighter is willing to follow the seller's instructions.[492] Article 71(2) CISG does not require the freighter to follow the seller's instructions. Of practical importance is the right to stoppage in cases in which the diminishing of the buyer's capacity to perform only becomes apparent after the seller has already given the goods to a freighter since in other cases the seller already prevents the handing over of the goods to a carrier. The exercise of the right to prevent the handing over of the goods is independent from the legal position in regard to property. The seller can exercise the right to prevent the handing over of the goods even if the buyer is already the owner of goods, for example because the document of title to goods had been already sent to the buyer. Effects has this "right of stoppage in transitu" only in regard to the seller-buyer relationship (Article 71(2)(2nd s) CISG; that means the seller does not act in accordance with law if the seller prevents the handing over of the goods by the freighter. On the other hand, the buyer breaches the contract if the buyer persuades the freighter to hand over the goods and thereby jeopardises the seller's right to stoppage.[493]

The right to stoppage, however, does not have any effect in regard to third parties who have gotten the rights in the goods, for example, in regard to a carrier who got a lieu; or in regard to a customer of the buyer who by handing over the document of title to goods is already owner of the goods. They can claim the goods because the right to stoppage is only supposed to protect the performance between buyer and seller.

6.1.7 Duty to Give Notice

266. If a party suspends its own performance it has to give notice without delay. The notice only has to be dispatched and any error or miscommunication or its failure to arrive does not deprive that party of the right to rely on the notice (Article 27 CISG). If the party fails to give notice it does not lose the right to suspend its performance but it allows the other party to claim damages if it could have prevented the right to stoppage being exercised if it had known about its execution, so that the contract would have been executed within the contractually agreed timeframe.[494]

---

compare also Bennett in Bianca/Bonell, Art 71 para 2.1; Hornung in Schlechtriem/Schwenzer, *Commentary*, Art 71 para 22: "The right to suspend performance enables the innocent party to suspend his own acts of performance and so to deviate from the contractual timetable without thereby breaching the contract.

[492] See para 250.

[493] Magnus in *Staudinger*, Art 71 para 54 with further references.

[494] Controversial: others argue that the failure to hive notice make the right to stoppage lapse: the AG Frankfurt decided ((31 Jan 1991) CISG-online 34 = IPRax 1991, 345 with comment by Jayme) that the right to stoppage lapsed because the seller had not notified the buyer without delay. In regard to

267. The "endangered" party can avert the exercise of the right to stoppage if it gives adequate assurance for the performance of the obligation. As described in the previous paragraph, notice of the intended exercise of the right to stoppage should ensure that the "endangered" party can make an attempt to avoid the exercise of the right. Adequate assurance can be given in form of the usual securities like bank guarantees but also through other evidence that the diminished capacity to perform has been re-established.[495] Mere declaration of the will to perform is not adequate.[496]

Example: The buyer, with seat in Switzerland, had bought 10 photocopiers from the company which worked as the selling agent for the manufacturer X. Delivery was agreed for 1 December 2007. At the beginning of November 2007 the Swiss buyer receives information that the manufacturer was bankrupt. The buyer gave notice that it would stop its payment of the purchase price which was due on 25 November 2007. The seller provided the buyer with evidence that it had purchased photocopiers from another supplier to be able to fulfil it contractual obligations. Such "evidence" of the ability to deliver despite the bankruptcy of the delivery source has to be adequate assurance under Article 71(3) CISG.

It should, without doubt, be an adequate assurance if the seller assigns its (free of any objections) delivery claims against its suppliers. However, the mere declaration that the photocopiers have already been purchased is not sufficient.

6.1.8 End of the In-Between-State

268. The exercise of the right to stoppage result in an in-between-state, since the contract as such stays in existence. If the non-ability to perform which in the first instance had lead to the exercise of the right to stoppage becomes a breach of contract after a certain time period because either the time at which the performance was due has passed or that the requirements of an anticipatory breach under Article 72 CISG are fulfilled the creditor can lift the in-between-state by declaring the contract avoided. Whether the omission after the notice and the request of the creditor to give adequate assurance fulfils the requirement of fundamental breach is doubtful: in the authors' view this is just an indication for a threatened breach of contract.[497] An express refusal can be seen, however, in certain circumstances as the refusal to perform. The in-between-state state is not only ordered by the avoidance of the contract but also by the end of the situation which endangered the

---

the different opinion and the consequences of the failure to give notice (loss of the right to stoppage or damages) see Magnus in *Staudinger*, Art 71 paras 46, 47; P Huber in *MünchKomm*, Art 71 para 19.

[495] Compare Hornung in Schlechtriem/Schwenzer, Art 71 para 38; Neumayer/Ming, Art 71 para 11.

[496] Compare Hornung in Schlechtriem/Schwenzer, Art 71 para 38 fn 79.

[497] See in regard to other opinions Honnold, *Uniform Law for International Sales*, § 392; like the authors: Ziegel, *Remedial Provisions,* 9–35; differentiating Hornung in Schlechtriem/Schwenzer, *Commentary*, Art 71 para 40 with further references.

performance[498] as well as if adequate assurance is given under Article 71(3) CISG. The party which would suspend its performance has to perform again or has to make the necessary preparations and has to, if the endangerment of the performance comes to fruition to utilise the assurance.

6.2   Anticipatory Breach

6.2.1 Requirements

269. Avoidance of the contract due to a party's breach generally requires that an obligation which is due has not been performed or is not in conformity with the contract. Nonetheless, there are cases in which it would not be opportune to compel the creditor, in light of a pending breach of contract, to wait until performance is due to then invoke Articles 49(1)(a) CISG or Article 72(1) CISG or Article 64(1)(a) CISG. The CISG, therefore, allows in Article 72(1) CISG the possibility to avoid the contract before a party's performance is due, if it is obvious that one party will fundamentally breach the contract. The requirement for the applicability of Article 72 CISG, however, is always that the obligation in question is not due – that the breach of contract is in the future.[499] If a party does not perform an obligation already due an avoidance of the contract is only possible under Articles 49 or 64 CISG.[500] (As a special case of an anticipatory breach to be seen) Article 73(2) CISG sets out that in case of an instalment contract the creditor may declare the contract avoided if the creditor has grounds to conclude that a fundamental breach of future instalments will occur.[501] The threshold in regard to the burden of proof is lower.[502]

270. The anticipated breach of contract has to be "clear" which means that it has to be expected with a high degree of probability.[503] That can be assumed if

---

[498] See para 264.

[499] It has to be noted that the possibility of remedies for an anticipatory breach is point of major departure from English law – see for further discussion Bridge, *International Sale of Goods*, 12.31–12.34.

[500] BGH (15 Feb 1995) CISG-online 149 = NJW 1995, 2101.

[501] The scenario set out in Art 73(3) CISG – where a close connection exists between future instalments and a non-conformity of one instalments indicates a fundamental breach in regard to all past and future instalments.

[502] See also para 279.

[503] Compare Bennett in Bianca/Bonell, Art 72 para 2.2; Hornung in Schlechtriem/ Schwenzer, *Commentary*, Art 72 paras 11, 12. In regard to the attempts to define the probability more detailed in Art 72 CISG see: Schlechtriem, *Einheitliches UN-Kaufrecht*, 88, 89. The wording evidential threshold – to "clearly" expect a fundamental breach- caused considerable problems in Vienna (see Schlechtriem, *Einheitliches UN-Kaufrecht*, 88, 89). The idea was probably to tighten, by using the particular wording, the requirements for the avoidance of a contract before performance was due in contrast to the requirements for a right to retention under Art 71 CISG. This is in line with the general value the CISG affords the avoidance of a contract in comparison with the right to retention. The creditor can, therefore, if the expected breach is not fundamental, stop his or her own performance under Art 71 CISG and wait until the signs have deepened that a fundamental breach will "clearly" occur and then avoid the contract.

the debtor declares that he or she does not want to perform or does not want to perform in accordance with the conditions stipulated in the contract before the performance is due (a case especially recognised by Article 72(3) CISG). Other scenarios which will most likely will lead to a "clear" anticipatory breach of the contract are: if the particular good was destroyed; if an embargo prevents either the export or the import of the goods; if the plant where the goods were supposed to be manufactured, burned down and cannot be re-erected in time for delivery; if the manufacturer cancelled the agency agreement in regard to the goods with the agent and stops delivery of the goods to the agent[504] etc.

The breach of previous contracts can in certain circumstances be a "clear" indication that the future performance of the new performance is jeopardised.

Example: A German shoe merchant ordered shoes from an Italian seller but it was, in regard to a previous contract, two months behind with its payment. The seller had not received the purchased price payment of that older contract three months after the conclusion of the new contract. The Italian seller demanded, therefore, the payment of the purchase price from the old contract within a week and assurance in regard to the payment of the purchase price of the new contract. The German buyer did not react. The Italian seller avoided the new contract and sold some of the already manufactured shoes as covering purchase and claimed damages. The OLG Düsseldorf allowed the claim and held that the seller could avoid the second contract under Articles 72(1), (2) CISG because of the buyer's non-performance of the first contract and the resulting "clear" fear that the buyer would not pay the purchase price in regard to the second contract either.[505]

271. Most importantly, it has to be a "fundamental breach" which is imminent. That means that the breach of the seller or buyer obligation(s), would performance have been due, would have met the requirements of a fundamental breached as set out in paras 188, 189, 241, 243. If, for example, political unrest or a fire in the manufacturing plant mean that at the time performance is due the party cannot perform but performance later is possible again the significance of the delivery date is of utmost importance. It is especially important whether the parties agreed to a specific date.[506] The same is true if a breach of the buyer's obligations is imminent: If the buyer has applied for insolvency proceedings to be commenced so that a purchase price payment on time is clearly unlikely, or is the harbour, in which the buyer is supposed to take delivery blocked off due to war and the buyer cannot take delivery at any other place the seller does not need to wait for the buyer's performance to become due but can avoid the contract according to the same requirements according to which the seller could avoid the contract if the buyer had performed at the due date.

---

[504] Compare BGH (15 Feb 1995) CISG-online 149 = NJW 1995, 2101, where the Court, however, assumed a current breach of contract.

[505] OLG Düsseldorf (14 Jan 1994) CISG-online 119.

[506] See para 113.

272. The desire to maintain the contract between the parties as long as possible is evidenced again Article 72(2) CISG.[507] Article 72(2) CISG stipulates that the party ("if time allows") has to give reasonable notice of its intention to avoid the contract to the other party. This allows the other party to provide adequate assurance of its performance.[508] The debtor, however, forfeits this chance if he or she declares that he or she does not want to and will not perform the contract (Article 72(3) CISG). The debtor can give adequate assurance to avert the avoidance of the contract by offering a security which will cover a potential damages claim of the creditor. Assurance can also be provided by securing the performance owed as such, for example, the seller assigns its claims against its supplier or proves in another way that it will be able to perform its obligations despite the appearance of an imminent breach of contract.[509] If the liquidator, in the example above para 270, declares that he will perform the contract instead of the buyer then that is an adequate assurance of the purchase price payment from the bankruptcy's assets. Mere confirmations, promises, or declarations of intent of the debtor are insufficient.

273. As special case is the debtor's unequivocal refusal to perform before the performance is due. This case stood at the beginning of the development of the anticipatory breach[510] and is especially dealt with in Article 72(3) CISG: If the debtor clearly stipulates that he or she will not perform his or her obligations under the contract the creditor does not have to give notice of his or her intention to avoid the contract to give the debtor the possibility to avert the avoidance by giving adequate assurance. Article 72(2) CISG is not applicable to the refusal to perform the contract. This does not only make it easier for the creditor to avoid the contract but it also takes account of the different doctrinal justifications for the avoidance. The avoidance of the contract due to the refusal to perform is in the end the acknowledgment that the parties have autonomy to shape the contract between them which includes for the debtor to decide to force the avoidance of the contract by non-performing, including the acceptance of the consequences for it.[511] The requirement is that the debtor's refusal has to be in relation to an obligation which is so fundamental that its non-performance would amount to a fundamental breach, The pronouncement to not perform an ancillary duty when it is due does not justify the avoidance of the contract under Articles 72(1), (3) CISG. The refusal not to perform has to be clear and unequivocal. The interpretation of the declaration refusing performance is carried out in accordance with Article 8 CISG.[512] In

---

[507] See in regard to the history of the provision: Schlechtriem, *Einheitliches UN-Kaufrecht*, 88.

[508] Compare the comparable regime in regard to the right to retention para 266 as well as para 274.

[509] Compare Magnus in *Staudinger*, Art 71 paras 48, 49.

[510] Compare Hornung in Schlechtriem/Schwenzer, *Commentary*, Art 72 para 8.

[511] Hornung in Schlechtriem/Schwenzer, Commentary, Art 72 para 8. The English decision *Vitol SA v Norelf Ltd* ((1995) 3 WLR 549, 553 et seq) is clearly based on the idea that a refusal to perform a contract is in a way the offer to terminate the contract which the other party can accept and would have to if it wanted to rely on any remedies; see also in regard to the CISG (even though wrongly applied) the Australian decision *Downs Investment P/L v Perwaja Steel SDN BHD* (12 Oct 2001) CISG-online 955 (Supreme Court of Queensland).

[512] See in regard to Art 8 paras 54 et seq.

practice it often is important under Article 8(2) CISG how a reasonable person in the shoes of the addressee of the declaration had to understand the declaration; that means the objective meaning of the declaration is decisive.

6.2.2 *Notice and Aversion of the Avoidance of the Contract*

274. If the creditor (who fears an imminent breach of contract) wants to avoid the contract he or she has to notify the debtor of his or her intention (unless the debtor has refused performance)[513] "if time allows" (Article 72(2) CISG). The reason for the notice is, as already noted in para 272, to allow the other party to give adequate assurances in regard to their performance and therewith to avert the avoidance of the contract. Whether the notice also has to be "reasonable in the circumstances" is controversial. The German text of Article 72(2) CISG differs in regard to that requirement from the English and French text which only requires "reasonable" notice.[514] However, in the authors' view the difference in the text will not lead to different results in practical terms. The additional German requirement that the notice has to be "reasonable in the circumstances" is closely linked with the time requirement "if time allows." Is a notice as such unreasonable, for example, if either in the remaining time the debtor would have no opportunity to provide adequate assurance, where a security could not compensate for the non-performance, or because due to war it is clear that the debtor will not be able to perform? In the latter case, notice is a mere formality and, therefore is not reasonable.

6.2.3 *Limitation of the Right to Avoid the Contract?*

Article 72 CISG does not stipulate a limitation of the right to avoid the contract. This can result in an in-between-state and a possibility to speculate for the party who is true to contract at the expense of the party breaching the contract since the creditor has a choice between the avoidance of the contract and to wait for performance until performance is due which the creditor does not have to exercise at a certain point in time. The literature has proposed a number of solutions to this issue.[515] In the authors' view a general principle should be developed stemming from Articles 49(2)(b), 64(2)(b) and especially 73(2) CISG[516] which allows to close the gap in Article 72 CISG in accordance with Article 7(2) CISG.[517] The rule should be that the creditor has to notify the debtor of his or her intention to avoid the contract within a reasonable time after it has become obvious that the other party will commit a fundamental breach of contract or after the creditor received notification that the debtor unequivocally refused to perform the contract. If the

---

[513] See para 273.

[514] See in regard to the controversy Magnus in *Staudinger*, Art 72 para 21, Hornung in Schlechtriem/Schwenzer, *Commentary*, Art 72 paras 15, 16.

[515] Compare on the one hand Hornung in Schlechtriem/Schwenzer, *Commentary*, Art 72 para 32 and on the other hand Schmidt-Kessel, RIW 1996, 62.

[516] See in regard to CISG, Art 73(2) para 280.

[517] See in regard to CISG, Art 7(2) paras 45 et seq.

unreasonable delay in notifying the debtor of the intention to avoid leads to an increased damage the creditor's damages claim should be reduced accordingly under Article 77 CISG.[518]

6.2.4 Damages

275a. Article 72 CISG only governs the right to avoid the contract. The question arises whether an anticipatory breach of a contract is equal to a current breach of contract in that any loss resulting from the anticipated breach can be claimed as damages. If the debtor declares or if it is obvious that the debtor will not perform or will not perform in conformity with the contract and the creditor/buyer as precautionary measure makes a cover purchase, or the seller/creditor stores the goods which have been already rejected by the buyer, it is questionable whether the resulting costs can be claimed as damages, especially if the contract, contrary to any expectation, is performed later. In the authors' view the question has to be answered in the affirmative if the debtor unequivocally refused to perform his or her obligations under the contract (Article 72(3) CISG) or if the debtor refused to provide adequate assurance for his or her performance (Article 72(2) CISG) since such conduct are equal to a current breach of contract.

6.3   Installment Contracts

276. In the case of a contract for delivery of goods by instalments the performance can be breached in regard to each installment: non-performance of an installment, performance not in time, or a performance not in conformity with the contract. The question arises whether the right to avoid the contract in regard to the particular installment also can encompass all future instalments and even past instalments which have been faultless. In other words, the question is whether a faulty performance of one installment can lead to right to avoid the entire contract. Generally the contract can only be avoided in regard to the installment in question (Article 73(1) CISG).[519] An anticipatory breach in regard to future instalments is governed by Article 73(2) CISG and requires "good grounds" to conclude that a fundamental breach of the contract will occur with respect to future instalments. Article 73(3) CISG stipulates the requirements which have to be met to avoid the entire contract in respect of past and future instalments because the debtor fundamentally breached the contract in regard to one instalment.[520]

277. The breach of the contract in regard to one instalment in contracts for delivery of goods by instalments are generally breaches of the seller's obligations who does not perform his or her obligations, who does not perform in time or who does not perform in conformity with the contract. Article 73 CISG is, however,

---

[518] See paras 315, 316.

[519] The requirements to be able to avoid a contract: non-performance, late performance or non-conformity with the contract (the latter only in exceptional circumstances see paras 115, 197).

[520] See paras 278–282.

also applicable to a breach of the buyer's obligations. Cases included are where the seller has to deliver in instalments and the buyer has to pay in instalments accordingly, or if the buyer does not take delivery of an instalment in time or refuses to take delivery.

Example: The textile trading company with its seat in the Netherland concluded a contract with the buyer which had its seat in Hamburg, Germany over the delivery of 225,000 yards of cotton-corduroy piece goods. The delivery was supposed to take place in instalments. A first delivery of 45,000 yards was paid for; after the second instalment of 15,219 yards the buyer neither took delivery of the instalment nor paid the invoice. The German buyer informed the seller that the buyer was generally prepared to take delivery of the second instalment but the buyer had problems with its customer in Morocco and was, therefore, delaying the taking of the delivery. In the subsequent correspondence the Dutch seller asked the German buyer several times, including setting additional time limits, to take delivery of the 15,219 yards and to pay the instalment. In the end, the seller avoided the contract and claimed damages. The BGH relied on Article 75 ULIS (Article 73 CISG's predecessor) and held that the buyer due to its non-performance of its obligations in regard to one instalment gave the seller good grounds to conclude that the buyer would not perform its obligations in regard to future instalments. The seller could, therefore, avoid the contract.[521] The wording of the ULIS is more akin now to the wording in regard to an anticipatory breach than an actual breach.[522]

277a. Unlike the CISG's fundamental breach approach, the common law view is to ask whether the breach has gone to the root of the contract[523] rather than just asking whether a party has good grounds for believing that a fundamental breach will occur.[524]

Generally, in the case of instalments, the buyer may reject all of the goods subject to whether the goods have been partially accepted under s 11(4) of the UK Sale of Goods Act 1979. Whether a party can repudiate an entire contract depends much on the terms of the contract and the circumstances of the case.[525] If the obligation is severable from the other installations then only compensation for the breach in relation to the severable instalment is recoverable.[526] Although there is no specific definition of 'severability', this can often be inferred from a buyer

---

[521] BGH (28 Mar 1979) NJW 1979, 1779, 1780 (in regard to the ULIS).

[522] The BGH (28 Mar 1979) NJW 1979, 1779, 1780 saw the German judge made rules in regard to the avoidance of a contract as the model for the ULIS.

[523] *Maple Flock Co Ltd v Universal Furniture Products (Wembley) Ltd* [1934] 1 KB 148.

[524] CISG, Art 73(2) although Bridge, *International Sale of Goods*, § 12.30 does not believe that the two approaches will be different in practice.

[525] SGA 1979 (UK) s 31(2).

[526] A similar view is taken in the UCC where a party may revoke an agreement provided the instalments are interdependent on each other, § 2–608 UCC. See also Honnold, *Uniform Law for International Sales*, § 402.

effecting separate payments or, in some instances, the severability can be otherwise inferred from the terms of the contract.[527]

Under the common law, no distinction is made between goods that are defective and goods that have not been delivered and the principles applying to the severability of the deliveries apply equally to both outcomes.[528]

6.3.1 Limitation of the Right to Avoid the Particular Installment

278. Article 73(2) CISG is based, as already mentioned in para 276, on the general principle that the creditor can only avoid the contract in regard to the particular instalment in question as far as the requirements of a fundamental breach are met or if an anticipatory breach of contract is imminent (Article 72 CISG). That is in line with Article 51(1) CISG.[529] The buyer can avoid the contract due to the inadequate performance or non-performance instalment only in regard to that particular instalment and only in regard that particular instalment will the buyer be freed in regard to his or her duty to take delivery and to pay the purchase price. The seller, however, cannot avoid the entire contract solely because the buyer does not take delivery of an instalment. The general limitation of avoidance to the non-performed, performed not in conformity with the contract or late performance is again based on the principle to sustain contracts as long as possible.

6.3.2 Application of the Right to Avoid Future Instalments

279. Article 73(2) CISG allows the avoidance of the contract in regard to future instalments, that means in regard to instalments which are not due and which might have been performed in conformity with the contract. In that far the issue is the same as the one in regard to anticipatory breach: inadequacy or non-performance of an instalment has to give rise to the assumption that also the future instalment will not be performed adequately as well. The wording of Article 73(2) CISG sets out the necessary evidentiary threshold lower than in Article 72(1) CISG in regard to anticipatory breach: it does not have to be clear that future instalments will not be performed adequately but it is sufficient that the creditor has a "good ground" for the assumption that future performance will be affected. The different wording, however, should not lead to a very different threshold for when the creditor can reasonably assume that future performance will be inadequate.[530] The threshold has to be developed depending on the function and the severity of the intervention in the particular contract.[531] Since a breach of contract

---

[527] *Jackson v Rotax Motor and Cycle Co* [1910] 2 KB 937; Benjamin, Sale of Goods, § 8–073.

[528] *The Mihalis Angelos* [1971] QB 164 at 196; *Texaco Ltd v Eurogulf Shipping Co Ltd* [1987] 2 Lloyd's Rep 541 at 544. See also Benjamin, *Sale of Goods*, § 8-076.

[529] See paras 191–195; see there also in regard to the demarcation between Art 51 and Art 73 CISG.

[530] See in regard to the accidental nature of the wording of Art 73 CISG in Vienna see Schlechtriem, *Einheitliches UN-Kaufrecht*, 89; compare also Hornung in Schlechtriem/Schwenzer, *Commentary*, Art 73 para 23 fn 38 with extensive references in regard to the comparisons of the thresholds in Art 71, 71, and 73 CISG.

[531] Compare Hornung in Schlechtriem/Schwenzer, *Commentary*, Art 73 para 23.

has already occurred in the cases of Article 73 CISG it is evident that, in comparison to Article 72 CISG, the prognosis is easier to make how the debtor's performance is most likely to be. Therefore, a lower threshold is necessary for Article 73 CISG than in regard to Article 72 CISG. In regard to Article 71, as already discussed under para 262, a further weakening of the threshold in respect of the probability that a further breach will occur is justified because the retention of the creditor's own performance is in comparison to the avoidance of the contract the weaker remedy. The requirement, however, is that due to the breach of contract a fundamental breach of contract in respect to future instalments can be expected. It has been examined whether the breach of an obligation in regard to one instalment interferes with the performance of the future instalments in a way which meets the threshold of "fundamental" under Article 25 CISG.[532]

280. The avoidance of future instalments has to be made known within a reasonable time period to reach certainty in regard to fate of the contract. Further, clarity has to be reached to avoid the possibility that the creditor waits with his or her decision to avoid the contract to see whether the market might change and to speculate differently at the expense of the debtor. The requirement set out in Article 49(2) CISG that the notice of avoidance has to be made generally in respect of late delivery of an instalment or delivery of non-conform goods within a reasonable time period after the party knew or ought to have known of the breach or the delivery.[533]

281. Avoidance of future instalments is not only possible if the breach of contract in regard to one instalment is fundamentally affecting all future instalments but also if the non-performance or the non-conformity of an instalment affects the interdependence of current and future deliveries and the future deliveries could not be used for the purpose contemplated by the parties at the time of the conclusion of the contract (Article 73(3) CISG).

6.3.3 Retrospectively of the Avoidance in Regard to Already Performed Instalments

282. The retrospective effect of the avoidance of a contract is a radical measure since it also encompasses already performed, contract conform performances. Therefore, Article 73(3) CISG allows such a retrospective effect only if the interdependence of the instalments means that the non-conformity, the non-performance, or the late performance of one instalment results in that the already performed instalments cannot be used as stipulated in the contract. Decisive whether the instalments are interdependent is the agreed purpose of the instalments at the time of the contract conclusion is decisive in this respect.

---

[532] See in regard to CISG, Art 25 paras 111 et seq.
[533] See in regard to CISG, Art 49(2) para 200.

Example:	The German seller sold a factory to the Austrian buyer. The factory consists of several interdependent units which are delivered in instalments. If one of the units does not conform to the contract and cannot be repaired the buyer has to be able to claim the taking back of the already delivered units even though they were in conformity with the contract since in isolation, without the non-conforming unit, they are useless for the buyer.

The retrospectively of the avoidance, therefore, does not depend on whether the already delivered instalments as such are usable and could maybe be used in a different way, that means different as stipulated in the contract but solely whether they can be used in the way stipulated in the contract. Again the notice of avoidance should be made within a reasonable time.

6.3.4 Other Remedies then Avoidance?

283. Article 73 CISG governs only the right to avoid the contract in regard to instalment contracts. The question arises whether, like Article 51 CISG,[534] the creditor can claim other remedies. The price reduction in the event that the instalments do not conform to the contract is particularly important. In the authors' view the price reduction does not only apply in regard to the non-conforming instalment but also applies in the case of Article 73(3) CISG. In that case the value of the whole contract has to be evaluated in relation to the value of the whole contract as tainted by the non-conform instalment. The devaluation of the whole contract can be far greater than the devaluation of the individual instalment.

Damages claims under Articles 74 to 76 CISG are also a possibility; especially is the breach of an obligation in regard to one instalment can be sufficient to trigger a damages claim under Article 74 CISG, independent from the question whether the breach leads to the avoidance of the future instalments or even the already performed instalments. Damages might encompass the devaluation of future instalments.

6.3.5 Avoidance After the Granting of an Additional Time Period?

284. If one instalment has not been performed it is questionable whether the contract can be avoided under Article 49(1)(b) CISG by setting an additional time period.[535]

Example:	The Dutch seller sold the German buyer 225,000 yards of cotton-corduroy piece goods. The delivery was supposed to take place in instalments. A first delivery of 45,000 yards was paid for; after the second instalment of 15,219 yards the buyer neither took delivery of the instalment nor paid the invoice. The buyer informed the seller that they were generally prepared to take delivery of the second

---

[534] See para 193.
[535] See in regard to CISG, Art 49(1)(b) para 189.

instalment but the buyer had problems with its customer in Morocco and was, therefore, delaying the taking of the delivery. In the subsequent correspondence the Dutch seller asked the German buyer several times, including setting an additional time limit, to take delivery of the 15.219 yards and to pay the instalment. Can the seller only avoid the contract in regard to the second instalment or also in regard to the future instalments?[536]

In the authors' view one has to differentiate: In regard to the individual instalment it has to be possible to avoid that part of the contract under Article 49(1)(b) CISG if the performance of the instalment is delayed (in this case there is a delay in the taking of the delivery) even if Article 73(1) CISG requires that the breach in regard to the instalment is a fundamental one. If the debtor lets the additional time period pass then the breach does become a fundamental one. Whether the fundamental breach which was achieved under Article 49(1)(b) CISG in regard of one instalment also extends to the future instalments has to be decided in accordance with Article 73(2) CISG: it depends, therefore, whether good grounds existed which lead to the conclusion that a fundamental breach of contract will occur in respect to future instalments. The prognosis is independent of whether the breach occurred was a fundamental breach. However, of course the occurred breach has an influence since if the setting of an additional time period has not led to a performance there will be a high likelihood that future instalments will not be performed in conformity with the contract. The likelihood is even higher if the debtor has seriously refused performance in regard to one instalment at the time it was due. Furthermore, the avoidance of the entire contract (future and past instalments) should be possible to be effected by setting an additional time period (Article 49(1)(b) CISG) if the requirements of Article 73(3) CISG are met. That means, if the instalments are interdependent that the breach of contract in regard to one instalment means that neither past nor future instalments can be used for the contractual purpose.

6.3.6 Breach of Other Obligations

285. In regard to instalment contracts, the parties can also agree to additional obligations between them. Those obligations can be so fundamental for the creditor that their breach amounts to a fundamental breach of the entire contract under the CISG.

Example: Pan African Export, a company with seat in the US, contracted with the French manufacturer of "Bonaventure" jeans for the delivery of those jeans in instalments. The buyer was only allowed to on-sell the jeans to Africa and South America, which the seller had made clear during the contract negotiations since the seller had already several exclusive buyers (on-sellers) on the European market and especially

---

[536] Compare BGH (28 Mar 1979) NJW 1979, 1779, 1780 (in regard to ULIS) see also the discussion of the case in para 277.

in Spain where the jeans were very popular. However, some of the jeans delivered to the American buyer appeared on the Spanish market. The seller refused further deliveries. The buyer's damages claim was rejected since the Cour d'appel de Grenoble found that the buyer had committed a fundamental breach under Article 25 CISG by on-selling the jeans to the Spanish market. The Court held that the seller could avoid the contract also in the future under Article 73(2) CISG.

7 Damages

286. The CISG differentiates between the damages claim, the debtor's discharge of a damages claim and the extent of damages.: the most important requirement in regard to a damages claim is the breach of an obligation which the debtor has to perform due to the contract between the parties or due to the CISG (Article 45(1)(b) CISG) in regard to the seller's breach of an obligation and liability and Article 61(1)(b) CISG in regard to the buyer's breach of an obligation and liability). The reason why and in what way the obligation was breached by the debtor is in the first instance immaterial: whether the debtor does not perform his or her obligation and whether the reason for that is impossibility of performance or another reason; whether the obligation is not performed at the time agreed upon; whether the obligation is not performed in conformity with the contract; or whether the performance of the obligation has already been refused before it was due.[537] The debtor can, however- if certain requirements are met-, escape liability (Articles 79, 80 CISG). In regard to the question of discharge of liability the reason why and in what way the debtor breached the obligation in question is of importance. The extent of the available damages is governed by Articles 74–77 CISG. Comparable to the common law damages under the CISG are generally seen as monetary damages.[538] The damages claim can be made cumulative with the avoidance of the contract.

7.1. Responsibility and Discharge of the Debtor

287. If the debtor breaches a contractual obligation the creditor can invoke the CISG remedies outlined in paras 176 et seq for the buyer and in paras 235 et seq for the seller. Generally, the availability of the remedies do not depend on whether the breach is the debtor's fault or whether the breach has a different reason, for example, is due to an act of God. The CISG only requires that the debtor was at fault in respect of the breach of the obligation in regard to the damages claim.[539]

---

[537] See para 275a.

[538] The English version of the CISG is very clear about that (unlike, for example, the German version) "damages....consist of a sum equal to the loss..."

[539] That other remedies do not depend on whether the breach of the obligation was the debtor's fault is set out in Art 79(5) CISG. It would not be conform, of course, with the legal framework of the

Article 80 CISG governs an all-embracing discharge of the debtor's duty to perform which encompasses all of the creditor's remedies if the creditor is responsible for the debtor's breach of an obligation under the contract.[540]

The debtor's discharge requires that the debtor is not responsible for the breach of an obligation. The debtor's responsibility is assumed; the debtor has to prove the discharging circumstances.

7.1.1 Basis for the Possibility to Discharge the Debtor's Liability

288. Article 79 CISG is based on the principle that the debtor is not liable for a breach of an obligation if the reason for the breach was neither controllable nor foreseeable. Rules of discharging the debtor's liability can also be found in Article 7.1.7(1) UNIDROIT Principles and Article 8:108(1) European Principles of Contract Law (however, both only extend to the performance claim). The formulation of Article 79 CISG was very controversial during the drafting of the CISG. The final wording of Article 79 CISG is a compromise. This compromise was supposed to cover the divergent dogmatic – theoretical differences between the member states in regard to the issue of the possibility for the debtor to discharge the debtor's liability which already had been fought over in the formulation of Article 79 CISG's predecessor, Article 74 ULIS. The compromise holds the danger, however, that when Article 79 CISG is applied or interpreted that seemingly overcome differences which are often based on domestic legal doctrine will again surface. Especially the following issues might be prone to different application or interpretation:[541] First, the wording of Article 79 CISG is supposed to avoid the fault-principle which is a prevalent requirement in Germanic jurisdictions. However, sometimes authors suspect that it is still quite influential.[542] Since the reform of the German law of obligations the differences between the requirements to allow a discharge of liability are slight.[543] Secondly, it is still unclear which breaches and which reasons are governed by Article 79 CISG and, therefore, discharge liability. On the one hand, it is unclear whether initial performance impediments which already existed at the time of the conclusion of the contract are covered (which should be case in the author's view)[544] or whether a strict guarantee-liability is set out by

---

CISG to allow that specific performance could be claimed after performance was made impossible. As already set out in para 119, in such a case the court can decide under Art 28 CISG whether to grant specific performance and which defence the debtor can invoke. A possible responsibility of the impossibility to perform by the debtor and the debtor's duty to pay damages is unaffected and is solely governed by Art 79 CISG.

[540] See para 297.

[541] See in regard to the following: Fischer, *Die Unmöglichkeit der Leistung*, 79 et seq, 292 et seq (in regard to the claim to performance), 314 et seq (in regard to the application of Art 79 CISG if the goods do not conform with the contract.

[542] See Nicholas, *Prerequisites*, 286 (in regard to the drafting history), 287: "I have some difficulty …. In accepting that the exception does not turn on fault".

[543] See already in regard to the pre-reform difference Stoll in Schlechtriem/Schwenzer, Art 79 para 9 fn 36: "It is pointless to ask the question whether the discharge of liability under Article 79 CISG in theory is rather a discharge is based on an objective fault principle." (translation from German original); see also Roßmeir, RIW 2000, 407: non-fault liability.

[544] See in regard to the opposite view: Fischer, *Die Unmöglichkeit der Leistung*, 249 et seq, 251.

Article 79 CISG. Thirdly, the question whether Article 79 CISG is applicable if non-conform goods were delivered is unresolved.[545] And it is unclear whether and for which "third party" and their non-performance the debtor especially the seller is liable.[546]

7.1.2 Requirements

289. The discharge of liability requires first and foremost under Article 79(1) CISG that the performance impediment lies outside the debtor's sphere of influence. The most obvious case is performance impediment due to force majeure.[547] Performance impediments which the debtor could have avoided because he or she was in charge of the preparation, the organisation and the implementation of the processes necessary for the performance are not governed by Article 79 CISG since the debtor guarantees his or her ability to perform in regard to the processes. Particularly, the debtor is not relieved if he or she cannot procure the goods or the materials to manufacture the goods due to financial difficulties, for example, due to foreclosure. The organisation of the manufacturing process and the energy supply of the seller's company, the readiness of the workers and their willingness to work etc, is therefore, generally in the risk sphere of the debtor.[548] If the debtor does not want to take the risk for possible disruptions which fall into his or her organisational sphere the debtor has to exempt him or herself in regard to a particular disruption from liability. In regard to an impediment which lies outside the debtor's sphere of influence the debtor is liable if he or she could have reasonably foreseen the impediment at the time of the conclusion of the contract or if the impediment already existed and the debtor knew or ought to have known about it and, therefore, should have been taken into consideration of the time of the conclusion of the contract. Even though the application of Article 79(1) CISG in regard to the performance impediments which already existed at the time of the conclusion of contract is doubtful, taking into account the genesis of Article 79 CISG[549] in the authors' view the reasons to interpret Article 79(1) CISG separate from its genesis are more persuasive. If the initial performance impediments would be excluded from the ambit of Article 79(1) CISG then it would be questionable under which principle the debtor would be liable: liability without the possibility

---

[545] See already BGH (24 Mar 1999) CISG-online 396, as well as para 292; extensive references in Fischer, *Die Unmöglichkeit der Leistung*, 341 et seq.

[546] See paras 293, 294.

[547] Under domestic law insurmountable performance impediments can lead to a void contract, however, the regime of CISG prevails over the domestic law in that regard (see para 36). An embargo which has been imposed by the UN, the EU, or a national Government can have different effects: it can make the contract void and does not face as a questions of the validity of the contract under Art 4(2nd s)(a) CISG, in the ambit of the CISG. Mostly, however, an embargo does not lead to an invalid contract but only to the cancellation or postponement of the delivery, taking delivery or payment duties. It is an insurmountable – may be only temporal, however, – impediment and relieves the debtor in regard to his or her performance, unless it was reasonable foreseeable at the time of the conclusion of the contract.

[548] Huber/Mullis, *The CISG*, 260.

[549] Compare Fischer, *Die Unmöglichkeit der Leistung*, 249 et seq, 253 (dismissing).

to discharge the liability, that means, a strict guarantee, or a gap and reverting back to domestic law which is applicable through private international law rules, or the forming of a principle under Article 7(2) CISG on the basis of which general principles? The timing of the performance impediment can be by chance either before or after the conclusion of the contract so, for example, when the goods in the seller's storage were destroyed by fire or were seized by one of the seller's suppliers such change should not be decisive about the debtor's liability. Significance should be placed on the responsibility for the actual or especially potential knowledge of already existing performance impediments. The liability for initial performance impediments is not alone dependent on the debtor's knowledge but also dependent on whether the initial impediment can be overcome later. Both factors, however, influence each other. If an already existing performance impediment was known or ought to have been known then a contract concluded despite the impediment demands a heightened guarantee comparable to efforts by the debtor to overcome the impediment.[550] If the debtor wants to avoid the heightened liability the impediment has to be taken into account in the contract. In regard to non-foreseeable impediments which occur after the conclusion of the contract and which are outside the debtor's sphere of influence the debtor only has to make those efforts which are reasonable in the circumstances to avoid and to overcome such a later impediment and its consequences.

289a. Article 79 CISG governs all contractual duties, however, the content of the duty has an impact on the control the debtor has over the reasons for the disturbance. Financial constraints are generally regarded as surmountable (and needs to be taken into account at the time of the conclusion of the contract), even if payment has to be made in a foreign currency and foreign exchange control hinders the payment.[551]

Example: The Austrian seller sold goods to a Bulgarian company. The payment was supposed to be effected by opening a letter of credit. Bulgaria issued a moratorium after the conclusion of the contract to the effect that no European bank was willing to open a letter of credit for a Bulgarian debtor since there was not guarantee that the bank would be able to claim the money back from the Bulgarian debtor. The arbitral tribunal of the International Chamber of Commerce did not see a reason in this impediment to relieve the Bulgarian buyer from its obligation to pay the purchase price since the moratorium was not a proven insurmountable impediment for the buyer.[552]

If the seller has to manufacture the goods him-or herself then the entire manufacturing sphere including the procurement of the material is part of the seller's

---

[550] See in regard to the guarantee for goods which are supplied by the seller's suppliers, para 292.

[551] Compare Tribunal of International Commercial Arbitration at the Russian Federation Chamber of Commerce and Industry (17 Oct 1995) CISG-online 207: the lack of free convertible bank credit of the Russian buyer/payment debtor does not relieve the buyer to pay the purchase price to the German seller.

[552] ICC Arbitral Awards (1 Jan 1992), CISG-online 36 = JDI 1993, 1028.

responsibility.[553] Article 79(1) CISG governs also the duty to deliver goods which are in conformity with the contract. That means the seller has to manufacture accordingly and/or to procure the material or goods accordingly from the supplier.[554] Especially in regard to goods which have to be obtained from a supplier it cannot make a difference whether the supplier had manufactured the goods already non-conforming to the contract between the seller and the buyer at the time of the conclusion of the contract and, therefore, an initial performance impediment existed or whether the supplier only manufactures after the conclusion of the contract between the buyer and the seller; that means the impediment only occurred later.

290. What the debtor has to do to avoid or to get rid of an impediment which occurs in the debtor's sphere of responsibility depends on the content of the contract: "guarantees" can heighten the liability for an impediment, the contracting out of liability or limitations on the debtor's liability can diminish the debtor's responsibility for an impediment. Often an interpretation of the contract under Article 8 CISG, taking into account also the parties' usages and practices (Article 9 CISG), will be necessary to ascertain whether the debtor has taken certain risks. Whether and to which extent the debtor, for example, has taken the risk to procure the goods in a heavily fluctuating market or in light of a risk of war has to be ascertained in regard to the actual circumstances of the parties and in regard to the particular contract. However, it has to be noted though that the general tendency is to interpret the circumstances which allow the debtor's exclusion from liability narrowly. Especially, the debtor has generally to assume liability for his or her financial position.

7.1.3 Economic Impossibility and Change of the Inherent Basis of the Contract

291. When and to what extent economic hardship should have the effect to relieve the debtor of his or her liability to perform was a controversial issue during the preparatory work on the CISG. The majority view in the end was probably that not only factual but also economic impossibility could relieve the debtor of his or her liabilities.[555] An impediment under Article 79(1) CISG is not only, as the change of wording from "circumstances" (Article 74 ULIS) to "impediments" in Article 79(1) CISG might suggest, an economic event which prevents the performance in its entirety, but also one which makes the performance economically prohibitive.[556] However, the debtor's discharge of his or her liability due to an

---

[553] See already para 289.

[554] See para 292.

[555] Compare Schlechtriem, *Einheitliches UN-Kaufrecht*, 96.

[556] General opinion, compare: Magnus in *Staudinger*, Art 79 para 24; Herber/Czerwenka, *Internationales Kaufrecht*, Art 79 para 8; Honnold, *Uniform Law for International Sales*, § 432.2; Enderlein/Maskow/Strohbach, Art 79 para 6.3; Neumayer/Ming, Art 79 para 14; comprehensive Gruber, *Geldwertschwankungen*, 538 et seq, 540–553; different opinion: Stoll in Schlechtriem (3 ed) Art 79 para 39, but also para 40 (there has to be a certain limit up to which the debtor is liable); especially French authors are against the possibility to relieve the debtor from his or her liability due to an

economic impediment has to be an exception. Only if the interpretation of the contract under Article 8 CISG, taking into account good faith in international trade (Article 7(1) CISG) prohibits that a particular, unforeseeable, exorbitant risk should be taken by the debtor can economic impediment lead to a discharge of the debtor's obligations. Generally, the debtor will have to endure economic hardship.

Example:	The Italian seller sold the Swedish buyer steel. The seller demanded an adjustment of the contract or the termination of the contract since the market price of steel had risen by 30% since the conclusion of the contract. The Court denied the adjustment as well as the termination of the contract: even if the CISG was applicable (which the Court denied) and Article 79 CISG would be applicable because of "eccessiva onerosità sopravenuta" ("unreasonable hardship"), in the case before it the Court could not find such "unreasonable hardship."[557]

However, the debtor's discharge of liability in cases of grave economic hardship is only one goal; the other is the, from a legal policy point of view desired, possibility to adjust the contract which is not possible by way of gap-filling under the CISG. Article 6.2.3 of the UNIDROIT- Principles and Article 6:111 (2) of the Principles of European Contract Law offer solutions which are more proper.[558] A solution would be to take account of, especially Article 6.2.3 of the UNIDROIT-Principles, as a trade usage under Article 9(2) CISG, as far as the requirements of Article 9(2) CISG are met.[559]

7.1.4 Non-conformity of the Goods

292. The duty to pay damages due to goods which are not conforming with the contract (Articles 35, 45(1)(b) CISG) or due to goods which are not free from any right or claim of a third party or not free from any right or claim of a third party based on industrial property or other intellectual property (Articles 41, 42 CISG) has also to be evaluated in accordance with Article 79 CISG, so that the seller might be able discharge his or her duty to delivery goods which are conforming with the contract. The application of Articles 79(1) or 79(2) CISG has to be an exception: the seller will always be liable in regard to non-conforming goods which the seller manufactured him or herself.[560] If the seller has to procure the sold goods him- or herself the seller generally[561] guarantees with the conclusion of the contract

---

economic impediment since French jurisprudence refuses the theory of "imprévision", compare Tallon in Bianca/Bonell, Art 79 para 3.1.2; Audit para 182.

[557] Tribunale Civile Monza (14 Jan 1993) CISG-online 540 = G.it. 1994, I, 145 (comment by Bonell).

[558] UNIDROIT – Principles, Art 6.2.3 and the Principles of European Contract Law, Art 6:111 allow in the case of hardship the re-negotiation of the contract. In case the parties can not agree the court can terminate the contract or can "adapt the contract with a view to restoring its equilibrium" (UNIDROIT-Principles, Art 6.2.3).

[559] See in regard to the requirements of Art 9(2) CISG para 61.

[560] Compare Stoll/Gruber in Schlechtriem/Schwenzer, *Commentary*, Art 79 para 39.

[561] The contract might contain clauses like "Sale and delivery of the goods shall be subject to correct and punctual supply to ourselves" which might alter the seller's responsibility.

that the seller will procure the goods and that the goods will be in conformity with the contract.[562]

Example: The buyer ran a vine nursery in Austria dealing, inter alia, with the cultivation and refinement of vines as well as the sale of these vines. In the grafting process, the buyer used a special wax in order to protect the vines from drying out and in order to reduce the risk of infection. The wax, which the buyer also in part resold, was purchased for many years from the German seller, whose owner also ran a vine nursery. The German seller in turn obtained the wax from the FW company. The manufacturer of the wax was the company S Werke GmbH. The buyer ordered "black vine wax" as in previous years. The wax which was thereupon delivered to the buyer was a type of wax newly developed by S Werke, as requested by the seller. The seller had neither actually received accepted nor inspected the wax prior to delivery to the buyer. The delivery took place in the original packaging directly from the manufacturer, S Werke, as requested by the seller via the FW Company. The buyer partially used the wax for the treatment of its own vines. In addition, the buyer also sold the wax and vines which had been treated in its nursery with the wax to other nurseries which, in turn, treated their vines with the wax and also delivered vines that had been treated with the help of the wax to other customers.

The wax was defective and the buyer complained of major damage to vines treated with the wax. The buyer claimed damages from the seller. The seller refused to compensate the buyer. The seller attributed the alleged damages to frost and argued that it was exempt from any liability as an intermediary pursuant to Article 79 CISG because the reason for the damages were out of its control. The Court confirmed the seller's liability without deciding whether or not Article 79 was arplicable, stating that even if it were applicable, it would not exclude the seller's liability since the defect in the wax was not an impediment beyond the seller's control. Although it was not the case here, the Court stated that when defects of the goods are caused by the seller's supplier, the seller is only exempt from liability under Article 79 if the failure to perform is due to an impediment beyond the control of the seller and each of the seller's suppliers. Thus, the Court left open the question of whether or not Article 79 of the CISG can be raised as a defence against all kinds of non-performance, including the delivery of defective goods. The Court also pointed out that the exemption provided under Article 79 does not alter the allocation of risk. Liability of the seller resulted from its failure to comply with its obligation to deliver conforming goods; it made no

---

[562] Compare: von Caemmerer, AcP 178 (1978), 148; Neumayer/Ming, Art 79 para 10 fn 46; Schlechtriem in *FS Welser*, 975, 983, 987 et seq; limiting Stoll in Schlechtriem (3 ed) Art 79 para 47: for the hidden non-conformity of the goods which the seller procured from a third party is the seller not liable if the non-conformity could not be detected in the ordinary course of a examination. Similar Stoll/Gruber in Schlechtriem/ Schwenzer, *Commentary*, Art 79 para 40.

difference whether the defect was the fault of the seller or its supplier.[563]

The Austrian Court's decision should be followed. The decision levels out the difference resulting from divergent opinions, set out in para 288, whether initial performance impediments and a breach in regard to the conformity of the goods with the contract are at all governed by Article 79 CISG. Following the BGH's decision the CISG comes closer to most jurisdictions which make the seller liable for damages due to the non-conformity of the goods without allowing the possibility for the discharge of that liability (independent from whether the non-conformity already existed before the time of the conclusion of the contract or developed later). The strict guarantee applies in the authors' view also in regard to mistakes in the development of a good.[564] Limits should only be made in regard to the extent of the damages, especially in regard to the foreseeability of the consequential harm caused by a defect.[565]

7.1.5 Liability for Personnel and Third Parties

293. The seller is responsible under Article 79(1) CISG for its own employees, and that is independent of whether they have caused the performance impediment.

Example: The supplier with seat in Switzerland delivered to a German car manufacturer forged axle shafts. Due a mistake by one its employees, the forge not reach the right temperature and the material could be sufficiently moulded and, therefore, hairline cracks developed in one batch of axle shafts. The Swiss supplier has to assume responsibility for the non-conformity of the axle shafts which was caused by its employee not withstanding whether the employees was at faultor not.

A difficult question raises a strike of the seller's employees. As far as the strike could have been avoidable by the seller the seller cannot discharge his or her liability

---

[563] BGH (24 Mar 1999) CISG-online 396 = NJW 1999, 2440 et seq; comment by Hohloch, JuS 1999, 1235, 1236; Rathjen, RIW 1999, 561 et seq; Schlechtriem, JZ 1999, 794–797; Stoll in Lindmaier/Möhring, CISG No 6/7.

[564] It has to be noted though that the BGH has in its decision of 9 Feb 2002 (main issue was colliding standard form contracts) (CISG-online 651 = NJW 2002, 1651, see para 92) directed the Appeal Court to allow a discharge of the seller's liability if the seller could prove that the non-conformity "could not have been detected before processing the supplied materials/goods using the available examination methods most carefully ("auch bei sorgfältiger Anwendung der gebotenen Untersuchungsmethoden vor der Weit-erverarbeitung nicht erkennbar gewesen ware") and if the non-conformity laid outside the seller's sphere of influence. Unfortunately, as feared by common law jurists, an back-door introduction of the "fault" criterium seems to be discernable from that passage of the judgment since non-conformity of the goods even though not detectable using the available scientific knowledge and methods is the seller's risk. That is different to liability under any product liability legislation or jurisprudence. The seller should, when negotiating the characteristics of the goods under Art 35(1) CISG, only agree to the delivery of goods which conform with the current scientific and technical standards- if there are faults in the development of the goods the seller is then not liable.

[565] See para 300.

even if the price would have been considerable concession to the employees. General, especially political strikes, in which the seller or his or her suppliers are caught can be, on the other hand, reason to discharge the seller of his or her responsibility under Article 79 CISG unless the strike was foreseeable at the time of the conclusion of the contract or could have been reasonably avoided.[566]

294. Whether or not the debtor is responsible for third parties was very controversial in Vienna.[567] The result of the negotiations was a stricter liability since the requirements of Article 79(1) CISG do not only have to be fulfilled in regard to the seller but also in regard to the third party, especially the sub-contractor, which the seller has to prove. Third parties under Article 79(2) CISG are only persons contractor independently participate in the performance and who perform directly to the creditor, for example, the sub-contractor but also in certain circumstances the supplier.[568] The German Bundesgerichtshof did not clearly differentiate in the "vine wax decision"[569] whether the seller's responsibility for his or her supplier who directly delivered to the buyer has to be examined under Article 79(1) CISG or Article 79(2) CISG since both paragraphs were cited by the Bundesgerichtshof. However, the wording "the seller could only discharge his or her responsibility if the defect of the goods was due to circumstances which was outside the seller's own and the seller's suppliers sphere of influence" suggests that the requirements in regard to the discharge of the liability have to be met cumulatively and, therefore, Article 79(2) CISG is the relevant paragraph. On the other hand, the allocation of the risk in regard to the procurement of conform goods suggests a refusal of the discharge of liability due to Article 79(1) CISG. That is especially true for the suppliers which the seller uses to supply materials for the manufacture of the goods: the manufacturing of conforming goods always takes place in the seller's sphere of influence and is, therefore, the seller's risk. However, exception might have to been made if the buyer, for example, has stipulated the use of certain suppliers, as the buyer's own sister firm. In the authors' view the seller possibly can then discharge its liability under Article 80 CISG.[570]

7.1.6 Passing Impediment

295. A passing impediment, for example, an embargo, only discharges from the performance for the time of its existence (Article 79(3) CISG). The importance of this paragraph, however, is very limited since the debtor's duty to perform during

---

[566] Compare Stoll/Gruber in Schlechtriem/Schwenzer, *Commentary*, Art 79 para 35; Saenger, CISG, Art 79 para 6. In addition, if a supplier is picketed it is important for the question whether it was avoidable for the seller whether the seller had to rely on the supplier or whether there were other suppliers the seller could have used: Compare Stoll/Gruber in Schlechtriem/Schwenzer, *Commentary*, Art 79 para 36.

[567] See Schlechtriem, *Einheitliches UN-Kaufrecht*, 97, 98. See overview of the issue by Huber/Mullis, *The CISG*, 263.

[568] Controversial, see Stoll/Gruber in Schlechtriem/Schwenzer, *Commentary*, Art 79 para 25: performance taker; Magnus in *Staudinger*, Art 79 paras 38–40.

[569] See para 292.

[570] See para 297. Herbots/Pauwles in *FS Neumayer*, 335, 341 et seq, 350 with further references.

discharging performance impediments stays unaltered. Practically, Article 79(3) CISG is especially important in regard to damages due to delay. However, during the time of the original performance impediment other impediments can develop which discharge the debtor finally under Article 79(1) CISG. If during a performance impediment an economical impediment develops it can if it meets certain criteria be a reason under Article 79(1) CISG to discharge the debtor's liability (but only in exceptional circumstances).[571]

7.1.7 Duty to Give Notice

296. The party which cannot perform its obligations has to notify the other party of the impediment and its consequences in regard to the performance (Article 79(4) CISG). The notice has to, contrary to Article 27 CISG, reach the other party (Article 79(4)(2nd s) CISG). A breach of the notice requirement results in the debtor's duty to pay damages for the damages incurred by the creditor due to the failure to give notice (Article 79(2)(2nd s) CISG even if the debtor is discharged in regard to the performance of his or her obligations due to a performance impediment. Of course, the notice can be combined with the offer to adjust the contract which under Articles 29, 14 et seq, 18(1) CISG can also be accepted impliedly.

7.1.8 Seller Causing Non-performance

297. Under Article 80 CISG the debtor can be discharged from performance entirely if the creditor has caused the performance impediment.[572] In regard to the scenarios in which the debtor's duty to pay damages is discharged under Article 80 CISG it has to be noted that most scenarios will already be covered by Article 79(1) CISG since an impediment which was caused by the creditor is generally neither avoidable nor controllable by the debtor. Only in cases where the seller's conduct was foreseeable offers Article 80 CISG wider protection than Article 79(1) CISG in regard to damages claims.

Example: The buyer has prevented the seller's timely performance to manufacture and to deliver a certain machine by not making drawings for the manufacturing of the machine available in time or by not getting the import papers in time. Even if such impediments were already to be taken into account at the time of the conclusion of the contract is the seller discharged under Article 80 CISG if, for example, the buyer claims damages for the non-timely delivery of the machine.

Article 80 discharges not only from the duty to pay damages but also excludes other remedies of the seller and the reliance on defences which are based on the inappropriate behaviour of the other party.

---

[571] Compare in regard to the suggestions in Vienna: Schlechtriem, *Einheitliches UN-Kaufrecht*, 99.

[572] The article has evolved from an application of former East Germany in Vienna, see Schlechtriem, *Einheitliches UN-Kaufrecht*, 100.

Example:	The buyer claims damages resulting from a claimed delivery delay. The seller defends him or herself arguing that the buyer had not opened a letter of credit in time. The buyer on the other hand points out that the delayed opening of a letter of credit was due to the seller had not let the buyer know certain information crucial for the issuing of the letter of credit. The seller can, therefore, not rely on the delayed opening of the letter of credit.[573]

The requirement for a discharge from the duty to perform according to the contract under Article 80 CISG is that there is a causal connection between the creditor's conduct and the breach of the obligation. It is, however, not decisive whether the creditor has caused the performance impediment in accordance with Article 79 CISG.

298. The debtor's discharge only occurs "as far as" the seller's conduct was the cause of the performance impediment. The limitation "as far as" only limits the application of Article 80 CISG. However, in the authors' view Article 80 CISG is also applicable in regard to other remedies "as far as" an adaptation is possible, for example, in regard to damages claims.[574] If the debtor's causing of the performance impediment is at the same time the breach of a contractual duty, for example, the omission of contractually agreed co-operation duties (compare Article 60(a) CISG) then the creditor can, of course, as debtor be liable for damages due to the breach of the obligation to cooperate.

7.2   Extent of the Damages Claim

299. In regard to the extent of the damages claim due to a breach of an obligation which the debtor has to accept responsibility for three principle rules have to be taken into account:

First, only material damage can be compensated; secondly the principle of total reparation applies; and damages without or in addition to avoidance of the contract.

7.2.1 Material Damage

299a. Only material damage which can be calculated in monetary terms has to be compensated in money. Damages for emotional harm, ("dommage moral") and damages for pain and suffering are not recoverable under the CISG.[575] In Schlechtriem's view, damages for pain and suffering and emotional harm cannot

---

[573] OGH (6 Feb 1996) CISG-online 224 = öst ZfRV 1996, 248 et seq; see also Rathjen, RIW 1999, 561, 565.

[574] Other view: Stoll in Schlechtriem (3 ed) Art 80 para 5; like here Magnus in *Staudinger*, Art 80 para 15; Stoll/Gruber in Schlechtriem/Schwenzer, *Commentary*, Art 80 para 10 (also in regard to other remedies like avoidance); Bach/Stieber, IHR 2006, 97, 99 (in regard to avoidance). In the authors' view is Art 80 CISG not applicable in regard to avoidance since it is not divisible.

[575] See CISG, Art 5 and para 39 for a more detailed discussion.

be recovered through domestic law since Articles 74 et seq govern damages exclusively in regard to contracts to which the CISG is applicable. However, it can be argued that practically if a breach of contract results in pain and suffering of the other party that act or omission will generally also fulfil the requirement of a tort especially negligence. Since tort law fulfils a regulatory function within society,[576] damages for pain and suffering should not be excluded by the CISG if they are available under domestic law.

The loss of "good will" is considered a material damage (devaluation of the company) which, however, might be hard to value and to prove.[577]

7.2.2 Total Reparation and Foreseeability

300. Generally, the principle of total reparation applies: namely that all damage caused by the breach must be compensated. A limitation of the damages which can be compensated through limiting causal theories like the German principle that only damages which can be "adequately" linked to a breach of duty are not applicable under the CISG and are not necessary. Limitations of the damages which will be compensated under the CISG are achieved through the requirement of forseeability.[578] The requirement of foreseeability limits damages to those which are generally to be expected at the time of the conclusion of the contract or which could at the time of the conclusion of the contract be foreseen by the debtor.[579] Since the principle of total reparation means that the creditor's economic situation after the breach of contract has to be compared with the situation the creditor would have been in if the breach would have not occurred. Generally positive developments for the creditor, caused by the breach of contract, have to be taken into account, for example, saved expenses for the erection of a conveyer belt which the seller has not delivered. However, the subtraction of economic advantages should only be allowed if it is not inconsistent with the aim and object of the duty to compensate for the breach.

7.2.3 Damages Without or in Addition to Avoidance

301. Under the CISG, a buyer may either claim damages due to a breach of the contract (Article 74) or avoid the contract and claim damages for breach of the duty that led to the avoidance (Articles 75, 76 CISG).[580]

---

[576] Posner, *Economic Analysis of Law*, 196–198.

[577] Compare like here: Honsell, SJZ 1992, 362; Stoll/Gruber in Schlechtriem/Schwenzer, *Commentary*, Art 74 para 12 ("generally"); different view: Magnus in *Staudinger*, Art 74 para 27; see for a general overview and discussion: AC-CISG Opinion No 6 (by Gotanda), CISG-online/cisg-ac.

[578] See Honnold, *Uniform Law for International Sales*, §§ 406–408.

[579] See in regard to latter para 302.

[580] See paras 310 et seq; compare also Roßmeir, RIW 2000, 407, 408 et seq.

7.3   Limitation on the Recovery of Damages Through the Requirement of Forseeability

302. Articles 74 et seq limit the damages claim of the creditor due to a breach of a contractual obligation to those damages which were foreseeable to occur as consequences of a breach of contract for the debtor at the time of the conclusion of the contract taking into account all circumstances which the debtor knew or ought to have known. The burden of proof in regard to the foreseeability lies with the aggrieved party.[581] The basic idea behind the principle comes from Article 1150 French Code Civile. The rule was, via the law of Louisiana, first stated in the text book of Sedgwick. From there it was made famous in the English decision of *Hadley v Baxendale* in 1854[582] and was elevated to the principle of the limitation of damages due to a breach of contract in the common law jurisdictions. Ernst Rabel used the principle then in his draft for a uniform sales law.[583]

The legal policy behind the principle is easy to understand and plausible: The limitation to the damages which could be foreseen or ought to have been foreseen at the time of the conclusion of the contract should allow the parties to calculate the risk of the particular contract, that means, to be able to assess whether the benefits of the contract outweigh the possible risks associated with it. The risk is circumscribed by the agreed contractual obligations and is limited by the purpose of those obligations.[584] Which of the creditor's interest and to what extent they are protected is first and foremost a matter of agreement between the parties. Guarantees, for example, in regard to the suitability of a good for an unusual use, can extend the seller's liability; product descriptions, limitations of liability and exclusions of liability can limit the liability. If there is not specific contractual agreement in regard to unusual risks then the seller has to be protected against being

---

[581] Compare OLG Bamberg (13 Jan 1999) CISG-online 516 = TranspR – IHR 2000, 17, 18 (simplified): The seller had delivered certain goods late. The buyer could not as planned use the goods for manufacturing cheaply in Turkey due to the late delivery but had to manufacture more expensively in Germany. The increase in price of the manufacturing was not known to the seller at the time of the conclusion of the contract and the seller also could not have known. The buyer had the burden of proof that the seller ought to have known of the consequence a delivery delay would have.

[582] *Hadley v Baxendale* (1854) 9 Ex. 341, 156 Eng Rep 145 (Chancery) The plaintiff, Hadley, operated a mill. The crankshaft of the mill broke, thus forcing the mill to shut down. Hadley contracted with the defendant, Baxendale, to deliver the crankshaft to engineers for repair by a certain date. Baxendale failed to deliver on the date in question, causing Hadley to lose some business. Hadley sued for the profits he lost due to Baxendale's late delivery, and the jury awarded Hadley damages of £25. Baxendale appealed, contending that he did not know that Hadley would suffer any particular damage by reason of the late delivery. The Court held hat Baxendale could only be held liable for losses that were generally foreseeable, or if Hadley had mentioned his special circumstances in advance

[583] Compare in regard to the history of "foreseeability" König, 75 et seq; Faust, 51 et seq.

[584] The foreseeabilty principle as an instrument to limit recoverable damage is founded on the same principle as the German principle that the recoverable damage has to be limited in accordance with the purpose of the breached duty or obligation (compare Schlechtriem in *Recht in Ost und West*, 505–518). Generally of a different view: Faust, 66 et seq, 336 (summary): the foreseeability principle forces the communication of information and the sharing of information between creditor and debtor (it should be noted though, that information sharing and communication is only one aspect of risk allocation).

liable for such risks whose extent the seller could not have ascertained at the time of the conclusion of the contract and, therefore, which the seller could calculate and could not form part of the basis for the seller's decision whether to enter into the contract. Damages which have to be usually expected and losses of the buyer due to a breach of obligations by the seller are on the other hand "foreseeable" and have been agreed upon by the seller when concluding the contract. The same is true for the buyer if the breach results in a "normal" loss for the seller, for example, if the buyer does not take delivery. In contrast, unusual losses of the seller which cannot be expected generally in the course of a breach of contract are only part of the buyer's liability if the buyer knew them and the buyer nevertheless agreed to take the risk, for example, to take delivery at a fixed date if the seller would incur a contractual penalty for not clearing his or her storage in time etc.

The principle, however, is only practicable if in the particular case the expectations and the knowledge of the parties does not have to be ascertained (which hardly ever will be satisfactorily possible) if a standardisation can be used.[585] The following scenarios are such examples:[586]

7.3.1 Value of the Goods

303. If the seller does not deliver the goods the buyer can always claim the value of the goods which the goods would have had if seller had delivered them. The buyer can claim the goods' objective value as foreseeable damage even if due to the lack of a market price the abstract calculation of the damages has to be ruled out or if a cover purchase is not possible in the particular case. If the goods do not conform with the contract the usual or customary repair- or return transport costs are part of the damages; costs in regard to the preservation of the goods are compensated under Articles 85 et seq CISG.

7.3.2 Resale Profits

304. Resale profits, which the buyer loses because of the non-delivery of the goods or because the goods are not in conformity with the contract are only recoverable under Article 74 CISG in regard to the usual gross profit margin (different in regard to the concrete calculation on the basis of a reasonable cover purchase, see Article 75 CISG). The buyer has to try, due to the buyer's duty to mitigate damages,[587] to make cover purchases as soon as reasonably possible if the damages can be mitigated through a cover purchase. Unusually high profits, contract penalties and probably also damage awards to the buyer's customers can only be recovered if at the time of the conclusion of the contract the particular risk has been pointed out or ought to have been recognised so that when concluding the contract the seller has subsumed the particular risks. A later notification in regard

---

[585] Very clear to the foreseeability principle as risk allocation Perillo, *Hardship and its Impact on Contractual Obligations*, 4 et seq; OGH (14 Jan 2002) CISG-online 643 = IHR 2002, 76, 80, 81: generally objective standard.

[586] Compare in regard to the scenarios also Faust, 166 et seq, 196.

[587] See paras 315, 316.

to such risks which were not foreseeable for the debtor at the time of the conclusion of the contract cannot burden the other party additionally.

7.3.3 Damages for Subsequent Loss of Business

305. The classification of damages for subsequent loss of business is uncertain. Damages for subsequent loss of business can be recovered, in the authors' view (following the Court in *Hadley*[588]), if at the time of conclusion of the contract the party had been informed about the risk of such loss or if the potential loss was clearly recognisable. Otherwise it has to be assumed that that a commercially operating business owner takes precautions for the case of a delayed or defective delivery.[589]

7.3.4 Consequential Damages

306. Consequential damages cause special difficulties, especially consequential harm caused by a defect like damage to the buyer's property (due to Article 5 CISG liability for death or personal injury falls outside the scope of the CISG), or the ruin of material which is processed together with the defective goods, the loss of customers and goodwill due to the resale of defect goods or the non-delivery of customers due to the delayed delivery of the seller, legal costs,[590] etc. It is indeed always foreseeable at the time of the conclusion of the contract that delivery of dangerously defective goods will cause consequential loss. In those circumstances where defective goods cause indirect loss to property, the foreseeability requirement merely acts as a rule to determine whether the loss which actually occurred lies within the typical risks which the seller created by delivering the defective goods.

Example: The seller with seat in Germany sold the buyer which had its seat in Alsace glue for the fastening of ceiling boards. It was agreed that the glue had certain characteristics in regard to its adhesive qualities and its weight bearing capacity which the seller had specified. If the ceiling boards fell from the ceiling after a while and damaged the buyer's property since the glue did not have the adhesive qualities agreed upon, or if the buyer had installed the ceiling boards for a customer and has now to repair the installation or has to pay damages then it depends for the question of what the scope of the damages is the buyer can recover what the intended use of the glue was or

---

[588] (1854) 9 Ex Ch 341, see para 302 fn 1056 in regard to the facts of the case.

[589] Compare, von Caemmerer, AcP 178 (1978) 147; generous Magnus in *Staudinger*, Art 74 para 40: stoppage of production is foreseeable if the goods were to be used for the production.

[590] In regard to legal costs as part of damages: see Schlechtriem, IHR 2006, 49–53, especially in regard to the so-called American rule according to which each party has to pay generally their own legal costs and, therefore, parties in regard to a contract which might be adjudicated in the United States take the risk to pay their own legal costs. In regard to Germany, however, see OLG Düsseldorf (22 Jul 2004) CISG-online 916 = IHR 2005, 29: damages in regard to legal costs under Art 61(1), 74 CISG.

what the seller could reasonable foresee what the use of the glue would be. If it was foreseeable that buyer would use the glue to fulfil its own contracts then the risk associated with those contracts is covered. The seller has not only to compensate for the cost of the unsuitable glue but also the costs the buyer has incurred because the buyer had to repair his or her work done with the glue.[591]

Also the loss of goodwill due to defective, non-conform goods or the delayed delivery of goods can be recoverable if the buyer is clearly a reseller in a volatile market.

Example: A Dutch cheese exporter sold and delivered Gouda-cheese to the German cheese importer. The cheese was to a small percentage (3 per cent) defective. The German buyer claimed damages because due to the delivery of defective cheese it lost four big customers and therewith a substantial amount of profit. Also, other business relationships had been damaged. The BGH took into account whether a reasonable "ideal type" debtor had to reckon on that its own defective performance to a middle man would lead to a loss of customers and therewith to a loss of profits. In the particular case the BGH thought it possible that the competition of the German cheese market was as such that a loss of customers in this situation was possible.[592]

However, it could be misleading to make the recoverability of consequential damages dependent on the probability of their occurrence and the security that they can be proven.

Example: The seller, manufacturer of wooden products in British Columbia, Canada sold 88 truck loads of cedar chips to Louisiana-Pacific Corp in Oregon, USA. The buyer on took delivery of 13 truck loads. In regard to the other 75 truckloads the buyer had not given the necessary information in regard to their shipment and had refused to take delivery with the claim that in so far a contract had not been concluded. The seller claimed damages for loss of profit in regard to the 75 truck loads. The Court in the first instance had denied that the lost profits were recoverable since the market was so volatile for wood chips so that a sound basis for the calculation of the lost profits was impossible. The Court wrongly applied US law[593] and approved the decision of the first instance which did not think it was a legal question but a question of fact which was for the jury to decide. If the CISG would have been applied to the case the question would have been a legal question which would have been to be decided by

---

[591] The case draws from BGH (29 May 1968) BGHZ 50, 200, 204 and clearly demonstrates that scope of the damages depends on the duties of the seller in regard to certain characteristics of the goods.

[592] BGH (20 Mar 1980) WM 1980, 36 to ULIS; critical to the decision Weitnauer, IPRax 1981, 83–85.

[593] *GPL Treatment Ltd v Louisiana-Pacific Corp* (11 Apr 1996) (SC Oregon) CISG-online 202 = 133 Or App 633 = 894 P2d 470; in regard to the application of the CISG to this case see the dissenting opinion of Judge Leeson, 133 Or App 633, 646.

the judge. Generally the question would have been decided in regard to recoverability of the loss of profits from the resale as "foreseeable". Only the amount of the lost profits could be seen as a question of fact for which the procedural rules of the lex fori is applicable.[594] The consideration of evidence and the degree of conviction of the judge are generally seen as part of the procedural rules and therewith fall within the lex fori. However, the expected difference of how different domestic laws deal with those questions make it plausible to develop a uniform rule.[595]

307. Despite of its clear basis the foreseeability rule can, in regard to particular heads of damages, cause considerable difficulties for courts which value each heads of damages separately instead of, like the German courts, taking a more holistic approach.

Example:	The US Rotorex Corp had sold 1800 compressors to the Delchi Carrier SpA which had its seat in Villasanta, Italy which were to be delivered in three instalments and which the buyer wanted to build into air conditioning. After two deliveries had been made and had been paid the buyer discovered that the compressors from the first delivery were defective and claimed inter alia damages. The following heads of damages were individually listed: costs of the preparation of the production of the air-conditions and the procurement of special materials and parts for the machines, costs for repair incurred by having to purchase spare parts and the man-hourly rates necessary to do the necessary repairs; additional investigation and testing costs, storage costs after the repair had failed and the buyer had avoided the contract and rejected the compressors; loss due to the interruption of business since no production could take place without the compressors, loss of sales due to the delayed production, costs for the delivery of substitute compressors, necessary adjustment of the design to the substitute compressors, lost profits from other expected sales. The United States District Court held[596] that those were heads of damages which were recoverable because they were foreseeable losses due to the seller's breach of contract: the costs for the repair (parts and man-hours), the additional costs for the cover purchase of other compressor – air transport costs (which mitigated the buyer's damages), the costs for storage of the rejected compressors and a part of the lost profits in regard to future sales. The Court, however, denied the recoverability in regard to a part of the asserted profit possibilities since the party could not sufficiently prove the probability of their coming into existence. The costs which the buyer incurred due to his or her expectation to be able to manu-

---

[594] Compare to this case to the cheese case of the BGH (para 306); in regard to lowering the threshold in respect of the proof of the loss or damage see AC-CISG Opinion No 6 (by Gotanda) sub 2: "reasonable certainty" is sufficient.

[595] As the AC-CISG Opinion suggests in its Opinion No 6 (by Gotanda) sub 2.1: the question of proof is a substantive matter and, therefore within the scope of the CISG.

[596] *Delchi Carrier SpA v Rotorex Corp* (6 Dec 1995) US Court of Appeals (2nd Circ) CISG-online 140 = 10 F 3rd 1024.

facture were also not seen to be recoverable since they have already been considered under "lost profits".

7.3.5 Frustrated Expenditure

308. Futile expended costs[597] are recoverable up to the amount of the expected (and foreseeable) profit. The debtor is not liable for a creditor's lost bargain.[598] If the buyer builds a storage facility to store the soon to be delivered goods which turn out useless, then the seller has not delivered the goods and the buyer can claim these costs as damages.[599] Such costs should be seen, unless the contrary is proven, as part of the lost profits.[600]

7.4   Details in Regard to the Damages Calculation

7.4.1 Performance Interest without Avoidance of the Contract?

309. If the creditor does not avoid the contract – or cannot avoid the contract – then the creditor can claim damages next to the performance of the contract under Article 74 CISG, like damages caused by delay or consequential damages caused by a defect.[601] The buyer can generally only claim "damages instead of performance," that means, liquidation of the contract and the compensation of the performance interest can only be claimed by the buyer after the avoidance of the contract under Articles 75, 76 CISG. If, however, the requirements of avoidance are met undisputed, for example, when one party categorically refuses performance, exceeds a fixed date, or performance is impossible, the performance interest should be recoverable without that the party has to declare avoidance of the contract under Article 74 (1ˢᵗ s) CISG if the creditor relinquishes his or her right to performances.[602] The relinquishment of performance demands, if necessary, the rejection of the goods. The buyer is entitled to reject the goods if the buyer could avoid the contract or could have avoided the contract. The point in time when avoidance is possible is also important for the calculation of damages on the basis of a concrete cover purchase and the necessary acts to mitigate the damages.

In the authors' view one should go one step further and award the performance interest under Article 74 (1ˢᵗ s) CISG without that the contract has been or could

---

[597] Compare in regard to the possible expenditure: Schmidt-Ahrendts, IHR 2006, 63, 68.

[598] Compare Magnus in *Staudinger*, Art 74 para 53 with further references; other view Stoll in *FS Neumayer*, 330, 331 limit in regard to the costs of the contract.

[599] Clearly as classification as loss and not costs in regard to the rewinding of the contract: Schmidt-Ahrendts, IHR 2006, 63, 70 et seq.

[600] Controversial: other view Stoll in *FS Neumayer*, 313 et seq, 322 et seq.

[601] See already para 301.

[602] Compare Stoll/Gruber in Schlechtriem/Schwenzer, *Commentary*, Art 75 para 5, but also already Art 74 para 2 (performance interest), para 14 (non-performance damages); from the courts: Hans OLG Hamburg (28 Feb 1997) CISG-online 261.

have been avoided.[603] If the seller delivers defective goods the buyer has to conclude a cover purchase to deliver to the buyer's customers or to continue with the manufacturing process. Therefore, the buyer must be able to calculate the damages according to the cover purchase. Of course, the buyer cannot demand in addition still the original performance: damages instead of performance is not compatible with a claim to performance (compare Articles 46(1), 62 CISG).[604] Under Article 77 CISG, to mitigate loss, the creditor might be obliged to do a cover purchase, for example, the buyer by rising prices, or the seller if the prices decline if it is foreseeable that at a later point in time at which the contract can be avoided the damage from a cover purchase would be higher.[605] The situation is different if the debtor has not committed a breach or an anticipator breach under Article 72 CISG yet[606] by either not performing in time or by delivering defect goods. The creditor in such cases who precautionary makes a cover purchase, for example, because of the rumours of the debtor's situation and in regard to Article 77 CISG, does that on his own risk: if the debtor performs in conformity with the contract than the cautious creditor has to bear the cost of the (in the end unnecessary) cover purchase. However, if the creditor can in the end avoid the contract and has a claim in regard to the performance interest then the cover purchase cannot be held against the creditor if the creditor wants to calculate the damages in accordance with Article 76 CISG (market price): Article 77 CISG does not stipulate that a cover purchase has to be done as "reasonable measure" before the breach of contract has happened (compare the wording in Article 77 CISG. "….resulting from the breach.").

7.4.2 Avoidance of the Contract and Damages

310. Article 75 CISG allows in case of the avoidance of the contract a concrete calculation of damages in form of the difference between contract price and the price of a cover purchase. Further damage which is not already part of the calculation under Article 75 CISG can often be claimed under Article 74 CISG.

Example: The sold goods were polluted and breached the express guarantee of absolute purity so the non-conformity of the goods fulfils the requirement of a fundamental breach. The buyer can avoid the contract and make a cover purchase but additionally the buyer can claim further losses and costs, for example, loss of customers or necessary tests of the cover purchase as far as they were caused by the breach

---

[603] See AC-CISG Opinion No 6 (by Gotanda) sub 8; Schlechtriem in *FS Georgiades*, 383, 384 et seq; OLG München (15 Sep 2004) IHR 2005, 70, 71; in contrast: Huber in *FS für Horst Konzen*, 331, 343; as well probably OLG Düsseldorf (22 Jul 2004) CISG-online 916 = IHR 2005, 29, 30 sub 4 (obiter dictum).

[604] Details in regard to the calculation of damages under Art 74 CISG in such cases and especially if the debtor later offers performance or performs: see Schlechtriem in *FS Georgiades*, 383, 384 et seq.

[605] See para 315.

[606] See in regard to anticipatory breach paras 269 et seq.

of the contract and were foreseeable for the seller at the time of the conclusion of the contract.[607]

Example: The buyer of scrap metal refuses to take delivery. As a result the seller avoids the contract and makes a cover resale. The seller had to cancel the ship which had been chartered to transport the scrap metal to the buyer. To charter the ship anew incurred higher costs. The additional costs are "further" costs and were in the view of the Court foreseeable. The costs could be recovered under Article 75 (2nd half s) in conjunction with Article 74 CISG.[608]

311. To avoid this, the party which has suffered the breach of contract starts to speculate at the expense of the party which breached the contract, especially waiting on how the market develops, Article 75 CISG determines that the requirement for the damages calculation in regard to a cover purchase is that the cover purchase has been made in a reasonable manner and within a reasonable time. Those requirements for a cover purchase are the same as the requirements of the duty to mitigate under Article 77 CISG which the party who has suffered the breach of contract has to meet. Those requirements would apply even if they would not be explicitly mentioned in Article 75 CISG. Article 75 CISG does not completely exclude the possibility to speculate in regard to the costs since the creditor can to a certain degree wait with the avoidance of the contract taking into account any market developments.[609] If the price rises for the cover purchase due to unreasonable waiting then the creditor's damages claim will have to be reduced in accordance with Article 77 CISG.[610]

311a. A cover purchase in "a reasonable manner" has to, other than in regard to the price, conform to the conditions of the avoided contract, especially in regard to time and place of the delivery. That is difficult in cases of an anticipatory breach (Articles 72, 73(2) CISG)[611] since the time of delivery when the buyer needs the goods or the seller will have the goods at his or her disposal might still be far away in the future. Article 75 CISG, however, can be read (and is read by the majority) that the crucial time for the calculation of the cover purchase is the time of the avoidance of the contract: If the goods are to be delivered in August 2008 but the seller refuses delivery of the goods (performance of the contract) already in spring 2007 (see Article 72(3) CISG) than it is questionable whether the buyer can or has to make the cover purchase in spring 2007 (substantial storage costs

---

[607] Compare also the case of *Delchi Carrier v Rotorex*, above para 307; see in regard to frustrated expenditure see para 308: frustrated expenditure is caught through calculating the concrete difference which covers the costs necessary to gain profit and treated as if the contract would have been performed.

[608] Compare *Downs Investment P/L v Perwaja Steel SDN BHD* (12 Oct 2001) (SCt Queensland) CISG-online 955.

[609] Different the ULIS which in such cases, if certain requirements were met, stipulated an ipso facto avoidance of the contract; critical, therefore, to the way the CISG governs this issue: Hellner, *Ipso facto avoidance*, 85–99.

[610] See also para 313.

[611] See in regard to the requirements of an anticipatory breach paras 269 et seq.

might ensue if the buyer only needs the goods in August 2008) or whether the buyer can or has to make the cover purchase in August 2008. In Schlechtriem's view the cover purchase has to be made at the original time of delivery unless the duty to mitigate dictates an early purchase.[612] In Butler's view the creditor's duty to mitigate loss under Article 77 CISG demands that it depends on the circumstances when a cover purchase should be made. That means if it reasonable certain that the price for the cover purchase will fall closer to August 2008 then the creditor has to wait with the cover purchase. However, if, on the contrary, all indicators predict that the prices will rise in the next six months the creditor has to make the cover purchase earlier unless the storage costs will outweigh any price rise. In short, it depends on the circumstance what a reasonable business person in the shoes of the creditor would have done.

312. Article 76 CISG provides for the abstract calculation of damages as a second possibility to calculate damages, that means, damages are calculated as the difference between the contract price and the market price of the goods. The market price rule is only applicable, of course, if no cover purchase was made.

"Market price" is under Article 55 CISG the price "generally charged at the time of the conclusion of the contract for such goods sold under comparable circumstances in the trade concerned." Often the market price can be ascertained by looking at the listing at the commodity exchange but also other information is sufficient, for example, specialised publications like "The Metal Bulletin." The price at the place of delivery is decisive. If the market price cannot be ascertained at the place of delivery the market price at the place has to be taken into account (Article 76(2) CISG).

313. In regard to the calculation of the market price it can be difficult which time is the relevant one to form the basis of the calculation. Again, like in the case of the cover purchase, problems arise specifically if the contract is avoided before performance is due and in cases of avoidance due to an anticipatory breach under Article 72 CISG. In Vienna it was decided to take the time of the declaration of avoidance to avoid giving the courts too much discretion in regard to the establishment of the time when the creditor could have first avoided the contract. The danger that the party who suffered the breach waits with its declaration of avoidance and speculates at the expense of the defaulting party exists as well and can only be controlled through the duty to mitigate damages under Article 77 CISG so that the time of the possible avoidance of the contract might gain relevance.

The time of the calculation cannot only be the time of the declaration of avoidance but also the time of the taking of the delivery of the goods if the goods have been already delivered to the party which avoids the contract (Article 76(1)(2nd s) CISG). The latter point time which was included in the CISG as a compromise can be quite a burden for the contract performing party if at the time when the party takes delivery of the goods the party could not know about the breach of contract

---

[612] Compare Schlechtriem, *FS Hellner*, sub II.

and, therefore, could not avoid the contract, for example, in regard to concealed defects in the goods characteristics.

313a. The application of Article 76 CISG to the avoidance by anticipatory breach is not only difficult in respect of the time of the calculation of the difference between contract and market price but also in regard to the determination of the relevant market price because Article 76(1)(1st s) CISG does calculate the market price for goods to be delivered at the time of avoidance instead, like numerous national legal systems,[613] at the time of performance which can be substantially later.[614] Schlechtriem, like in regard to the concrete calculation of damages under Article 75 CISG, is of the view that in the calculation of the market price under Article 76 CISG in the case of an anticipatory breach, the time of performance is determinative for the calculation of damages. Those prices can be determined, if required, by looking at the listings of the commodity market. Article 76(1) CISG should, therefore be read: The party claiming damages can demand "the difference between the price agreed upon in the contract and the market price at the time of the avoidance of the contract for goods which are available at the time of delivery." Only if such prices for goods are not available should the market price for goods which can be delivered at the time of avoidance be relevant.[615]

314. Also if damages are calculated under Article 76 CISG further damages can be recovered under Article 74 (2nd s) CISG, for example, the loss of customers or goodwill, costs to get the goods back if the buyer has refused to take delivery, etc. Lost volume, for example, the loss due to more expensive production costs due to reduce production capacity can generally be claimed. Of course, those losses have to have been foreseeable and have to be shown. Frustrated expenditure is already included in the abstract damages calculation.[616]

7.5   Duty to Mitigate Damages

315. Article 77 (1st s) CISG obliges the party which wants to claim damages, due to the breach of contract of the other party, to take reasonable measures to mitigate the damage caused by the breach of contract. A breach of this obligation results under Article 77 (2nd s) CISG accordingly to a decrease of the damages claimed by the creditor who has been the victim of a breach of contract. The obligation to mitigate damages exists only in regard to damages claims and not in regard to claims in regard to the performance of the contract.[617] What the obligation to

---

[613] See Schlechtriem, *FS Hellner*, sub III.2.b.

[614] See para 311a.

[615] See in regard to details and to measure which are necessary to mitigate the damage: Schlechtriem, *FS Hellner*, sub III.

[616] See also paras 308, 310.

[617] Compare in regard to the discussion in Vienna: Schlechtriem, *Einheitliches UN-Kaufrecht*, 92, 93; further Stoll/Gruber in Schlechtriem/Schwenzer, *Commentary*, Art 77 para 4 with further references.

mitigate damages entails depends on the circumstances in the particular case, that means, it depends on the conduct of a reasonable person in the shoes of the creditor who has a damages claim. Trade usages and practices (Article 9 CISG)[618] as well as special habits which exist between the parties have to be taken into account.[619] Especially the obligation to mitigate can mean for the creditor to have to make a timely cover purchase[620] or to repair a defect before the defect can cause consequential damage to other property of the creditor.

316. If the creditor breached his or her obligation to mitigate damages than the damages claim is reduced *on demand of the debtor* to the amount which was lost because the creditor did not mitigate in time (Article 77 (2nd s) CISG).[621] The burden of proof for the existence of an obligation to mitigate and its breach, including the reasonableness of a possible mitigation measure lies with the debtor. The obligation to mitigate damages is only taken into account if the debtor raises it as a defence since it requires the creditor to demand damages.[622]

8   Interest

317. The questions surrounding interest were very controversial in Vienna and caused considerable difficulties.[623] The applications and suggestions reflected different legal persuasions, divergent dogmatic classifications of the duty to pay interest and colliding practical needs: on the one hand the duty to pay interest was rejected outright by the Islamic states on religious grounds. Other states thought a special provision governing interest was superfluous since the lost use of capital could be recovered as damages under Article 74 CISG. Delegations which thought a specific provision covering interest was necessary did not want to classify interest as a head of damages to allow the duty to pay interest to continue in case the debtor could discharge his or her performance due to an impediment under Article 79 CISG. Futile were especially attempts to find a measure for the "right" interest rate. Against the use of the discount rate in the creditor's country (Article 83 ULIS) it was argued that the discount rate was not an, internationally corresponding, meaningful indicator for the costs of capital usage in the particular states. Especially no agreement could be reached whether the credit cost in the creditor's or debtor's state should be decisive. In regard to Article 84 CISG[624] it was thought,

---

[618] See in regard to CISG, Art 9 paras 43 et seq.

[619] Stoll/Gruber in Schlechtriem/Schwenzer, *Commentary*, Art 77 para 7.

[620] See already paras 309, 313; Stoll/Gruber in Schlechtriem/Schwenzer, *Commentary*, Art 77 para 9. See also Honnold, *Uniform Law for International Sales*, § 418.

[621] See Stoll/Gruber in Schlechtriem/Schwenzer, *Commentary*, Art 77 para 12.

[622] Different the majority view: the obligation to mitigate has to be taken into account by the courts ipso iure, see Stoll/Gruber in Schlechtriem/Schwenzer, *Commentary*, Art 77 para 12.

[623] See Meyer, *FS Otte*, 246 et seq. Also Honnold, *Uniform Law for International Sales*, § 418.

[624] CISG, Art 84(1) states: "If the seller is bound to refund the price, he must also pay interest on it, form the date on which the price was paid."

and also today a part of the literature still thinks,[625] that interest was an adjustment of profits, that means, an enrichment of the debtor so that the common interest on the debtor's financial market was supposed to be decisive. Behind the discussion, however, was that some socialist states did not want to be referred to their internally, administratively held, low interest in regard to their outstanding debts, but wanted to base the interest on the interest of their debtors which had very high interest at the time, since the socialist states had to pay the high interest when they were borrowing money from those states.[626] Article 78 CISG as worded in the CISG is, therefore, the result of a compromise which is not satisfactory. Article 78 CISG ascertains that interest has to be paid generally for a money debt which is due but it does not provide any guidance from which point in time the interest has to be paid and especially what the rate of interest is.

318. If the courts apply the CISG they generally are faced with Article 78 CISG since generally either the claim is for the purchase price plus interest or damages plus interest. The duty to pay interest starts with date performance was due and is generally accepted this has to be determined like the due date itself from the CISG.[627] It is doubtful, however, how to determine the interest rate. The numerous solutions can only be outlined here:[628] Some suggest that the gap which exists in regard to the interest rate should be closed through a substantive uniform norm developed in accordance with Article 7(2) CISG. The ICC, for example, used LIBOR[629] in an arbitral award as a generally widely accepted, and therefore suitable for the gap-filling, interest rate.[630] However, since the majority of delegations in Vienna rejected to agree on a particular interest rate, in the authors' view that excludes the possibility to find a substantive uniform rule in regard to the rate of interest under Article 7(2) CISG.[631] Furthermore, the CISG does not contain any principle which could be used to develop such a uniform substantive rule in regard to the rate of interest.[632] Therefore, the only option is to resort to the applicable domestic law.[633] However, even in regard to the application of domestic law the views are disparate: in the Germany jurisprudence and literature the majority view is that that subsidiary law applicable to the contract is decisive.[634] On the other hand the other part

---

[625] Hornung in Schlechtriem/Schwenzer, *Commentary*, Art 84 para 13: adjustment of profit; see also Neumayer/Ming, Art 78 para 2, p 514.

[626] See in regard to a more detailed summary of events and discussion: Schlechtriem, *Einheitliches UN-Kaufrecht*, 93, 94.

[627] See para 319.

[628] See in regard to a more detailed description: Bacher in Schlechtriem/Schwenzer, *Commentary*, Art 78 para 22 et seq; Königer, 83 et seq; Roßmeir, RIW 2000, 407, 412 et seq.

[629] LIBOR = London Interbank Offered Rate.

[630] Compare Arbitral Awards of the ICC Paris (1 Jan 1993) CISG-online 71 = JDI 1993, 1040 (in regard to Art 84 CISG).

[631] Compare Frigge, *Externe Lücken und Internationales Privatrecht*, 79.

[632] See paras 45 et seq.

[633] For EU Member States that can be the Directive "Late Payments in Commercial Transactions" (2000/35/EU) or the according domestic provisions (converted directive); compare Meyer, *FS Otte*, 241, 249, 262 et seq; Schroeter, *UN-Kaufrecht und Gemeinschaftsrecht*, 239, 240.

[634] Extensive references to the different views Bacher in Schlechtriem/Schwenzer, *Commentary*, Art 78 paras 27 et seq; Witz in Witz/Salger/Lorenz, *Internationales Einheitliches Kaufrecht*, Art 78 paras 7

of the literature and jurisprudence argues that the question of interest is not determined by the law applicable to the contract but that special rules in regard to the
determination of the applicable domestic law apply. How to determine this special
rule is again controversial. Some want to develop a uniform rule determining the
applicable domestic law in regard to interest on the basis of Article 7(2) CISG. As
a rule to determine the applicable law as the seat of the creditor's business, because the claim for interest was very similar to a claim for damages,[635] the law of
the debtor's seat of business because the debtor is enriched by the unjustified use of
the capital and the enrichment took place at the debtor's seat of business,[636] to the
law of the agreed currency or (maybe in the alternative) the law of the place of
payment. In the authors' view the will of the drafters of the CISG (or their
incompetence to come to an agreement in regard to the issue of interest) has to be
respected so that a gap-filling under Article 7(2) CISG is not possible (neither by
developing a uniform substantive norm in regard to the interest rate nor in regard
to developing a uniform rule which determines the applicable law).[637] More modest
but equally diverse are suggestions which want to modify the private international
law rules of the member states. However, to achieve a uniform application it is desirable to use the domestic law applicable to the contract[638] especially as in Europe
through the endeavour to formulate a uniform private international law, notably in
regard to contracts, a certain uniform basis to determine the applicable law already
exists.[639]

It is uncertain whether and according to which law compound interest can be
recovered. Article 78 CISG is not applicable to the question of compound interest
but the law applicable in regard to the question of the interest rate. Due to the uncertainties surrounding the law applicable in regard to the interest rate parties
should agree upon the interest rate or to agree on the measure to be applied or at
least to agree on the applicable law in regard to the interest rate.[640]

319. A uniform solution governs, on the other hand, the start of the duty to
pay interest: since generally the non-payment at the time the payment was due
amounts to a breach of the contract, the debtor has the duty to pay interest start at

---

et seq; Dettmeier in Lüderitz, Art 78 paras 7, 8; Magnus in *Staudinger*, Art 78 paras 12, 13;
Königer, 102 et seq.

[635] Compare Arbitral Award of the International Arbitral Tribunal of the Bundeskammer der
gewerblichen Wirtschaft in Österreich (15 Jun 1994) CISG-online 120, 121 = RIW 1995, 590
et seq with commentary by Schlechtriem in RIW 1995, 593.

[636] Compare Neumayer/Ming, Art 78 para 2, p. 514.

[637] If one does approve of a possibility to fill a gap in accordance with Art 7(2) CISG then the best
possible option would be to develop a uniform rule alongside Art 84(1) CISG so Hornung in
Schlechtriem/Schwenzer, *Commentary*, Art 84 para 13: In accordance with the governing principle
of equalisation of benefits the conditions at the seller's place of business who had the benefit of the
purchase price are the relevant factors for calculation.

[638] See also Königer, 74 et seq who rejects a special application; further Meyer, *FS Otte*, who notes
that an analysis of international jurisprudence to the CISG shows a preference for the law applicable to the contract in regard to finding the law applicable to interest.

[639] Compare in regard to the European international private law: Kreuzer, RabelsZ 70 (2006) 1, 13
et seq.

[640] Witz in Witz/Salger/Lorenz, *Internationales Einheitliches Kaufrecht*, Art 78 para 13.

the time performance was due.[641] The time when performance is due depends on the contractual agreement between the parties or the CISG[642] which prevails over the domestic law which has incorporated the EU Directive "Late Payments in Commercial Transactions".[643] The decisiveness of the due date ensues already from the fact that Article 78 CISG mentions not only the purchase price but also "any other sum that is in arrears". The provision would have been clearer if "that is in arrears" would have been also repeated after "price" to make clear that it is not only any other sum which has to be in arrears.[644] As far as the CISG does not stipulate a different or more special regulation, like for the purchase price in Articles 58(1)(1st s) or (2), (3) CISG, the time the performance is due is at the time the pecuniary claim, for example, a damages claim, comes into existence. Pay back claims due to the reduction of the purchase price will incur interest from the time the purchase price had been paid.[645] Of course trade usages, habits or practices can also be determinative for the duty to pay interest, the start of the interest payments, and the interest rate.[646]

The debtor has to pay interest even if the debtor can discharge him or herself in regard to the delayed payment. The CISG governs interest payable from the due date not interest for delay.[647]

9   Restitution

9.1   Introduction

320. The reversal of the performance might be necessary if the buyer demands substitute delivery, but especially in case of the avoidance of the contract due to a fundamental breach of the other party. Articles 81 to 84 CISG have been adopted without change from the ULIS; the only major change was the consideration of the need to return the goods when the buyer demanded substitute delivery. The governance of the unwinding of the contract was one of weak parts in the ULIS and unfortunately the CISG has not brought great improvements.[648] Especially

---

[641] Compare, however, in contrast to the general opinion: Bacher in Schlechtriem/Schwenzer, *Commentary*, Art 78 paras 7 et seq; Dettmeier in Lüderitz, Art 78 paras 2 et seq; Witz in Witz/Salger/Lorenz, Art 78 para 5. In regard to the relationship to the Directive "Late Payments in Commercial Transactions" (2000/35/EU) see para 345a as well as Meyer, *FS Otte*, 256, 257.

[642] See paras 217 et seq.

[643] (2000/35/EU); see para 345a.

[644] Bacher in Schlechtriem/Schwenzer, *Commentary*, Art 78 para 10.

[645] Bacher in Schlechtriem/Schwenzer, *Commentary*, Art 78 para 11 with further references.

[646] Compare Juzgado Nacional de 1° Instancia en lo Comercial N°10, Buenos Aires (23 Oct 1991) CISG-online 460: Court decided that in international trade the interest rate for an obligation payable in US dollars is the prime rate.

[647] That is the idea behind Art 78(1st s), see para 317; in regard to the relationship to the Directive "Late Payments in Commercial Transactions" (2000/35/EU) see para 345a; compare Meyer, *FS Otte*, 257, 258.

[648] See in regard to the reasons already in regard to the ULIS: Leser in Dölle, before Art 78–81 paras 39–41 and Art 81 para 39: Those questions belong to the hardest in contract law. Leser notes that

gaps have not been closed and solutions which have not proved worthwhile have been kept. In particular are three fundamental decisions of the drafters of the CISG to understand Articles 81 to 84 CISG.

9.1.1 Barrier to Avoid the Contract

321. The CISG generally requires for the buyer to avoid the contract or to demand substitute goods from the seller before it is possible for the buyer to make restitution of the goods substantially in the condition in which the buyer received them (Article 82(1) CISG).[649] Damage to the goods or total loss of the goods before avoidance or the demand for substitute goods have the effect to bar the avoidance of the contract. If the goods are damaged or are getting lost after the buyer has declared avoidance only questions in regard to damages for the breach of restitutionary duties arise. It would have been more akin with modern thinking not to make the right to avoid or to demand substitute delivery dependent on the possibility of intact restitution of the goods which forces an arbitrary differentiation dependent on the time of the loss of the goods or the time of the damage but to generally regulate restitution of the goods as a liability problem.[650] A question left open by the CISG in what responsibility a restitution debtor has where there is a valid avoidance of the contract and the subsequent damage occurs.[651]

9.1.2 Equal Treatment of Avoidance and Substitute Delivery

322. As already set out in regard to the buyer's claim for substitute performance the CISG assumes that the demand for substitute delivery has, in practice, generally the effect that the contract is avoided in regard to the delivered non-conform goods in conjunction with the seller's obligation to delivery contract conform goods, since the already delivered (non-conform) goods have to be given back to the seller that means the non-conform goods have to be, if necessary, transported back and/or often have to be stored for a while. Costs and risks develop which are similar to the once developing in regard to the avoidance of a contract. The claim for substitute delivery has, therefore, the same narrow requirements as the right to avoid the contract.[652] Consistently Articles 82 and 83 CISG govern the right to avoidance and substitute delivery the same, especially the "block" of the right to avoidance due to the goods having perished or deteriorated is also applicable to the right to claim substitute goods (Article 82(1) CISG) while the

---

all the different domestic solutions which extend to fundamental questions like causal connection of the contract and transfer of property on the one hand and the German "abstraction" principle on the other have prevented that a core of uniform solutions could be developed on a comparative basis which could have been the basis for a workable and convincing solution. The attempt of a comprehensive overview has been made by Schlechtriem, *Restitution*, 11 et seq, 695 et seq; see also Hellwege, *Rückabwicklung gegenseitiger Verträge*, 576 et seq.

[649] See para 325.

[650] Compare UNIDROIT Principles, Art 7.36 (Restitution) and PECL, Artt 9:305 et seq which only allow restitution in exceptional circumstance.

[651] See para 331.

[652] See paras 103, 117, 186.

buyer retains in both cases all other remedies under the contract and the CISG (Article 83 CISG).

Open and questionable is whether the buyer in the case of a substitute delivery has to compensate for the use the buyer got from defect goods before substitution, for example, the use of a truck or a machine like in the case of avoidance of the contract (Article 84(2) CISG). With the substitute delivery the seller only fulfils his or her duty from the contract, and it does not seem clear that buyer should incur costs from that. On the other hand the buyer receives new goods which (maybe) have a longer life expectancy.[653] The argument that the buyer has an advantage by the longer life of the substitute goods is correct but cannot justify the compensation for the use of defective goods before substitute delivery.[654] The core of the problem is that and in how far the buyer has to pay compensation for the better value the buyer might have got from the substitute goods under Article 46(3) CISG. It is clear, for example, in regard to the substitution of a truck whose value depends on the model and year of manufacture and where the value of the substituted truck can be considerably higher than the original one. In the authors' view the principle set out in Article 84(2) CISG that the buyer must account for benefits which the buyer has derived from the delivery of the defective goods or parts of them has to applied by filling the gap left in regard to substitution of the goods in accordance with Article 7(2) CISG.

9.1.3 Structure of the Articles 81 et seq CISG

323. Articles 81 et seq CISG only govern the consequences of the avoidance of a contract and the mentioned "block" of the right to avoid the contract. The requirements which have to be fulfilled to be able to avoid the contract are governed together with other remedies of the parties (Articles 49 and 64 CISG).[655] Articles 81 and 84 CISG have to be applied analogously as far as parties avoid the contract jointly (compare Article 29(1) CISG) and have not contractually agreed to restitute any performance already received. Parties can contract out of the restitution "block" under Article 82 CISG. The consequence if one party avoids the contract not knowing that the goods which have to be given back perished or deteriorated cannot, in the authors' view, be found in the CISG but is governed by the applicable domestic law, challenge of declarations, determined through the private international law rules of the forum. [656]

---

[653] So the official reasoning for the duty compensate for the use of goods before they have to be returned in the BGB § 439 IV BGB in conjunction with §§ 346, 347 BGB: The question is, however, in the German law of obligation controversial and the BGH has the question submitted to the ECJ (in regard to Artt 3(2) to (4) of the European Union Directive 1999/44/EC (25 May 1999) on certain aspects of the sale of consumer goods and associated guarantees which does not stipulate a duty to pay user charges for the time the buyer uses a defective good) (reference for a preliminary ruling on 16 Aug 2006) (see also: http://eur-lex.europa.eu/LexUriServ/site/en/oj/2006/c_310/c_31020061216en00050005.pdf); see a discussion in Beck, JR 2006, 177–181.

[654] See Beck, JR 2006, 177–181.

[655] See in regard to how a contract can be avoided just by the creditor's declaration Art 26 CISG, para 108.

[656] But compare Hornung in Schlechtriem/Schwenzer, *Commentary,* before Artt 81–84 para 5 who suggest to develop a gap filling rule under Art 7(2) CISG from the Art 81 et seq.

9.2 Block of the Right to Avoid the Contract and to Demand Substitute Delivery

324. Article 82 CISG "blocks" the right to avoid the contract and the buyer's right to claim substitute goods if the goods perished or deteriorated substantially unless the loss, destruction and the deterioration did not occur through the buyer's conduct (Article 82(2)(a) CISG).

The buyer loses his or her right to avoid the contract under Article 82(1) CISG if he or she cannot give the goods back at all notwithstanding whether the goods were destroyed, seized, sold or used in any other way unless that happened in the normal course of business (Article 82(2)(c) CISG). Only a substantial deterioration of the goods "blocks" the right to avoid the contract or to demand any minor deterioration do not "block" the right (bagatelle regulation).[657] What amounts to a "substantial deterioration" should be determined according the usage of the goods, the view of businesses of the same kind, and maybe the special circumstance of the particular case.[658] In addition, however, the core principle of the CISG to avoid the reversal of a contract should not be forgotten in the analysis. Therefore, minimal damage, caused by the buyer, to the goods should already in certain circumstances, in the authors' view, exclude the buyer's right to avoid the contract and the buyer should be referred to his or her right to claim damages due to the breach of the seller's duty which was the reason for the buyer's right to avoid the contract. This should be especially true for damages of the goods through their use.[659]

Example:	The buyer with seat in Germany detects five months after the purchase of a truck from a French dealer that the truck is stolen and the accompanying papers and all identification features (for example the chassis number) were forged or changed. The truck gets damaged at an accident at the building side. Its frame is bent out of shape. Some damage remains despite the repair at a panel beater, which does not have any bearing on the use of the truck but which does diminishes its value. In the authors' preferred interpretation of Article 82(1) CISG the buyer cannot avoid the contract due to the defect of title. The buyer can only claim damaged or demand the relief of the owner's right.[660]

325. The "block" of the right to avoid the contract is only applicable to the buyer. The seller can avoid the contract, for example, if the payment of the purchase price or the taking of delivery was delayed and any setting of any additional time period was futile if the goods perished at the buyer and the seller knew

---

[657] See Hornung in Schlechtriem/Schwenzer, *Commentary,* Art 82 para 11.
[658] Hornung in Schlechtriem/Schwenzer, *Commentary,* Art 82 para 11
[659] But see also paras 327, 329.
[660] But see para 327.

that.[661] The "block" is only effective if the loss, destruction, or the substantial deterioration of the goods occurred before the seller avoided the contract;[662] If the damage to the defective goods which have to be given back occurs later then only liability questions arise[663] but not a "block" or a retrospective loss of the already exercised right to avoid the contract. It is questionable how the "block" comes to effect in time for buyer's right to claim substitute goods under Article 46(2) CISG. The exercise of that remedy has constitutive effect. It could be argued that also damage to the goods after the buyer's demand to substitute the goods does not "block" the right to claim substitute goods but only a reaction of the seller. In the authors' view, however, due to the similarities between avoidance and the right to claim substitute goods in regard to the risk problems they should be treated the same: the buyer has to restitute once the buyer's claim of the substitution of the goods is executed; a loss, destruction, or substantial deterioration of the goods which occurred after the execution of the claim can only result in liability claims for the breach of the restitution duty but not the loss of the asserted right to substitute goods.[664]

9.3   Exceptions of the "Block" to Avoid the Contract or to Claim Substitute Goods

9.3.1 Loss, Destruction or Deterioration Not Caused by the Buyer

326. The right to avoid the contract and the right to demand substitute goods remain if the damage to the goods which have to be given back has not been caused by the buyer. Acts of God but also a loss of the goods due to their defect leave the buyer's right to claim substitute goods or to avoid the contract intact. Also a consequential defect which leads to the damage of the total destruction of the good, does not fall in the buyer's sphere of responsibility, at least not as long as the buyer could not recognise the defect and prevent further damage.

Example: The truck which was sold by a German seller to a French buyer crashes into an excavation because its breaks are blocked due to a defect. The buyer's right to avoid the contract if the defect of the breaks was in the circumstance a fundamental breach or another fundamental breach in regard to the buyer's rights has occurred remains despite the substantial damage of the truck.[665]

---

[661] Compare Hornung in Schlechtriem/Schwenzer, *Commentary,* Art 82 para 13; see already para 320.

[662] Compare instead of the majority: Hornung in Schlechtriem/Schwenzer, *Commentary,* Art 82 paras 7, 8.

[663] See para 332.

[664] Like here Magnus in *Staudinger,* Art 82 para 14: the same (=avoidance) is true for the demand to substitute goods; other view probably (not quite clear) Piltz, *Internationales Kaufrecht,* § 5 para 169.

[665] Compare Hornung in Schlechtriem/Schwenzer, *Commentary,* Art 82 para 19.

327. It is still uncertain what exactly "is not due to his act or omission" means. Of course a destruction of the goods due to an act of God cannot be put down to an act of the buyer although maybe the flooding, the lighting strike, or the seizure only resulted in the loss of the goods because the buyer took delivery – without the buyer taking delivery the goods (maybe) would have not been destroyed but would have been safe at the seller's place of business (Article 82(2)(a) CISG). Article 82(2)(a) CISG, however, can only be understood to govern the buyer's culpable conduct.[666] The English text of the CISG "due to" makes it clear that it has to be at least conduct that the buyer has to accept responsibility for.[667] Such responsibility is to be assumed if the buyer not only causes the possibility of damage to the goods but also enhances or heightens through his or her conduct. That can also occur through the conduct of the buyer's employees. However, the buyer does not bear the risk for damage which is outside the buyer's sphere of influence and for unforeseeable and inevitable events whose onset the buyer has not influenced by his or her own conduct heightening the risk. The use of the bought goods as agreed is, therefore, by itself in the authors' view not a risk heightening conduct unless the buyer already knows that a reason for avoidance exists (Article 82(2)(c) CISG).

9.3.2 Damage of the Goods Through Examination

328. If the damage to the goods (or even their loss) is caused by the necessary examination carried out under Article 38 CISG the buyer also does not lose his or her right to avoid the contract (Article 82(2)(b) CISG). An example is the opening of the packaging to (at a random basis) take small samples for test, by which those samples are used up.

9.3.3 As Agreed Usage

329. In practice, the most important exception from the "block" to avoid the contract is set out in Article 82(2)(c) CISG: the buyer has sold all of the non-conform[668] goods or some of the goods in his or her normal cause of business which accordingly get worn out, used up, or changed. However, Article 82(2)(c) CISG further requires that the buyer did not know or ought to have known about the non-conformity of the goods did not know beforehand. On-sale as an exception to the "block" to avoidance of the contract also requires that the on-sale occurred in the "normal cause of business" so that the pawning of the goods or also their squandering, to get through financial difficult times, should not be covered by the exception. The goods must also be used for their intended purpose, for example, to process raw materials, to burn of fossil energy, etc. On the other hand the burning of new car tyres or building towers are not governed by the exception. In regard to the changing of the goods the bagatelle limit of Article 82(1) CISG

---

[666] Compare Hornung in Schlechtriem/Schwenzer, *Commentary,* Art 82 para 20.

[667] Krebs, *Die Rückabwicklung im UN-Kaufrecht,* 103, 104.

[668] See in regard to the term "non-conform" (including goods tainted with protective rights but not including goods whose title is defective) Mohs, IHR 2002, 62, 63.

applies.[669] A further requirement of this exception is that the on-sale, use or change occurred before the buyer knew or ought to have known of the reason for the avoidance.

Example: The German buyer had cut to size and used marble bought from the Italian seller, after the alleged defects had been already discovered. The Court held that the buyer could not avoid the contract.[670]

9.4   Effects of Avoidance

330. The avoidance of the contract under the CISG does not annihilate the contract but only extinguishes the duty to perform so far as they have not been performed (Article 81(1)(1st s) CISG). The contract as such, as Leser has formulated it, "alters its course;"[671] it continues to exist, so that not only damages claims keep their basis but also, for example, agreements in regard to dispute resolution like jurisdiction clauses and arbitration clauses, but also other special contractual agreements which govern the avoidance or other disturbances of the contract, for example, penalty clauses, special arrangement in regard to the restitution of performance or the estimated amount of damages (Article 82(1)(2nd s) CISG). It is uncertain what the effect avoidance has on property ownership. Avoidance in jurisdictions with a Roman law tradition[672] has the effect to retrospectively annihilate the contract, therefore, due to the causa – dependency of the ownership the property would be re-invested in the "original" owner. Since under Article 4 (2nd s)(b) CISG the question of ownership is not a question which falls in the ambit of the CISG but has to be decided under the domestic property law which is applicable in accordance with the private international law rules of the forum (generally the lex rei sitae) it could be argued that in regard to goods which are in Spain, France or Italy the avoidance of the contract has also the effect that the property gets re-invested in the seller. The seller could then not only claim the goods back under Article 81(2)(1st s) CISG but also if necessary, with a better position than other creditors, invoke his or her property rights.[673] In the authors' view is the incidental question whether the causa of the ownership transfer ceases to exist when the contract is avoided to be answered in accordance with the lex contractus (the law applicable to the contract – that means here the CISG) and not the lex rei sitae. An explicit provision is, however, missing in the CISG so that the

---

[669] See para 324.

[670] OLG Koblenz (27 Sep 1991) CISG-online 30. Compare also OLG Düsseldorf (10 Feb 1994) CISG-online 115 = NJW – RR 1994, 506, 507 in regard to the sale of defective textiles by the buyer who obviously did not follow the normal cause of business.

[671] Critical to this line of thinking which has originated in German law: Krebs, *Die Rückabwicklung im UN-Kaufrecht*, 50, 51. Of practical importance is the effect of avoidance in regard to cause dependent transfer of ownership, see Hornung in Schlechtriem/Schwenzer, *Commentary*, Art 81 paras 9a-c.

[672] See Krebs, *Die Rückabwicklung im UN-Kaufrecht*, 52; Berg, *Rückabwicklung*, 77, 78, 81; Hornung, *Rückabwicklung*, 50 et seq, 116.

[673] Hornung in Schlechtriem/Schwenzer, *Commentary*, Art 81 para 9c.

effect of the avoidance has to be ascertained by interpreting Article 81(2)(1st s) CISG under Article 7(1) CISG. The result should be that the causa of the ownership transfer, that means, the sale of goods contract is not retrospectively annihilated by the avoidance of the contract (see Article 81(1)(2nd s) CISG but is altered into a restitutionary relationship: restitution is, therefore, only possible if the requirements under the CISG are met (unless the parties contracted out). Property rights under the domestic law (which are often contrary to the restitutionary provisions set out in the CISG) are, however, excluded since it is assumed that the causa for the contract is still in existence.

9.4.1 Duties in Regard to Restitution

331. As far as the contract has been in total or part performed the recipients have to give back the performance (Article 81(2)(1) CISG). The restitution has to be step-by-step (Article 81(2nd s)(2) CISG) so that each party can hold back the performance which it has to give back until the party's performance is given back or at least offered back. The duty to restitution of one party corresponds with the duty to accept back the performance of the other.

Example: The German buyer of shoes refused one part of the delivery as defective and the other part as delivery which exceeded the order. Against the purchase price claim of the Italian seller because of the perfect goods the buyer argued that he or she was only willing to pay the purchase price step-by-step against the taking back of the shoes which were not conform with the contract and the additional performance. The LG Krefeld upheld the buyer's argument and approved the application of Article 81(2) (2nd s) also in regard to this case.

In the case of the deterioration or the loss of the goods the party who has to provide restitution of the goods has to pay damages: the provisions in regard to damages in respect of the primary duties of the "active" contract (that means that part of the contract which has not been avoided) apply like a mirror image if the party cannot discharge its liability to restitute the goods intact under Article 79(1) CISG.[674] That is especially true for the deterioration or loss of the goods after the avoidance of the contract since often in cases of the loss of the goods or their substantial deterioration before the avoidance of the contract the avoidance "block" under Article 82(1) CISG will apply. Cases where damages claims might arise even before the avoidance of the contract are if the threshold of Article 82(1) CISG is not met, that means, when the damage is not significant or if Article 82(2) CISG is applicable.[675] In regard to the liability under Article 79 CISG the same questions arise as in the case of the breach of primary duties by already at the time of the conclusion of

---

[674] Compare Hornung in Schlechtriem/Schwenzer, *Commentary*, Art 82 para 13; Magnus in *Staudinger*, Art 82 para 15 noting the duty to maintain the goods under Art 86 CISG.

[675] The buyer will most likely be able to discharge the liability under Art 79 CISG in the latter case.

the contract existing causes for the disturbance:[676] it depends on whether and in how far the party who has to restitute reasonably could be expected to take into account the possibility of a duty to restitute already before the avoidance of the contract (Article 79(1) CISG).

The CISG does not provide for the question where the duty to restitute has to be performed and who has to bear the costs of the restitution. Both questions are gaps under Article 7(2) which should be closed on the basis of the principles set out in the CISG. In regard to the place where the duty to restitute should have to be performed the regulation in regard to the primary duties should be applied like a mirror image.[677]

If the parties agreed that the delivery of the goods should take place at the buyer's place of business that does not change in regard to the performance of the duty to restitute the buyer has to put the goods to the seller's disposal at the buyer's place of business. The buyer who has to restitute has to send the goods back to the seller by handing them over to the carrier if the contract for the sale of goods involves carriage of the goods;[678] place of performance for the restitution is also buyer's place of business.[679] Conceivable and also with good reasons justifiable, however, would be to for the determination of the place of performance for the restitution: the party which breached the contract would then have to be burdened more- in regard to the duty to restitute the place of performance would be the place of the creditor; in regard to the claim to restitution the place of performance would be debtor.[680]

The costs associated with the restitution of the performance are in the authors' view damages which the party responsible for conduct leading to the avoidance of the contract has to bear. If the reason that the contract can be avoided is caused by a party who can discharge his or her liability under Article 79(1) CISG the party who has not breached the contract has to bear the costs of the restitution.[681]

9.4.2 Restitution of Gained Benefits

332. The buyer must give back the defective goods and also all benefits which the buyer gained from their use (Article 84(2)(a) CISG). "Benefits" from the goods can, in the case that restitution of the original performance is not possible, be surrogates like commodum ex re as well as commodum ex negotiatione.[682] However, especially fruits derived from the goods, benefits from its use, and other benefits have to be restituted and, if necessary, have to be calculated in monetary

---

[676] See para 289.

[677] OGH (29 Jun 1999) CISG-online 483 = TranspR – IHR 1999, 48; not clear Kantonsgericht Wallis (21 Feb 2005) CISG-online 1193 = IHR 2006, 155 et seq sub 4b (place of performance for the restitution of the goods is (always?) the buyer's place of business); different the BGH in regard to ULIS (place of performance is place of performance in regard to the primary duites) BGHZ 78, 275, 260, 261 (25 Sep 1980).

[678] Compare OGH (29 Jun 1999) CISG-online 483 = TranspR – IHR 1999, 48.

[679] Hornung in Schlechtriem/Schwenzer, *Commentary*, Art 81 para 18 with further references.

[680] Compare LG Krefeld (24 Nov 1992) CISG-online 62.

[681] Hornung in Schlechtriem/Schwenzer, *Commentary*, Art 81 para 19.

[682] Compare Hornung in Schlechtriem/Schwenzer, *Commentary*, Art 84 paras 25–27.

terms. The value of rent or licence fees, for example, can serve as a model for the calculation of benefits from its use. The CISG is silent in regard to the costs which can be associated with the attainment of benefits. In accordance with the basic idea of the restitution of gained benefits only net benefits should be deducted.[683] The buyer has also to restitute the benefits he or she has gained in using the defective goods (which the buyer has to restitute) while waiting for the substitute goods.[684] The buyer, on the other hand, does not have to restitute benefits which he or she has not enjoyed; the CISG does not compel the buyer to use the goods in a way that they generate benefits.

Buyer's expenditures on the goods are also not extensively covered by the CISG and how to deal with them is uncertain. Often a gap is assumed which only could be closed by applying the applicable domestic law.[685] Desirable, however, would be a uniform gap-filling based on the principle in Article 84 CISG but also in consideration of Article 86(2nd s) CISG: expenditures on the goods which are beneficial for the seller have to be compensated by the seller if and in as far as they have brought the seller a usable benefit which the seller otherwise would have had to pay for him-or herself. The classical differentiation between necessary, useful and luxury expenditures can only be an indication.

333. Under Article 84(2)(b) CISG the buyer owes the seller all benefits the buyer has derived from the goods or part of them even if it is impossible for him or her to make restitution of all or part of the goods. The same is true in case of substitute deliveries where the defective goods cannot be given back without that the claim to substitute delivery is already "blocked".[686] The general principle set out in Article 84(2)(b) CISG is also applicable to others, in their nature, not restitutionable performances and the benefits derived from them: Article 84(2)(b) CISG contains in the authors' view which allows gap-filling through the development of uniform rules. For example, if the seller also had to perform services (without breaching the threshold of Article 3(2) CISG)[687] then the value of the benefits which the buyer derived from the services is to be recompensed if the contract is avoided. The value of the services as stipulated in the contract should be the basis on which the value of the benefit should be determined. Otherwise a reasonable measure should be applied.

Example: The seller of a computer system has also agreed to train the buyer's employees in the use of the computers. The contract is avoided due to the malfunctioning of the computers. The computers have to be given back to the seller and the value of the training services has to be reimbursed. If in the purchase price the teaching was an itemised

---

[683] See Hornung in Schlechtriem/Schwenzer, *Commentary*, Art 84 para 20.

[684] See already para 322.

[685] Compare Hornung in Schlechtriem/Schwenzer, *Commentary*, Art 84 para 20c; for the differentiation between necessary, useful and luxury expenditures on the goods Krebs, *Die Rückabwicklung im UN-Kaufrecht*, 77, 78; both with further references.

[686] See para 324.

[687] See in regard to CISG, Art 3(2) para 27.

head so that value has to be used otherwise the market value of such training has to be reimbursed.

334. The paid purchase price is to be reimbursed to the buyer with interest (Articles 81(2)(1ˢᵗ s), 84(1) CISG). The interest is to be calculated in accordance with the explanation to Article 78 CISG.[688]

10   Preservation of the Goods and Self-help Sale

335. If a contract is breached then the fate of the goods has to be determined along with the remedies. If the buyer does not take delivery of the goods the CISG provides that the seller should store the goods if at all possible in a way that protects their value or has to use them in the most profitable way. A comparable situation can evolve if the buyer declines to take delivery where he or she already has got them – the buyer cannot simply leave them to their fate. A regulation of a contractual breach in regard to the fate of the goods also to take account of the costs which can arise unplanned but is a necessary measure to safeguard the goods or to use them in the most profitable way. The CISG provides for a possible debtor's discharge of liability if the creditor's performance is delayed in Article 80 CISG[689] and for the transition of risk in the case of a delayed taking of delivery in Article 69 CISG. However, the CISG especially provides for duties in regard to the preservation of the goods of the respective debtor (Articles 85 to 87 CISG) including the possibility to store the goods with third parties (Article 87 CISG) and the possibility of a self-help sale (Article 88 CISG). The CISG goes further and is more comprehensive in regard to the possessing party's duty to preserve the goods along with the right to on-sell the goods under certain requirements than the common law. Under section 36 of the Sale of Goods Act 1979 (UK), for example, rejected goods do not entail an obligation on the part of the buyer to return the goods to the seller. Furthermore under most common law systems, the seller cannot compel the buyer (as one can under Article 62 CISG) to accept delivery by recovering the purchase price. Hence there is little requirement for a rule requiring the seller to preserve the goods as the seller cannot transfer this loss to the buyer as they can under CISG Article 62.[690]

10.1   Preservation of the Goods

336. Article 85 CISG stipulates the seller's duties in case the buyer does not take timely delivery of the goods or in case the performance was to be step-by-step, does not pay the purchase price in regard to the goods which are still in his or

---

[688] See para 317 et seq; Compare also Hornung in Schlechtriem/Schwenzer, *Commentary*, Art 84 para 13: basic idea of the equalisation of the benefits, but abstract possibility of the benefits at the seat of the seller, not the actual circumstances are deceisive.

[689] Para 297.

[690] Honnold, *Uniform Law for International Sales*, § 454.

her possession and over which the seller can still dispose of: the seller "must take such steps as are reasonable in the circumstances" (Article 85(1) CISG). That is especially important in cases in which the risk has already transferred onto the buyer although the seller is still in possession of the goods (compare Article 69(1) CISG). The seller can demand compensation for the costs arising from those measures even if the requirements of a damages claim due to a breach of a buyer's duty are not met. The seller can retain the goods until his or her expenditure replacement claim is met (Article 85(2nd s) CISG).[691] In regard to the interest of the parties the comparable situation is that the goods are offered to the buyer but that the buyer can refuse the goods either under Article 52 CISG (refusing the taking of delivery)[692] or under Article 86(1)(1st s) CISG (exercising, for example, his or her right to avoid the contract). Article 86(1)(1st s) CISG like Article 85(1st s) CISG is based on the basic idea that the party in whose sphere of influence the goods are has responsibility for them. Article 86(1)(1st s) CISG compels the buyer, like the seller is compelled under Article 85(1st s) CISG, to reasonable preservation measures in regard to the goods. However, it also gives the buyer a compensation claim for the expenditure incurred and a right to retain it until he or she is reimbursed in regard to those expenditures (Article 86(1)(2nd s) CISG. A buyer's breach of the duty to take care of the goods which results in the damage of the goods or destroys them will often lead to a loss of the right to avoid the contract and a loss of the right to demand substitute goods.[693] The duty to take care of the goods set out in Article 86(1)(1st s) CISG, however, further demands from the buyer to protect the goods from insignificant damage.

337. If the buyer is not in possession of the goods but have the goods been sent to him (or a third place) and were offered to him or her then the buyer has to take possession of the goods for the seller despite the buyer's right to refuse taking delivery as far as the buyer can do this without paying the purchase price and without great inconvenience or substantial costs (Article 86(2)(1st s) CISG). An exception only exists if the seller or a person who is authorised to take charge of the goods for the seller is present at the destination. Article 86(2) CISG obliges the buyer to temporarily take possession of the goods even if he or she can avoid the contract or maybe even already has avoided the contract, or the buyer demanded his or her right to substitute delivery and therefore wants to and can refuse the goods, or if the buyer could refuse the taking of the delivery due to a right of retention.

338. "Reasonable preservation measures" does not mean that the seller under Article 85 CISG or the buyer under Article 86 CISG has to take every possible precaution. What is in the particular circumstances "reasonable" depends on the goods (perishable, durable, weather-proof, fragile, etc), the probability and size of

---

[691] Magnus in *Staudinger*, Art 85 para 17.
[692] See in regard to Art 52 para 208.
[693] Compare CISG Art 82(1) and para 330.

the possible damage and other circumstances.[694] The risk that the costs of the pre-servation measures will not be reimbursed by the other party cannot be consi-dered since the party whose duty the preservation is can if necessary recuperate the costs through a self-help sale under Article 88 CISG.[695]

339. The party whose duty is the preservation of the goods can (to preserve the goods) demand the costs for their preservation especially their storage from the other party provided that the expense incurred is not unreasonable (Article 87 CISG). If the storage causes unreasonable costs then the other party has only to reimburse the reasonable costs.[696] Storage costs, for example, would be unreason-able if they are higher than the goods' value, unless that there is a special persona interest at play.

Example: A Russian museum sells an altar painting from an unknown artist to a New York art dealer. The buyer finds out due to an expert opinion that the painting is a stolen work of art and the seller could not val-idly transfer ownership of the painting. In regard to the avoidance of the contract and the taking back of the painting by the Russian seller, a prolonged argument. Since the dealer does not have suitable storage (thief-proof, acclimatised), he stores it at a storage facility specialised for such paintings. The costs which exceed the value of the painting should not be unreasonable in these particular circum-stances.[697]

Storage of the goods with a third party does not affect performance.

10.2 Self-help Sale

340. Article 88(1) CISG allows the party who has to take care of the goods to sell the goods in self-help. In regard to perishable goods or goods whose manage-ment incurs unreasonably high costs the party even has a duty to take reasonable measures to sell the goods. The risk that goods deteriorate under Article 88(1) CISG exists only in regard to physical deterioration but not in regard to an immi-nent drop-off in price.

Example: The Islamic Republic Iran bought from US company electronic equipment. Since the buyer did not pay, the seller exercised its right to a self-help sale in regard to the non-delivered equipment. The Iran-

---

[694] Compare Magnus in *Staudinger*, Art 85 para 10.

[695] Compare Bacher in Schlechtriem/Schwenzer, *Commentary*, Art 88 para 17 in regard to the situation governed by Art 85 CISG.

[696] Magnus in *Staudinger*, Art 87 paras 3, 4.

[697] A self-help sale is not possible until the ownership of the painting is not ascertained.

United States Claims Tribunal[698] assumed that the self-help sale was in accordance with the "recognised rules of the international law of commercial sales" as they are incorporated into Article 88 CISG. This is a generous application of Article 88 CISG, since it was open whether the sale was a cover sale or a self-help sale; in the latter case the seller would have had to explain the reasons which allowed him a self-help sale.[699]

10.2.1 Normal Self-help Sale

341. Under Article 88(1) CISG the party who is bound to preserve the goods can make a self-help sale "by any appropriate means." "Appropriate means" also encapsulates differences which originate from the different regulations or common usages of self-help sales in the different jurisdictions so that domestic law and domestic customs indirectly influence the interpretation of Article 88(1) CISG. An "appropriate measure" can, therefore, for example, also be the public auction of the goods or its open sale by a broker in accordance with § 373(2) HGB. The person who is bound to preserve the goods also can, however, sell the goods him-or herself or take them him-or herself to the market price.[700]

10.2.2 Notice of the Self-help

342. The party who can make or even has to make a self-help sale has to give a "reasonable" notice to the other party of its intention to do so (Article 88(1) CISG). The qualification of this notice had caused great difficulties in Vienna whereby "reasonable" (in the Swiss version "in time") was to make sure to give the other party time and opportunity to prevent the self-help sale. Without notice the self-help sale is illegal: The self-help seller has to pay damages the other party has incurred by the self-help sale.[701] An objection against the intention of a self-help sale due to the notice has, however, no effect.[702] If the seller has fixed an additional time period in accordance with Article 63(1) CISG for the buyer to take delivery in the authors' view, the possibility of a self-help sale until the expiry of the additional time period is "blocked" (compare Article 63(2) CISG).

10.2.3 Emergency Sale

343. In regard to perishable goods and goods which incur unreasonable management costs the party who is bound to preserve the goods can immediately try in a reasonable manner to sell the goods. A notice of its intention to make a self-help

---

[698] An arbitral tribunal which governed claims situated in the Hague, the Iran-United States Claims Tribunal governed claims that arose from the nationalising of assets by Iran of US nationals following the Iranian revolution.

[699] Iran-United States Claims Tribunal (28 Jul 1989) CISG-online 9 = XV YbComArb (1990) 220.

[700] Magnus in *Staudinger*, Art 88 para 13.

[701] Bacher in Schlechtriem/Schwenzer, *Commentary*, Art 88 para 8.

[702] Magnus in *Staudinger*, Art 88 para 10 with further references.

sale is then only necessary as far as it is possible (Article 88(2)(2nd s) CISG). That means that the other party can be so timely notified that the other party could still react and prevent a self-help sale.[703] If the party does not make a self-help emergency sale in light of perishable goods and the goods perish so the buyer, analogous to Article 82(1) CISG, can lose the right to avoid the contract and could not demand substitute delivery; in any case the party who is bound to preserve the goods has to pay damages in the amount of the proceeds which could have reasonable expected from a self-help sale.

10.2.4 Clearance and Transfer of the Proceeds from the Self-help Sale

344. The proceeds from the self-help sale have generally to be paid to the other party who was supposed to take delivery of the goods or who was to take them back. The costs for the preservation and the sale can be subtracted (Articles 88(3)(1st s) and (2) CISG). Further claims of the party who has to pay the proceeds, for example, damages claims or a claim for the purchase price – in the case of a self-help sale by the seller due to the refusal to take delivery of the goods by the buyer – can be set off against the claim for the proceeds. However, in what way set-off will occur- through a set-off declaration (or ipso iure) or whether it is a substantive or procedural defence has to be determined by the contract law applicable to the contract which is determined by the private international law of the forum.[704] The party who is bound to preserve the goods has, in the view of authors, to render an account.[705]

11 Part IV – Final Provisions

345. Part IV of the CISG contains in Article 89 to 101 the public international framework of the CISG. Within the framework of this book details do not need to be discussed especially since by coming into force of the CISG some of the Articles have lost their importance through performance. A few explanations should, therefore, be enough: The signing of a state which wants to take over the Convention means that the state commits itself under public international law which is subject to the ratification of the Convention, the acceptance or approval by the responsible state organs (compare Article 91(2) CISG). The respective ratification, acceptance and approval documents have to be deposited with the Secretary-General of the United Nations (Article 91(4) CISG). For the CISG to come into force, ten ratification, acceptance, approval or accession instruments had to be deposited with the Secretary-General of the United Nations. The requirement was fulfilled on 11 December 1986 when the USA, China, and Italy deposited their

---

[703] Magnus in *Staudinger*, Art 88 para 18.

[704] Controversial: see Bacher in Schlechtriem/Schwenzer, *Commentary*, Art 88 para 18; other view probably Magnus in *Staudinger*, Art 88 para 25 (the party who had to hand over the proceeds can keep the proceeds in total or in part when other claims exist).

[705] Compare Magnus in *Staudinger*, Art 88 para 26.

ratification certificates. The CISG could, therefore, come into force under Article 99(2) CISG twelve months later on 1 January 1988. As of 1 January 2008 the CISG has been ratified by 70 states.[706]

345a. Under Article 90 CISG other international agreements prevail over the CISG. That, however, does not apply to European Union legislation, regulations and directives, even if they are based on the EEC and EC Treaties,[707] public international law instrument. The question is very controversial and uncertain. Directives are implemented by the national legislature into domestic law in so far it is a matter of domestic law making. Since the CISG member states would commit a breach of contract (the CISG) if they would implement a directive which does not conform to the CISG, it has to be assumed that in so far a limitation of the implementation was wanted.[708] If the EU enacts regulations which collide with the CISG the EU acts as legislator which is as such not a member of the CISG and, therefore, is not bound to adhere to the CISG, however, the European Commission attributes the CISG the status of "quasi-acquis" and treats the CISG in its memoranda on European contract law often like part of Community law.[709] Since it can be assumed that the Commission is committed to the principle of consistent law-making it can be concluded that the EU's law-making including regulations are enacted with the immanent limitation that they do not prevail over conflicting CISG provisions. The domestic legislator which when enacting the regulation attributes the conflicting provisions of the CISG priority over the regulation does not breach Community law. This applies, for example, in regard to the EU Directive "Late Payments in Commercial Transactions,"[710] E-Commerce Regulation[711] and Directive on certain Aspects of the Sale of Consumer Goods and Associated Guarantees.[712] If a national legislator wants to back out of the CISG in favour of the unifying legislative act of the EU then the state has to make a declaration under Articles 94(1) or (2) CISG.[713]

346. Article 98 CISG contains the principle that reservations when signing or ratifying, accepting, approving, or acceding the Convention is generally not possible as far as it is not expressly authorised in the final provisions of the Convention.

---

[706] To check the number of ratifications, see UNCITRAL website: http://www.uncitral.org/ uncitral/en/uncitral_texts/sale_goods/1980CISG_status.html (last accessed 1 Jan 2008).

[707] Or in future perhaps the European Constitution.

[708] Compare instead of the majority Piltz, IHR 2002, 2, 4; Schlechtriem in Schlechtriem/Schwenzer, *Commentary*, Art 90 paras 3, 4, 12 to 13; Magnus in *Staudinger*, Art 90 para 10 with further references to different opinions especially also in regard to the "way out" via Art 94 CISG.

[709] KOM (2001) 398, 10, 52, as well as appendix III, 59–65 et passim.

[710] (2000/35/EU); see para 319.

[711] EU-Regulation 2000/31/EG of the European Parliament and the Council of 3 Jun 2000. ABR.2 178/1, see para 70b.

[712] Directive 1999/44/EC.

[713] See Magnus in *Staudinger*, Art 90 para 4; extensively Schroeter, *UN-Kaufrecht und Gemeinschaftsrecht*, 10, 346 et seq, 354 et seq; in regard to the issue of the "excessive" effect of such declarations – complete exclusion of the CISG – see Schroeter, *UN-Kaufrecht und Gemeinschaftsrecht*, 357 et seq (exclusion only of single CISG provisions); Schlechtriem in Schlechtriem/ Schwenzer, *Commentary*, Art 94 para 4.

A reservation, change, or limitation of any part of the CISG at its ratification would be a breach of the state's public international law duty under Article 98 CISG which the state has assumed with its signature. Reservations are set out in Articles 92, 93, 94, 95, and 96 CISG.[714] The reservation under Article 95 CISG which allows implementing the CISG without Article 1(1)(b) CISG[715] and the reservation in Article 96 which allows excluding the free form of contracts both have special significance.

12   Addition: Statute of Limitation

347. The CISG does not contain provisions in regard to a statute of limitation.[716] The 1974 the United Nations Convention on the Limitation Period in the International Sale of Goods has been adopted.[717] The Limitation Convention was signed in 1974 on the basis of the travaux prèparatoires for the CISG. Since the travaux pèparatoires differed in several aspects from the final version of the CISG an adaptation of the Limitation Convention to those changes became necessary, and the respective Protocol amending the Convention on the Limitation Period to adjust the scope of the application in accordance the CISG was attached as Annex II. The Protocol entered into force on 1 August 1988.[718]

The Limitation Convention has been ratified by a number of states, including, for example, Mexico and the USA, other states like France, Germany, and Italy have not.[719]

If the private international law of the forum which is not a member state of the Limitation Convention refers to a state which is a member of the Limitation Convention then the Limitation Convention is applicable in that forum if its application requirements are met. Core provision of the Limitation Convention is Article 8 of the Convention which stipulates a limitation period of four years.[720]

348. Article 8 of the Limitation Convention prescribes a shorter time than other parallel instruments in the common law. In New Zealand for example, a cause of action in contract must be taken within 6 years from which the breach occurred.[721] Although not entirely uniform within its specific federal jurisdictions, Australia and Canada also prescribe similar limitation time periods which

---

[714] See in regard to the states which have ratified the CISG and the reservations made – Appendix 2.

[715] See para 18.

[716] See also already para 162.

[717] See Landfermann, RabelZ 39 (1975) 253 et seq.

[718] Amending Protocol, Art IX(1); as of 1 Jan 2008 19 countries have acceded to the protocol; see in regard to list of signatory states (amended and unamended version): http://www.uncitral.org/uncitral/en/uncitral_texts/sale_goods/1974Convention_status.html (last accessed 1 Jan 2008).

[719] See in regard to list of signatory states (amended and unamended version): http:// www.uncitral.org/uncitral/en/uncitral_texts/sale_goods/1974Convention_status.html last accessed 1 Jan 2008); see also in regard to text and materials: cisg-online.

[720] See for a more detailed discussion on the Limitation Convention: Müller-Chen in Schlechtriem/Schwenzer, *Commentary,* Limitation Convention 1974.

[721] Limitation Act 1950 (NZ), s 4(1)(a); *White v Taupo Totara Timber Co* [1960] NZLR 547.

also accrue from the time the contract was breached. This however, does not deny a party who is victim of a latent defect a remedy as the party usually will have recourse through the tort of negligence.[722]

---

[722] *Kamploops v Nielsen* (1984) 10 DLR (4th) 641 (Canada); *Hamlin v Ivercargill City Council* [1996] 1 NZLR 513 (New Zealand).

Appendix

1   Useful Sources

There are several sources which provide useful academic commentary on the CISG as well as a compilation of CISG case law from courts and arbitral tribunals:[1]

1.1   Databases

1. Pace Database (www.cisg.law.pace.edu): offers structured information on case law, literature, "Travaux Prépertoires" (e.g. the so-called "Secretariat Commentary"), the status (Contracting States) etc. Many of the foreign decisions are translated into English and the site contains a large number of articles in full text. Unfortunately, the search engine is not particularly user friendly. The database is more accessible if one has already some understanding of the issue.
2. CISG-Online (www.cisg-online.ch), offers different search forms on case law and a similar (but somewhat more limited) content than the Pace Database. The advantage of this database is that every decision is numbered individually so that they can be easily identified. This is the reason why this book quotes the decisions simply by reference to their CISG-Online Number (where available). CISG-Online also offers information on printed versions of the decisions and cross-references to English translations on Pace-Database. Again the search engine limits the accessibility of the database and the fact that cases cannot be searched according to subject-matter can be frustrating at times.

CISG-online (www.cisg-online.ch) provides the published opinions of the CISG-Advisory Council:

CISG-AC Opinion no 1, Electronic Communications under CISG, 15 August 2003. Rapporteur: Professor Christina Ramberg, Gothenburg, Sweden.

CISG-AC Opinion no 2, Examination of the Goods and Notice of Non-Conformity - Articles 38 and 39, 7 June 2004. Rapporteur: Professor Eric Bergsten, Emeritus, Pace University New York.

CISG-AC Opinion no 3, Parol Evidence Rule, Plain Meaning Rule, Contractual Merger Clause and the CISG, 23 October 2004. Rapporteur: Professor Richard Hyland, Rutgers Law School, Camden, NJ, USA.

---

[1] This part relies heavily on a similar chapter in Huber/Mullis, *The CISG*, pp. 10 et seq.

CISG-AC Opinion no 4, Contracts for the Sale of Goods to Be Manufactured or Produced and Mixed Contracts (Article 3 CISG), 24 October 2004. Rapporteur: Professor Pilar Perales Viscasillas, Universidad Carlos III de Madrid.

CISG-AC Opinion no 5, The buyer's right to avoid the contract in case of non-conforming goods or documents, 7 May 2005, Badenweiler (Germany). Rapporteur: Professor Dr. Ingeborg Schwenzer, LL.M., Professor of Private Law, University of Basel.

CISG-AC Opinion no 6, Calculation of Damages under CISG Article 74, Spring 2006, Stockholm (Sweden). Rapporteur: Professor John Y. Gotanda, Villanova University School of Law, Villanova, Pennsylvania, US.

3. UNITRAL Database (www.uncitral.org), featuring CLOUT (www.uncitral.org/uncitral/en/case_law.html), the official case law database of UNCITRAL which provides abstracts of decisions rather than the full decision. The site also provides an up-to-date list of Contracting States and other relevant issues (www.uncitral.org/ uncitral/en/uncitral_texts/sale_goods/1980CISG_status.html).
4. Autonomous network of CISG Databases (www.cisg.law.pace.edu/network.html): A network of national or regional databases on the CISG.

1.2   Commentaries

Another rewarding source (of interpreting the CISG) are commentaries. The leading commentaries published in English are:

- Peter Schlechtriem/Ingeborg Schwenzer (Editors); Commentary on the UN Convention on the International Sale of Goods (CISG); 2nd ed., (2005).
- John Honnold, Uniform Law of International Sales, 3rd ed., (1999).
- Cesare Massimo Bianca/Michael Joachim Bonell (Editors); Commentary on the International Sales Law; The 1980 Vienna Sales Convention; (1987).

1.3   Texts

A very useful instrument for finding relevant case law on the CISG is the UNCITRAL Digest which presents an overview of relevant case law on every article of the CISG. The Digest has been prepared by eminent scholars in this area. The Digest tries to limit itself to simply referring to the content of decisions without trying to evaluate or criticise them. The digest provides easy access to relevant decisions on a particular issue. A draft of it (the so-called Draft Digest) has been published, however, together with the proceedings of a Conference at the University of Pittsburgh where scholars (including the persons charged with drafting the Digest) commented on the Draft Digest and on the case law referred to there.

A good reference for important case law on the CISG is the new casebook "International Sales Law", edited by Ingeborg Schwenzer and Christiana Fountoulakis (*International Sales Law*, Routledge-Cavendish, London, 2007).

The newly published textbook by Peter Huber and Alastair Mullis *The CISG: A new textbook for students and practitioners* (Sellier European Law Publishers, München, 2007) provides easy access to the CISG. The structure the book has adopted makes it easy to gain an overview of important issues and the structure of the CISG.

1.4   CISG Advisory Council Opinions

The CISG Advisory Council (CISG-AC) is a private initiative of eminent scholars in the field. Its aim is to promote the uniform application of the CISG by issuing opinions relating to the interpretation and application of the Convention on request (for instance of international organisations, professional associations and adjudication bodies) or on its own initiative. As of April 2008 the CISG-AC has issued six opinions. The opinions of the CISG-AC are regularly published on the relevant website (e.g. Pace, CISG-Online).

2   Further Conventions

2.1   Convention on the Limitation Period in the International Sale of Goods

2.1.1   *Convention on the Limitation Period in the International Sale of Goods as Amended by the Protocol Amending the Convention on the Limitation Period in the International Sale of Goods- Introductory Note*

Introductory Note

1. The Convention on the Limitation Period in the International Sale of Goods (hereinafter called the 1974 Limitation Convention) was concluded at New York on 14 June 1974. A Protocol to the 1974 Limitation Convention (hereinafter called the 1980 Protocol) was concluded at Vienna on 11 April 1980.

2. The 1974 Limitation Convention and the 1980 Protocol both entered into force on 1 August 1988, in accordance with articles 44/(1) of the 1974 Limitation Convention and IX (1) of the 1980 Protocol.

3. In accordance with paragraph 2 of article XIV of the 1980 Protocol, the text of the 1974 Limitation Convention as amended by the 1980 Protocol has been prepared by the Secretary-General and will be found hereinafter.

4. The present text includes the relevant amendments to the articles of the 1974 Limitation Convention, as provided for by the 1980 Protocol. For ease of reference, the text of the original provisions of the 1974 Limitation Convention which

have been amended by the 1980 Protocol are reproduced in footnotes. The present text also incorporates substantive provisions (final clauses) of the 1980 Protocol as required, including editorial additions. The relevant articles of the 1980 Protocol which have been incorporated in the present text of the 1974 Limitation Convention as amended have, for clarity, been assigned *bis* numbers with the indication in parenthesis of the corresponding number of the 1980 Protocol.

2.1.2 Convention on the Limitation Period in the International Sale of Goods as Amended by the Protocol Amending the Convention on the Limitation Period in the International Sale of Goods

Preamble

<u>The States Parties to the present Convention,</u>

<u>Considering</u> that international trade is an important factor in the promotion of friendly relations amongst States,

<u>Believing</u> that the adoption of uniform rules governing the limitation period in the international sale of goods would facilitate the development of world trade,

<u>Have agreed</u> as follows:

Part I. Substantive provisions

Sphere of Application

Article 1

1. This Convention shall determine when claims of a buyer and a seller against each other arising from a contract of international sale of goods or relating to its breach, termination or invalidity can no longer be exercised by reason of the expiration of a period of time. Such a period of time is hereinafter referred to as "the limitation period".

2. This Convention shall not affect a particular time-limit within which one party is required, as a condition for the acquisition or exercise of his claim, to give notice to the other party or perform any act other than the institution of legal proceedings.

3. In this Convention:

(a) "buyer", "seller" and "party" mean persons who buy or sell, or agree to buy or sell, goods, and the successors to and assigns of their rights or obligations under the contract of sale;

(b) "creditor" means a party who asserts a claim, whether or not such a claim is for a sum of money;

(c) "debtor" means a party against whom a creditor asserts a claim;

(d) "breach of contract" means the failure of a party to perform the contract or any performance not in conformity with the contract;

(e) "legal proceedings" includes judicial, arbitral and administrative proceedings;

(f) "person" includes corporation, company, partnership, association or entity, whether private or public, which can sue or be sued;

(g) "writing" includes telegram and telex;

(h) "year" means a year according to the Gregorian calendar.

Article 2

For the purposes of this Convention:

(a) a contract of sale of goods shall be considered international, if at the time of the conclusion of the contract, the buyer and the seller have their places of business in different States;

(b) the fact that the parties have their place of business in different States shall be disregarded whenever this fact does not appear either from the contract or from any dealings between, or from information disclosed by, the parties at any time before or at the conclusion of the contract;

(c) where a party to a contract of sale of goods has places of business in more than one State, the place of business shall be that which has the closest relationship to the contract and its performance, having regard to the circumstances known to or contemplated by the parties at the time of the conclusion of the contract;

(d) where a party does not have a place of business, reference shall be made to his habitual residence;

(e) neither the nationality of the parties nor the civil or commercial character of the parties or of the contract shall be taken into consideration.

Article 3[1]

1. This Convention shall apply only

(a) if, at the time of the conclusion of the contract, the places of business of the parties to a contract of international sale of goods are in Contracting States; or

(b) if the rules of private international law make the law of a Contracting State applicable to the contract of sale.

2. This Convention shall not apply when the parties have expressly excluded its application.

Article 4[2]

This Convention shall not apply to sales:

(a) of goods bought for personal, family or household use, unless the seller, at any time before or at the conclusion of the contract, neither knew nor ought to have known that the goods were bought for any such use;

(b) by auction;

(c) on execution or otherwise by authority of law;

(d) of stocks, shares, investment securities, negotiable instruments or money;

(e) of ships, vessels, hovercraft or aircraft;

(f) of electricity.

Article 5

This Convention shall not apply to claims based upon:

(a) death of, or personal injury to, any person;

(b) nuclear damage caused by the goods sold;

(c) a lien, mortgage or other security interest in property;

(d) a judgement or award made in legal proceedings;

(e) a document on which direct enforcement or execution can be obtained in accordance with the law of the place where such enforcement or execution is sought;

(f) a bill of exchange, cheque or promissory note.

Article 6

1. This Convention shall not apply to contracts in which the preponderant part of the obligations of the seller consists in the supply of labor or other services.

2. Contracts for the supply of goods to be manufactured or produced shall be considered to be sales, unless the party who orders the goods undertakes to supply a substantial part of the materials necessary for such manufacture or production.

Article 7

In the interpretation and application of the provisions of this Convention, regard shall be had to its international character and to the need to promote uniformity.

The Duration and Commencement of the Limitation Period

Article 8

The limitation period shall be four years.

Article 9

1. Subject to the provisions of articles 10, 11 and 12 the limitation period shall commence on the date of which the claim accrues.

2. The commencement of the limitation period shall not be postponed by:

(a) a requirement that the party be given a notice as described in paragraph 2 of article 1, or

(b) a provision in an arbitration agreement that no right shall arise until an arbitration award has been made.

Article 10

1. A claim arising from a breach of contract shall accrue on the date on which such breach occurs.

2. A claim arising from a defect or other lack of conformity shall accrue on the date on which the goods are actually handed over to, or their tender is refused by, the buyer.

3. A claim based on fraud committed before or at the time of the conclusion of the contract or during its performance shall accrue on the date on which the fraud was or reasonably could have been discovered.

Article 11

If the seller has given an express undertaking relating to the goods which is stated to have effect for a certain period of time, whether expressed in terms of a specific period of time or otherwise, the limitation period in respect of any claim arising from the undertaking shall commence on the date on which the buyer notifies the seller of the fact on which the claim is based, but not later than on the date of the expiration of the period of the undertaking.

Article 12

1. If, in circumstances provided for by the law applicable to the contract, one party is entitled to declare the contract terminated before the time for performance is due, and exercises this right, the limitation period in respect of a claim based on any such circumstances shall commence on the date on which the declaration is made to the other party. If the contract is not declared to be terminated before performance becomes due, the limitation period shall commence on the date on which performance is due.

2. The limitation period in respect of a claim arising out of a breach by one party of a contract for the delivery of or payment for goods by instalments shall, in relation to each separate instalment, commence on the date on which the particular breach occurs. If, under the law applicable to the contract, one party is entitled to declare the contract terminated by reason of such breach, and exercises this right, the limitation period in respect of all relevant instalments shall commence on the date on which the declaration is made to the other party.

Cessation and Extension of the Limitation Period

Article 13

The limitation period shall cease to run when the creditor performs any act which, under the law of the court where the proceedings are instituted, is recognized as commencing judicial proceedings against the debtor or as asserting his claim in such proceedings already instituted against the debtor, for the purpose of obtaining satisfaction or recognition of his claim.

Article 14

1. Where the parties have agreed to submit to arbitration, the limitation period shall cease to run when either party commences arbitral proceedings in the manner provided for in the arbitration agreement or by the law applicable to such proceedings.

2. In the absence of any such provision, arbitral proceedings shall be deemed to commence on the date on which a request that the claim in dispute be referred to arbitration is delivered at the habitual residence or place of business of the other party or, if he has no such residence or place of business, then at his last known residence or place of business.

Article 15

In any legal proceedings other than those mentioned in articles 13 and 14, including legal proceedings commenced upon the occurrence of:

(a) the death or incapacity of the debtor,

(b) the bankruptcy or any state of insolvency affecting the whole of the property of the debtor, or

(c) the dissolution or liquidation of a corporation, company, partnership, association or entity when it is the debtor, the limitation period shall cease to run when the creditor asserts his claim in such proceedings for the purpose of obtaining satisfaction or recognition of the claim, subject to the law governing the proceedings.

Article 16

For the purposes of articles 13, 14 and 15, any act performed by way of counterclaim shall be deemed to have been performed on the same date as the act performed in relation to the claim against which the counterclaim is raised, provided that both the claim and the counterclaim relate to the same contract or to several contracts concluded in the course of the same transaction.

Article 17

1. Where a claim has been asserted in legal proceedings within the limitation period in accordance with article 13, 14, 15 or 16, but such legal proceedings have ended without a decision binding on the merits of the claim, the limitation period shall be deemed to have continued to run.

2. If, at the time such legal proceedings ended, the limitation period has expired or has less than one year to run, the creditor shall be entitled to a period of one year from the date on which the legal proceedings ended.

Article 18

1. Where legal proceedings have been commenced against one debtor, the limitation period prescribed in this Convention shall cease to run against any other party jointly and severally liable with the debtor, provided that the creditor informs such party in writing within that period that the proceedings have been commenced.

2. Where legal proceedings have been commenced by a subpurchaser against the buyer, the limitation period prescribed in this Convention shall cease to run in relation to the buyer's claim over against the seller, if the buyer informs the seller in writing within that period that the proceedings have been commenced.

3. Where the legal proceedings referred to in paragraphs 1 and 2 this article have ended, the limitation period in respect of the claim of the creditor or the buyer against the party jointly and severally liable or against the seller shall be deemed not to have ceased running by virtue of paragraphs 1 and 2 of this article, but the creditor or the buyer shall be entitled to an additional year from the date on which the legal proceedings ended, if at that time the limitation period had expired or had less than one year to run.

Article 19

Where the creditor performs, in the State in which the debtor has his place of business and before the expiration of the limitation period, any act, other than the acts described in articles 13, 14, 15 and 16, which under the law of that State has the effect of recommencing a limitation period, a new limitation period of four years shall commence on the date prescribed by that law.

Article 20

1. Where the debtor, before the expiration of the limitation period, acknowledges in writing his obligation to the creditor, a new limitation period of four years shall commence to run from the date of such acknowledgement.

2. Payment of interest or partial performance of an obligation by the debtor shall have the same effect as an acknowledgement under paragraph (1) of this article if it can reasonably be inferred from such payment or performance that the debtor acknowledges that obligation.

Article 21

Where, as a result of a circumstance which is beyond the control of the creditor and which he could neither avoid nor overcome, the creditor has been prevented from causing the limitation period to cease to run, the limitation period shall be extended so as not to expire before the expiration of one year from the date on which the relevant circumstance ceased to exist.

Modification of the Limitation Period by the Parties

Article 22

1. The limitation period cannot be modified or affected by any declaration or agreement between the parties, except in the cases provided for in paragraph (2) of this article.

2. The debtor may at any time during the running of the limitation period extend the period by a declaration in writing to the creditor. This declaration may be renewed.

3. The provisions of this article shall not affect the validity of a clause in the contract of sale which stipulates that arbitral proceeding shall be commenced within a shorter period of limitation than that prescribed by this Convention, provided that such clause is valid under the law applicable to the contract of sale.

General Limit of the Limitation Period

Article 23

Notwithstanding the provisions of this Convention, a limitation period shall in any event expire not later than ten years from the date on which it commenced to run under articles 9, 10, 11 and 12 of this Convention.

Consequences of the Expiration of the Limitation Period

Article 24

Expiration of the limitation period shall be taken into consideration in any legal proceedings only if invoked by a party to such proceedings.

Article 25

1. Subject to the provisions of paragraph (2) of this article and of article 24, no claim shall be recognized or enforced in any legal proceedings commenced after the expiration of the limitation period.

2. Notwithstanding the expiration of the limitation period, one party may rely on his claim as a defence or for the purpose of set-off against a claim asserted by the other party, provided that in the latter case this may only be done:

(a) if both claims relate to the same contract or to several contracts concluded in the course of the same transaction; or

(b) if the claims could have been set-off at any time before the expiration of the limitation period.

Article 26

Where the debtor performs his obligation after the expiration of the limitation period, he shall not on that ground be entitled in any way to claim restitution even if he did not know at the time when he performed his obligation that the limitation period had expired.

Article 27

The expiration of the limitation period with respect to a principal debt shall have the same effect with respect to an obligation to pay interest on that debt.

Calculation of the Period

Article 28

1. The limitation period shall be calculated in such a way that it shall expire at the end of the day which corresponds to the date on which the period commenced to run. If there is no such corresponding date, the period shall expire at the end of the last day of the last month of the limitation period.

2. The limitation period shall be calculated by reference to the date of the place where the legal proceedings are instituted.

Article 29

Where the last day of the limitation period falls on an official holiday or other dies non juridicus precluding the appropriate legal action in the jurisdiction where the creditor institutes legal proceedings or asserts a claim as envisaged in articles 13, 14 or 15, the limitation period shall be extended so as not to expire until the end of the first day following that official holiday or dies non juridicus on which such proceedings could be instituted or on which such a claim could be asserted in that jurisdiction.

International Effect

Article 30

The acts and circumstances referred to in articles 13 through 19 which have taken place in one Contracting State shall have effect for the purposes of this Convention in another Contracting State, provided that the creditor has taken all reasonable steps to ensure that the debtor is informed of the relevant act or circumstances as soon as possible.

Part II. Implementation

Article 31

1. If a Contracting State has two or more territorial units in which, according to its constitution, different systems of law are applicable in relation to the matters dealt with in this Convention, it may, at the time of signature, ratification or accession, declare that this Convention shall extend to all its territorial units or only to one or more of them, and may amend its declaration by submitting another declaration at any time.

2. These declarations shall be notified to the Secretary-General of the United Nations and shall state expressly the territorial units to which the Convention applies.

3. If a Contracting State described in paragraph (1) of this article makes no declaration at the time of signature, ratification or accession, the Convention shall have effect within all territorial units of that State.

ⁱ4. If, by virtue of a declaration under this article, this Convention extends to one or more but not all of the territorial units of a Contracting State, and if the place of business of a party to a contract is located in that State, this place of business shall, for the purposes of this Convention, be considered not to be in a Contracting State, unless it is in a territorial unit to which the Convention extends.

Article 32

Where in this Convention reference is made to the law of a State in which different systems of law apply, such reference shall be construed to mean the law of the particular legal system concerned.

Article 33

Each Contracting State shall apply the provisions of this Convention to contracts concluded on or after the date of the entry into force of this Convention.

Part III. Declarations and Reservations

Article 34[4]

1. Two or more Contracting States which have the same or closely related legal rules on matters governed by this Convention may at any time declare that the Convention shall not apply to contracts of international sale of goods where the parties have their places of business in those States. Such declarations may be made jointly or by reciprocal unilateral declarations.

2. A Contracting State which has the same or closely related legal rules on matters governed by this Convention as one or more non-Contracting States may at any time declare that the Convention shall not apply to contracts of international sale of goods where the parties have their places of business in those States.

3. If a State which is the object of a declaration under paragraph (2) of this article subsequently becomes a Contracting State, the declaration made shall, as from the date on which this Convention enters into force in respect of the new Contracting State, have the effect of a declaration made under paragraph (1), provided that the new Contracting State joins in such declaration or makes a reciprocal unilateral declaration.

Article 35

A Contracting State may declare, at the time of the deposit of its instrument of ratification or accession, that it will not apply the provisions of this Convention to actions for annulment of the contract.

Article 36

Any State may declare, at the time of the deposit of its instrument of ratification or accession, that it shall not be compelled to apply the provisions of article 24 of this Convention.

Article 36 bis (Article XII of the Protocol)

Any State may declare at the time of the deposit of its instrument of accession or its notification under article 43 bis that it will not be bound by the amendments to article 3 made by article I of the 1980 Protocol.[5] A declaration made under this article shall be in writing and be formally notified to the depositary.

Article 37[6]

This Convention shall not prevail over any international agreement which has already been or may be entered into, and which contains provisions concerning the matters governed by this Convention, provided that the seller and buyer have their places of business in States parties to such agreement.

Article 38

1. A Contracting State which is a party to an existing convention relating to the international sale of goods may declare, at the time of the deposit of its instrument of ratification or accession, that it will apply this Convention exclusively to contracts of international sale of goods as defined in such existing convention.

2. Such declaration shall cease to be effective on the first day of the month following the expiration of twelve months after a new convention on the international sale of goods, concluded under the auspices of the United Nations, shall have entered into force.

Article 39

No reservation other than those made in accordance with articles 34, 35, 36, 36 bis and 38 shall be permitted.

Article 40

1. Declarations made under this Convention shall be addressed to the Secretary-General of the United Nations and shall take effect simultaneously with the entry of this Convention into force in respect of the State concerned, except declarations made thereafter. The latter declarations shall take effect on the first day of the month following the expiration of six months after the date of their receipt by the Secretary-General of the United Nations.* Reciprocal unilateral declarations under article 34 shall take effect on the first day of the month following the expiration of six months after the receipt of the latest declaration by the Secretary-General of the United Nations. [7]

2. Any State which has made a declaration under this Convention may withdraw it at any time by a notification addressed to the Secretary-General of the United Nations. Such withdrawal shall take effect on the first day of the month following the expiration of six months after the date of the receipt of the notification by the Secretary-General of the United Nations. In the case of a declaration made under article 34 of this Convention, such withdrawal shall also render inoperative, as from the date on which the withdrawal takes effect, any reciprocal declaration made by another State under that article.*[ii]

Part IV. Final Clauses

Article 41

This Convention[8] shall be open until 31 December 1975 for signature by all States at the Headquarters of the United Nations.

Article 42

This Convention[8] is subject to ratification. The instruments of ratification shall be deposited with the Secretary-General of the United Nations.

Article 43

This Convention[8] shall remain open for accession by any State. The instruments of accession shall be deposited with the Secretary-General of the United Nations.

Article 43 bis (Article X of the Protocol)

If a State ratifies or accedes to the 1974 Limitation Convention after the entry into force of the 1980 Protocol, the ratification or accession shall also constitute a ratification or an accession to the Convention as amended by the 1980 Protocol if the State notifies the depositary accordingly.

Article 43 ter (Article VIII (2) of the Protocol)

Accession to the 1980 Protocol by any State which is not a Contracting Party to the 1974 Limitation Convention shall have the effect of accession to that Convention as amended by the Protocol, subject to the provisions of article 44 bis.

Article 44

1. This Convention shall enter into force on the first day of the month following the expiration of six months after the date of the deposit of the tenth instrument of ratification or accession.

2. For each State ratifying or acceding to this Convention after the deposit of the tenth instrument of ratification or accession, this Convention shall enter into force on the first day of the month following the expiration of six months after the date of the deposit of its instrument of ratification or accession.

Article 44 bis (Article XI of the Protocol)

Any State which becomes a Contracting Party to the 1974 Limitation Convention, as amended by the 1980 Protocol, shall, unless it notifies the depositary to the contrary, be considered to be also a Contracting Party to the Convention, unamended, in relation to any Contracting Party to the Convention not yet a Contracting Party to the 1980 Protocol.

Article 45

1. Any Contracting State may denounce this Convention by notifying the Secretary-General of the United Nations to that effect.

2. The denunciation shall take effect on the first day of the month following the expiration of twelve months after receipt of the notification by the Secretary-General of the United Nations.

Article 45 bis (Article XIII (3) of the Protocol)

Any Contracting State in respect of which the 1980 Protocol ceases to have effect by the application of paragraphs (1) and (2)[9] of article XIII of 1980 Protocol shall remain a Contracting Party to the 1974 Limitation Convention, unamended, unless it denounces the unamended Convention in accordance with article 45 of that Convention.

Article 46

The original of this Convention, of which the Chinese, English, French, Russian and Spanish texts are equally authentic, shall be deposited with the Secretary-General of the United Nations.

2.1.3 Explanatory Note by the UNCITRAL Secretariat on the Convention on the Limitation Period in the International Sale of Goods and the Protocol amending the Convention on the Limitation

Period in the International Sale of Goods[10]

Introduction. 1. The Convention on the Limitation Period in the International Sale of Goods (New York, 1974) provides uniform international legal rules governing the period of time within which a party under a contract for the international sale of goods must commence legal proceedings against the other party to assert a claim arising from the contract or relating to its breach, termination or invalidity. This period is referred to in the Convention as the "limitation period". The basic aims of the limitation period are to prevent the institution of legal proceedings at such a late date that the evidence relating to the claim is likely to be unreliable or lost and to protect against the uncertainty and injustice that would result if a party were to remain exposed to unasserted claims for an extensive period of time.

2. The Limitation Convention grew out of the work of the United Nations Commission on International Trade Law (UNCITRAL) towards the harmonization and unification of international sales law, which also resulted in the United Nations Convention on Contracts for the International Sale of Goods (Vienna, 1980) (hereinafter referred to as the "United Nations Sales Convention"). During that work it was observed that, while most legal systems limited or prescribed a claim from being asserted after the lapse of a specified period of time, numerous disparities existed among legal systems with respect to the conceptual basis for doing so. As a result there were disparities in the length of the period and in the rules governing the limitation or prescription of claims after that period. Those disparities created

difficulties in the enforcement of claims arising from international sales transactions, and thus burdened international trade.

3. In view of those problems UNCITRAL decided to prepare uniform international legal rules on the limitation period in the international sale of goods. On the basis of a draft Convention prepared by UNCITRAL, a diplomatic conference convened in New York by the General Assembly adopted the Limitation Convention on 14 June 1974. The Limitation Convention was amended by a Protocol adopted in 1980 by the diplomatic conference that adopted the United Nations Sales Convention, in order to harmonize the Limitation Convention with the latter Convention.

4. The Limitation Convention entered into force on 1 August 1988. As of 31 January 1990, 11 States had ratified or acceded the Convention. Czechoslovakia, Dominican Republic, Ghana, Norway and Yugoslavia are parties to the unamended Convention. Argentina, Egypt, German Democratic Republic, Hungary, Mexico and Zambia are parties to the Convention as amended by the 1980 Protocol.

A. Scope of Application. 5. The Convention applies to contracts for the sale of goods between parties whose places of business are in different States if both of those States are Contracting States. Under the 1980 Protocol the Convention also applies if the rules of private international law make the law of a Contracting State applicable to the contract. However, in becoming a party to the Protocol a State may declare that it will not be bound by that provision. Each Contracting State must apply the Convention to contracts concluded on or after the date of the entry into force of the Convention.

6. The application of the Convention is excluded in certain situations. Firstly, the Convention will not apply if the parties to a sales contract expressly exclude its application. This provision gives effect to the basic principle of freedom of contract in the international sale of goods. Secondly, the Convention will not apply in certain cases where matters covered by the Convention are governed by other Conventions. Thirdly, Contracting States are permitted to deposit declarations or reservations excluding the application of the Convention in the following situations: two or more Contracting States may exclude the application of the Convention to contracts between parties having their places of business in those States when the States apply to those contracts the same or closely related legal rules. So far, one State has availed itself of that declaration. In addition, a State may exclude the application of the Convention to actions for annulment of the contract. No State has thus far availed itself of such a declaration.

7. Since the Convention applies only in respect of international sales contracts, it clarifies whether contracts involving certain services are covered. A contract for the supply of goods to be manufactured or produced is considered to be a sales contract unless the party who orders the goods undertakes to supply a substantial part of the materials necessary for their manufacture or production. Furthermore,

when the preponderant part of the obligations of the party who furnishes the goods consists in the supply of labor or other services, the Convention does not apply.

8. The Convention contains a list of types of sales that are excluded from the Convention, either because of the purpose of the sale (goods bought for personal, family or household use (under the 1980 Protocol sales of those goods are covered by the Convention if the seller could not have known that they were bought for such use)), the nature of the sale (sales by auction, on execution or otherwise by law) or the nature of the goods (stocks, shares, investment securities, negotiable instruments, money, ships, vessels, aircraft or electricity (the 1980 Protocol adds hovercraft)).

9. The Convention makes it clear that it applies only to the usual type of commercial claims based on contract. It specifically excludes claims based on death or personal injury; nuclear damage; a lien, mortgage or other security interest; a judicial judgment or award; a document on which direct enforcement or execution can be obtained; and a bill of exchange, cheque or promissory note. The limitation periods for those claims are generally subject to particular rules and it would not necessarily be appropriate to apply in respect of those claims the rules applicable to ordinary commercial contractual claims.

B. Duration and Commencement of Limitation Period. 10. The duration of the limitation period under the Convention is four years. The period cannot be modified by agreement of the parties, but it can be extended by a written declaration of the debtor during the running of the period. Also, the contract of sale may stipulate a shorter period for the commencement of arbitral proceedings, if the stipulation is valid under the law applicable to the contract. Rules are provided as to how the period should be calculated.

11. A limitation period of four years' duration was thought to accomplish the aims of the limitation period and yet to provide an adequate period of time to enable a party to an international sales contract to assert his claim against the other party. Circumstances where an extension or recommencement of the limitation period would be justified are dealt with in particular provisions of the Convention.

12. With respect to the time when the limitation period commences to run, basic rule is that it commences on the date on which the claim accrues. The Convention establishes when claims for breach of contract, for defects in the goods or other lack of conformity and for fraud are deemed to accrue. Special rules are provided for the commencement of the limitation period in two particular cases: where the seller has given the buyer an express undertaking (such as a warranty or guarantee) relating to the goods which is stated to have effect for a certain period of time, and where a party terminates the contract before the time for performance is due. Rules are also provided in respect of claims arising from the breach of an instalment contract and claims based on circumstances giving rise to a termination of such a contract.

C. Cessation and Extension of Limitation Period. 13. Having established the time of commencement and the length of the limitation period, the Convention sets forth rules concerning the cessation of the period. The period ceases to run when the claimant commences judicial or arbitral proceedings against the debtor, or when he asserts his claim in existing proceedings. A counterclaim is deemed to have been asserted on the same date as the date when the proceedings in which the counterclaim is asserted were commenced, if the counterclaim and the claim against which it is raised relate to the same contract or to several contracts concluded in the course of the same transaction.

14. Judicial or arbitral proceedings commenced by a claimant within the limitation period might terminate without a binding decision on the merits of the claim, for example, because the court or arbitral tribunal lacks jurisdiction or because of a procedural defect. The creditor would normally be able to pursue his claim by commencing new proceedings. Thus, the Convention provides that if the original proceedings end without a binding decision on the merits the limitation period will be deemed to have continued to run. However, by the time the original proceedings have ended, the limitation period might have expired, or there might remain insufficient time for the claimant to commence new proceedings. To protect the claimant in those cases the Convention grants him an additional period of one year to commence new proceedings.

15. The Convention contains rules to resolve in a uniform manner questions concerning the running of the limitation period in two particular cases. Firstly, it provides that where legal proceedings have been commenced against one party to the sales contract, the limitation period ceases to run against a person jointly and severally liable with him if the claimant informs that person in writing within the limitation period that the proceedings have been commenced. Secondly, it provides that where proceedings have been commenced against a buyer by a party who purchased the goods from him, the limitation period ceases to run in respect of the buyer's recourse claim against the seller if the buyer informs the seller in writing within the limitation period that the proceedings against the buyer have been commenced. Where the proceedings in either of those two cases have ended, the limitation period in respect of the claim against the jointly and severally liable person or against the seller will be deemed to have continued to run without interruption, but there will be an additional year to commence new proceedings if at that time the limitation period has expired or has less than a year to run.

16. One effect of the provision mentioned above relating to the buyer is to enable him to await the outcome of the claim against him before commencing an action against his seller. This enables the buyer to avoid the trouble and expense of instituting proceedings against the seller and the disruption of their good business relationship if it turns out that the claim against the buyer was not successful.

17. Under the Convention the limitation period recommences in two cases: if the creditor performs in the debtor's State an act that, under the law of that State, has

the effect of recommencing a limitation period, or if the debtor acknowledges in writing his obligation to the creditor or pays interest or partially performs the obligation from which his acknowledgement can be inferred.

18. The Convention protects a creditor who was prevented from taking the necessary acts to stop the running of the limitation period in extreme cases. It provides that when the creditor could not take those acts as a result of a circumstance beyond his control and which he could neither avoid nor overcome, the limitation period will be extended so as to expire one year after the date when the circumstance ceased to exist.

D. Overall Limit of Limitation Period. 19. Since the limitation period may, under the circumstances noted above, be extended or recommence, the Convention establishes an overall time period of 10 years, from the date on which the limitation period originally commenced to run, beyond which no legal proceedings to assert the claim may be commenced under any circumstances. The theory behind that provision is that enabling proceedings to be brought after that time would be inconsistent with the aims of the Convention in providing a definite limitation period.

E. Consequences of Expiration of Limitation Period. 20. The principal consequence of the expiration of the limitation period is that no claim will be recognized or enforced in legal proceedings commenced thereafter. The expiration of the limitation period will not be taken into consideration in legal proceedings unless it is invoked by a party to the proceedings. However, in light of views expressed at the diplomatic conference that adopted the Convention that the limitation or prescription of actions was a matter of public policy and that a court should be able to take the expiration of the limitation period into account on its own initiative, a Contracting State is permitted to declare that it will not apply that provision. No State has thus far made such a declaration.

21. Even after the limitation period has expired a party can in certain situations raise his claim as a defense to or set-off against a claim asserted by the other party.

F. Other Provisions and Final Clauses. 22. Other provisions of the Convention deal with implementation of the Convention in States having two or more territorial units where different legal systems exist. A series of provisions deals with declarations and reservations permitted under the Convention and with procedures for making and withdrawing them. The permitted declarations and reservations have been mentioned above; no others may be made under the Convention.

23. The final clauses contain the usual provisions relating to the Secretary-General of the United Nations as depositary of the Convention. The Convention is subject to ratification by States that signed the Convention by 31 December 1975 and for accession by States that did not do so. The Chinese, English, French, Russian and Spanish texts of the Convention are equally authentic.

24. The Secretary-General of the United Nations is also the depositary of the 1980 Protocol amending the Convention, which is open for accession by all States. Since the Protocol has already received the necessary number of accessions, the Convention as amended by the Protocol will enter into force on the same date as the unamended Convention, i.e. on 1 August 1988.

25. A State that ratifies or accedes to the Convention after the Convention and Protocol come into force will become a party to the Convention as amended by the Protocol if it notifies the depositary accordingly. The Convention as amended will enter into force for that State on the first day of the month following the expiration of 6 months after the date of deposit of its instrument of ratification or accession. Accession to the Protocol by a State that is not a Contracting Party to the Convention constitutes accession to the Convention as amended by the Protocol.

* * *

Notes. [1] Text as amended in accordance with article I of the 1980/Protocol. States that make a declaration under article 36/bis (article XII of the 1980 Protocol) will be bound by article 3 as originally adopted in the Limitation Convention, 1974. Article/3 as originally adopted reads as follows:

"Article 3

1. This Convention shall apply only if, at the time of the conclusion of the contract, the places of business of the parties to a contract of international sale of goods are in Contracting States.

2. Unless this Convention provides otherwise, it shall apply irrespective of the law which would otherwise be applicable by virtue of the rules of private international law.

3. This Convention shall not apply when the parties have expressly excluded its application."

[2] Text of paragraphs (a) and (e) as amended in accordance with article II of the 1980 Protocol. Paragraphs (a) and (e) of article 4 as originally adopted in the Limitation Convention, 1974, prior to its amendment under the 1980 Protocol, read as follows:

(a) of goods bought for personal, family or household use;
(e) of ships, vessels, or aircraft;

[3] New Paragraph 4, added in accordance with article III of the 1980 Protocol.

[4] Text as amended in accordance with article IV of the 1980 Protocol. Article 34 as originally adopted in the Limitation Convention, 1974, prior to its amendment under the 1980 Protocol, read as follows:

"Article 34

Two or more Contracting States may at any time declare that contracts of sale between a seller having a place of business in one of these States and a buyer having a place of business in another of these States shall not be governed by this Convention, because they apply to the matters governed by this Convention the same or closely related legal rules."

[5] Such a State will then be bound by article 3 of the unamended Convention. For its text, see footnote under article 3.

[6] Text as amended in accordance with article V of the Protocol. Article 37 as originally adopted in the Limitation Convention, 1974, prior to its amendment under the 1980 Protocol, read as follows:

"Article 37

This Convention shall not prevail over conventions already entered into or which may be entered into, and which contain provisions concerning the matters governed by this Convention, provided that the seller and buyer have their places of business in States parties to such a convention."

[7] Last sentence of paragraph 1 of article 40 (between asterisks) added in accordance with article VI of the 1980 Protocol.

[8] Refers to the 1974 Limitation Convention

[9] Paragraphs (1) and (2) of article XIII of the Protocol read as follows:

"(1) A Contracting State may denounce this Protocol by notifying the depositary to that effect.
(2) The denunciation shall take effect on the first day of the month following the expiration of twelve months after receipt of the notification by the depositary."

[10] This note has been prepared by the secretariat of the United Nations Commission on International Trade Law for informational purposes; it is not an official commentary on the Convention. A commentary on the unamended Convention prepared at the request of the United Nations Conference on Prescription (Limitation) in the International Sale of Goods appears in A/CONF.63/17 (reprinted in Yearbook of The United Nations Commission on International Trade Law, vol. X:1979 (United Nations Publication, Sales No. E.81.V.2), part three, chap. I and in UNCITRAL: The United Nations Commission on International Trade Law (United Nations Publication, Sales No. E.86.V.8), Annex II.B).

2.2   United Nations Convention on Contracts for the International Sale of Goods (1980)

Contents

2.2.1 *United Nations Convention on Contracts for the International Sale of Goods*

Preamble

Part I. Sphere of Application and General Provisions

Chapter I. Sphere of Application

Article 1
Article 2
Article 3
Article 4
Article 5
Article 6

Chapter II. General Provisions

Article 7
Article 8
Article 9
Article 10
Article 11
Article 12
Article 13

Part II. Formation of the Contract

Article 14
Article 15
Article 16
Article 17
Article 18
Article 19
Article 20
Article 21
Article 22
Article 23
Article 24

Part III. Sale of Goods

Chapter I. General Provisions

Chapter II. Obligations of the Seller

Section I. Delivery of the Goods and Handing Over of Documents

Section II. Conformity of the Goods and Third Party Claims

Section III. Remedies for Breach of Contract by the Seller

2.2.2 Explanatory Note by the Uncitral Secretariat on the United Nations Convention on Contracts for the International Sale of Goods

Introduction

Part One. Scope of Application and General Provisions

A. Scope of application
B. Party autonomy
C. Interpretation of the Convention
D. Interpretation of the contract; usages
E. Form of the contract

Part Two. Formation of the Contract

Part Three. Sale of Goods

A. Obligations of the seller
B. Obligations of the buyer
C. Remedies for breach of contract
D. Passing of risk
E. Suspension of performance and anticipatory breach
F. Exemption from liability to pay damages
G. Preservation of the goods

Part Four. Final Clauses

2.2.3 United Nations Convention on Contracts for the International Sale of Goods

Preamble

The States Parties to this Convention

Bearing in mind the broad objectives in the resolutions adopted by the sixth special session of the General Assembly of the United Nations on the establishment of a New International Economic Order, *Considering* that the development of international trade on the basis of equality and mutual benefit is an important element in promoting friendly relations among States,

Being of the opinion that the adoption of uniform rules which govern contracts for the international sale of goods and take into account the different social, economic and legal systems would contribute to the removal of legal barriers in international trade and promote the development of international trade,

Have agreed as follows:

Part I. Sphere of Application and General Provisions

Chapter I. Sphere of Application

Article 1

(1) This Convention applies to contracts of sale of goods between parties whose places of business are in different States:

(a) when the States are Contracting States; or

(b) when the rules of private international law lead to the application of the law of a Contracting State.

(2) The fact that the parties have their places of business in different States is to be disregarded whenever this fact does not appear either from the contract or from any dealings between, or from information disclosed by, the parties at any time before or at the conclusion of the contract.

(3) Neither the nationality of the parties nor the civil or commercial character of the parties or of the contract is to be taken into consideration in determining the application of this Convention.

Article 2

This Convention does not apply to sales:

(a) of goods bought for personal, family or household use, unless the seller, at any time before or at the conclusion of the contract, neither knew nor ought to have known that the goods were bought for any such use;

(b) by auction;

(c) on execution or otherwise by authority of law;

(d) of stocks, shares, investment securities, negotiable instruments or money;

(e) of ships, vessels, hovercraft or aircraft;

(f) of electricity.

Article 3

(1) Contracts for the supply of goods to be manufactured or produced are to be considered sales unless the party who orders the goods undertakes to supply a substantial part of the materials necessary for such manufacture or production.

(2) This Convention does not apply to contracts in which the preponderant part of the obligations of the party who furnishes the goods consists in the supply of labour or other services.

Article 4

This Convention governs only the formation of the contract of sale and the rights and obligations of the seller and the buyer arising from such a contract. In particular, except as otherwise expressly provided in this Convention, it is not concerned with:

(a) the validity of the contract or of any of its provisions or of any usage;

(b) the effect which the contract may have on the property in the goods sold.

Article 5

This Convention does not apply to the liability of the seller for death or personal injury caused by the goods to any person.

Article 6

The parties may exclude the application of this Convention or, subject to article 12, derogate from or vary the effect of any of its provisions.

Chapter II. General Provisions

Article 7

(1) In the interpretation of this Convention, regard is to be had to its international character and to the need to promote uniformity in its application and the observance of good faith in international trade.

(2) Questions concerning matters governed by this Convention which are not expressly settled in it are to be settled in conformity with the general principles on which it is based or, in the absence of such principles, in conformity with the law applicable by virtue of the rules of private international law.

Article 8

(1) For the purposes of this Convention statements made by and other conduct of a party are to be interpreted according to his intent where the other party knew or could not have been unaware what that intent was.

(2) If the preceding paragraph is not applicable, statements made by and other conduct of a party are to be interpreted according to the understanding that a reasonable

person of the same kind as the other party would have had in the same circumstances.

(3) In determining the intent of a party or the understanding a reasonable person would have had, due consideration is to be given to all relevant circumstances of the case including the negotiations, any practices which the parties have established between themselves, usages and any subsequent conduct of the parties.

Article 9

(1) The parties are bound by any usage to which they have agreed and by any practices which they have established between themselves.

(2) The parties are considered, unless otherwise agreed, to have impliedly made applicable to their contract or its formation a usage of which the parties knew or ought to have known and which in international trade is widely known to, and regularly observed by, parties to contracts of the type involved in the particular trade concerned.

Article 10

For the purposes of this Convention:

(a) if a party has more than one place of business, the place of business is that which has the closest relationship to the contract and its performance, having regard to the circumstances known to or contemplated by the parties at any time before or at the conclusion of the contract;

(b) if a party does not have a place of business, reference is to be made to his habitual residence.

Article 11

A contract of sale need not be concluded in or evidenced by writing and is not subject to any other requirement as to form. It may be proved by any means, including witnesses.

Article 12

Any provision of article 11, article 29 or Part II of this Convention that allows a contract of sale or its modification or termination by agreement or any offer, acceptance or other indication of intention to be made in any form other than in writing does not apply where any party has his place of business in a Contracting State which has made a declaration under article 96 of this Convention. The parties may not derogate from or vary the effect of this article.

Article 13

For the purposes of this Convention "writing" includes telegram and telex.

Part II. Formation of the Contract

Article 14

(1) A proposal for concluding a contract addressed to one or more specific persons constitutes an offer if it is sufficiently definite and indicates the intention of the offeror to be bound in case of acceptance. A proposal is sufficiently definite if it indicates the goods and expressly or implicitly fixes or makes provision for determining the quantity and the price.

(2) A proposal other than one addressed to one or more specific persons is to be considered merely as an invitation to make offers, unless the contrary is clearly indicated by the person making the proposal.

Article 15

(1) An offer becomes effective when it reaches the offeree.

(2) An offer, even if it is irrevocable, may be withdrawn if the withdrawal reaches the offeree before or at the same time as the offer.

Article 16

(1) Until a contract is concluded an offer may be revoked if the revocation reaches the offeree before he has dispatched an acceptance.

(2) However, an offer cannot be revoked:

(a) if it indicates, whether by stating a fixed time for acceptance or otherwise, that it is irrevocable; or

(b) if it was reasonable for the offeree to rely on the offer as being irrevocable and the offeree has acted in reliance on the offer.

Article 17

An offer, even if it is irrevocable, is terminated when a rejection reaches the offeror.

Article 18

(1) A statement made by or other conduct of the offeree indicating assent to an offer is an acceptance. Silence or inactivity does not in itself amount to acceptance.

(2) An acceptance of an offer becomes effective at the moment the indication of assent reaches the offeror. An acceptance is not effective if the indication of assent does not reach the offeror within the time he has fixed or, if no time is fixed, within a reasonable time, due account being taken of the circumstances of the transaction, including the rapidity of the means of communication employed by the offeror. An oral offer must be accepted immediately unless the circumstances indicate otherwise.

(3) However, if, by virtue of the offer or as a result of practices which the parties have established between themselves or of usage, the offeree may indicate assent by performing an act, such as one relating to the dispatch of the goods or payment of the price, without notice to the offeror, the acceptance is effective at the moment the act is performed, provided that the act is performed within the period of time laid down in the preceding paragraph.

Article 19

(1) A reply to an offer which purports to be an acceptance but contains additions, limitations or other modifications is a rejection of the offer and constitutes a counteroffer.

(2) However, a reply to an offer which purports to be an acceptance but contains additional or different terms which do not materially alter the terms of the offer constitutes an acceptance, unless the offeror, without undue delay, objects orally to the discrepancy or dispatches a notice to that effect. If he does not so object, the terms of the contract are the terms of the offer with the modifications contained in the acceptance.

(3) Additional or different terms relating, among other things, to the price, payment, quality and quantity of the goods, place and time of delivery, extent of one party's liability to the other or the settlement of disputes are considered to alter the terms of the offer materially.

Article 20

(1) A period of time of acceptance fixed by the offeror in a telegram or a letter begins to run from the moment the telegram is handed in for dispatch or from the date shown on the letter or, if no such date is shown, from the date shown on the envelope. A period of time for acceptance fixed by the offeror by telephone, telex

or other means of instantaneous communication, begins to run from the moment that the offer reaches the offeree.

(2) Official holidays or non-business days occurring during the period for acceptance are included in calculating the period. However, if a notice of acceptance cannot be delivered at the address of the offeror on the last day of the period because that day falls on an official holiday or a non-business day at the place of business of the offeror, the period is extended until the first business day which follows.

Article 21

(1) A late acceptance is nevertheless effective as an acceptance if without delay the offeror orally so informs the offeree or dispatches a notice to that effect.

(2) If a letter or other writing containing a late acceptance shows that it has been sent in such circumstances that if its transmission had been normal it would have reached the offeror in due time, the late acceptance is effective as an acceptance unless, without delay, the offeror orally informs the offeree that he considers his offer as having lapsed or dispatches a notice to that effect.

Article 22

An acceptance may be withdrawn if the withdrawal reaches the offeror before or at the same time as the acceptance would have become effective.

Article 23

A contract is concluded at the moment when an acceptance of an offer becomes effective in accordance with the provisions of this Convention.

Article 24

For the purposes of this Part of the Convention, an offer, declaration of acceptance or any other indication of intention "reaches" the addressee when it is made orally to him or delivered by any other means to him personally, to his place of business or mailing address or, if he does not have a place of business or mailing address, to his habitual residence.

Part III. Sale of Goods

Chapter I. General Provisions

Article 25

A breach of contract committed by one of the parties is fundamental if it results in such detriment to the other party as substantially to deprive him of what he is entitled to expect under the contract, unless the party in breach did not foresee and a reasonable person of the same kind in the same circumstances would not have foreseen such a result.

Article 26

A declaration of avoidance of the contract is effective only if made by notice to the other party.

Article 27

Unless otherwise expressly provided in this Part of the Convention, if any notice, request or other communication is given or made by a party in accordance with this Part and by means appropriate in the circumstances, a delay or error in the transmission of the communication or its failure to arrive does not deprive that party of the right to rely on the communication.

Article 28

If, in accordance with the provisions of this Convention, one party is entitled to require performance of any obligation by the other party, a court is not bound to enter a judgement for specific performance unless the court would do so under its own law in respect of similar contracts of sale not governed by this Convention.

Article 29

(1) A contract may be modified or terminated by the mere agreement of the parties.

(2) A contract in writing which contains a provision requiring any modification or termination by agreement to be in writing may not be otherwise modified or terminated by agreement. However, a party may be precluded by his conduct from asserting such a provision to the extent that the other party has relied on that conduct.

Chapter II. Obligations of the Seller

Article 30

The seller must deliver the goods, hand over any documents relating to them and transfer the property in the goods, as required by the contract and this Convention.

Section I. *Delivery of the goods and handing over of documents*

Article 31

If the seller is not bound to deliver the goods at any other particular place, his obligation to deliver consists:

(a) if the contract of sale involves carriage of the goods--in handing the goods over to the first carrier for transmission to the buyer;

(b) if, in cases not within the preceding subparagraph, the contract relates to specific goods, or unidentified goods to be drawn from a specific stock or to be manufactured or produced, and at the time of the conclusion of the contract the parties knew that the goods were at, or were to be manufactured or produced at, a particular place—in placing the goods at the buyer's disposal at that place;

(c) in other cases—in placing the goods at the buyer's disposal at the place where the seller had his place of business at the time of the conclusion of the contract.

Article 32

(1) If the seller, in accordance with the contract or this Convention, hands the goods over to a carrier and if the goods are not dearly identified to the contract by markings on the goods, by shipping documents or otherwise, the seller must give the buyer notice of the consignment specifying the goods.

(2) If the seller is bound to arrange for carriage of the goods, he must make such contracts as are necessary for carriage to the place fixed by means of transportation appropriate in the circumstances and according to the usual terms for such transportation.

(3) If the seller is not bound to effect insurance in respect of the carriage of the goods, he must, at the buyer's request, provide him with all available information necessary to enable him to effect such insurance.

Article 33

The seller must deliver the goods:

(a) if a date is fixed by or determinable from the contract, on that date;

(b) if a period of time is fixed by or determinable from the contract, at any time within that period unless circumstances indicate that the buyer is to choose a date; or

(c) in any other case, within a reasonable time after the conclusion of the contract.

Article 34

If the seller is bound to hand over documents relating to the goods, he must hand them over at the time and place and in the form required by the contract. If the seller has handed over documents before that time, he may, up to that time, cure any lack of conformity in the documents, if the exercise of this right does not cause the buyer unreasonable inconvenience or unreasonable expense. However, the buyer retains any right to claim damages as provided for in this Convention.

Section II. *Conformity of the goods and third party claims*

Article 35

(1) The seller must deliver goods which are of the quantity, quality and description required by the contract and which are contained or packaged in the manner required by the contract.

(2) Except where the parties have agreed otherwise, the goods do not conform with the contract unless they:

(a) are fit for the purposes for which goods of the same description would ordinarily be used;

(b) are fit for any particular purpose expressly or impliedly made known to the seller at the time of the conclusion of the contract, except where the circumstances show that the buyer did not rely, or that it was unreasonable for him to rely, on the seller's skill and judgement;

(c) possess the qualities of goods which the seller has held out to the buyer as a sample or model;

(d) are contained or packaged in the manner usual for such goods or, where there is no such manner, in a manner adequate to preserve and protect the goods.

(3) The seller is not liable under subparagraphs *(a)* to *(d)* of the preceding paragraph for any lack of conformity of the goods if at the time of the conclusion of the contract the buyer knew or could not have been unaware of such lack of conformity.

Article 36

(1) The seller is liable in accordance with the contract and this Convention for any lack of conformity which exists at the time when the risk passes to the buyer, even though the lack of conformity becomes apparent only after that time.

(2) The seller is also liable for any lack of conformity which occurs after the time indicated in the preceding paragraph and which is due to a breach of any of his obligations, including a breach of any guarantee that for a period of time the goods will remain fit for their ordinary purpose or for some particular purpose or will retain specified qualities or characteristics.

Article 37

If the seller has delivered goods before the date for delivery, he may, up to that date, deliver any missing part or make up any deficiency in the quantity of the goods delivered, or deliver goods in replacement of any non-conforming goods delivered or remedy any lack of conformity in the goods delivered, provided that the exercise of this right does not cause the buyer unreasonable inconvenience or unreasonable expense. However, the buyer retains any right to claim damages as provided for in this Convention.

Article 38

(1) The buyer must examine the goods, or cause them to be examined, within as short a period as is practicable in the circumstances.

(2) If the contract involves carriage of the goods, examination may be deferred until after the goods have arrived at their destination.

(3) If the goods are redirected in transit or redispatched by the buyer without a reasonable opportunity for examination by him and at the time of the conclusion of the contract the seller knew or ought to have known of the possibility of such redirection or redispatch, examination may be deferred until after the goods have arrived at the new destination.

Article 39

(1) The buyer loses the right to rely on a lack of conformity of the goods if he does not give notice to the seller specifying the nature of the lack of conformity within a reasonable time after he has discovered it or ought to have discovered it.
(2) In any event, the buyer loses the right to rely on a lack of conformity of the goods if he does not give the seller notice thereof at the latest within a period of two years from the date on which the goods were actually handed over to the buyer, unless this time-limit is inconsistent with a contractual period of guarantee.

Article 40

The seller is not entitled to rely on the provisions of articles 38 and 39 if the lack of conformity relates to facts of which he knew or could not have been unaware and which he did not disclose to the buyer.

Article 41

The seller must deliver goods which are free from any right or claim of a third party, unless the buyer agreed to take the goods subject to that right or claim. However, if such right or claim is based on industrial property or other intellectual property, the seller's obligation is governed by article 42.

Article 42

(1) The seller must deliver goods which are free from any right or claim of a third party based on industrial property or other intellectual property, of which at the time of the conclusion of the contract the seller knew or could not have been unaware, provided that the right or claim is based on industrial property or other intellectual property:

(a) under the law of the State where the goods will be resold or otherwise used, if it was contemplated by the parties at the time of the conclusion of the contract that the goods would be resold or otherwise used in that State; or

(b) in any other case, under the law of the State where the buyer has his place of business.

(2) The obligation of the seller under the preceding paragraph does not extend to cases where:

(a) at the time of the conclusion of the contract the buyer knew or could not have been unaware of the right or claim; or

(b) the right or claim results from the seller's compliance with technical drawings, designs, formulae or other such specifications furnished by the buyer.

Article 43

(1) The buyer loses the right to rely on the provisions of article 41 or article 42 if he does not give notice to the seller specifying the nature of the right or claim of the third party within a reasonable time after he has become aware or ought to have become aware of the right or claim.

(2) The seller is not entitled to rely on the provisions of the preceding paragraph if he knew of the right or claim of the third party and the nature of it.

Article 44

Notwithstanding the provisions of paragraph (1) of article 39 and paragraph (1) of article 43, the buyer may reduce the price in accordance with article 50 or claim damages, except for loss of profit, if he has a reasonable excuse for his failure to give the required notice.

Section III. *Remedies for breach of contract by the seller*

Article 45

(1) If the seller fails to perform any of his obligations under the contract or this Convention, the buyer may:

(a) exercise the rights provided in articles 46 to 52;

(b) claim damages as provided in articles 74 to 77.

(2) The buyer is not deprived of any right he may have to claim damages by exercising his right to other remedies.

(3) No period of grace may be granted to the seller by a court or arbitral tribunal when the buyer resorts to a remedy for breach of contract.

Article 46

(1) The buyer may require performance by the seller of his obligations unless the buyer has resorted to a remedy which is inconsistent with this requirement.

(2) If the goods do not conform with the contract, the buyer may require delivery of substitute goods only if the lack of conformity constitutes a fundamental breach of contract and a request for substitute goods is made either in conjunction with notice given under article 39 or within a reasonable time thereafter.

(3) If the goods do not conform with the contract, the buyer may require the seller to remedy the lack of conformity by repair, unless this is unreasonable having regard to all the circumstances. A request for repair must be made either in conjunction with notice given under article 39 or within a reasonable time thereafter.

Article 47

(1) The buyer may fix an additional period of time of reasonable length for performance by the seller of his obligations.

(2) Unless the buyer has received notice from the seller that he will not perform within the period so fixed, the buyer may not, during that period, resort to any remedy for breach of contract. However, the buyer is not deprived thereby of any right he may have to claim damages for delay in performance.

Article 48

(1) Subject to article 49, the seller may, even after the date for delivery, remedy at his own expense any failure to perform his obligations, if he can do so without unreasonable delay and without causing the buyer unreasonable inconvenience or uncertainty of reimbursement by the seller of expenses advanced by the buyer. However, the buyer retains any right to claim damages as provided for in this Convention.

(2) If the seller requests the buyer to make known whether he will accept performance and the buyer does not comply with the request within a reasonable time, the seller may perform within the time indicated in his request. The buyer may not, during that period of time, resort to any remedy which is inconsistent with performance by the seller.

(3) A notice by the seller that he will perform within a specified period of time is assumed to include a request, under the preceding paragraph, that the buyer make known his decision.

(4) A request or notice by the seller under paragraph (2) or (3) of this article is not effective unless received by the buyer.

Article 49

(1) The buyer may declare the contract avoided:

(a) if the failure by the seller to perform any of his obligations under the contract or this Convention amounts to a fundamental breach of contract; or

(b) in case of non-delivery, if the seller does not deliver the goods within the additional period of time fixed by the buyer in accordance with paragraph (1) of article 47 or declares that he will not deliver within the period so fixed.

(2) However, in cases where the seller has delivered the goods, the buyer loses the right to declare the contract avoided unless he does so:

(a) in respect of late delivery, within a reasonable time after he has become aware that delivery has been made;

(b) in respect of any breach other than late delivery, within a reasonable time:

(i) after he knew or ought to have known of the breach;

(ii) after the expiration of any additional period of time fixed by the buyer in accordance with paragraph (1) of article 47, or after the seller has declared that he will not perform his obligations within such an additional period; or

(iii) after the expiration of any additional period of time indicated by the seller in accordance with paragraph (2) of article 48, or after the buyer has declared that he will not accept performances.

Article 50

If the goods do not conform with the contract and whether or not the price has already been paid, the buyer may reduce the price in the same proportion as the value that the goods actually delivered had at the time of the delivery bears to the value that conforming goods would have had at that time. However, if the seller remedies any failure to perform his obligations in accordance with article 37 or article 48 or if the buyer refuses to accept performance by the seller in accordance with those articles, the buyer may not reduce the price.

Article 51

(1) If the seller delivers only a part of the goods or if only a part of the goods delivered is in conformity with the contract, articles 46 to 50 apply in respect of the part which is missing or which does not conform.

(2) The buyer may declare the contract avoided in its entirety only if the failure to make delivery completely or in conformity with the contract amounts to a fundamental breach of the contract.

Article 52

(1) If the seller delivers the goods before the date fixed, the buyer may take delivery or refuse to take delivery.

(2) If the seller delivers a quantity of goods greater than that provided for in the contract, the buyer may take delivery or refuse to take delivery of the excess quantity. If the buyer takes delivery of all or part of the excess quantity, he must pay for it at the contract rate.

Chapter III. Obligations of the Buyer

Article 53

The buyer must pay the price for the goods and take delivery of them as required by the contract and this Convention.

Section I. *Payment of the price*

Article 54

The buyer's obligation to pay the price includes taking such steps and complying with such formalities as may be required under the contract or any laws and regulations to enable payment to be made.

Article 55

Where a contract has been validly concluded but does not expressly or implicitly fix or make provision for determining the price, the parties are considered, in the absence of any indication to the contrary, to have impliedly made reference to the price generally charged at the time of the conclusion of the contract for such goods sold under comparable circumstances in the trade concerned.

Article 56

If the price is fixed according to the weight of the goods, in case of doubt it is to be determined by the net weight.

Article 57

(1) If the buyer is not bound to pay the price at any other particular place, he must pay it to the seller:

(a) at the seller's place of business; or

(b) if the payment is to be made against the handing over of the goods or of documents, at the place where the handing over takes place.

(2) The seller must bear any increase in the expenses incidental to payment which is caused by a change in his place of business subsequent to the conclusion of the contract.

Article 58

(1) If the buyer is not bound to pay the price at any other specific time, he must pay it when the seller places either the goods or documents controlling their disposition at the buyer's disposal in accordance with the contract and this Convention. The seller may make such payment a condition for handing over the goods or documents.

(2) If the contract involves carriage of the goods, the seller may dispatch the goods on terms whereby the goods, or documents controlling their disposition, will not be handed over to the buyer except against payment of the price.

(3) The buyer is not bound to pay the price until he has had an opportunity to examine the goods, unless the procedures for delivery or payment agreed upon by the parties are inconsistent with his having suchan opportunity.

Article 59

The buyer must pay the price on the date fixed by or determinable from the contract and this Convention without the need for any request or compliance with any formality on the part of the seller.

Section II. *Taking delivery*

Article 60

The buyer's obligation to take delivery consists:

(a) in doing all the acts which could reasonably be expected of him in order to enable the seller to make delivery; and

(b) in taking over the goods.

Section III. *Remedies for breach of contract by the buyer*

Article 61

(1) If the buyer fails to perform any of his obligations under the contract or this Convention, the seller may:

(a) exercise the rights provided in articles 62 to 65;

(b) claim damages as provided in articles 74 to 77.

(2) The seller is not deprived of any right he may have to claim damages by exercising his right to other remedies.

(3) No period of grace may be granted to the buyer by a court or arbitral tribunal when the seller resorts to a remedy for breach of contract.

Article 62

The seller may require the buyer to pay the price, take delivery or perform his other obligations, unless the seller has resorted to a remedy which is inconsistent with this requirement.

Article 63

(1) The seller may fix an additional period of time of reasonable length for performance by the buyer of his obligations.

(2) Unless the seller has received notice from the buyer that he will not perform within the period so fixed, the seller may not, during that period, resort to any remedy for breach of contract. However, the seller is not deprived thereby of any right he may have to claim damages for delay in performance.

Article 64

(1) The seller may declare the contract avoided:

(a) if the failure by the buyer to perform any of his obligations under the contract or this Convention amounts to a fundamental breach of contract; or

(b) if the buyer does not, within the additional period of time fixed by the seller in accordance with paragraph (1) of article 63, perform his obligation to pay the price or take delivery of the goods, or if he declares that he will not do so within the period so fixed;

(2) However, in cases where the buyer has paid the price, the seller loses the right to declare the contract avoided unless he does so:

(a) in respect of late performance by the buyer, before the seller has become aware that performance has been rendered; or

(b) in respect of any breach other than late performance by the buyer, within a reasonable time:

(i) after the seller knew or ought to have known of the breach; or

(ii) after the expiration of any additional period of time fixed by the seller in accordance with paragraph (1) of article 63, or after the buyer has declared that he will not perform his obligations within such an additional period.

Article 65

(1) If under the contract the buyer is to specify the form, measurement or other features of the goods and he fails to make such specification either on the date agreed upon or within a reasonable time after receipt of a request from the seller, the seller may, without prejudice to any other rights he may have, make the specification himself in accordance with the requirements of the buyer that may be known to him.

(2) If the seller makes the specification himself, he must inform the buyer of the details thereof and must fix a reasonable time within which the buyer may make a different specification. If, after receipt of such a communication, the buyer fails to do so within the time so fixed, the specification made by the seller is binding.

Chapter IV. Passing of Risk

Article 66

Loss of or damage to the goods after the risk has passed to the buyer does not discharge him from his obligation to pay the price, unless the loss or damage is due to an act or omission of the seller.

Article 67

(1) If the contract of sale involves carriage of the goods and the seller is not bound to hand them over at a particular place, the risk passes to the buyer when the goods are handed over to the first carrier for transmission to the buyer in accordance with the contract of sale. If the seller is bound to hand the goods over to a carrier at a particular place, the risk does not pass to the buyer until the goods are handed over to the carrier at that place. The fact that the seller is authorized to retain documents controlling the disposition of the goods does not affect the passage of the risk.

(2) Nevertheless, the risk does not pass to the buyer until the goods are clearly identified to the contract, whether by markings on the goods, by shipping documents, by notice given to the buyer or otherwise.

Article 68

The risk in respect of goods sold in transit passes to the buyer from the time of the conclusion of the contract. However, if the circumstances so indicate, the risk is assumed by the buyer from the time the goods were handed over to the carrier who issued the documents embodying the contract of carriage.

Nevertheless, if at the time of the conclusion of the contract of sale the seller knew or ought to have known that the goods had been lost or damaged and did not disclose this to the buyer, the loss or damage is at the risk of the seller.

Article 69

(1) In cases not within articles 67 and 68, the risk passes to the buyer when he takes over the goods or, if he does not do so in due time, from the time when the goods are placed at his disposal and he commits a breach of contract by failing to take delivery.

(2) However, if the buyer is bound to take over the goods at a place other than a place of business of the seller, the risk passes when delivery is due and the buyer is aware of the fact that the goods are placed at his disposal at that place.

(3) If the contract relates to goods not then identified, the goods are considered not to be placed at the disposal of the buyer until they are clearly identified to the contract.

Article 70

If the seller has committed a fundamental breach of contract, articles 67, 68 and 69 do not impair the remedies available to the buyer on account of the breach.

Chapter V. Provisions Common to the Obligations of the Seller and of the Buyer

Section I. *Anticipatory breach and instalment contracts*

Article 71

(1) A party may suspend the performance of his obligations if, after the conclusion of the contract, it becomes apparent that the other party will not perform a substantial part of his obligations as a result of:

(a) a serious deficiency in his ability of perform or in his creditworthiness; or

(b) his conduct in preparing to perform or in performing the contract.

(2) If the seller has already dispatched the goods before the grounds described in the preceding paragraph become evident, he may prevent the handing over of the goods to the buyer even though the buyer holds a document which entitles him to obtain them. The present paragraph relates only to the rights in the goods as between the buyer and the seller.

(3) A party suspending performance, whether before or after dispatch of the goods, must immediately give notice of the suspension to the other party and must continue with performance if the other party provides adequate assurance of his performance.

Article 72

(1) If prior to the date for performance of the contract it is clear that one of the parties will commit a fundamental breach of contract, the other party may declare the contract avoided.

(2) If time allows, the party intending to declare the contract avoided must give reasonable notice to the other party in order to permit him to provide adequate assurance of his performance.

(3) The requirements of the preceding paragraph do not apply if the other party has declared that he will not perform his obligations.

Article 73

(1) In the case of a contract for delivery of goods by instalments, if the failure of one party to perform any of his obligations in respect of any instalment constitutes a fundamental breach of contract with respect to that instalment, the other party may declare the contract avoided with respect to that instalment.

(2) If one party's failure to perform any of his obligations in respect of any instalment gives the other party good grounds to conclude that a fundamental breach of contract will occur with respect to future installments, he may declare the contract avoided for the future, provided that he does so within a reasonable time.

(3) A buyer who declares the contract avoided in respect of any delivery may, at the same time, declare it avoided in respect of deliveries already made or of future deliveries if, by reason of their interdependence, those deliveries could not be used for the purpose contemplated by the parties at the time of the conclusion of the contract.

Section II. *Damages*

Article 74

Damages for breach of contract by one party consist of a sum equal to the loss, including loss of profit, suffered by the other party as a consequence of the breach. Such damages may not exceed the loss which the party in breach foresaw or ought to have foreseen at the time of the conclusion of the contract, in the light of the facts and matters of which he then knew or ought to have known, as a possible consequence of the breach of contract.

Article 75

If the contract is avoided and if, in a reasonable manner and within a reasonable time after avoidance, the buyer has bought goods in replacement or the seller has resold the goods, the party claiming damages may recover the difference between the contract price and the price in the substitute transaction as well as any further damages recoverable under article 74.

Article 76

(1) If the contract is avoided and there is a current price for the goods, the party claiming damages may, if he has not made a purchase or resale under article 75, recover the difference between the price fixed by the contract and the current price at the time of avoidance as well as any further damages recoverable under article 74. If, however, the party claiming damages has avoided the contract after taking

over the goods, the current price at the time of such taking over shall be applied instead of the current price at the time of avoidance.

(2) For the purposes of the preceding paragraph, the current price is the price prevailing at the place where delivery of the goods should have been made or, if there is no current price at that place, the price at such other place as serves as a reasonable substitute, making due allowance for differences in the cost of transporting the goods.

Article 77

A party who relies on a breach of contract must take such measures as are reasonable in the circumstances to mitigate the loss, including loss of profit, resulting from the breach. If he fails to take such measures, the party in breach may claim a reduction in the damages in the amount by which the loss should have been mitigated.

Section III. *Interest*

Article 78

If a party fails to pay the price or any other sum that is in arrears, the other party is entitled to interest on it, without prejudice to any claim for damages recoverable under article 74.

Section IV. *Exemption*

Article 79

(1) A party is not liable for a failure to perform any of his obligations if he proves that the failure was due to an impediment beyond his control and that he could not reasonably be expected to have taken the impediment into account at the time of the conclusion of the contract or to have avoided or overcome it or its consequences.
(2) If the party's failure is due to the failure by a third person whom he has engaged to perform the whole or a part of the contract, that party is exempt from liability only if:

(a) he is exempt under the preceding paragraph; and

(b) the person whom he has so engaged would be so exempt if the provisions of that paragraph were applied to him.

(3) The exemption provided by this article has effect for the period during which the impediment exists.

(4) The party who fails to perform must give notice to the other party of the impediment and its effect on his ability to perform. If the notice is not received by the other party within a reasonable time after the party who fails to perform knew or ought to have known of the impediment, he is liable for damages resulting from such nonreceipt.

(5) Nothing in this article prevents either party from exercising any right other than to claim damages under this Convention.

Article 80

A party may not rely on a failure of the other party to perform, to the extent that such failure was caused by the first party's act or omission.

Section V. *Effects of avoidance*

Article 81

(1) Avoidance of the contract releases both parties from their obligations under it, subject to any damages which may be due. Avoidance does not affect any provision of the contract for the settlement of disputes or any other provision of the contract governing the rights and obligations of the parties consequent upon the avoidance of the contract.

(2) A party who has performed the contract either wholly or in part may claim restitution from the other party of whatever the first party has supplied or paid under the contract. If both parties are bound to make restitution, they must do so concurrently.

Article 82

(1) The buyer loses the right to declare the contract avoided or to require the seller to deliver substitute goods if it is impossible for him to make restitution of the goods substantially in the condition in which he received them.
(2) The preceding paragraph does not apply:

(a) if the impossibility of making restitution of the goods or of making restitution of the goods substantially in the condition in which the buyer received them is not due to his act or omission;

(b) the goods or part of the goods have perished or deteriorated as a result of the examination provided for in article 38; or

(c) if the goods or part of the goods have been sold in the normal course of business or have been consumed or transformed by the buyer in the course of normal use before he discovered or ought to have discovered the lack of conformity.

Article 83

A buyer who has lost the right to declare the contract avoided or to require the seller to deliver substitute goods in accordance with article 82 retains all other remedies under the contract and this Convention.

Article 84

(1) If the seller is bound to refund the price, he must also pay interest on it, from the date on which the price was paid.

(2) The buyer must account to the seller for all benefits which he has derived from the goods or part of them:

(a) if he must make restitution of the goods or part of them; or

(b) if it is impossible for him to make restitution of all or part of the goods or to make restitution of all or part of the goods substantially in the condition in which he received them, but he has nevertheless declared the contract avoided or required the seller to deliver substitute goods.

Section VI. *Preservation of the goods*

Article 85

If the buyer is in delay in taking delivery of the goods or, where payment of the price and delivery of the goods are to be made concurrently, if he fails to pay the price, and the seller is either in possession of the goods or otherwise able to control their disposition, the seller must take such steps as are reasonable in the circumstances to preserve them. He is entitled to retain them until he has been reimbursed his reasonable expenses by the buyer.

Article 86

(1) If the buyer has received the goods and intends to exercise any right under the contract or this Convention to reject them, he must take such steps to preserve them as are reasonable in the circumstances. He is entitled to retain them until he has been reimbursed his reasonable expenses by the seller.

(2) If goods dispatched to the buyer have been placed at his disposal at their destination and he exercises the right to reject them, he must take possession of them on behalf of the seller, provided that this can be done without payment of the price and without unreasonable inconvenience or unreasonable expense. This provision does not apply if the seller or a person authorized to take charge of the goods on his behalf is present at the destination. If the buyer takes possession of the goods

under this paragraph, his rights and obligations are governed by the preceding paragraph.

Article 87

A party who is bound to take steps to preserve the goods may deposit them in a warehouse of a third person at the expense of the other party provided that the expense incurred is not unreasonable.

Article 88

(1) A party who is bound to preserve the goods in accordance with article 85 or 86 may sell them by any appropriate means if there has been an unreasonable delay by the other party in taking possession of the goods or in taking them back or in paying the price or the cost of preservation, provided that reasonable notice of the intention to sell has been given to the other party.

(2) If the goods are subject to rapid deterioration or their preservation would involve unreasonable expense, a party who is bound to preserve the goods in accordance with article 85 or 86 must take reasonable measures to sell them. To the extent possible he must give notice to the other party of his intention to sell.

(3) A party selling the goods has the right to retain out of the proceeds of sale an amount equal to the reasonable expenses of preserving the goods and of selling them. He must account to the other party for the balance.

Part IV. Final Provisions

Article 89

The Secretary-General of the United Nations is hereby designated as the depositary for this Convention.

Article 90

This Convention does not prevail over any international agreement which has already been or may be entered into and which contains provisions concerning the matters governed by this Convention, provided that the parties have their places of business in States parties, to such agreement.

Article 91

(1) This Convention is open for signature at the concluding meeting of the United Nations Conference on Contracts for the International Sale of Goods and will remain open for signature by all States at the Headquarters of the United Nations, New York until 30 September 1981.

(2) This Convention is subject to ratification, acceptance or approval by the signatory States.

(3) This Convention is open for accession by all States which are not signatory States as from the date it is open for signature.

(4) Instruments of ratification, acceptance, approval and accession are to be deposited with the Secretary-General of the United Nations.

Article 92

(1) A Contracting State may declare at the time of signature, ratification, acceptance, approval or accession that it will not be bound by Part II of this Convention or that it will not be bound by Part III of this Convention.

(2) A Contracting State which makes a declaration in accordance with the preceding paragraph in respect of Part II or Part III of this Convention is not to be considered a Contracting State within paragraph (1) of article 1 of this Convention in respect of matters governed by the Part to which the
declaration applies.

Article 93

(1) If a Contracting State has two or more territorial units in which, according to its constitution, different systems of law are applicable in relation to the matters dealt with in this Convention, it may, at the time of signature, ratification, acceptance, approval or accession, declare that this Convention is to extend to all its territorial units or only to one or more of them, and may amend its declaration by submitting another declaration at any time.

(2) These declarations are to be notified to the depositary and are to state expressly the territorial units to which the Convention extends.
(3) If, by virtue of a declaration under this article, this Convention extends to one or more but not all of the territorial units of a Contracting State, and if the place of business of a party is located in that State, this place of business, for the purposes of this Convention, is considered not to be in a Contracting State, unless it is in a territorial unit to which the Convention extends.

(4) If a Contracting State makes no declaration under paragraph (1) of this article, the Convention is to extend to all territorial units of that State.

Article 94

(1) Two or more Contracting States which have the same or closely related legal rules on matters governed by this Convention may at any time declare that the Convention is not to apply to contracts of sale or to their formation where the par-

ties have their places of business in those States. Such declarations may be made jointly or by reciprocal unilateral declarations.

(2) A Contracting State which has the same or closely related legal rules on matters governed by this Convention as one or more non-Contracting States may at any time declare that the Convention is not to apply to contracts of sale or to their formation where the parties have their places of business in those States.

(3) If a State which is the object of a declaration under the preceding paragraph subsequently becomes a Contracting State, the declaration made will, as from the date on which the Convention enters into force in respect of the new Contracting State, have the effect of a declaration made under paragraph (1), provided that the new Contracting State joins in such declaration or makes a reciprocal unilateral declaration.

Article 95

Any State may declare at the time of the deposit of its instrument of ratification, acceptance, approval or accession that it will not be bound by subparagraph (1) (b) of article 1 of this Convention.

Article 96

A Contracting State whose legislation requires contracts of sale to be concluded in or evidenced by writing may at any time make a declaration in accordance with article 12 that any provision of article 11, article 29, or Part II of this Convention, that allows a contract of sale or its modification or termination by agreement or any offer, acceptance, or other indication of intention to be made in any form other than in writing, does not apply where any party has his place of business in that State.

Article 97

(1) Declarations made under this Convention at the time of signature are subject to confirmation upon ratification, acceptance or approval.

(2) Declarations and confirmations of declarations are to be in writing and be formally notified to the depositary.

(3) A declaration takes effect simultaneously with the entry into force of this Convention in respect of the State concerned. However, a declaration of which the depositary receives formal notification after such entry into force takes effect on the first day of the month following the expiration of six months after the date of its receipt by the depositary. Reciprocal unilateral declarations under article 94 take effect on the first day of the month following the expiration of six months after the receipt of the latest declaration by the depositary.

(4) Any State which makes a declaration under this Convention may withdraw it at any time by a formal notification in writing addressed to the depositary. Such withdrawal is to take effect on the first day of the month following the expiration of six months after the date of the receipt of the notification by the depositary.

(5) A withdrawal of a declaration made under article 94 renders inoperative, as from the date on which the withdrawal takes effect, any reciprocal declaration made by another State under that article.

Article 98

No reservations are permitted except those expressly authorized in this Convention.

Article 99

(1) This Convention enters into force, subject to the provisions of paragraph (6) of this article, on the first day of the month following the expiration of twelve months after the date of deposit of the tenth instrument of ratification, acceptance, approval or accession, including an instrument which contains a declaration made under article 92.

(2) When a State ratifies, accepts, approves or accedes to this Convention after the deposit of the tenth instrument of ratification, acceptance, approval or accession, this Convention, with the exception of the Part excluded, enters into force in respect of that State, subject to the provisions of paragraph (6) of this article, on the first day of the month following the expiration of twelve months after the date of the deposit of its instrument of ratification, acceptance, approval or accession.

(3) A State which ratifies, accepts, approves or accedes to this Convention and is a party to either or both the Convention relating to a Uniform Law on the Formation of Contracts for the International Sale of Goods done at The Hague on 1 July 1964 (1964 Hague Formation Convention) and the Convention relating to a Uniform Law on the International Sale of Goods done at The Hague on 1 July 1964 (1964 Hague Sales Convention) shall at the same time denounce, as the case may be, either or both the 1964 Hague Sales Convention and the 1964 Hague Formation Convention by notifying the Government of the Netherlands to that effect.

(4) A State party to the 1964 Hague Sales Convention which ratifies, accepts, approves or accedes to the present Convention and declares or has declared under article 92 that it will not be bound by Part II of this Convention shall at the time of ratification, acceptance, approval or accession denounce the 1964 Hague Sales Convention by notifying the Government of the Netherlands to that effect.

(5) A State party to the 1964 Hague Formation Convention which ratifies, accepts, approves or accedes to the present Convention and declares or has declared under article 92 that it will not be bound by Part III of this Convention shall at the time

of ratification, acceptance, approval or accession denounce the 1964 Hague Formation Convention by notifying the Government of the Netherlands to that effect.

(6) For the purpose of this article, ratifications, acceptances, approvals and accessions in respect of this Convention by States parties to the 1964 Hague Formation Convention or to the 1964 Hague Sales Convention shall not be effective until such denunciations as may be required on the part of those States in respect of the latter two Conventions have themselves become effective. The depositary of this Convention shall consult with the Government of the Netherlands, as the depositary of the 1964 Conventions, so as to ensure necessary co-ordination in this respect.

Article 100

(1) This Convention applies to the formation of a contract only when the proposal for concluding the contract is made on or after the date when the Convention enters into force in respect of the Contracting States referred to in subparagraph (1) (a) or the Contracting State referred to in subparagraph (1) *(b)* of article 1.

(2) This Convention applies only to contracts concluded on or after the date when the Convention enters into force in respect of the Contracting States referred to in subparagraph (1)(a) or the Contracting State referred to in subparagraph *(1)(b)* of article 1.

Article 101

(1) A Contracting State may denounce this Convention, or Part II or Part III of the Convention, by a formal notification in writing addressed to the depositary.

(2) The denunciation takes effect on the first day of the month following the expiration of twelve months after the notification is received by the depositary. Where a longer period for the denunciation to take effect is specified in the notification, the denunciation takes effect upon the expiration of such longer period after the notification is received by the depositary.

DONE at Vienna, this day of eleventh day of April, one thousand nine hundred and eighty, in a single original, of which the Arabic, Chinese, English, French, Russian and Spanish texts are equally authentic.

IN WITNESS WHEREOF the undersigned plenipotentiaries, being duly authorized by their respective Governments, have signed this Convention.

2.2.4 *Explanatory Note by the Uncitral Secretariat on the United Nations Convention on Contracts for the International Sale of Goods**

Introduction

1. The United Nations Convention on Contracts for the International Sale of Goods provides a uniform text of law for international sales of goods. The Convention was prepared by the United Nations Commission on International Trade Law (UNCITRAL) and adopted by a diplomatic conference on 11 April 1980.

* This note has been prepared by the Secretariat of the United Nations Commission on International Trade Law for informational purposes; it is not an official commentary on the Convention.

2. Preparation of a uniform law for the international sale of goods began in 1930 at the International Institute for the Unification of Private Law (UNIDROIT) in Rome. After a long interruption in the work as a result of the Second World War, the draft was submitted to a diplomatic conference in The Hague in 1964, which adopted two conventions, one on the international sale of goods and the other on the formation of contracts for the international sale of goods.

3. Almost immediately upon the adoption of the two conventions there was widespread criticism of their provisions as reflecting primarily the legal traditions and economic realities of continental Western Europe, which was the region that had most actively contributed to their preparation. As a result, one of the first tasks undertaken by UNCITRAL on its organization in 1968 was to enquire of States whether or not they intended to adhere to those conventions and the reasons for their positions. In the light of the responses received, UNCITRAL decided to study the two conventions to ascertain which modifications might render them capable of wider acceptance by countries of different legal, social and economic systems. The result of this study was the adoption by diplomatic conference on 11 April 1980 of the United Nations Convention on Contracts for the International Sale of Goods, which combines the subject matter of the two prior conventions.

4. UNCITRAL's success in preparing a Convention with wider acceptability is evidenced by the fact that the original eleven States for which the Convention came into force on 1 January 1988 included States from every geographical region, every stage of economic development and every major legal, social and economic system. The original eleven States were: Argentina, China, Egypt, France, Hungary, Italy, Lesotho, Syria, United States, Yugoslavia and Zambia.

5. As of 31 January 1988, an additional four States, Austria, Finland, Mexico and Sweden, had become a party to the Convention.

6. The Convention is divided into four parts. Part One deals with the scope of application of the Convention and the general provisions. Part Two contains the rules governing the formation of contracts for the international sale of goods. Part Three deals with the substantive rights and obligations of buyer and seller arising from the contract. Part Four contains the final clauses of the Convention concerning such matters as how and when it comes into force, the reservations and declarations that are permitted and the application of the Convention to international sales where both States concerned have the same or similar law on the subject.

Part One. Scope of Application and General Provisions

A. Scope of application

7. The articles on scope of application state both what is included in the coverage of the Convention and what is excluded from it. The provisions on inclusion are the most important. The Convention applies to contracts of sale of goods between parties whose places of business are in different States and either both of those States are Contracting States or the rules of private international law lead to the law of a Contracting State. A few States have availed themselves of the authorization in article 95 to declare that they would apply the Convention only in the former and not in the latter of these two situations. As the Convention becomes more widely adopted, the practical significance of such a declaration will diminish.

8. The final clauses make two additional restrictions on the territorial scope of application that will be relevant to a few States. One applies only if a State is a party to another international agreement that contains provisions concerning matters governed by this Convention; the other permits States that have the same or similar domestic law of sales to declare that the Convention does not apply between them.

9. Contracts of sale are distinguished from contracts for services in two respects by article 3. A contract for the supply of goods to be manufactured or produced is considered to be a sale unless the party who orders the goods undertakes to supply a substantial part of the materials necessary for their manufacture or production. When the preponderant part of the obligations of the party who furnishes the goods consists in the supply of labour or other services, the Convention does not apply.

10. The Convention contains a list of types of sales that are excluded from the Convention, either because of the purpose of the sale (goods bought for personal, family or household use), the nature of the sale (sales by auction, on execution or otherwise by law) or the nature of the goods (stocks, shares, investment securities, negotiable instruments, money, ships, vessels, hovercraft, aircraft or electricity). In many States some or all of such sales are governed by special rules reflecting their special nature.

11. Several articles make clear that the subject matter of the Convention is restricted to the formation of the contract and the rights and duties of the buyer and

seller arising from such a contract. In particular, the Convention is not concerned with the validity of the contract, the effect which the contract may have on the property in the goods sold or the liability of the seller for death or personal injury caused by the goods to any person.

B. Party autonomy

12. The basic principle of contractual freedom in the international sale of goods is recognized by the provision that permits the parties to exclude the application of this Convention or derogate from or vary the effect of any of its provisions. The exclusion of the Convention would most often result from the choice by the parties of the law of a non-contracting State or of the domestic law of a contracting State to be the law applicable to the contract. Derogation from the Convention would occur whenever a provision in the contract provided a different rule from that found in the Convention.

C. Interpretation of the Convention

13. This Convention for the unification of the law governing the international sale of goods will better fulfill its purpose if it is interpreted in a consistent manner in all legal systems. Great care was taken in its preparation to make it as clear and easy to understand as possible. Nevertheless, disputes will arise as to its meaning and application. When this occurs, all parties, including domestic courts and arbitral tribunals, are admonished to observe its international character and to promote uniformity in its application and the observance of good faith in international trade. In particular, when a question concerning a matter governed by this Convention is not expressly settled in it, the question is to be settled in conformity with the general principles on which the Convention is based. Only in the absence of such principles should the matter be settled in conformity with the law applicable by virtue of the rules of private international law.

D. Interpretation of the contract; usages

14. The Convention contains provisions on the manner in which statements and conduct of a party are to be interpreted in the context of the formation of the contract or its implementation. Usages agreed to by the parties, practices they have established between themselves and usages of which the parties knew or ought to have known and which are widely known to, and regularly observed by, parties to contracts of the type involved in the particular trade concerned may all be binding on the parties to the contract of sale.

E. Form of the contract

15. The Convention does not subject the contract of sale to any requirement as to form. In particular, article 11 provides that no written agreement is necessary for the conclusion of the contract. However, if the contract is in writing and it

contains a provision requiring any modification or termination by agreement to be in writing, article 29 provides that the contract may not be otherwise modified or terminated by agreement. The only exception is that a party may be precluded by his conduct from asserting such a provision to the extent that the other person has relied on that conduct.

16. In order to accommodate those States whose legislation requires contracts of sale to be concluded in or evidenced by writing, article 96 entitles those States to declare that neither article 11 nor the exception to article 29 applies where any party to the contract has his place of business in that State.

Part Two. Formation of the Contract

17. Part Two of the Convention deals with a number of questions that arise in the formation of the contract by the exchange of an offer and an acceptance. When the formation of the contract takes place in this manner, the contract is concluded when the acceptance of the offer becomes effective.

18. In order for a proposal for concluding a contract to constitute an offer, it must be addressed to one or more specific persons and it must be sufficiently definite. For the proposal to be sufficiently definite, it must indicate the goods and expressly or implicitly fix or make provision for determining the quantity and the price.

19. The Convention takes a middle position between the doctrine of the revocability of the offer until acceptance and its general irrevocability for some period of time. The general rule is that an offer may be revoked. However, the revocation must reach the offeree before he has dispatched an acceptance. Moreover, an offer cannot be revoked if it indicates that it is irrevocable, which it may do by stating a fixed time for acceptance or otherwise. Furthermore, an offer may not be revoked if it was reasonable for the offeree to rely on the offer as being irrevocable and the offeree has acted in reliance on the offer.

20. Acceptance of an offer may be made by means of a statement or other conduct of the offeree indicating assent to the offer that is communicated to the offerer. However, in some cases the acceptance may consist of performing an act, such as dispatch of the goods or payment of the price. Such an act would normally be effective as an acceptance the moment the act was performed.

21. A frequent problem in contract formation, perhaps especially in regard to contracts of sale of goods, arises out of a reply to an offer that purports to be an acceptance but contains additional or different terms. Under the Convention, if the additional or different terms do not materially alter the terms of the offer, the reply constitutes an acceptance, unless the offeror without undue delay objects to those terms. If he does not object, the terms of the contract are the terms of the offer with the modifications contained in the acceptance.

22. If the additional or different terms do materially alter the terms of the contract, the reply constitutes a counter-offer that must in turn be accepted for a contract to be concluded. Additional or different terms relating, among other things, to the price, payment, quality and quantity of the goods, place and time of delivery, extent of one party's liability to the other or settlement of disputes are considered to alter the terms of the offer materially.

Part Three. Sale of Goods

A. Obligations of the seller

23. The general obligations of the seller are to deliver the goods, hand over any documents relating to them and transfer the property in the goods, as required by the contract and this Convention. The Convention provides supplementary rules for use in the absence of contractual agreement as to when, where and how the seller must perform these obligations.

24. The Convention provides a number of rules that implement the seller's obligations in respect of the quality of the goods. In general, the seller must deliver goods that are of the quantity, quality and description required by the contract and that are contained or packaged in the manner required by the contract. One set of rules of particular importance in international sales of goods involves the seller's obligation to deliver goods that are free from any right or claim of a third party, including rights based on industrial property or other intellectual property.

25. In connection with the seller's obligations in regard to the quality of the goods, the Convention contains provisions on the buyer's obligation to inspect the goods. He must give notice of any lack of their conformity with the contract within a reasonable time after he has discovered it or ought to have discovered it, and at the latest two years from the date on which the goods were actually handed over to the buyer, unless this time-limit is inconsistent with a contractual period of guarantee.

B. Obligations of the buyer

26. Compared to the obligations of the seller, the general obligations of the buyer are less extensive and relatively simple; they are to pay the price for the goods and take delivery of them as required by the contract and the Convention. The Convention provides supplementary rules for use in the absence of contractual agreement as to how the price is to be determined and where and when the buyer should perform his obligation to pay the price.

C. Remedies for breach of contract

27. The remedies of the buyer for breach of contract by the seller are set forth in connection with the obligations of the seller and the remedies of the seller are set forth in connection with the obligations of the buyer. This makes it easier to use and understand the Convention.

28. The general pattern of remedies is the same in both cases. If all the required conditions are fulfilled, the aggrieved party may require performance of the other party's obligations, claim damages or avoid the contract. The buyer also has the right to reduce the price where the goods delivered do not conform with the contract.

29. Among the more important limitations on the right of an aggrieved party to claim a remedy is the concept of fundamental breach. For a breach of contract to be fundamental, it must result in such detriment to the other party as substantially to deprive him of what he is entitled to expect under the contract, unless the result was neither foreseen by the party in breach nor foreseeable by a reasonable person of the same kind in the same circumstances. A buyer can require the delivery of substitute goods only if the goods delivered were not in conformity with the contract and the lack of conformity constituted a fundamental breach of contract. The existence of a fundamental breach is one of the two circumstances that justifies a declaration of avoidance of a contract by the aggrieved party; the other circumstance being that, in the case of non-delivery of the goods by the seller or non-payment of the price or failure to take delivery by the buyer, the party in breach fails to perform within a reasonable period of time fixed by the aggrieved party.

30. Other remedies may be restricted by special circumstances. For example, if the goods do not conform with the contract, the buyer may require the seller to remedy the lack of conformity by repair, unless this is unreasonable having regard to all the circumstances. A party cannot recover damages that he could have mitigated by taking the proper measures. A party may be exempted from paying damages by virtue of an impediment beyond his control.

D. Passing of risk

31. Determining the exact moment when the risk of loss or damage to the goods passes from the seller to the buyer is of great importance in contracts for the international sale of goods. Parties may regulate that issue in their contract either by an express provision or by the use of a trade term. However, for the frequent case where the contract does not contain such a provision, the Convention sets forth a complete set of rules.

32. The two special situations contemplated by the Convention are when the contract of sale involves carriage of the goods and when the goods are sold while in transit. In all other cases the risk passes to the buyer when he takes over the goods or from the time when the goods are placed at his disposal and he commits a breach of contract by failing to take delivery, whichever comes first. In the frequent case when the contract relates to goods that are not then identified, they must be identified to the contract before they can be considered to be placed at the disposal of the buyer and the risk of their loss can be considered to have passed to him.

E. Suspension of performance and anticipatory breach

33. The Convention contains special rules for the situation in which, prior to the date on which performance is due, it becomes apparent that one of the parties will not perform a substantial part of his obligations or will commit a fundamental breach of contract. A distinction is drawn between those cases in which the other party may suspend his own performance of the contract but the contract remains in existence awaiting future events and those cases in which he may declare the contract avoided.

F. Exemption from liability to pay damages

34. When a party fails to perform any of his obligations due to an impediment beyond his control that he could not reasonably have been expected to take into account at the time of the conclusion of the contract and that he could not have avoided or overcome, he is exempted from paying damages. This exemption may also apply if the failure is due to the failure of a third person whom he has engaged to perform the whole or a part of the contract. However, he is subject to any other remedy, including reduction of the price, if the goods were defective in some way.

G. Preservation of the goods

35. The Convention imposes on both parties the duty to preserve any goods in their possession belonging to the other party. Such a duty is of even greater importance in an international sale of goods where the other party is from a foreign country and may not have agents in the country where the goods are located. Under certain circumstances the party in possession of the goods may sell them, or may even be required to sell them. A party selling the goods has the right to retain out of the proceeds of sale an amount equal to the reasonable expenses of preserving the goods and of selling them and must account to the other party for the balance.

Part Four. Final Clauses

36. The final clauses contain the usual provisions relating to the Secretary-General as depositary and providing that the Convention is subject to ratification, acceptance or approval by those States that signed it by 30 September 1981, that it is open to accession by all States that are not signatory States and that the text is equally authentic in Arabic, Chinese, English, French, Russian and Spanish.

37. The Convention permits a certain number of declarations. Those relative to scope of application and the requirement as to a written contract have been mentioned above. There is a special declaration for States that have different systems of law governing contracts of sale in different parts of their territory. Finally, a State may declare that it will not be bound by Part II on formation of contracts or Part III on the rights and obligations of the buyer and seller. This latter declaration was included as part of the decision to combine into one convention the subject matter of the two 1964 Hague Conventions.

2.3   CISG Member States

2.3.1 1980 – United Nations Convention on Contracts for the International Sale of Goods

This page is updated whenever the UNCITRAL Secretariat is informed of changes in status of the Convention.

Readers are also advised to consult the United Nations Treaty Collection for authoritative status information on UNCITRAL Conventions deposited with the Secretary-General of the United Nations.

The UNCITRAL Secretariat also prepares yearly a document containing the Status of Conventions and Enactments of UNCITRAL Model Laws, which is available on the web page of the corresponding UNCITRAL Commission Session.

State	Signature	Ratification, Accession, Approval, Acceptance or Succession	Entry into force
Argentina (a)		19 July 1983 (b)	1 January 1988
Australia		17 March 1988 (b)	1 April 1989
Austria	11 April 1980	29 December 1987	1 January 1989
Belarus (a)		9 October 1989 (b)	1 November 1990
Belgium		31 October 1996 (b)	1 November 1997
Bosnia and Herzegovina		12 January 1994 (c)	6 March 1992
Bulgaria		9 July 1990 (b)	1 August 1991
Burundi		4 September 1998 (b)	1 October 1999
Canada (d)		23 April 1991 (b)	1 May 1992
Chile (a)	11 April 1980	7 February 1990	1 March 1991
China (e)	30 September 1981	11 December 1986 (f)	1 January 1988
Colombia		10 July 2001 (b)	1 August 2002
Croatia (g)		8 June 1998 (c)	8 October 1991
Cuba		2 November 1994 (b)	1 December 1995
Cyprus		7 March 2005 (b)	1 April 2006
Czech Republic (h), (i)		30 September 1993 (c)	1 January 1993
Denmark (j)	26 May 1981	14 February 1989	1 March 1990
Ecuador		27 January 1992 (b)	1 February 1993
Egypt		6 December 1982 (b)	1 January 1988

El Salvador		27 November 2006 (b)	1 December 2007
Estonia (k)		20 September 1993 (b)	1 October 1994
Finland (j)	26 May 1981	15 December 1987	1 January 1989
France	27 August 1981	6 August 1982 (f)	1 January 1988
Gabon		15 December 2004 (b)	1 January 2006
Georgia		16 August 1994 (b)	1 September 1995
Germany (l), (m)	26 May 1981	21 December 1989	1 January 1991
Ghana	11 April 1980		
Greece		12 January 1998 (b)	1 February 1999
Guinea		23 January 1991 (b)	1 February 1992
Honduras		10 October 2002 (b)	1 November 2003
Hungary (a), (n)	11 April 1980	16 June 1983	1 January 1988
Iceland (j)		10 May 2001 (b)	1 June 2002
Iraq		5 March 1990 (b)	1 April 1991
Israel		22 January 2002 (b)	1 February 2003
Italy	30 September 1981	11 December 1986	1 January 1988
Kyrgyzstan		11 May 1999 (b)	1 June 2000
Latvia (a)		31 July 1997 (b)	1 August 1998
Lesotho	18 June 1981	18 June 1981	1 January 1988
Liberia		16 September 2005 (b)	1 October 2006
Lithuania (a)		18 January 1995 (b)	1 February 1996
Luxembourg		30 January 1997 (b)	1 February 1998
Mauritania		20 August 1999 (b)	1 September 2000
Mexico		29 December 1987 (b)	1 January 1989
Moldova		13 October 1994 (b)	1 November 1995
Mongolia		31 December 1997 (b)	1 January 1999
Montenegro		23 October 2006 (c)	3 June 2006
Netherlands	29 May 1981	13 December 1990 (o)	1 January 1992
New Zealand		22 September 1994 (b)	1 October 1995
Norway (j)	26 May 1981	20 July 1988	1 August 1989
Paraguay (a)		13 January 2006 (b)	1 February 2007
Peru		25 March 1999 (b)	1 April 2000
Poland	28 September 1981	19 May 1995	1 June 1996
Republic of Korea		17 February 2004 (b)	1 March 2005

Romania		22 May 1991 (b)	1 June 1992
Russian Federation (a), (p)		16 August 1990 (b)	1 September 1991
Saint Vincent and the Grenadines (i)		12 September 2000 (b)	1 October 2001
Serbia (q)		12 March 2001 (c)	27 April 1992
Singapore (i)	11 April 1980	16 February 1995	1 March 1996
Slovakia (h), (i)		28 May 1993 (c)	1 January 1993
Slovenia		7 January 1994 (c)	25 June 1991
Spain		24 July 1990 (b)	1 August 1991
Sweden (j)	26 May 1981	15 December 1987	1 January 1989
Switzerland		21 February 1990 (b)	1 March 1991
Syrian Arab Republic		19 October 1982 (b)	1 January 1988
The former Yugoslav Republic of Macedonia		22 November 2006 (c)	17 November 1991
Uganda		12 February 1992 (b)	1 March 1993
Ukraine (a)		3 January 1990 (b)	1 February 1991
United States of America (i)	31 August 1981	11 December 1986	1 January 1988
Uruguay		25 January 1999 (b)	1 February 2000
Uzbekistan		27 November 1996 (b)	1 December 1997
Venezuela (Bolivarian Republic of)	28 September 1981		
Zambia		6 June 1986 (b)	1 January 1988

2.3.2 Parties: 70

(a) Declarations and reservations. This State declared, in accordance with articles 12 and 96 of the Convention, that any provision of article 11, article 29 or Part II of the Convention that allowed a contract of sale or its modification or termination by agreement or any offer, acceptance or other indication of intention to be made in any form other than in writing, would not apply where any party had his place of business in its territory.

(b) Accession.

(c) Succession.

(d) Declarations and reservations. Upon accession, Canada declared that, in accordance with article 93 of the Convention, the Convention would extend to Alberta, British Columbia, Manitoba, New Brunswick, Newfoundland and Labrador, Nova Scotia, Ontario, Prince Edward Island and the Northwest Territories. (Upon accession, Canada declared that, in accordance with article 95 of the Convention, with respect to British Columbia, it will not be bound by article 1, paragraph (b), of the Convention. In a notification received on 31 July 1992, Canada withdrew that declaration). In a declaration received on 9 April 1992, Canada extended the application of the Convention to Quebec and Saskatchewan. In a notification received on 29 June 1992, Canada extended the application of the Convention to the Yukon Territory. In a notification received on 18 June 2003, Canada extended the application of the Convention to the Territory of Nunavut.

(e) Declarations and reservations. Upon approving the Convention, the People's Republic of China declared that it did not consider itself bound by sub-paragraph (b) of paragraph (1) of article 1 and article 11, nor the provisions in the Convention relating to the content of article 11.

(f) Approval.

(g) Upon succeeding to the Convention, Croatia has decided, on the basis of the Constitutional Decision on Sovereignty and Independence of the Republic of Croatia of 25 June 1991 and the Decision of the Croatian Parliament of 8 October 1991, and by virtue of succession of the Socialist Federal Republic of Yugoslavia in respect of the territory of Croatia, to be considered a party to the Convention with effect from 8 October 1991, the date on which Croatia severed all constitutional and legal connections with the Socialist Federal Republic of Yugoslavia and took over its international obligations.

(h) The former Czechoslovakia signed the Convention on 1 September 1981 and deposited an instrument of ratification on 5 March 1990, with the Convention entering into force for the former Czechoslovakia on 1 April 1991. On 28 May and 30 September 1993, respectively, Slovakia and the Czech Republic, deposited instruments of succession, with effect from 1 January 1993, the date of succession of both States.

(i) Declarations and reservations. This State declared that it would not be bound by paragraph 1 (b) of article 1.

(j) Declarations and reservations. Upon ratifying the Convention, Denmark, Finland, Norway and Sweden declared, in accordance with article 92, paragraph 1, that they would not be bound by Part II of the Convention ("Formation of the Contract"). Upon ratifying the Convention, Denmark, Finland, Norway and Sweden declared, pursuant to article 94, paragraph 1 and 94, paragraph 2, that the Convention would not apply to contracts of sale where the parties have their places of business in Denmark, Finland, Iceland, Sweden or Norway. In a notification effected on 12

March 2003, Iceland declared, pursuant to article 94, paragraph 1, that the Convention would not apply to contracts of sale or to their formation where the parties had their places of business in Denmark, Finland, Iceland, Norway or Sweden.

(k) Declarations and reservations. On 9 March 2004, Estonia withdrew the reservation made upon ratification mentioned in footnote (a).

(l) The Convention was signed by the former German Democratic Republic on 13 August 1981 and ratified on 23 February 1989 and entered into force on 1 March 1990.

(m) Declarations and reservations. Upon ratifying the Convention, Germany declared that it would not apply article 1, paragraph 1 (b) in respect of any State that had made a declaration that that State would not apply article 1, paragraph 1 (b).

(n) Declarations and reservations. Upon ratifying the Convention, Hungary declared that it considered the General Conditions of Delivery of Goods between Organizations of the Member Countries of the Council for Mutual Economic Assistance to be subject to the provisions of article 90 of the Convention.

(o) Acceptance.

(p) The Russian Federation continues, as from 24 December 1991, the membership of the former Union of Soviet Socialist Republics (USSR) in the United Nations and maintains, as from that date, full responsibility for all the rights and obligations of the USSR under the Charter of the United Nations and multilateral treaties deposited with the Secretary-General.

(q) The former Yugoslavia signed and ratified the Convention on 11 April 1980 and 27 March 1985, respectively. On 12 March 2001, the former Federal Republic of Yugoslavia declared the following:

"The Government of the Federal Republic of Yugoslavia, having considered [the Convention], succeeds to the same and undertakes faithfully to perform and carry out the stipulations therein contained as from April 27, 1992, the date upon which the Federal Republic of Yugoslavia assumed responsibility for its international relations."

Bibliography

Abderrahmane, Ben "La conformité des merchandises dans la Convention du 11 avril 1980 sur les contrats de vente internationale de merchandises", Droit et Pratique Du Commerce International 1989, 551 (cited: Abderrahmane, Droit et Pratique Du Commerce International 1989, 551)

Achilles, Wilhelm-Albrecht, *Kommentar zum UN-Kaufrechtsübereinkommen (CISG)* (Neuwied, Kriftel: Luchterhand, Berlin, 2000) (cited: Achilles, *Kommentar*)

Ahrens, Hans-Jürgen "Die gesetzlichen Grundlagen der Grenzbeschlagnahme von Produktpiratteriewaren nach dem deutschen nationalen Recht" Der Betriebsberater 1997, 902 (cited: Ahrens, BB 1997, 902)

Amato, Paul "UN Convention on Contracts for the International Sale of Goods – The Open Price Term and Uniform Application: An Early Interpretation by the Hungarian Courts" (1993) 13 The Journal of Law and Commerce, 1 (cited: Amato, (1993) 13 J L & Comm, 1)

Audit, Bernard *La vente internationale de marchandises* (L.G.D.J., Paris, 1990) (cited: Audit, *Vente internationale*)

Aue, Joachim *Mängelgewährleistung im UN-Kaufrecht unter besonderer Berücksichtigung stillschweigender Zusicherungen* (Lang, Frankfurt aM, 1989) (cited: Aue, *Mängelgewährleistung*)

Baasch Andersen, Camilla "The Uniform International Sales Law and the Global Jurisconsultorium" (2005) 24 The Journal of Law and Commerce, 159 (available at www.cisg.law.pace.edu) (cited: Baasch Andersen, (2005) 24 J L & Comm, 159)

Bach, Ivo/Stieber, Christoph "Anmerkung zu AG Berlin (Mitte)" Internationales Handelsrecht 2006, 59 (cited, Bach/Stieber, IHR 2006, 59, *Anmerkung*)

Bach, Ivo/Stieber, Christoph "Die beiderseitig verursachte Unmöglichkeit im CISG" Internationales Handelsrecht 2006, 97 (cited: Bach/Stieber, IHR 2006, 97)

Beatson, Jack (ed) *Anson's Law of Contract* (28 ed, Oxford University Press, Oxford, 2002) (cited: Beatson, *Anson's Law of Contract*)

Beck, Simon "Nutzungsherausgabe bei kaufrechtlicher Ersatzlieferung" Juristische Rundschau 2006, 177 (cited: Beck, JR 2006, 177)

Benicke, Christoph "Verlust der Rechtsmängelrechte durch verspätete Rüge" in Lindenmayer/Möhring *Kommentierte BGH-Rechtsprechung* 2006, 1822 (cited: Benicke in Lindenmayer/Möhring)

Benjamin, Judah *Benjamin's Sale of Goods* (5 ed, Sweet & Maxwell, London, 1997) (cited: Benjamin, *Sale of Goods*)

Berg, Daniel Friedrich *Die Rückabwicklung gescheiterter Verträge im spanischem und deutschem Recht*, Schriften der Deutsch-Spanischen Juristenvereinigung Vol 8 (Peter Lang, Frankfurt aM, 2003) (cited: Berg, *Rückabwicklung*)

Bergsten, Eric/Miller, Anthony "The Remedy of Reduction of Price" (1979) 27 American Journal of Comparative Law 255 (cited: Bergsten/Miller, (1979) 27 Am J Comp L, 255)

Bianca, Cesare Massimo/Bonell, Michael Joachim *Commentary on the International Sales Law* (Giuffrè, Mailand, 1987) (cited: commentator in Bianca/ Bonell, *Commentary*)

Blodgett, Paul C "The United Nations Convention on the Sale of Goods and the 'Battle of the Forms'" (1989) 18 Colorado Law 423 (cited: Blodgett (1989) 18 Col Law, 423)

Bonell, Michael "Vertragsverhandlungen und culpa in contrahendo nach dem Wiener Kaufrechtsübereinkommen" Recht der Internationalen Wirtschaft 1990, 693 (cited: Bonell, RIW 1990, 693)

Brandi-Dohrn, Matthias *Gewährleistung bei Hard-und Softwaremängeln* (2nd ed, Beck, München, 1994) (cited: Brandi-Dohrn, *Gewährleistung*)

Bridge, Michael *The International Sale of Goods – Law and Practice* (Oxford University Press, Oxford, 2007) (cited: Bridge, *International Sale of Goods*)

Bucher, Eugen "Preisvereinbarung als Voraussetzung der Vertragsgültigkeit beim Kauf – Zum angeblichen Widerspruch zwischen Art. 14 und Art. 55 des 'Wiener Kaufrechts'" in Sturm, Fritz (ed) *Mélanges Paul Piotet: Recueil de travaux offerts à M.P. Piotet* (Staempfli, Bern, 1990) 371 (cited: Bucher, *FS Piotet*, 371)

Bucher, Eugen "Preisvereinbarung als Voraussetzung der Vertragsgültigkeit beim Kauf; zum angeblichen Widerspruch zwischen Art. 14 und Art. 55 des 'Wiener Kaufrecht'" in Bucher, Eugen (ed) *Wiener Kaufrecht* (Stämpfli, Bern, 1991) 53 (cited: Bucher, *Preisvereinbarung*, 53)

Bucher, Eugen "Überblick über die Neuerungen des Wiener Kaufrechts; dessen Verhältnis zur Kaufrechtstradition und zum nationalen Recht" in Bucher, Eugen (ed) *Wiener Kaufrecht* (Stämpfli, Bern, 1991) 13 (cited: Bucher, *Neuerungen*, 13)

Burrows, Andrew/Todd, Stephen *Contract Law in NZ* (2 ed, Brookers, Wellington, 2002) (cited: Burrows/Todd, *Contract Law*)

Burrows, John/Finn, Jeremy/Todd, Stephen *Law of Contract in New Zealand* (3 ed, LexisNexis NZ Ltd, Wellington, 2007) (cited: Burrows/Finn/Todd, *Law of Contract*)

Butler, Petra "The Doctrine of Parole Evidence Rule and Consideration – A Deterrence to the Common Law Lawyer?" SIAC *Celebrating Success: 25 Years United Nations Convention on Contracts for the International Sale of Goods* (SIAC, 2006, Singapore) 54 (cited: Butler, "Doctrine of Parole Evidence Rule and Consideration", 54)

Bydlinski, Peter "Das allgemeine Vertragsrecht" in Doralt, Peter (ed) *Das UNCITRAL-Kaufrecht im Vergleich zum österreichischen Recht* (Manz, Wien, 1985) 57 (cited: Bydlinski, *Allgemeines Vertragsrecht*, 57)

Bydlinski, Peter "Der Sachbegriff im elektronischen Zeitalter: zeitlos oder anpassungsbedürftig?"Archiv für die civilistische Praxis 198 (1998) 288 (cited: Bydlinski, AcP 198 (1998) 288)

Center for Comparative and Foreign Law Studies (ed) *UNILEX, International Case Law and Bibliography on the UN Convention on Contracts for the International Sale of Goods* (Loose-leaf) (Transnational Juris Publications, Irvington-on-Hudson, NY, 1995) (cited: *UNILEX*)

Cherednychenko, Olga "The Constitutionalisation of Contract Law: Something New under the Sun?" 8.1 (March 2004) EJCL http://www.ejcl.org/81/ art81-3.html (last accessed 1 Feb 2008) (cited: Cherednychenko, 8.1 (March 2004) EJCL http://www.ejcl.org/81/art81-3.html)

Chiomenti, Cristina "Does the Choice of National Rules Entail an Implicit Exclusion of the CISG?" (2005) European Legal Forum I, 141 (cited: Chiomenti, (2005) European Legal Forum I, 141)

Cohn, Ernst "The Defence of Uncertainty: a Study in the Interpretation of the Uniform Law on International Sales Act 1967" (1974) 23 International and Comparative Law Quarterly, 520 (cited: Cohn, (1974) 23 Int'l & Comp L Q, 520)

Conrad, Thomas *Die Lieferung mangelhafter Ware als Grund für eine Vertragsaufhebung im einheitlichen UN-Kaufrecht* (Schulthess, Zürich, 1999) (cited: Conrad, *Die Lieferung mangelhafter Ware*)

Coote, Brian "The Instantaneous Transmission of Acceptances" (1971) 4 New Zealand University Law Review, 331 (cited: Coote, (1971) 4 NZULR, 331)

Cox, Trevor "Chaos versus Uniformity: The Divergent News of Software in the International Community" (2000) 4 Vindobona Journal of International Commercial Law and Arbitration, 3 (cited: Cox, (2000) 4 VJ, 3)

Cuncannon, Fionnghuala "The Case for Specific Performance as the Primary Remedy for Breach of Contract in New Zealand" (2004) 35 Victoria University of Wellington Law Review, 657 (cited: Cuncannon, (2004) 35 VUWLR, 657)

Dicey, Albert/Morris, John/Collins, Lawrence *The Conflict of Laws* (14th ed, Sweet & Maxwell, London, 2006) (cited: Dicey, *Conflict of Laws*)

Diedrich, Frank "Anwendbarkeit des Wiener Kaufrechts auf Softwareüberlassungsverträge" Recht der Internationalen Wirtschaft 1993, 441 (cited: Diedrich, "Anwendbarkeit des Wiener Kaufrechts", RIW 1993, 441)

Diedrich, Frank "Anwendung der 'Vorschaltlösung' im Internationalen Kaufrecht" Recht der Internationalen Wirtschaft 1993, 758 (cited: Diedrich, RIW 1993, 758)

Diedrich, Frank "Lückenfüllung im Internationalen Einheitsrecht" Recht der Internationalen Wirtschaft 1995, 353 (cited: Diedrich, RIW 1995, 353)

Diedrich, Frank "The CISG and Computer Software Revisited" (2002) 6 Vindobona Journal of International Commercial Law and Arbitration, 55 (cited: Diedrich, (2002) 6 VJ, 55)

DiMatteo, Larry/Dhooge, Lucien/Greene, Stephanie/Maurer, Virginia/Pagnattaro, Marisa *International Sales Law: A Critical Analysis of CISG Jurisprudence* (Cambridge University Press, NY, 2005) (cited: DiMatteo/Dhooge/ Greene/Maurer/Pagnattaro, *International Sales Law*)

Dölle, Hans (ed) *Kommentar zum Einheitlichen Kaufrecht* (Beck, München, 1976) (cited: Dölle, *Kommentar*)

Durry, Georges *La Distinction De La Responsabilité Contractuelle Et De La Responsabilité Delictuelle* (McGill University Press, Montreal, 1986) (cited: Durry, *La Distinction De La Responsabilité Contractuelle*)

Enderlein, Fritz/Graefrath, Bernhard "Nochmals: Deutsche Einheit und internationales Kaufrecht" Betriebsberater 1991, Suppl No 6, 8 (cited: Enderlein/ Graefrath, BB 1991, Suppl No 6, 8)

Enderlein, Fritz/Maskow Dietrich/Strohbach Heinz *Internationales Kaufrecht* (Haufe, Berlin, 1991) (cited: commentator in Enderlein/Maskow/Strohbach, *Internationales Kaufrecht*)

Enderlein, Fritz/Maskow Dietrich *International Sales Law* (Oceana Publ, Dobbs Ferry, New York, 1992) (cited: Enderlein/Maskow, *International Sales Law*)

Enderlein, Fritz "Die Verpflichtung des Verkäufers zur Einhaltung des Lieferzeitraums und die Rechte des Käufers bei dessen Nichteinhaltung nach dem UN-Übereinkommen über Verträge über den internationalen Warenkauf" Praxis des Internationalen Privat- und Verfahrensrechts 1991, 313 (cited: Enderlein, IPRax 1991, 313)

Endler, Maximillian/Daub, Jan "Internationale Softwareüberlassung und UN-Kaufrecht" Computer und Recht 1993, 601 (cited: Endler/Daub, CR 1993)

Farnsworth, E Allan "Duties of Good Faith and Fair Dealing under the UNIDROIT Principles, Relevant International Conventions, and National Laws" (1995) 3 Tulane Journal of International Conventions and Comparative Law, 47 (cited: Farnsworth, Tul J Int'l and Comp L, 47)

Faust, Florian *Die Voraussehbarkeit des Schadens gemäß Art. 74 Satz 2 CISG* (Mohr Siebeck, Tübingen, 1996) (cited: Faust, *Die Voraussehbarkeit*)

Fawcett, James/Harris, Jonathan/Bridge, Michael *International Sale of Goods in the Conflict of Laws* (Oxford University Press, Oxford, 2005) (cited: Fawcett/Harris/Bridge, *International Sale of Goods*)

Ferrari, Franco "Einige kurze Anmerkungen zur Anwendbarkeit des UN-Kaufrechts beim Vertragsschluß über Internet" (2000) European Law Forum, 301 (cited: Ferrari, (2000) European L Forum, 301)

Ferrari, Franco "Italienische CISG-Rechtsprechung - Eine Übersicht" Zeitschrift für Internationales Handelsrecht 2001, 179 (cited: Ferrari, IHR 2001, 179)

Ferrari, Franco "The Relationship Between International Uniform Contract Law Conventions" (2003) 22 The Journal of Law and Commerce, 57 (cited: Ferrari, (2003) 22 J L & Com, 57)

Ferrari, Franco "Uniform Interpretation of the 1980 Uniform Sales Law" (1994) 24 Georgia Journal of International & Comparative Law, 183 (cited: Ferrari, (1994) 24 GA J Int'l & Comp L, 183)

Fischer, Jörg *Die Unsicherheitseinrede* (Lang, Frankfurt aM, 1988) (cited: Fischer, *Die Unsicherheitseinrede*)

Fischer, Nicole H *Die Unmöglichkeit der Leistung im internationalen Kauf- und Vertragsrecht* (Duncker & Humblot, Berlin, 2001) (cited: Fischer, *Die Unmöglichkeit der Leistung*)

Flannigan, Robert "The Legal Construction of Rights of First Refusal" (1997) 76 Canadian Bar Rev 1 (cited: Flannigan, (1997) 76 Canadian Bar Rev, 1)

Frense, Astrid *Grenzen der formularmäßigen Freizeichnung im einheitlichen Kaufrecht* (Recht und Wirtschaft, Heidelberg, 1993)

Frigge, Bettina *Externe Lücken und Internationales Privatrecht nach dem UN-Kaufrecht (Art 7 Abs 2)* (Lang, Frankfurt aM, 1994) (cited: Frigge, *Externe Lücken und Internationales Privatrecht*)

Gabriel, Henry *Contracts for the Sale of Goods: A Comparison of Domestic and International Law* (Oceana Publ, Dobbs Ferry, New York, 2004) (cited: Gabriel, *Contracts for the Sale of Goods*)

Galston, Nina/Smit, Hans (ed) *International Sales: The United Nations Convention on Contracts for the International Sale of Goods* (Matthew Bender, Albany, New York, 1984) (cited: Galston/Smith (ed) *International Sales*)

Geldsetzer, Annette *Einvernehmliche Änderung und Aufhebung von Verträgen* (Nomos, Baden-Baden, 1993) (cited: Geldsetzer, *Einvernehmliche Änderung*)

Grebler, Eduardo "The Convention on International Sale of Goods and Brazilian Law: Are the Differences Irreconcilable?" (2005–2006) 25 Journal of Law & Commerce, 467 (cited: Grebler, 25 J L & Com, 467)

Grossfeld, Bernhard/Winship, Peter "The Law Professor Refugee" (1992) 18 Syracuse Journal of International Law and Commerce, 3 (cited: Grossfeld, (1992) 18 Syracuse J Int'l L & Com, 3)

Gruber, Georg *Geldwertschwankungen und handelsrechtliche Verträge in Deutschland und Frankreich* (Berlin, Duncker & Humblot, 2002) (cited: Gruber, *Geldwertschwankungen*)

Hager, Günter *Die Rechtsbehelfe des Verkäufers wegen Nichtabnahme der Ware nach amerikanischem, deutschem und einheitlichem Haager Kaufrecht,* (Metzner, Frankfurt am Main, 1975) (cited: Hager, *Rechtsbehelfe des Verkäufers*)

Halsbury's Laws of England, vol 41 (Reissue, LexisNexis, Bath, 2005) Sale of Goods and Supply of Services (cited: *Halsbury's Laws of England*)

Hartnell, Helen "Rousing the Sleeping Dog: The Validity Exception to the Convention on Contracts for the International Sales of Goods" (1996) 18 Yale Journal of International Law, 77 (cited: Hartnell, (1996) 18 Yale J Int'l L, 77)

Hawes, Cynthia et al. *Butterworths Introduction to Commercial Law* (5 ed LexisNexis NZ Ltd, Wellington, 2005) (cited: Hawes et al., *Butterworths Introduction to Commercial Law*)

Hawes, Cynthia with Hon Justice Smellie (consulting ed) *The Laws of New Zealand* (LexisNexis, Wellington, 2007) Sale of Goods, part VII, para 357 (last updated 1 March 2007) www.lexisnexis.com (cited: *The Laws of New Zealand*)

Hellner, Jan "Ipso facto avoidance" in Horst Ehmann (ed) *Privatautonomie, Eigentum und Verantwortung, Festgabe für Hermann Weitnauer zum 70. Geburtstag*, (Duncker & Humblot, Berlin, 1980) 85 (cited: Hellner, *Ipso facto avoidance*)

Hellwege, Phillip *Die Rückabwicklung gegenseitiger Verträge als einheitliches Problem* (Mohr Siebeck, Tübingen, 2004) (cited: Hellwege, *Rückabwicklung gegenseitiger Verträge*)

Henninger, Michael *Die Frage der Beweislast im Rahmen des UN-Kaufrechts, zugleich eine rechtsvergleichende Grundlagenstudie zur Beweislast* (V. Florentz, München, 1995) (cited: Henninger, *Die Frage der Beweislast*)

Herber, Rolf/Czerwenka, Beate *Internationales Kaufrecht, Kommentar zu dem Übereinkommen der Vereinten Nationen vom 11. April 1980 über Verträge über den internationalen Warenkauf* (Beck, München, 1991) (cited: Herber/Czerwenka, *Internationales Kaufrecht*)

Herber, Rolf "Anwendungsbereich des UNCITRAL-Kaufrechtsübereinkommens" in Peter Doralt (ed) *Das UNCITRAL-Kaufrecht im Vergleich zum österreichischen Recht* (Manz, Wien, 1985) 28 (cited: Herber, *Anwendungsbereich*)

Herber, Rolf "Anwendungsvoraussetzungen und Anwendungsbereich des Einheitlichen Kaufrechts" in Peter Schlechtriem (ed), *Einheitliches Kaufrecht und nationales Obligationenrecht* (Nomos, Baden-Baden, 1987) 97 (cited: Herber, *Anwendungsvoraussetzungen*)

Herber, Rolf "Das Arbeiten des Ausschusses der Vereinten Nationen für internationales Handelsrecht (UNCITRAL)" Recht der Internationalen Wirtschaft 1974, 577; Recht der Internationalen Wirtschaft 1976, 125; Recht der Internationalen Wirtschaft 1977, 314; Recht der Internationalen Wirtschaft 1980, 81 (cited: Herber, RIW 1974, 577; RIW 1976, 125; RIW 1977, 314; RIW 1980, 81)

Herber, Rolf "Internationales Handelsrecht – ein für die Praxis wichtiges, doch für sie bisher zu wenig erschlossenes Rechtsgebiet" Zeitschrift für Transportrecht 1999, 1 (cited: Herber, Z TranspR 1999, 1)

Herber, Rolf "Mangelfolgeschäden nach dem CISG und nationales Deliktsrecht" Internationales Handelsrecht 2001, 187 (cited: Herber, IHR 2001, 187)

Herbots, Jacques/Pauwles, François "Responsabilité du fait d'auxiliaires dans la convention de Vienne d'un point de vue de droit compare" in *Festschrift Neumayer* (Basel, Recht und Gesellschaft, 1997) (cited: Herbots/Pauwles in *FS Neumayer*)

Heuzé, Vincent *La vente internationale de marchandises – Droit uniforme* (GLN Joly, Paris, 1992) (cited: Heuzé, *La vente internationale*)

Heuzé, Vincent *Traité des Contracts: La vente international de marchandise* (2 ed, GLN Joly, Paris, 2000) (cited: Heuzé, *Traité des Contracts*)

Hillman, Robert "Article 29 (2) of the United Nations Convention on Contracts for the International Sale of Goods: A New Effort at Clarifying the Legal Effect of 'No Oral Modification' Clauses" (1988) 21 Cornell International Law Journal, 449 (cited: Hillman, (1988) 21 Cornell Int'l L J, 449)

Hirner, Matthias *Der Rechtsbehelf der Minderung nach dem UN-Kaufrecht (CISG)* (Lang, Frankfurt aM, 2000) (cited: Hirner, *Rechtsbehelf der Minderung*)

Hoeren, Thomas "Informationspflichten im Internet – Im Lichte des neuen UWG" Wertpapier-Mitteilungen 2004, 2461 (cited: Hoeren, WM 2004, 2461)

Hohloch, Gerhard "Rechtsprechungsübersicht – Entlastung des Verkäufers und Zulässigkeit eines Grundurteils" Juristische Schulung, 1999, 1235 (cited: Hohloch, JuS 1999, 1235)

Holl, Volker/Keßler, Oliver "'Selbstgeschaffenes Recht der Wirtschaft' und Einheitsrecht – Die Stellung der Handelsbräuche und Gepflogenheiten im Wiener UN-Kaufrecht" Recht der Internationalen Wirtschaft 1995, 457 (cited: Holl/Keßler, RIW 1995, 457)

Honnold, John (ed) *Documentary History of the Uniform Law for International Sales. The Studies, Deliberations and Decisions that led to the 1980 United Nations Convention with Introductions and Explanations* (Kluwer Law and Taxation, Deventer, 1989) (cited: Honnold (ed) *Documentary History*)

Honnold, John *Uniform Law for International Sale under the 1980 United Nations Convention* (3 ed, Kluwer Law International, The Hague, 1999) (cited: Honnold, *Uniform Law for International Sales*)

Honsell, Heinrich/Schnyder, Anton K/Straub, Ralf Michael (eds) *Kommentar zum UN-Kaufrecht* (Springer, Heidelberg, 1997) (cited: Honsell et al. (eds) *Kommentar zum UN-Kaufrecht*)

Honsell, Heinrich "Die Vertragsverletzung des Verkäufers nach dem Wiener Kaufrecht" Schweizerische Juristen-Zeitung 1992, 345 (cited: Honsell, SJZ 1992, 345)

Honsell, Heinrich *Schweizerisches Obligationenrecht*, Besonderer Teil (8 ed, Stämpfli Verlag, Bern, 2006) (cited: Honsell, OR BT)

Hornung, Rainer *Die Rückabwicklung gescheiterter Verträge nach französischem, deutschem und nach Einheitsrecht* (Nomos, Baden-Baden, 1997) (cited: Hornung, Rückabwicklung)

Huber, Peter/Mullis, Alastair *The CISG: A new textbook for students and practitioners* (Sellier European Law Publishers, München, 2007) (cited: Huber/Mullis, *The CISG*)

Huber, Peter "Neues deutsches Kaufrecht und UN-Kaufrecht" in *Festschrift für Horst Konzen* (Mohr Siebeck, Tübingen, 2006) (cited: Huber in *FS für Horst Konzen*)

Huber, Ulrich "Der UNCITRAL-Entwurf eines Übereinkommens über internationale Warenkaufverträge" Rabels Zeitschrift 43 (1979) 413 (cited: Huber, RabelsZ 43 (1979))

Huber, Ulrich *Leistungsstörungen* (Bd I) (Mohr Siebeck, Tübingen, 1999) (cited: Huber, *Leistungsstörungen*)

Hyland, Richard "Conformity of Goods to the Contract Under the United Nations Sales Convention and the Uniform Commercial Code" in Schlechtriem, Peter (ed) *Einheitliches Kaufrecht und nationales Obligationenrecht* (Nomos, Baden-Baden, 1987) 305 (cited: Hyland in Schlechtriem (ed), *Einheitliches Kaufrecht*)

Janal, Ruth *Sanktionen und Rechtsbehelfe bei der Verletzung verbraucherschützender Informations- und Dokumentationspflichten im elektronischen Geschäftsverkehr* (Tenea Verlag für Medien, Berlin, 2003) (cited: Janal, *Sanktionen und Rechtsbehelfe*)

Janssen, André "Die Einbeziehung von allgemeinen Geschäftsbedingungen in internationale Kaufverträge und die Bedeutung der UNIDROIT – und der Lando-Principles" Internationales Handelsrecht 2004, 194 (cited: Janssen, IHR 2004, 194)

Janssen, André "Nach welchem Recht richtet sich die Einbeziehung von Allgemeinen Geschäftsbedingungen in den Niederlanden?" Internationales Handelsrecht 2005, 155 (cited: Janssen, IHR 2005, 155)

Jung, Reinhard *Die Beweislastverteilung im UN-Kaufrecht* (Lang, Frankfurt aM, 1996) (cited: Jung, *Beweislastverteilung*)

Karollus, Martin *UN-Kaufrecht* (Springer, Wien, 1991) (cited: Karollus, *UN-Kaufrecht*)

Kastely, Amy "The Right to Require Performance in International Sales: Towards an International Interpretation of the Vienna Convention" 63 (1988) Washington Law Review, 607 (cited: Kastely, (1988) 63 Wash L Rev, 607)

Kegel, Gerhard/Schurig, Klaus *Internationales Privatrecht* (8 ed, Beck, 2000) (cited: Kegel/Schurig, *Internationales Privatrecht*)

Kelso, J Clark "The United Nations Convention on Contracts for the International Sale of Goods: Contract Formation and the Battle of the Forms" (1983) 21 Columbia Journal Transnational Law, 529 (cited: Kelso, (1983) 21 Colum J Transnat'l L, 529)

Kern, Christoph "Ein einheitliches Zurückbehaltungsrecht im UN-Kaufrecht?" Zeitschrift für Europäisches Privatrecht 2000, 837 (cited: Kern, ZEuP 2000, 837)

Kern, Christoph "Leistungsverweigerungsrechte im UN-Kaufrecht" in Will, Michael (ed) *Rudolf Meyer zum Abschied* (1999) 19 Schriftenreihe deutscher Jura-Studenten in Genf, 73 (cited: Kern in Will (ed) *Rudolf Meyer*, 73)

Kindler, Peter "Sachmängelhaftung, Aufrechnung und Zinssatzbemessung: Typische Fragen des UN-Kaufrechts in der gerichtlichen Praxis" Praxis des Internationalen Privat- und Verfahrensrechts 1996, 16 (cited: Kindler, IPRax 1996, 16)

Koch, Robert *The Concept of Fundamental Breach of Contract under the United Nations Convention on Contracts for the International Sale of Goods*, (Kluwer Law International, The Hague, 1999) 35 (cited, Koch, 35)

Kock, Annette *Nebenpflichten im UN-Kaufrecht, dargestellt am Beispiel der Pflichten des Verkäufers* (S. Roderer Verlag, Regensburg, 1995) (cited: Kock, *Nebenpflichten*)

Köhler, Martin *Die Haftung nach UN-Kaufrecht im Spannungsverhältnis zwischen Vertrag und Delikt* (Mohr Siebeck, Tübingen, 2003) (cited: Köhler, *Haftung nach UN-Kaufrecht*)

Koller, Thomas/Stadler, Michael "Verunreinigter Paprika – ein Prüfungsfall des UN-Kaufrechts (CISG) mit prozessualen Aspekten" recht 2004, 10 (cited: Koller/Stadler, recht 2004, 10)

Koller, Thomas/Stalder, Michael "Die Vertragswidrigkeit der Ware im UN-Kaufrecht (CISG) bei national unterschiedlichen öffentlichrechtlichen Beschaffenheitsvorschriften" in *Gauchs Welt, Festschrift für Peter Gauch zum 65. Geburtstag* (Schulthess, Zürich, 2004) 477 (cited: Koller/Stadler *FS Gauch*)

Koller, Thomas "Das Regressrecht des CISG-Importeurs gegen den CISG-Verkäufer bei Produkthaftungsfällen Körperschäden" in Bucher, Eugen/Canaris, Claus-Wilhelm/Honsell, Heinrich/Koller, Thomas (eds) *Norm und Wirkung, Festschrift Wolfgang Wiegand* (Staempfli, Bern, 2005) 422 (cited: Koller in Bucher et al. (eds) *Norm und Wirkung*)

König, Detlev "Voraussehbarkeit des Schadens als Grenze vertraglicher Haftung – zu Art. 82, 86, 87 EKG" in Leser, Hans/v Marschall, Wolfgang (eds) *Das Haager Einheitliche Kaufgesetz und das Deutsche Schuldrecht, Kolloquium zum 65. Geburtstag von Ernst von Caemmerer* (C.F. Müller, Karlsruhe, 1973) 75 (cited: König, "Voraussehbarkeit des Schadens")

Königer, Ursula *Die Bestimmung der gesetzlichen Zinshöhe nach dem deutschen Internationalen Privatrecht. Eine Untersuchung unter besonderer Berücksichtigung der Artt. 78 und 84 I UN-Kaufrecht (CISG)* (Duncker & Humblot, Berlin, 1997) (cited: Königer)

Koziol, Helmut/Welser, Rudolf *Grundriß des bürgerlichen Rechts*, vol I, Allgem Teil (12 ed), vol II, Schuldrecht (11 ed) (Manz, Wien, 2000/2002) (cited: Koziol/Welser, *Grundriß des bürgerlichen Rechts*)

Kramer, Ernst "Konsensprobleme im Rahmen des UN-Kaufrechts" in Fischer-Czermak, Constance/Kletecka, Andreas/Schauer, Martin/Zankl, Wolfgang (eds) *Festschrift Rudolf Welser* (Manz, Wien, 2004) 539 (cited: Kramer in *FS Welser)*

Kramer, Ernst "Neues aus Gesetzgebung, Praxis und Lehre zum Vertragsschluss" Basler Juristische Mitteilungen 1995, 1 (cited: Kramer, BJM 1995)

Kramer, Ernst "Uniform Interpretation von Einheitsprivatrecht" Juristische Blätter (Österreich) 1996, 137 (cited as Kramer, öst JBl 1996, 137)

Kramer, Ernst "Modifizierte Auftragsbestätigung. Schweigen als Annahme des geänderten Antrags" (Urteilsanmerkung zu BGH NJW 1995, 1671) Entscheidungen zum Wirtschaftsrecht 1995, 639 (cited: Kramer, EWiR 1995, 639)

Krebs, Markus "Das UN-Kaufrecht ist nicht anwendbar auf Garantieverträge des Verkäufers mit Abnehmern des Käufers" (2001) 1 European Law Forum, 16 (cited: Krebs, (2001) 1 European L Forum, 16)

Krebs, Markus *Die Rückabwicklung im UN-Kaufrecht* (Beck, München, 2000) (cited: Krebs, *Die Rückabwicklung im UN-Kaufrecht*)

Kren-Kostkiewicz, Jolanta/Schwander, Ivo "Zum Anwendungsbereich des UN-Kaufrechtsübereinkommens" in Majoros, Ferenc (ed) *Emptio-Venditio inter nations, Festschrift für Karl Heinz Neumayer* (VRG-Verlag, Basel, 1997) 33 (cited: Kren-Kostkiewicz/Schwander, *FS Neumayer*)

Kreuzer, Karl "Stand und Perspektiven des Europäischen Internationalen Privatrechts- Wie europäisch soll das Europäische Internationale Privatrecht sein?" RabelsZ 70 (2006) 1 (cited: Kreuzer, RabelsZ 70 (2006) 1)

Landfermann, Hans-Georg, "Das UNCITRAL-Übereinkommen über die Verjährung beim internationalen Warenkauf" Rabels Zeitschrift 39 (1975) 253 (cited: Landfermann, RabelsZ 39 (1975) 253)

Lando, Ole/Beale, Hugh (ed) *Principles of European Contract Law* Part I and II (Kluwer International, The Hague, 2000) (cited: Lando, *Principles of European Contract Law Part I and II*)

Lando, Ole/Clive, Eric/Zimmermann, Reinhard (ed) *Principles of European Contract Law* Part III (Kluwer International, The Hague, 2003) (cited: Lando, *Principles of European Contract Law Part III*)

Lavers, Richard M "CISG: To Use, or Not to Use?" (1993) International Business Law, 11 (cited: Lavers, (1993) Int'l Bus Law, 11)

Leible, Stephan/Sosnitza, Olaf "Rechtsprechungsübersicht zum Recht des Internet und des E-Commerce im Jahr 2004" Der Betriebsberater 2005, 725 (cited: Leible/Sosnitza, BB 2005, 725)

Leser, Hans/Marschall von Bieberstein, Wolfgang (ed) *Das Haager Einheitliche Kaufgesetz und das Deutsche Schuldrecht. Kolloquium zum 65. Geburtstag von Ernst von Caemmerer* (C.F. Müller, Karlsruhe, 1973) (cited: Leser/ von Bieberstein, *Das Haager Einheitliche Kaufgesetz*)

Leser, Hans "Vertragsaufhebung und Rückabwicklung unter dem UN-Kaufrecht" in Peter Schlechtriem (ed), *Einheitliches Kaufrecht und nationales Obligationenrecht,* (Nomos, Baden-Baden, 1987) 225 (cited: Leser in Schlechtriem (ed) *Einheitliches Kaufrecht*, 225)

Lessiak, Rudolf "UNCITRAL-Kaufrechtsabkommen und Irrtumsanfechtung" Österreichische Juristischen Blätter 1989, 487 (cited: Lessiak, öst JBl 1989, 487)

Lohmann, Arnd, *Parteiautonomie und UN-Kaufrecht* (Mohr Siebeck, Tübingen, 2005) (cited: Lohmann, *Parteiautonomie*)

Lookofsky, Joseph "*Understanding the CISG in the U.S.A.: a compact guide to the 1980 United Nations Convention on Contracts for the International Sale of Goods*" (Kluwer Law International, Boston, 1995) (cited: Lookofsky, *Understanding the CISG*)

Lookofsky, Joseph "In Dubio pro Conventione? Some Thoughts about Opt-Outs, Computer Programs and pre-emption under the 1980 Vienna Sales Convention (CISG)" (2003) 13 Duke Journal of Comparative & International Law, 263 (cited as Lookofsky, (2003) 13 Duke J of Comp & Int'l L, 263)

Lookofsky, Joseph "The 1980 United Nations Convention on Contracts for the International Sale of Goods" in Herborts, Jacques/Blanpain, Roger (eds) *International Encyclopaedia of Laws – Contracts*, Suppl. 29 (Kluwer Law International, The Hague, 2000) 37 (cited: Lookofsky, 2000 "The 1980 United Nations Convention", 37)

Lookofsky, Joseph *Understanding the CISG in Scandinavia* (DJOF Publishing, Copenhagen, 1996) (cited: Lookofsky, *Understanding the CISG in Scandinavia*)

Lüderitz, Alexander (ed) *Kommentar zum EKG und CISK* in Hans Soergel, *Bürgerliches Gesetzbuch mit Einführungsgesetz und Nebengesetzen,* vol 3,

Schuldrecht II (12 ed, Kohlhammer, Stuttgart, 1991) (cited: commentator in Soergel)

Lurger, Briggitta "Die wesentliche Vertragsverletzung nach Art. 25 CISG" Internationales Handelsrecht 2001, 91 (cited: Lurger, IHR 2001, 91)

Lutz, Henning "The CISG and Common Law Courts: Is There Really a Problem?" 35 (2004) VUWLR, 711 (cited: Lutz, 35 (2004) VUWLR, 711)

Magnus, Ulrich (ed) "UN-Kaufrecht" in Julius Staudinger *von Staudingers Kommentar zum Bürgerlichen Gesetzbuch mit Einführungsgesetz und Nebengesetzen,* (13 ed, Sellier/de Gruyter, Berlin, 1995, Neubearbeitung 1999) (cited: Magnus in *Staudinger*)

Magnus, Ulrich "Aktuelle Entwicklungen des UN-Kaufrechts" Zeitschrift für Europäisches Privatrecht 2002, 523 (cited: Magnus, ZEuP 2002, 523)

Magnus, Ulrich "Aufhebungsrecht des Käufers und Nacherfüllungsrecht des Verkäufers im UN-Kaufrecht" in Schwenzer, Ingeborg/Hager, Günter *Festschrift Peter Schlechtriem* (Mohr Siebeck, Tübingen, 2003) 599 (cited: Magnus in *FS Schlechtriem*, 599)

Magnus, Ulrich "Das UN-Kaufrecht tritt in Kraft!" Rabels Zeitschrift 51 (1987) 123 (cited: Magnus, RabelsZ 51 (1987) 123)

Magnus, Ulrich "Das UN-Kaufrecht und die Erfüllungsortzuständigkeit in der neuen EuGVO" Internationales Handelsrecht 2002, 45 (cited: Magnus, IHR 2002, 45)

Magnus, Ulrich "Die allgemeinen Grundsätze im UN-Kaufrecht" Rabels Zeitschrift 59 (1995) 467 (cited: Magnus, RabelsZ 59 (1995) 467)

Magnus, Ulrich "Die Rügeobliegenheit des Käufers im UN-Kaufrecht" TransportRecht- Internationales Handelsrecht 1999, 29 (cited: Magnus, TranspR 1999, 29)

Magnus, Ulrich "Stand und Entwicklungen des UN-Kaufrechts" Zeitschrift für Europäisches Privatrecht 1995, 202 (cited: Magnus, ZEuP 1995, 202)

Magnus, Ulrich "Zum räumlichen internationalen Anwendungsbereich des UN-Kaufrechts und zur Mängelrüge" Praxis des Internationalen Privat- und Verfahrensrechts 1993, 390 (cited: Magnus, IPRax 1993, 390)

Marly, Jochen *Softwareüberlassungsverträge* (3 ed, Beck, München, 2000) (cited: Marly, *Softwareüberlassungsverträge*)

Maskow, Dietrich *The Convention on the International Sale of Goods from the Perspective of the Socialist Countries,* in *La Vendita Internazionale* (Giuffré Editoré, Milan, 1981) (cited: Maskow, *Convention on the International Sale of Goods*)

McLauchlan, David "Defying Common Sense in Contract – The 'Exact Compliance' Rule/Earlier Court of Appeal Decisions" [2005] New Zealan Law Journal 300 (cited: McLauchlan, [2005] NZLJ, 300)

McLauchlan, David "The Agreement to Negotiate in Good faith: A Non-justiciable Contract?" (2005) 11 New Zealand Business Law Quarterly, 454 (cited: McLauchlan, (2005) 11 NZBLQ, 454)

McManus, John *The Law of Contracts* (Irwin Law Inc, Toronto, 2005) (cited: McManus, *The Law of Contracts*)

Meyer, Justus "'Zahlungsverzug' im UN-Kaufrecht und UN-Vertragsrecht" in *Gesetz, Recht und Rechtsgeschichte* in Baumann, Wolfgang/Dickhuth-Harrach, Hans-Jürgen/Marotzke, Wolfgang (eds) *Festschrift für Gerhard Otte* (Sellier European Law Publishers, München, 2005) 241 (cited: Meyer, *FS Otte*, 241)

Meyer, Justus "Verbraucherverträge im UN-Kaufrecht und EU-Vertragsrecht" in Hay, Peter (ed) *Balancing of Interests - Liber Amicorum* (Verlag Recht und Wirtschaft, Frankfurt am Main, 2005) 297 (cited: Meyer in Hay (ed) 297)

Mohs, Florian "Anmerkung zu BGer (13 November 2003)" Internationales Handelsrecht 2004, 219 (cited: Mohs, IHR 2004, 219)

Mohs, Florian "Die Vertragswidrigkeit im Rahmen des Art. 82 Abs. 2 lit. c CISG" Internationales Handelsrecht 2002, 59 (cited: Mohs, IHR 2002)

Mowbray, Jacqueline "The Application of the United Nations Convention on Contracts for the International Sale of Goods to E-Commerce Transactions: The Implications for Asia" (2003) 7 Vindobona Journal of International Commercial Law & Arbitration, 121 (cited Mowbray, VJ, 121)

Müller, Tobias *Ausgewählte Fragen der Beweislastverteilung im UN-Kaufrecht im Lichte aktueller Rechtsprechung, Beiträge zum Internationalen Wirtschaftsrecht* (Sellier European Law Publishers, München, 2005) (cited: Müller, *Beweislastverteilung*)

Neumayer, Karl/Ming, Catherine *Convention de Vienne sur les contrats de vente internationale de marchandises, Commentaire* (CEDIDAC, Lausanne, 1993) (cited: Neumayer/Ming)

Neumayer, Karl "Offene Fragen zur Anwendung des Abkommens der Vereinten Nationen über den internationalen Warenkauf" Recht der Internationalen Wirtschaft 1994, 99 (cited: Neumayer, RIW 1994, 99)

New Zealand Law Commission, *The United Nations Convention on Contracts for the International Sale of Goods: New Zealand's Proposed Acceptance* NZLC 23 (Wellington, 1992) (cited: New Zealand Law Commission, *United Nations Convention on Contracts*)

Nicholas, Barry "Prerequisites and Extent of Liability for Breach of Contract under the U.N. Convention" in Peter Schlechtriem (ed) *Einheitliches Kaufrecht und nationales Obligationenrecht* (Nomos, Baden-Baden, 1987) 283 (cited: Nicholas, *Prerequisites*)

Nicholas, Barry "The Vienna Convention on International Sales Law" (1989) 105 The Law Quarterly Review, 201 (cited: Nicholas (1989) 105 LQR, 201)

Niggemann, Friedrich "Die Bedeutung des Inkrafttretens des UN-Kaufrechts für den deutsch-französischen Wirtschaftsverkehr" Recht der Internationalen Wirtschaft 1991, 372 (cited: Niggemann, RIW 1991, 372)

O'Brien, John *Smith's Conflict of Laws* (2 ed, Cavendish, London, 1999) (cited: *Smith's Conflict of Laws*)

Palandt, Otto *Bürgerliches Gesetzbuch mit Einführungsgesetzen* (64 ed, Beck, München, 2005) (cited: commentator in Palandt)

Paterson, Jeannie/Robertson, Andrew/Heffey, Peter *Principles of Contract Law* (2 ed, Lawbook Co, Sydney, 2005) (cited: Paterson et al., *Principles of Contract Law*)

Perales Viscasillas, Pilar "'Battle of the Forms' under the 1980 United Nations Convention on contracts for the International Sale of Goods" (1998) 10 Pace International Law Review, 97 (cited: Perales, (1998) 10 Pace Int'l L Rev, 97)

Perillo, Joseph *Hardship and its Impact on Contractual Obligations: A Comparative Analysis* (Centre for Comparative and Foreign Law Studies, Rome, 1996) (cited: Perillo, *Hardship and its Impact on Contractual Obligations*)

Piliounis, Peter "The Remedies of Specific Performance, Price Reduction and Additional Time (Nachfrist) under the CISG: Are these worthwhile changes or additions to English Sales Law?" (2000) 12 Pace International Law Review 1 (cited: Piliounis, (2000) 12 Pace Int'l L Rev 1)

Piltz, Burghard "Anwendbares Recht in grenzüberschreitenden Verträgen" Praxis des Internationalen Privat- und Verfahrensrechts 1994, 191 (cited: Piltz, IPRax 1994, 191)

Piltz, Burghard "Gerichtsstand des Erfüllungsortes in UN-Kaufverträgen" Internationales Handelsrecht 2006, 53 (cited: Piltz, IHR 2006, 53)

Piltz, Burghard "Gestaltung von Exportverträgen nach der Schuldrechtsreform" Internationales Handelsrecht 2002, 2 (cited: Piltz, IHR 2002, 2)

Piltz, Burghard "INCOTERMS 2000 – ein Praxisüberblick" Recht der Internationalen Wirtschaft 2000, 485 (cited: Piltz, RIW 2000, 485)

Piltz, Burghard "Neue Entwicklungen im UN-Kaufrecht" Neue Juristische Wochenschrift 1994, 1101 (cited: Piltz, NJW 1994, 1101)

Piltz, Burghard "Neue Entwicklungen im UN-Kaufrecht" Neue Juristische Wochenschrift 2005, 2127 and 3128 (cited: Piltz, NJW 2005, 2127 and 3128)

Piltz, Burghard *Internationales Kaufrecht: Das UN-Kaufrecht in praxisorientierter Darstellung* (Beck, München, 1993) (cited: Piltz, *Internationales Kaufrecht*)

Piltz, Burghard *UN-Kaufrecht: Gestaltung von Export- und Importverträgen Wegweiser für die Praxis* (3 ed, Economica, Heidelberg, 2001) (cited: Piltz, *UN-Kaufrecht*)

Possner, Richard *Economic Analysis of Law* (4th ed, Little Brown, Boston, 1992) (cited: Posner, *Economic Analysis of Law*)

Prosser, William/Keeton, W Page et al. (eds) *On the Law of Torts* (5th ed, West Publishing Co, Minnesota, 1984) (cited: Prosser/Keeton, *On the Law of Torts*)

Pünder, Hermann "Das Einheitliche UN-Kaufrecht – Anwendung kraft kollisionsrechtlicher Verweisung nach Art. 1 Abs. 1 lit. b UN-Kaufrecht" Recht der Internationalen Wirtschaft 1990, 869 (cited: Pünder, RIW 1990, 869)

Rabel, Ernst "Rapport sur ledroit comparé en metière de vente" (1929), in Hans G. Leser (ed), *Gesammelte Aufsätze*, vol III: *Arbeiten zur Rechtsvergleichung und zur Rechtsvereinheitlichung* (JCB Mohr, Tübingen, 1967) (cited: Rabel, *Rapport sur ledroit comparé en metière de vente*)

Rabel, Ernst *Recht des Warenkaufs* Vol. 1 & 2 (unveränderter Nachdruck der Ausgabe von 1936) (de Gruyter, Berlin, 1957, 1958) (cited: Rabel, *Recht des Warenkaufs* Vol. 1 & 2)

Ramberg, Christina "The E-Commerce Directive and formation of contracts in a comparative perspective" (2001) European Law Review, 429 (cited: Ramberg, (2001) European L Rev, 429)

Rathjen, Peter "Haftungsentlastung des Verkäufers oder Käufers nach Art 79, 80 CISG" Recht der Internationalen Wirtschaft 1999, 561 (cited: Rathjen, RIW 1999, 561)

Rebmann, Kurt/Säcker, Franz J (eds) *Münchener Kommentar zum Bürgerlichen Gesetzbuch* Vol 3 (4 ed Beck, München, 2004) (cited: commentator in *MünchKomm*)

Réczei, Láslò *The Rules of the Convention Relating to Its Field of Application and to its Interpretation* (Oceana Publ, Dobbs Ferry, New York, 1980) (cited: Réczei, *Rules of the Convention*)

Reifner, Christina "Stillschweigender Ausschluss des UN-Kaufrechts im Prozess?" Internationales Handelsrecht 2002, 57 (cited: Reifner, IHR 2002, 57)

Reinhart, Gert "Fälligkeitszinsen und UN-Kaufrecht" Praxis des Internationalen Privat- und Verfahrensrechts 1991, 376 (cited: Reinhart, IPRax 1991, 376)

Reinhart, Gert "Zur nachträglichen Änderung des Vertragsstatuts nach Art. 27 Abs. 2 EGBGB durch Parteiverinbarung im Prozeß" [On the subsequent modification by the parties in court of the law applicable to the contract under Arts 27(2) of the German Introductory Law to the Civil Code] (commenting on OLG Köln 22 February 1994, 22 U 202/93 - in German], Praxis des Internationalen Privat- und Verfahrensrechts 1995, 365 (cited: Reinhart, IPRax 1995, 365)

Reinhart, Gert *UN-Kaufrecht, Kommentar zum Übereinkommen der Vereinten Nationen vom 11.April 1980 über Verträge über den internationalen Warenkauf* (C.F. Müller, Heidelberg, 1991) (cited: Reinhart, *UN-Kaufrecht*)

Roßmeir, Daniela "Schadensersatz und Zinsen nach UN-Kaufrecht – Art 74-78 CISG" Recht der Internationalen Wirtschaft (2000) 407 (cited: Roßmeir, RIW 2000, 407)

Rudolph, Helga *Kaufrecht der Export- und Importverträge* (Haufe, Berlin, 1996) (cited: Rudolph, *Kaufrecht*)

Saenger, Ingo/Sauthoff, Elisabeth "Die Aufrechnung im Anwendungsbereich des CISG" Internationales Handelsrecht 2005, 189 (cited: Saenger/Sauthoff, IHR 2005, 189)

Saenger, Ingo "Übereinkommen der Vereinten Nationen über Verträge über den internationalen Warenkauf" in Bamberger, Heinz Georg/Roth, Herbert (eds) *Kommentar zum Bürgerlichen Gesetzbuch* (Beck, München, 2003) (cited: Saenger in Bamberger/Roth)

Schäfer, Friedericke "Die Wahl nichtstaatlichen Rechts nach Art 3 Abs 2 des Entwurfs einer Rom I VO: Auswirkungen auf das optionale Instrument des europäischen Vertragsrechts" Zeitschrift für Gemeinschaftsprivatrecht 2006, 54 (cited: Schäfer, GPR 2006, 54)

Schäfer, Friederike "Zur Anwendbarkeit des UN-Kaufrechts auf Werklieferungsverträge" Internationales Handelsrecht 2003, 118 (cited: Schäfer, IHR 2003, 118)

Scheifele, Bernd *Die Rechtsbehelfe des Verkäufers nach deutschem und UN-Kaufrecht* (Schäuble, Rheinfelden. 1986) (cited: Scheifele, *Rechtsbehelfe*)

Schilf, Sven "Writing in conformation: valid evidence of a sales contract? Reflections on a Danish case regarding usages, CISG and the UNIDROIT-Principles" (1999) Uniform Law Review, 1004 (cited: Schilf, (1999) Uniform L Rev, 1004)

Schlechtriem Peter, *Restitution und Bereicherungsausgleich in Europa* Vol 1 (Mohr Siebeck, Tübingen, 2000) (cited: Schlechtriem, *Restitution*)

Schlechtriem, Peter (ed) *Einheitliches Kaufrecht und nationales Obligationenrecht, Fachtagung Einheitliches Kaufrecht der Gesellschaft für Rechtsvergleichung, Freiburg i.Br. 16./17. 2. 1987* (Nomos, Baden-Baden, 1987) (cited: Schlechtriem (ed), *Einheitliches Kaufrecht und nationales Obligationenrecht*)

Schlechtriem, Peter (ed) *Kommentar zum Einheitlichen UN-Kaufrecht – CISG* (4 ed, Beck, München, 2004) (cited: commentator in Schlechtriem, *Kommentar zum Einheitlichen UN-Kaufrecht*)

Schlechtriem, Peter/Magnus, Ulrich *Internationale Rechtsprechung zu EKG und EAG* (Nomos, Baden-Baden, 1987) (cited: Schlechtriem/Magnus, *Internationale Rechtsprechung zu EKG und EAG*)

Schlechtriem, Peter/Schmidt-Kessel, Martin "Anmerkung zu BGH (25 June 1997)" Entscheidungen zum Wirtschaftsrecht 1997, 1097 (cited: Schlechtriem/Schmidt-Kessel, EWiR 1997, 1097)

Schlechtriem, Peter/Schwenzer, Ingeborg (eds) *Commentary on the UN-Convention on the International Sale of Goods (CISG)* (2 ed, OUP, Oxford, 2005) (cited: commentator in Schlechtriem/Schwenzer, *Commentary*)

Schlechtriem, Peter/Schwenzer, Ingeborg (eds) *Kommentar zum Einheitlichen UN-Kaufrecht – CISG* (4 ed, Beck, München, 2004) (cited: commentator in Schlechtriem/Schwenzer)

Schlechtriem, Peter "Anmerkung zu BGH (24 March 1999)" Juristenzeitung 1999, 794 (cited, Schlechtriem, JZ 1999, 794)

Schlechtriem, Peter "Anmerkung zu OLG Hamm (9 June 1995)" CISG-online 141

Schlechtriem, Peter "Aufhebung von CISG-Kaufverträgen wegen vertragswidriger Beschaffenheit der Ware" in von Baums, Theodor/Lutter, Marcus/Schmidt, Karsten/Wertenbruch, Johannes (eds) *Festschrift für Ulrich Huber* (Mohr Siebeck, Tübingen, 2006) 563 (cited: Schlechtriem, *FS Huber*)

Schlechtriem, Peter "Aufrechnung durch den Käufer wegen Nachbesserungsaufwand – deutsches Vertragsstatut und UN-Kaufrecht, Urteilsanmerkung zu OLG Hamm" Praxis des Internationalen Privat- und Verfahrensrechts 1996, 138 (cited: Schlechtriem, IPRax 1996, 138)

Schlechtriem, Peter "Auslegung, Lückenfüllung und Weiterentwicklung des CISG" in Bernhard, Christ/Kramer, Ernst (eds) Symposium für Frank Vischer (Helbing Lichtenhahn, Basel, 2005) translated by Martin Koehler "Interpretation, gap-filing and further development of the UN Sales Convention" (www.cisg.law.pace.edu) (cited: Schlechtriem in *Symposium Frank Vischer*)

Schlechtriem, Peter "Bemerkungen zur Geschichte des Einheitskaufrechts" in Schlechtriem, Peter (ed) *Einheitliches Kaufrecht und nationales Obligationenrecht*, (Nomos, Baden-Baden, 1987) 27 (cited: Schlechtriem, *Geschichte*)

Schlechtriem, Peter "Bindung an Erklärungen nach dem Einheitlichen Kaufrecht" in Majoros, Ferenc (ed) *Emptio-Venditio inter nationes, Festschrift für Karl Heinz Neumayer* (VRG-Verlag, Basel, 1997) 259 (cited: Schlechtriem in *FS Neumayer*)

Schlechtriem, Peter "Der Bezugspunkt der Schadensersatzverantwortung des Verkäufers für Sachmängel" in *Festschrift Welser* (Manz, Wien, 2004) (cited: Schlechtriem in *FS Welser*)

Schlechtriem, Peter "Erfüllung von Zahlungsansprüchen nach CISG am Ort der Niederlassung des Gläubigers" (Urteilsanmerkung zu OLG Düsseldorf 2 July 1993) Recht der Internationalen Wirtschaft 1993, 845 (cited: Schlechtriem, RIW 1993, 845)

Schlechtriem, Peter "Fristsetzungen bei Leistungsstörungen im Einheitlichen UN-Kaufrecht (CISG) und der Einfluß des § 326 BGB" in Friedrich Graf von Westphalen/Otto Sandrock (eds) *Lebendiges Recht – Von den Sumerern bis zur Gegenwart, Festschrift für Reinhold Trinkner zum 65. Geburtstag* (Recht und Wirtschaft, Heidelberg, 1995) 321 (cited: Schlechtriem, *Fristsetzungen*)

Schlechtriem, Peter "Gemeinsame Bestimmungen über Verpflichtungen des Verkäufers und des Käufers" in Schweizerisches Institut für Rechtsvergleichung (ed) Lausanner Kolloquium 1984 (Schulthess, Zürich, 1985) 149 (cited: Schlechtriem, *Gemeinsame Bestimmungen*)

Schlechtriem, Peter "International Einheitliches Kaufrecht und neues Schuldrecht" in Dauner-Lieb, Barbara/Konzen, Horst/Schmidt, Karsten (eds) *Das neue Schuldrecht in der Praxis* (Carl Heymanns, Köln, 2003), 71 (cited: Schlechtriem, "International Einheitliches Kaufrecht und neues Schuldrecht", 71)

Schlechtriem, Peter "Kaufmännisches Bestätigungsschreiben – Vertragsaufhebung nach Einheitskaufrecht" (Urteilsanmerkung zu OLG Köln 22 Feb 1994), Entscheidungen zum Wirtschaftsrecht 1994, 867 (cited: Schlechtriem, EWiR 1994, 867)

Schlechtriem, Peter "Kurzkommentar" Entscheidungen zum Wirstchaftsrecht 1994, 867 (cited: Schlechtriem "Kurzkommentar", EWiR 1994, 867)

Schlechtriem, Peter "Recent Developments in International Sales Law" (1983) 18 Israel Law Review 309 (www.cisg.law.pace.edu) (cited: Schlechtriem, (1983) 18 Israel L Rev, 309)

Schlechtriem, Peter "Rechtswahl im europäischen Binnenmarkt und Klausel-kontrolle" in Rauscher, Thomas/Mansel, Heinz-Peter (eds) *Festschrift Werner Lorenz zum 80. Geburtstag* (Sellier European Law Publishers, München, 2001) 565 (cited: Schlechtriem in *FS Lorenz*)

Schlechtriem, Peter "Schadenersatz und Erfüllungsinteresse" in *Festschrift für Apostolos Georgiades*, von Stathopoulos, Michalis/Beys, Kostas/Doris, Philippas (eds) (Beck, München, 2006) 383 (cited: Schlechtriem in *FS Georgiades*)

Schlechtriem, Peter "Verfahrenskosten als Schaden in Anwendung des UN-Kaufrechts" IHR 2006, 49 (cited: Schlechtriem, IHR 2006, 49)

Schlechtriem, Peter "Vertragsmäßigkeit der Ware als Frage der Beschaffenheits-vereinbarung" (Urteilsanmerkung zu BGH, NJW 1995, 2099), Praxis des Internationalen Privat- und Verfahrensrechts 1996, 12 (cited: Schlechtriem, IPRax 1996, 12)

Schlechtriem, Peter "Vertragsmäßigkeit der Ware und öffentlich-rechtliche Vorgaben" Praxis des Internationalen Privat- und Verfahrensrechts 1999, 388 (cited: Schlechtriem, IPRax 1999, 388)

Schlechtriem, Peter "Voraussehbarkeit und Schutzzweck einer verletzten Pflicht als Kriterium der Eingrenzung des ersatzfähigen Schadens im deutschen Recht" in *Recht in Ost und West, Festschrift zum 30-jährigen Jubiläum des Instituts für Rechtsvergleichung der Waseda University, Tokyo* (Waseda University Press, Tokyo, 1988) (cited: Schlechtriem in *Recht in Ost und West*)

Schlechtriem, Peter *Einheitliches UN-Kaufrecht* (Mohr Siebeck, Tübingen, 1981) (cited: Schlechtriem, *Einheitliches UN-Kaufrecht*)

Schlechtriem, Peter *Internationales UN-Kaufrecht* (4 ed, Mohr Siebeck, Tübingen, 2007) (cited: Schlechtriem, *Internationales UN-Kaufrecht*)

Schlechtriem, Peter *Kommentar zum Einheitlichen UN-Kaufrecht – CISG* (3 ed, Beck, München, 2000) (cited: commentator in Schlechtriem, 3 ed)

Schlechtriem, Peter *Schuldrecht, Besonderer Teil* (6 ed, Mohr Siebeck, Tübingen, 2003) (cited: Schlechtriem, *Schuldrecht BT*)

Schlosser, Peter/Pirrung, Jorg *Recht der internationalen privaten Schiedsgerichts-barkeit* (2 ed, Mohr Siebeck, Tübingen, 1989) (cited: Schlosser/ Pirrung, *Schiedsgerichtsbarkeit*)

Schluchter, Anne-Kathrin *Die Gültigkeit von Kaufverträgen unter dem UN-Kaufrecht: wie gestaltet sich die Ergänzung des Einheitsrechts mit deutschen und französischen Nichtigkeitsnormen?* (Nomos, Baden-Baden, 1996) (cited: Schluchter, *Gültigkeit von Kaufverträgen*)

Schmid, Christoph "Das Verhältnis von Einheitlichem Kaufrecht und nationalem Deliktsrecht am Beispiel des Ersatzes von Mangelfolgeschäden" Recht der Internationalen Wirtschaft 1996, 904 (cited: Schmidt, 1996, 904)

Schmid, Christoph *Das Zusammenspiel von Einheitlichem UN-Kaufrecht und nationalem Recht: Lückenfüllung und Normenkonkurrenz* (Duncker & Humblot, Berlin, 1996) (cited: Schmid, *Zusammenspiel von Einheit-lichem UN-Kaufrecht und nationalem Recht*)

Schmidt, Karsten (ed) *Münchener Kommentar zum Handelsgesetzbuch* Vol 6 (Handelsgeschäfte) (Beck, München, 2004) (cited: commentator in *MünchKomm HGB*)

Schmidt-Ahrendts, Nils "Der Ersatz "frustrierter Aufwendungen" im Falle der Rückabwicklung gescheiterter Verträge im Un-Kaufrecht" IHR 2006, 63 (cited: Schmidt-Ahrendts, IHR 2006, 63)

Schmidt-Kessel, Martin "Urteilsanmerkung zu BGH NJW 1995, 2101" Recht der Internationalen Wirtschaft 1996, 60 (cited: Schmidt-Kessel, RIW 1996, 60)

Schmidt-Kessel, Martin "Urteilsanmerkung zu BGH-Urteil 31.10.2002" Neue Juristische Wochenschrift 2002, 3444 (cited: Schmidt-Kessel, NJW 2002, 3444)

Schmitt, Hansjörg "Intangible Goods in Online-Kaufverträgen und der Anwendungsbereich des CISG" Computer and Recht 2001, 145 (cited: Schmitt, CR 2001, 145)

Schmitz, Dirk "UN-Kaufrecht (CISG) und Datentransfer via Internet" Zeitschrift Multimedia und Recht 2000, 256 (cited: Schmitz, MMR 2000, 256)

Schneider, Dirk *UN-Kaufrecht und Produkthaftpflicht* (Helbing & Lichtenhahn, Basel, 1995) (cited: Schneider, *UN-Kaufrecht*)

Schroeter, Ulrich "Entscheidungsanmerkung zu BGH, Urteil vom 11.1.2006 – VIII ZR 268/04 (Rüge eines Rechtsmangels im UN-Kaufrecht unter Angabe des Rechte beanspruchenden Dritten und dessen rechtlicher Schritte; complaint in regard to a legal defect under the CISG relying on the right of a third party and its legal action)" Entscheidungen zum Wirtschaftsrecht Art 43 CISG 1/06, 427 (cited: Schroeter, EWiR, Art 43)

Schroeter, Ulrich "Interpretation of Writing" (2002) 6 Vindobona Journal of International Commercial Law and Arbitration, 267 (cited: Schroeter, (2002) 6 VJ, 267)

Schroeter, Ulrich "Vienna Sales Convention: Applicability to 'Mixed Contracts' and Interaction with the 1968 Brussels Convention" (2001) 5 Vindobona Journal of International Commercial Law and Arbitration, 74 (cited: Schroeter, (2001) 5 VJ, 74)

Schroeter, Ulrich in "Die Anwendbarkeit des UN-Kaufrechts auf grenzüberschreitende Versteigerungen und Internet-Auktionen" ZEuP 2004, 20 (cited: Schroeter, ZEuP 2004, 20)

Schroeter, Ulrich *UN-Kaufrecht und Europäisches Gemeinschaftsrecht, Verhältnis und Wechselwirkungen* (Sellier European Law Publishers, München, 2005) (cited: Schroeter, *UN-Kaufrecht und Gemeinschaftsrecht*)

Schumacher, Florian "Kaufoptionsverträge und Verwendengsrisiko" Internationales Handelsrecht 2005, 147 (cited: Schumacher, IHR 2005, 147)

Schwenzer, Ingeborg/Mohs, Florian "Old Habits Die Hard: Traditional Contract Formation in a Modern World" Internationales Handelsrecht 2006, 239 III (cited: Schwenzer/Mohs, IHR 2006, 239 III)

Schwenzer, Ingeborg "Das UN-Abkommen zum internationalen Warenkauf" Neue Juristische Wochenschrift 1990, 602 (cited: Schwenzer, NJW, 1990, 602)

Secretariat's Commentary *Commentary on the Draft Convention on Contracts for the International Sale of Goods*, Secretariat, Official Records, at 20, U.N. Doc. A/CONF.97/5 (1979) (cited: Secretariat's Commentary OR)

Sharma, Rajeev "The United Nations Convention on Contracts for the International Sale of Goods: The Canadian Experience" (2005) 36 Victoria University of Wellington Law Review, 847 (cited: Sharma, (2005) 36 VUWLR, 847)

Shiffrin, Seanna Valentine "The Divergence of Contract and Promise" (2007) 120 Harvard Law Review, 3 (cited: Shiffrin, (2007) 120 Harv L Rev, 3)

Soergel, Hans/Siebert, Wolfgang *Bürgerliches Gesetzbuch mit Einführungsgesetzen und Nebengesetzen* (12 ed, Kohlhammer, Stuttgart, 1991) (cited: commentator in *Soergel*)

Soergel, Hans/Siebert, Wolfgang *Schuldrechtliche Nebengesetze 2: Übereinkommen der Vereinten Nationen über Verträge über den internationalen Warenkauf (CISG)* (13 ed, Kohlhammer, Stuttgart, 2000) (cited: commentator in *Soergel*)

Staudinger, Julius von *Staudingers Kommentar zum Bürgerlichen Gesetzbuch mit Einführungsgesetz und Nebengesetzen,* (13 ed, Sellier/de Gruyter, Berlin, 1993 onwards) (cited: commentator in *Staudinger*)

Stern, Elisabeth *Erklärungen im UNCITRAL-Kaufrecht* (Manz, Wien, 1990) (cited: Stern, *Erklärungen*)

Stoll, Hans "Das Statut der Rechtswahlvereinbarung – eine irreführende Konstruktion" in Meier, Isaak/Siehr, Kurt (eds) *Festschrift für Anton Heini* (Schulthess, Zürich, 1995) 429 (cited: Stoll in *FS Heini*)

Stoll, Hans "Ersatz für Vertrauensschaden nach dem Einheitlichen Kaufrecht" in *Festschrift Neumayer* (Basel, Recht und Gesellschaft, 1997) (cited: Stoll in *FS Neumayer*)

Stoll, Hans "Zur Haftung bei Erfüllungsverweigerung im Einheitlichen Kaufrecht" Rabels Zeitschrift 52 (1988) 617 (cited: Stoll, RabelsZ 52 (1988) 617)

Strohbach, Heinz "Rechtsanwendungskonvention" in Enderlein, Fritz/Maskow, Dietrich/Strohbach, Heinz *Internationales Kaufrecht* (Haufe, Berlin, 1991) 387 (cited: Strohbach in Enderlein/Maskow/Strohbach)

Sutton, Kenneth *Sales and consumer law in Australia and New Zealand* (4 ed, LBC Information Services, North Ryde (NSW), 1995) (cited: Sutton, *Sales and Consumer Law)*

Teklote, Stephan *Die Einheitlichen Kaufgesetze und das deutsche AGB-Gesetz* (Nomos, Baden-Baden, 1994) (cited: Teklote, *Einheitlichen Kaufgesetze*)

van Alstine, Michael P "Dynamic Treaty Interpretation" (1998) 146 University of Pennsylvania Law Review, 687 (cited: van Alstine, (1998) 146 U Pa L Rev, 687)

van Alstine, Michael P *Fehlender Konsens beim Vertragsschluß nach dem einheitlichen UN Kaufrecht* Arbeiten zur Rechtsvergleichung Vol 174 (Nomos, Baden-Baden, 1995) (cited: van Alstine, *Fehlender Konsens*)

Vékás, Lajos "The Foreseeability Doctrine in Contractual Damage Cases" (2002) 43 Acta Juridica Hungarica, 145 (cited: Vékás, (2002) 43 Acta Juridica Hungarica, 145)

Verzoni, Fernando "Electronic Commerce and the UN Convention on Contracts for the International Sale of Goods (CISG)" (2006) Nordic Journal of Commercial Law, 2 (cited: Verzoni, Nordic J Comm L, 2)

Vida, Sándor "Keine Anwendung des UN-Kaufrechtsübereinkommen bei Übertragung des Geschäftsanteils einer GmbH" Praxis des Internationalen Privat- und Verfahrensrechts 1995, 52 (cited: Vida, IPRax 1995, 52)

Vida, Sándor "Zur Anwendung des UN-Kaufübereinkommens in Ungarn" (Hauptstadtgericht Budapest, Urteil 24 März 1992) Praxis des Internationalen Privat- und Verfahrensrechts 1993, 263 (cited: Vida, IPRax 1993, 263) mäiz

Vilus, Jelena "Electronic Commerce: An Incentive for the Modernization and Harmonization of Contract Law?" (2003) 8 Uniform Law Review, 163 (cited: Vilus, (2003) 8 Unif L Rev, 163)

von Bernstorff, Christoph Graf "Ausgewählte Rechtsprobleme im Electronic Commerce" Recht der Internationalen Wirtschaft 2000, 181 (cited: von Bernstorff, RIW 2000, 181)

von Bernstorff, Christoph Graf "Der Abschluss elektronischer Verträge" Recht der Internationalen Wirtschaft 2002, 179 (cited: von Bernstorff, RIW 2002, 179)

von Caemmerer, Ernst/Schlechtriem, Peter (ed) *Kommentar zum Einheitlichen UN-Kaufrecht* (2 ed, Beck, München,1994) (cited: von Caemmerer/ Schlechtriem, *Kommentar*)

von Caemmerer, Ernst "Probleme des Haager Einheitlichen Kaufrechts" (1978) 178, Archiv fuer die civilistische Praxis, 121 (cited: von Caemmerer, (1978) 178 AcP, 121)

von Caemmerer, Ernst "Zahlungsort" in Flume (ed) *Internationales Recht und Wirtschaftsordnung, Festschrift für F.A. Mann zum 70. Geburtstag* (Beck, München, 1977) 108 (cited: *von Caemmerer, Zahlungsort*)

von Mehren, Arthur Taylor "The 'Battle of the Forms': A Comparative View" (1990) 38 American Journal of Comparative Law, 265 (cited: von Mehren, (1990) 38 Am J Comp L, 265)

Waddams, Stephen *The Law of Contract* (5 ed, Canada Law Book Co, Toronto, 2005) (cited: Waddams, *The Law of Contracts*)

Weber, Rolf "Vertragsverletzungsfolgen: Schadenersatz, Rückabwicklung, vertragliche Gestaltungsmöglichkeiten" in Bucher, Eugen (ed) *Wiener Kaufrecht* (Stämpfli, Bern, 1991) 165 (cited: Weber, "Vertragsverletzungsfolgen" 165)

Weitnauer, Hermann "Nichtvoraussehbarkeit eines Schadens nach Art. 82 S. 2 des Einheitlichen Gesetzes über den internationalen Kauf beweglicher Sachen" Praxis des Internationalen Privat- und Verfahrensrechts 1981, 83 (cited: Weitnauer, IPRax, 1981, 83)

Willier, William/Hart Frederick, *Uniform Commercial Code Reporter-Digest* (Matthew Bender, Albany, New York, release 155, 2005) (cited: Willier/ Hart, *Uniform Commercial Code*)

Winship, Peter "Changing Contract Practices in Light of the United Nations Sales Convention: A Guide for Practitioners" (1995) 29 International Lawyer, 525 (cited: Winship, (1995) 29 Int'l Lawyer, 525)

Winship, Peter "The Scope of the Vienna Convention on International Sales Contracts" in Galston, Nina/Smit, Hans (ed) *International Sales* (Matthew Bender, Albany, New York, 1984) ch. 1, 1 (cited: Winship, *Scope*)

Witz, Claude/Wolter, Gebhard "Das Ende der Problematik des unbestimmten Preises in Frankreich" Zeitschrift für Europäisches Privatrecht 1996, 648 (cited: Witz/Wolter, ZEuP 1996, 648)

Witz, Claude/Wolter, Gebhard "Die ersten Entscheidungen französischer Gerichte zum Einheitlichen UN-Kaufrecht" Recht der Internationalen Wirtschaft 1995, 810 (cited: Witz/Wolter, RIW 1995, 810)

Witz, Claude/Wolter, Gebhard "Die neuere Rechtsprechung französischer Gerichte zum Einheitlichen UN-Kaufrecht" Recht der Internationalen Wirtschaft 1998, 278 (cited Witz/Wolter, RIW 1998, 278)

Witz, Claude "Panorama, Droit uniforme de la vente internationale de marchandises: janvier 2005 – juin 2006" Dalloz, Recueil 2007, 530 (cited Wiltz, Dalloz 2007, 530)

Witz, Claude *Les premières applications jurisprudentielles du droit uniforme de la vente internationale* (L.G.D.J., Paris, 1995) (cited: Witz, Claude *Premières applications*)

Witz, Wolfgang/Salger, Hanns-Christian/Lorenz, Manuel, *Internationales Einheitliches Kaufrecht, Praktiker-Kommentar und Vertragsgestaltung zum CISG* (Verlag Recht und Wirtschaft, Heidelberg, 2000) (cited: Witz in Witz/Salger/Lorenz, *Internationales Einheitliches Kaufrecht*)

Witz, Wolfgang "Zurückbehaltungsrechte im internationalen Kauf – eine praxisorientierte Analyse zur Durchsetzung des Kaufpreisanspruchs im CISG" in Schwenzer, Ingeborg/Hager, Günter (ed) *Festschrift für Peter Schlechtriem zum 70. Geburtstag* (Mohr Siebeck, Tübingen, 2003) 291 (cited: Witz in *FS Schlechtriem*)

Witz, Wolfgang *Der unbestimmte Kaufpreis* (Metzner, Frankfurt aM, 1989) (cited: Witz, *Kaufpreis*)

Zahraa, Mahdi/Ghith, Aburima Abdullah "Specific Performance under the Vienna Sales Convention, English Law and Libyan Law" (2000) 15 Arab Law Quarterly, 304 (cited: Zahraa/Ghith, (2000) 15 Arab L Q, 304)

Ziegel, Jacob "The Remedial Provisions in the Vienna Sales Convention: Some Common Law Perspectives" in Galston. Nina/Smit, Hans (ed) *International Sales* (Matthew Bender, Albany, New York, 1984) ch. 9, 1 (cited: Ziegel, *Remedial Provisions*)

Zweigert, Konrad/Kötz, Hein *Einführung in die Rechtsvergleichung auf dem Gebiete des Privatrechts* Vol 1 & 2 (2 ed, Mohr Siebeck, Tübingen, 1984) (cited: Zweigert/Kötz, *Einführung*)

Index

*Note: Page numbers in **boldface** type indicate paragraph numbers in text.*

CPSIA information can be obtained
at www.ICGtesting.com
Printed in the USA
LVHW080450160721
692783LV00004B/44

9 783540 253143